ROMANTIC AND VICTORIAN:
Studies in Memory of William H. Marshall

William Harvey Marshall

Courtesy Jean Sardou

ROMANTIC AND VICTORIAN:
Studies in Memory of William H. Marshall

Edited by W. PAUL ELLEDGE *and*
RICHARD L. HOFFMAN

Rutherford ● *Madison* ● *Teaneck*
FAIRLEIGH DICKINSON UNIVERSITY PRESS

Associated University Presses, Inc.
Cranbury, New Jersey 08512

ISBN: 0-8386-7742-8
Printed in the United States of America

CONTENTS

PREFACE

Although commonplace enough, volumes of this sort remain anomolies in the corpus of literary criticism. Indigenously susceptible to the defects of a miscellany, they seldom manifest the thematic singularity of a monograph, the focal centrality of canonical analyses, the synthesizing coherence of historical or cultural studies. We have not been unaware of these dangers in compiling the present collection. But given our primary aim—accurately to reflect the variety, the depth, and the range of Professor Marshall's scholarly contributions to the profession—we have stipulated only that our contributors confine themselves to Romantic and Victorian subjects, or to general theories of literary interpretation incorporating or applicable to those subjects. To impose more rigid substantive prescriptions seemed to us needlessly restrictive of the critical minds and dispositions herein represented. If we have sacrificed ideological consistency and continuity, we have nevertheless throughout the book attempted to preserve and set forth, in units however small, the kind of scholarly integrity and intellectual energy uniformly exampled in Professor Marshall's work.

Following the studies by Professors Peckham and Stevenson, the essays are arranged to suggest a roughly chronological movement through the two periods, from Blake to Browning. The apparent departure from such a sequence, W. P. Albrecht's "Archibald Alison and the Sublime Pleasures of Tragedy," is included among discussions of second-generation Romantics because of its remarks on Keats and Hazlitt.

Of the many to whom we owe gratitude, we would here cite: Mrs. William H. Marshall, for her considerate and thoughtful cooperation during the early, planning stages; Mr. Thomas Yoseloff, the publisher, for his enthusiastic interest in and support of the project; Mr. Harold Cone for editorial assistance, and Mrs. Walter H. Deathridge for secretarial help. Our first and final debt is of course to the contributors, whose book this is, for their liberal donations of effort and time, their willingness to meet deadlines, and their patient, good-natured

7

endurance of our sometimes nagging and niggling queries, suggestions, revisions. They have, we trust, significantly advanced that solid, though humane, scholarly tradition to which Professor Marshall was so firmly committed.

W.P.E.
R.L.H.

WILLIAM HARVEY MARSHALL
(1925-1968)

William H. Marshall was born in Washington, D. C., on 16 October 1925, the first child and only son of Robert Wallace Marshall and Nettie Evelyn Heinline Marshall. He was raised principally in Wilmington, Delaware, and did his preparatory work both in its public schools and at the Tower Hill School, where, as he later wrote in an autobiographical sketch, he was "a totally undistinguished student, who spent most of his time reading good novels and writing bad ones."

"At the University of Virginia" during the years 1943 to 1946, the autobiographical sketch continues, "he moved rapidly to the study of literature, philosophy, history, and sociology; here he served as literary editor of several undergraduate magazines, to which he contributed occasional short stories, essays, and a kind of poetry. He graduated after six semesters (Phi Beta Kappa) and passed the next three years travelling through the United States, studying philosophy but with no particular direction, living in Paris, and teaching in a military school."

On 20 August 1949 he married Shirley Evelyn Repp, a native New Yorker, who attended De Pauw University, received her B.A. (with a major in science) from Beaver College, and taught high school in New York, New Jersey, and Virginia. Shirley Marshall was always deeply committed to her husband's wide and numerous scholarly interests. She worked with him untiringly on his books and articles and is herself a member of the Modern Language Association of America and the editor of a fine anthology of English poetry for children. Three daughters were born to the Marshalls: Judith Blanche (1951), Susan Jane (1954), and Barbara Jean (1957–1968).

A few weeks after his marriage, William Marshall began graduate work in English literature at the University of Virginia. He was awarded the M.A. in 1951, with a Master's thesis, "Thomas Traherne's Doctrine of Man," directed by Fredson Bowers. It was later (1958) published in small part and revised form in *Modern Language Notes*. The year follow-

9

ing his M.A. (1951–1952) he devoted, like the one preceding his graduate career at Virginia, to private-school teaching.

In 1952 he came as a doctoral candidate to the University of Pennsylvania, where his primary interests became the Romantic Period and, more specifically, Byron. He received his Ph.D. in 1956 with a dissertation entitled "The Liberal, 1822–1823," published by the University Press in 1960 as *Byron, Shelley, Hunt, and The Liberal.*

He was to remain at the University of Pennsylvania for almost all the rest of his life: as Assistant Instructor (1952–1956), Instructor (1956–1958), Assistant Professor (1958–1962), Associate Professor (1962–1965), and Professor (1965–1968). Here he taught, first the freshman and sophomore required English courses; later, advanced undergraduate courses in nineteenth-century English poetry and fiction, the Romantic poets, and the history of the English language; finally, graduate seminars in Byron, Coleridge, the Romantic critics, fiction, Dickens, Thackeray, and George Eliot. He directed doctoral dissertations on Byron, Coleridge, Wordsworth, and the Victorian novel; and, in the spring of 1962, he presented a "TV Seminar" in the nineteenth-century English novel over WCAU-TV (CBS affiliate), Philadelphia.

His committee work at Pennsylvania was scarcely less demanding than his teaching. At various times between 1960 and 1965 he served on the Executive Committees of the College and of the College for Women. He was a member of the Committee on Instruction of the Graduate School of Arts and Sciences (Humanities Quadrant) from 1962 to 1966 and of the Graduate School of Education in 1965-1966. He was Chairman of the Committee for an Association between the University of Pennsylvania and Morgan State College from 1964 to 1966 and a member of the Editorial Committee for the Haney Foundation Monograph Series from 1966 to 1968. In addition, he served as Assistant to the Dean of the College from 1958 to 1960; as Visiting Lecturer at Bryn Mawr College in 1964–1965; as Educational Consultant for the Humanities at the Philadelphia College of Textiles and Science in 1965; as teaching participant in the NDEA Institute in English at Philadelphia, summer 1967; and as Visiting Professor at Duke University during the spring semester of 1968.

His students will remember not only the excitement of his lectures and seminars (for he was an inspired and eloquent teacher), but also his warmth, his kindness, and his concern—

qualities not always found in "research-oriented" professors. Some measure of the scholarly respect and personal affection which he won from his students as well as from his peers may be gathered from the list of distinguished contributors to this volume. And some indication of his ever-widening range of interests in nineteenth-century literature and thought may be gleaned from the scope of their subjects.

But however great William Marshall's devotion to teaching, and however faithful his service to the University, his greatest commitment, undeniably, was to scholarship: to read, think, write, and publish were, he maintained unabashedly, the first duties of a scholar—and he labored incessantly to live his creed. As Chaucer remarked of his Parson, "first he wroghte, and afterward he taughte." His final bibliography lists seventy-three items: four scholarly books, three editions, fifty-two articles and notes, thirteen reviews, and a record of poetry readings. With the exceptions of three notes and his first book, this massive amount of work was produced in a single decade, 1958–1968.

A Summer Research Grant at Pennsylvania in 1960 helped him complete his second book, *The Structure of Byron's Major Poems* (1962), and a Guggenheim Fellowship (1963–1964) allowed him to start work on *The World of the Victorian Novel* (1967). The latter title reveals the main intellectual direction of his final years. Not that he meant, by any means, to abandon either poetry or the Romantic Period. Among his latest titles are three splendid anthologies of nineteenth-century verse: *The Major English Romantic Poets* (New York, second edition, 1966); *The Major Victorian Poets* (New York, 1966); and *Lord Byron: Selected Poems and Letters* (Boston, Riverside Editions, 1968). But it is significant that the last of his books to be published was *Wilkie Collins*, for the Twayne English Authors Series. And on 5 January 1968 he wrote to Mr. Thomas Y. Yoseloff, publisher of *The World of the Victorian Novel*, "I am slowly putting together plans for the book I am tentatively calling 'The Moral Moment,' a study of literary reflections during the nineteenth century of the transition from the traditional to the 'modern' moral orientation." Had he lived longer, his major contribution might well have been in the areas of nineteenth- and twentieth-century fiction and nonfictional prose.

In his last year at Pennsylvania, he accepted a position as Professor of English at the University of North Carolina—a post he was never to hold. On Sunday, 2 June 1968, near Durham, North Carolina, an automobile accident took his life and that of his youngest daughter, Barbara. They were buried in the Congressional Cemetery in Washington, the day after Robert Kennedy (a man very like him, in age and temperament) was shot. Shirley Marshall and her two daughters live in Chapel Hill, where Judy is a student at the University and where Susan attends Chapel Hill High School.

These facts, largely professional, present only one or two facets of the man. They hardly serve either to introduce Bill Marshall to those who never knew him or to recall him to those of us who did. The many other facets of his exuberant personality and his rich life were remarkably varied: his devotion to his wife and daughters; his delight in befriending, encouraging, and assisting young scholars; his affection for nineteenth-century houses and furniture—especially when they required his expert repair and refinishing; his fondness for the ocean and the shore; his joy in books and book collecting; his love of people and their talk; his total enjoyment of life and boundless energy in all things, expressing itself usually in wondrously violent extremes—either broad good humor (of the best Fieldingesque variety) or perspiring rage (he hated sham, professional incompetence, and meanness). Perhaps his quintessential qualities were zest, mischievousness, and—in its widest and fullest sense—goodness.

Of the hundreds of telephone calls I received from him over the years, my favorite is the one he introduced by telling me that, having finished his writing for the day, he was about to imbibe an especially large quantity of Scotch and then repair to his back yard for the night. His youngest daughter, Barbara, had elected, as her "half-day" boon, to spend that night with her father in a tent. (The Marshalls invented "half days" because birthdays—like Christmas and Easter—come, after all, but once a year.) I had another call early the following morning to assure me that all had gone well: the neighborhood German Shepherd had, "for the most part," left them alone for the night.

I think the most memorable of the many letters which poured in when Bill Marshall died was that which concluded by quoting from Yeats's *In Memory of Major Robert Gregory:* "What made us dream that he could comb grey hair?" The same poem provides a kind of answer, for what he never gave us time or cause to dream was that he "could share in that discourtesy of death."

Richard L. Hoffman

THE PUBLICATIONS OF WILLIAM H. MARSHALL

Books

Byron, Shelley, Hunt, and The Liberal. Philadelphia: University of Pennsylvania Press, 1960.

The Structure of Byron's Major Poems. Philadelphia: University of Pennsylvania Press, 1962.

Editor. *The Major English Romantic Poets, An Anthology.* New York: Washington Square Press, 1964 (softbound); second edition, 1966 (hardbound); 1967 (softbound).

Editor. *The Major Victorian Poets, An Anthology.* New York: Washington Square Press, 1966 (hardbound); 1967 (softbound).

The World of the Victorian Novel. New York and Cranbury, New Jersey: A. S. Barnes and Company, 1967.

Editor. *Lord Byron: Selected Poems and Letters.* Boston: Houghton Mifflin, 1968. Riverside Editions.

Wilkie Collins. New York: Twayne Publishers, Inc., 1970. Twayne English Authors Series.

Articles and Notes

"The Text of T. S. Eliot's 'Gerontion,'" *Studies in Bibliography*, IV (1951-1952), 213-217.

"The Misdating of a Letter: An Exoneration of Byron," *Notes and Queries*, n. s. IV (1957), 122-123.

"Leigh Hunt on Walt Whitman: A New Letter," *Notes and Queries*, n. s. IV (1957), 392-393.

"Thomas Traherne and the Doctrine of Original Sin," *Modern Language Notes*, LXXIII (1958), 161-165.

"Spenser and General Election," *Notes and Queries*, n. s. V (1958), 95.

"A News [*sic.* printer's error] Letter from Byron to John Hunt," *Notes and Queries*, n. s. V (1958), 122-124.

"Elizabeth Drury and the Heathens," *Notes and Queries*, n. s. V (1958), 533-534.

"A Possible Interpretation of Donne's *The Second Anniversary* (Lines 33-36)," *Notes and Queries*, n. s. V (1958), 540-541.

"Eliot's *The Waste Land*, 182," *Explicator*, XVII (1959), Item 42.

13

"Calvin, Spenser, and the Major Sacraments," *Modern Language Notes*, LXXIV (1959), 97-101.

"A Note on 'Prufrock,'" *Notes and Queries*, n. s. VI (1959), 188-189.

"*Queen Mab:* The Inconsistency of Ahasuerus," *Modern Language Notes*, LXXIV (1959), 397-400.

"Comments on Shelley in *The Beacon* and *The Kaleidoscope* (1821)," *Notes and Queries*, n. s. VI (1959), 224-226.

"Some Byron Comments on Pope and Boileau," *Philological Quarterly*, XXXVIII (1959), 252-253.

"The Structure of Coleridge's 'Reflections on Having Left A Place of Retirement,'" *Notes and Queries*, n. s. VI (1959), 319-321.

"Plato's Myth of Aristophanes and Shelley's Panthea," *The Classical Journal*, LV (1959), 121-123.

"A Coleridgean Borrowing from Plato," *The Classical Journal*, LV (1960), 371-372.

"'Caleb Williams' and 'The Cenci,'" *Notes and Queries*, n. s. VII (1960), 260-263.

"The Image of Steerforth and the Structure of *David Copperfield*," *Tennessee Studies in Literature*, V (1960), 57-65.

"Three New Leigh Hunt Letters," *Keats-Shelley Journal*, IX (1960), 115-123.

"Richard Feverel, 'The Original Man,'" *Victorian Newsletter*, no. 18 (Fall 1960), pp. 15-17.

"Dramatic Irony in *Henry Esmond*," *Revue des Langues Vivantes*, XXVII (1961), 35-42.

"Paradise Lost: Felix Culpa and the Problem of Structure," *Modern Language Notes*, LXXVI (1961), 15-20; reprinted in *Milton. Modern Essays in Criticism*, ed. Arthur E. Barker. New York: Oxford University Press (Galaxy), 1965, pp. 336-341.

"A Reading of Byron's *Mazeppa*," *Modern Language Notes*, LXXVI (1961), 120-124.

"Byron's *Parisina* and the Function of Psychoanalytic Criticism," *The Personalist*, XLII (1961), 213-223.

"The Structure of Coleridge's 'The Eolian Harp,'" *Modern Language Notes*, LXXVI (1961), 229-232.

"The Father-Child Symbolism in *Prometheus Unbound*," *Modern Language Quarterly*, XXII (1961), 41-45.

"Reference to a Popular Tradition in 'Don Juan' and 'Mazeppa,'" *Notes and Queries*, n. s. VIII (1961), 224-225.

"The Accretive Structure of Byron's 'The Giaour,'" *Modern Language Notes,* LXXVI (1961), 502-509.

"The Self, The World, and The Structure of *Jane Eyre,*" *Revue des Langues Vivantes,* XXVII (1961), 416-425.

"Coleridge, The Mariner, and Dramatic Irony," *The Personalist,* XLII (1961), 524-532.

"The Method of *A Tale of Two Cities,*" *The Dickensian,* LVII (1961), 183-189.

"The Byron Controversy Again," *Literature and Psychology,* XI (1961), 68-69.

"An Addition to the Hazlitt Canon: Arguments from External and Internal Evidence," *Papers of the Bibliographical Society of America,* LV (1961), 347-370.

"Point of View and Structure in *The Heart of Midlothian,*" *Nineteenth-Century Fiction,* XVI (1961), 257-262.

"Some English Verses of John Taylor Coleridge," *The Library Chronicle,* XXVIII (1962), 1-13.

"An Early Misattribution to Byron: Hunt's 'The Feast of the Poets,'" *Notes and Queries,* n. s. IX (1962), 180-182.

"Introduction" to *Jane Eyre* by Charlotte Brönte. New York: Collier Books, 1962.

" 'Pulpit Oratory,' I-III: Essays by John Hamilton Reynolds in Imitation of William Hazlitt," *The Library Chronicle,* XXVIII (1962), 88-105.

"Hareton Earnshaw: Natural Theology on the Moors," *The Victorian Newsletter,* no. 21 (Spring 1962), pp. 14-15.

"Introduction" to *The Ordeal of Richard Feverel* by George Meredith. New York: Washington Square Press, 1962.

"*The Way of All Flesh*: The Dual Function of Edward Overton," *Texas Studies in Literature and Language,* IV (1963), 583-590.

"Motivation in *Tess of the d'Urbervilles,*" *Revue des Langues Vivantes,* XXIX (1963), 224-231.

"The Conclusion of *Great Expectations* as the Fulfillment of Myth," *The Personalist,* XLIV (1963), 337-347.

"A Joyce-Santayana Parallel," *Notes and Queries,* n. s. X (1963), 379-380.

"An Expanding Theme in *The Last Puritan,*" *The Personalist,* XLV (1964), 27-40.

"The Use of Symbols in *The Way of All Flesh,*" *Tennessee Studies in Literature,* X (1965), 109-121.

"The Byron Collection in Memory of Meyer Davis, Jr.," *The*

Library Chronicle, XXXIII (1967), 8-29.

"The Byron Will of 1809," *The Library Chronicle,* XXXIII (1967), 97-114.

"A Selective Bibliography of Writings about George Eliot, to 1965," *Bulletin of Bibliography and Magazine Notes,* XXV (1967), 70-72.

"The Catalogue for the Sale of Byron's Books," *The Library Chronicle,* XXXIV (1968), 24-50.

"The Davis Collection of Byroniana," *Keats-Shelley Journal,* XVIII (1969), 9-11.

Reviews

"Leigh Hunt's Autobiography: The Earliest Sketches. Edited with an Introduction and Notes by Stephen F. Fogle," *Keats-Shelley Journal,* IX (1960), 131-133.

"Byron and the Spoiler's Art. By Paul West," *Keats-Shelley Journal,* XI (1962), 101-103.

"The Notebooks of Samuel Taylor Coleridge. Edited by Kathleen Coburn," *The Romantic Movement: A Bibliography,* in *Philological Quarterly,* XLI (1962), 665-666.

"A Life of Matthew G. Lewis. By Louis F. Peck," *Keats-Shelley Journal,* XII (1963), 116-118.

"The Poetic Voices of Coleridge. A Study of His Desire for Spontaneity and Passion for Order. By Max F. Schulz," *The Romantic Movement: A Bibliography,* in *Philological Quarterly,* XLIII (1964), 452-453.

"The Poems of William Barnes. Edited by Bernard Jones," *Modern Philology,* LXII (1964), 81-82.

"Captain Medwin, Friend of Byron and Shelley. By Ernest J. Lovell, Jr.," *Keats-Shelley Journal,* XIII (1964), 113-116.

"Ernest Pontifex, or The Way of All Flesh by Samuel Butler. Edited by Daniel F. Howard," *College Composition and Communication,* XVI (1965), 184-185.

"The Letters of Thomas Moore. Edited by Wilfred S. Dowden," *Journal of English and Germanic Philology,* LXIV (1965), 204-207.

"The Letters of Charles Armitage Brown. Edited by Jack Stillinger," *Journal of English and Germanic Philology,* LXVI (1967), 159-162.

"Selected Prose of John Hamilton Reynolds. Edited by Leonidas M. Jones," *Keats-Shelley Journal,* XVII (1968), 123-126.

"Byron and the Ruins of Paradise. By Robert F. Gleckner," *South Atlantic Quarterly*, LXVII (1968), 709-710.

"Matthew Arnold. The Poet as Humanist. By G. Robert Stange," *Comparative Literature Studies*, V (1968), 351-355.

Miscellaneous

"Words That Never Die—The Case For Poetry [a record of readings, with Norman Mailer, Shirley Marshall, Norman Rosten, and William Saroyan]," New York: Washington Square Press, 1965.

ROMANTIC AND VICTORIAN:
Studies in Memory of William H. Marshall

ON THE HISTORICAL
INTERPRETATION OF LITERATURE*
Morse Peckham

A theory of historical interpretation depends upon a theory of interpretation. And a theory of interpretation depends upon a theory of meaning. A theory of meaning depends upon a theory of language, and a theory of language depends in turn upon a theory of mind. If we had these theories in reasonably satisfactory shape we could begin to grapple with what effect the attribute "historical" has upon the term "interpretation." An initial confusion can be cleared up by distinguishing between "historical" and "historiographical." "History" is "past events," and "historiography" is "discourse that purports to discuss history." A literary work is an event if some human being is connected with it by behavior; either it is the deposit or consequence of writing behavior, or it is the stimulus of reading behavior. Of reading events two kinds may be distinguished: immediate, and mediated. To make this distinction it is necessary to return to the ground of theory construction: mind.

The word "mind" is the source of a common, virtually universal confusion. 1) One semantic function is "what happens between stimulus and response." 2) The other is "covert verbal or other semiotic behavior, such as subjective images, verbal, aural, tactile, etc., dreams, and so on." (Henceforth the discussion will be confined to verbal behavior.) When an individual says, "I thought so," it is never clear to others whether he engaged in covert verbal behavior before making the utterance, or whether the stimulus responsible for the utterance fulfilled certain expectancies, that is, simply seemed "right" to him. It is not clear if he is reporting that the prediction of covert verbal behavior has been confirmed, or if he is merely reporting a sense of gratification elicited by the stimulus responsible for his saying, "I thought so." Thus, the same duality of semantic

21

function is to be found in the various forms of "thought" as well as in the various forms of "mind." In the sense of "response" as "observable response," if only to the person generating it, that is, "private" or "privileged verbal response," what happens between stimulus and response is unobservable and inaccessible. "Observable response" is equivalent to "phenomenal response," while "what happens between stimulus and phenomenal response" is "physiologic response." Between physiological response and phenomenal response it is currently impossible to make a connection, and it is likely to remain impossible. The most recent research has shown that the "stochastic or indeterminate behavior of nerve cells, requiring statistical analysis in terms of probabilities of firing, and thus making any meaningful statement of the relation between an individual [phenomenal] response and a particular single stimulus impossible . . . the neurones at all levels of the nervous system are continually and spontaneously active."[1] (It is to be noted that the term "stimulus" now becomes in itself extremely vague; it depends upon the assumption that direct connection between stimulus and response is ascertainable. Since it is not, it is therefore impossible to identify a stimulus; one must speak of a "stimulus field.")

Immediate verbal response is the direct consequence—how we do not and probably cannot know—of physiological response, or brain activity. Mediated verbal response is response preceded by verbal behavior, covert or overt, from the individual generating the immediate verbal response. This is feedback. Any given utterance may be a mixture of the two; *i.e.*, while the speaker is performing the utterance, the utterance itself may enter his stimulus field and by feedback affect the rest of the utterance. Thus, whether reading behavior is immediate or mediated depends on whether the reader generates verbal behavior which affects his reading behavior.

From this several conclusions may be drawn. First, it is consistent with Grace Andrus de Laguna's proposal that language functions by coordinating behavior. Since response is always after stimulus, language functions in time. Thus, a higher explanatory level of language function is that it gives directions controlling behavior; but since the relation between stimulus field and response is stochastic, language gives directions only to one who has been conditioned to obey those directions, or to disobey them. Second, for this same reason of the indeterminate connection between stimulus and response it cannot be said that "meaning" is something immanent in language which the "mind" "extracts" from language. "Meaning" is an attribute of response, not of stimulus field. That is, meaning is a matter of cultural convention, or protocol. The question is not, "What is the meaning of the term or utterance," but, "What is the appropriate response to the term or utterance." In its most radical form, the meaning of an utterance is all possible responses. By this is meant not "all possible responses to that utterance" but, quite nakedly, "all possible responses." This is the full consequence of the proposition that meaning is a matter of cultural convention, or protocol.

A response to a verbal utterance, then, is either appropriate or inappropriate. It can be inappropriate in various ways, according to the judgment of the observer of the response, including the generator of the response. If we judge that the responder is ignorant of the appropriate response, then "inappropriate" means "incorrect," "wrong," "in error." If we judge that the responder is capable of the appropriate response but makes an inappropriate response, we call his response "ironic." Irony is possible because inappropriate responses are possible, and inappropriate responses are possible because responses are cultural conventions. Irony is of several sorts. 1) If we judge that the ironist is capable of the appropriate response, then our judgment includes a judgment that he has judged the utterance to which he is responding to be a response inappropriate for the situation in which it was generated. We may call this "judgmental irony." (Thus, we can call an incorrect response "ironic" if we judge that the response reveals the stimulus utterance as inappropriate for its situation, even though the responder, we assume, did not so judge it.) 2) If our judgment is that the ironist is concerned not with the appropriateness of the stimulus utterance for the situation in which it was generated, but only with the appropriateness of his response for the situation in which he generates that response, then we may call such irony "indifferent irony." In either kind of irony, given a situation in which the factors of the generative situation are identical with the factors of the response situation, except for the entrance of the utterance into the situation, we judge that the utterer and the ironist have judged the situation differently. The term we use to categorize ventionality of response, that is, meanings.) "Interpretation" categorizes the factors of situation, interests, and utterance. Any utterance necessarily involves interests, including the interests of the responder. In appropriate response the interests of utterer and responder are identical; in error, judgmental irony, and indifferent irony, they are divergent.

A response in which the only factor in the response situation different from the factors in the generative situation is judged to be the original utterance, and in which the original utterance has not been mediated by verbal or other semiotic behavior, covert or overt, on the part of the responder, is a "current situation." Any response situation in which the response is immediate but into which factors beyond the utterance are judged to have entered, is an "ironic situation." Any response situation in which the response is mediated by covert, or overt, verbal or other semiotic behavior on the part of the responder is a "historical situation." In historical situations the responder generates a further set of directions to control his behavior in responding to the original utterance. Such directions may be constructs of factors of the generative situation, of the response situation, of the interests of the utterer, or of the interests of the responder, or of all four. (Analysis of syntax and grammar of the utterance is a construct of factors of the generative situation.)

Loosely, "historical interpretation" may mean any one of these, or any combination of them. Hence, the extreme confusion over the term. "Objective historical interpretation" is response mediated by a construct of the interest factors of the utterer, of the factors of the generative situation, and of the relation between the two. "Augustinian historical interpretation," which I have named for the practitioner most responsible for its currency in European culture, is response mediated by a construct of the factors in the responder's situation, in his interests, and of the relation between the two. " 'Contextualist' or 'New Critical' historical interpretation" depends on the judgment that an ironic situation is a current situation. These last two are modes of indifferent irony. Any interpretational construct which omits any one of the four interpretational factors is influenced by those factors, since they are operant in all responses, even though they are not factors in the construct.

"Complete historical interpretation" attempts to include all four factors of interest and situation of utterer and responder. Complete historical interpretation can never be final. Since the response in a historical response situation which the generative situation preceded by a brief interval—say thirty seconds, or even less, so long as a mediated response took place—can be appropriate, there is no theoretical objection to the possibility of appropriateness for a response in a historical response situation which the generative situation preceded by hundreds or even thousands of years. The difficulty of appropriateness, however, is undeniably increased by the degree to which the situation has become ironic. The more ironic the situation, the greater the number and complexity of factors to be included in the interpretative construct and the greater the cultural distance to be overcome in establishing an identity of interests for speaker and responder, or complete historical interpreter. To establish such an identity requires a mediating construct.

"Historiography" is written discourse which is the deposit or consequence of historical interpretation. Confusion would be alleviated if "historiography" were confined to the deposit or consequence of complete historical interpretation.

The ambition of the complete historical interpretation of literature is to make a construct of an ironic and historical situation such that the attributes of the construct are those of a current situation. So long as it is remembered that the construct as an event is not identical with the original utterance as an event, confusion can be avoided, though certainty can never be achieved. The function of "historical research" is the improvement of the construct by identifying the factors of ironic situations. The function of "historical theory" is the improvement of the construct by identifying the interest factors of the complete historical interpreter.

NOTES

*Reprinted from *The Triumph of Romanticism* (Columbia, S. C., 1970) by permission of the author and the publisher. Copyright © 1970 by the University of South Carolina Press.

1. M. A. Boden, review of *The Uncertain Nervous System*, by B. Delisle Burns, *Mind*, LXXVIII (April 1969), 313.

THE MYSTIQUE OF
ROMANTIC NARRATIVE POETRY
Lionel Stevenson

An unacknowledged paradox inheres in many of the accepted definitions of the complex phenomenon known as Romanticism. Though varying as to other elements, the definitions usually agree in emphasizing that Romantic poetry is essentially subjective, and that for this reason none of the Romantic poets wrote in the objective genre of the novel (until Scott was belatedly impelled into it by circumstances), and all of them were inept when they attempted the most impersonal of genres, the drama. While this hypothesis is valid when confined to the achievements of the Romantic authors in the lyric and in poems of personal meditation, it ignores the conspicuous fact that many noteworthy poems by all the principal poets were in the primarily objective form of narrative.

It seems to be assumed that such poems are adequately marshaled under the Romantic banner because they present exotic settings or historical eras or exciting adventures or passionate love scenes or supernatural manifestations or humble rural tragedies; but exclusive reliance on subject-matter produces merely an elementary classification without much critical validity. A more sophisticated criterion is essential if narrative is to be regarded as a genuine and indeed eminent category of Romantic poetry.

The only extensive treatment of the subject, Karl Kroeber's *Romantic Narrative Art* (1960), is handicapped by the assumption that equal attention must be accorded to all narrative poems by Romantic (and pre-Romantic) writers. Scattered through the book are occasional hints of a valid definition, but they are obscured by the effort to deal exhaustively and indiscriminately with such unlike poems as *Tam O'Shanter, Peter Grimes, The Prelude, The Lady of the Lake, Christabel, Don Juan, La Belle*

Dame Sans Merci, and *Miss Kilmansegg and her Precious Leg.*
Hence, the book turns out to be a group of analyses of disparate
poems rather than a unified study. I propose to differentiate
among such poems and to eliminate a large proportion of them
from the category of essentially Romantic art.

If it is legitimate to describe Romantic poetry as dominantly
subjective, the concept has to apply equally to both sides of the
artistic communication—not only to the author's creative impulse but also to the reader's response. Any sensitive reader not
hopelessly shackled by text-book classifications must instinctively
feel that some narratives by the Romantics possess a peculiar
quality lacking in others by the same authors and their contemporaries. The quality can be designated by the term that
Scott popularized, "glamour," or by Matthew Arnold's more
sedate phrase, "natural magic"; but here again the mere use
of a label does not suffice to distinguish an aesthetic effect. The
prime necessity is to determine exactly what constitutes the
exceptional impact of these quintessentially Romantic works.

If the reader's participation in the effect of a poem is to be
enlisted, the only method is by stimulating his imagination to
work independently. Watts-Dunton's old definition of the
Romantic movement as "The Renascence of Wonder" can be
applied, not as a superficial reference to supernatural marvels,
but as an indication that the reader is led to wondering about
elements in the story that are not explicitly set forth, and thereby
to inventing them for himself. I do not imply, of course, that
readers consciously undertake the function of expanding the
story beyond the data provided by the author. The peculiar
power of a successful poem in this mode is that it hypnotizes
the reader into imagining events that he assumes to be in
the poem though actually they are absent.

Literal-minded readers are apt to be impervious to such
stimuli. This is the principal reason why so many critics in
the Romantic era, conditioned by the rationality of the preceding
century, dismissed poems by Coleridge or Keats as meaningless
or mad. Demanding full and clear explanation as the first
requisite of literary communication, they resisted any pressure
upon the reader to cooperate in the creative process. For a
similar reason, Bishop Percy, as a sound neoclassical intellectual,
felt obliged to write additional stanzas to fill the gaps in his
manuscript sources.

Two main methods are employed by the Romantic poets to

ensure as far as possible that the reader will assume his fair share. One is to render the details so vivid that he perceives them fully with his mental senses. Settings, appearance of the characters, dialogue, maintenance of suspense, are all devices to simulate the experience of being in a theater and witnessing a play, with the consequent illusion of immediacy. This technique is entirely compatible with the Romantic preference for "specificity," in contrast with the insistence upon "generality" in neoclassical aesthetics. Nor is the use of sensuous detail in the Romantic poems confined to supplying materials for full visualization; it also can serve to induce a mood. The reader's matter-of-fact common sense is anesthetized by the poem's atmosphere, which renders him joyous or melancholy, hopeful or timorous, to a higher degree than the actual events of the poem require. When thus stimulated, the reader's imagination may possibly be capable of taking off on a short independent flight before relapsing into lethargy.

Preparing the reader to exert his creative power, however, is only the preliminary step. More subtle tactics are involved in pointing the direction in which it is to move. If such a poem is to communicate its overtones successfully, it must establish contact with some fairly general background that is likely to be deep in the reader's mind—usually fairy tales, mythology, or familiar works of earlier literature. Part of the value of this relationship between poet and reader is that it allows room for alternative assumptions. Depending on each reader's individual temperament and his patterns of association, he will extrapolate to suit himself.

Two possible sources may be suggested for this strategy of indirect suggestion. One of them is the folk ballad, with its stark condensation and its rigorous focus upon action. Thomas Gray observed this phenomenon when he remarked of "Gil Morice" in a letter to Mason: "You may read it two-thirds through without guessing what it is about; and yet, when you come to the end, it is impossible not to understand the whole story." Actually, Gray was reading an eighteenth-century "improved" version; the genuine folk versions as found in the Percy manuscript and elsewhere are far more cryptic. Nowadays it is generally believed that most folk ballads were adequately explicit when first composed and became eroded by oral transmission until only a fragmentary skeleton of the story remained; yet it is these mere shards of ballads that impress the reader most strongly. We do not know where Usher's Well is located, or the name of the Wife who lived there, or how her sons met their death, or why she understood the significance of their birch-bark hats; but by combining vivid detail with pregnant silence the forty-eight lines constitute one of the most unforgettable of the ballad tales.

The other probable source for the implicative method is Macpherson's Ossianic poems. In order to produce the illusion of ancient legends that have lost their historical context, he depicts his heroes as stalking phantom-like through misty Highland landscapes in an aura of eerie forebodings to engage in inexplicable battles. Unlike authentic folk-ballads, these pseudo-epic fragments remain remote from a modern reader's imagination through lack of the specific details that promote a sense of immediacy. The Romantic poets, however, found the elusiveness of *Fingal* and its sequels intensely suggestive.

It is time now to test these hypotheses by applying them to some representative poets of the Romantic age. When we begin with Wordsworth, we find that his narrative poems rate very low on the scale of imaginative suggestion. His earliest pieces, *An Evening Walk* and *Descriptive Sketches*, which are narrative only in that they report a series of observations chronologically, are in the neoclassical genre of topographical verse, with all its informative precision. *Guilt and Sorrow*, still mainly neoclassical in manner, offers the sort of tale of humble life that later became Wordsworth's forte; but his method is not under control. The reader is indeed inadequately informed about some essential occurrences in the action, such as how the sailor lost his severance pay, how he murdered the traveler, and how the woman's family became impoverished; but we are not stimulated to invent fuller details. Rather, the summary of these crucial events merely exasperates us by its baldness. Though Wordsworth's later narrative poems are better proportioned, the stories are still recounted as explicitly as those of Crabbe. *Ruth, Michael,* and *Peter Bell,* with their exhaustive biographical data, are typical. The technique of suggestion is to be found to a slight degree in only two of Wordsworth's narratives. In *The Thorn* it is achieved through the cautious innuendos of the narrator, a retired seaman who fancies himself superior to the gossip and superstitions of the villagers and who therefore scrupulously avoids asserting as positive fact that Martha Ray murdered her infant. In *The Idiot Boy* we have only Johnny's imbecile mumbling as a basis for inferring what happened to him during his ride. In both poems, however, there is little demand upon the reader's inventiveness. Wordsworth's two narratives that use conventionally "Romantic" subjects, *Hart-Leap Well* and *The White Doe of Rylstone*, are no less explicit than the tales of humble life.

In his long poems, Scott ranks almost as low as Wordsworth by the test of suggestive implication. In a few brief imitations of the folk ballad he proves that he can exert the evocative spell. We know nothing as to why Proud Maisie is doomed to an early and virgin death, but we reconstruct a whole tragic story from the seventy-five-word dialogue between the lady and the robin-redbreast. In the long narratives, however, this authentic Romantic power is totally obscured. In *The Lay of the Last Minstrel* even the Lady of Branksome's skill in black magic is prosaically attributed to her father's majoring in necromancy at the University of Padua, with a graduate course at St. Andrew's. The subsequent poems are so meticulously informative about every detail and so thorough in the analysis of character that we need not be astonished by the ease of Scott's transition to the writing of prose fiction. Incidentally, my hypothesis may help to demolish the still-surviving fallacy that Scott's prose stories are to be denied the name of "novels" and to be ignominiously classified as "romances." It is more appropriate to say that *Marmion* and *The Lady of the Lake* are not poetical romances but historical novels in rhyme.

The narrative technique of Coleridge is utterly different, as can be seen by contrasting *The Lay of the Last Minstrel* with *Christabel*. The much-discussed similarities between the two poems in meter, setting, and theme only serve to emphasize the disparity. It seems indubitable that Coleridge's inability to finish the poem was due to his intuitive recognition that it had already achieved its full Romantic impact. Indeed, the laboriously written second canto is so inferior to the first that it seriously weakens the effect. The summary of the projected completion which Coleridge gave many years afterwards to the inquisitive Dr. Gillman is such a tissue of melodramatic absurdities that one must infer that he invented it on the spur of the moment as a mocking rebuke to an impertinent question. The first canto enthralls the reader by its sequence of hints that provoke curiosity. If Christabel wants to pray for her absent lover, why not in the castle chapel instead of under an oak on a cold night? If Geraldine was forcibly abducted and transported for two days tied on a horse's back, how can she be in a spotless white gown, with jewels entwined in her coiffure? What does Christabel see when Geraldine disrobes? If Geraldine is an evil witch, why does she seem to be suffering inner pangs? With these clues, as well as minor ones such as the mastiff's behavior, the fire's flaring, and Geraldine's collapse on the threshold, every reader can draw upon his private store of ideas about druidism, witchcraft, and perhaps lesbianism, and thus fill out the story as his taste dictates. At the same time, the visual details, from the last red leaf on the oak to the firelight glinting on Sir Leoline's shield and the lamp in Christabel's room fastened to an angel's feet by a two-fold silver chain, are so exact that even the weirdest supernatural conjectures become plausible. In the second part the interview with Sir Leoline and Bard Bracy's dream are disappointingly commonplace by comparison.

Coleridge's other attempt at a tale of chivalry, *The Ballad of the Dark Ladye*, was abandoned even more abruptly, but I suspect for the opposite reason. The existing portion adheres so slavishly to the clichés of the folk ballad (or of eighteenth-century imitations of it) that there is scarcely any imaginative stimulus at all. My guess is that the last three stanzas of the fragment, wherein the Dark Ladye wistfully describes her longed-for wedding, set Coleridge's imagination off on a more rewarding scene, the opening of *The Ancient Mariner*, and that he felt no impulse to return to the sterile ballad.

The Ancient Mariner is the only substantial narrative that Coleridge completed, and it seems clear and coherent enough to modern readers (except those whose minds have been obfuscated by a search for transcendental symbolism). It was regarded by Coleridge's contemporaries, however, as so obscure that in the revised version he provided the superfluous—indeed ludicrous—prose gloss as a contemptuous concession to obtuseness. In the poem such homely details as the diminishing view of kirk, hill, and lighthouse, and the presence of the mariner's brother and nephew in the crew combine to suggest that the setting is some little West-Country seaport (perhaps Dartmouth?), while the crossbow and the navigation by the position of the sun take us back before gunpowder and the compass to the time of Chaucer's Shipman, who was famous for

> his craft to rekene wel his tydes,
> His stremes, and his daungers hym bisides,
> His herberwe, and his moone, his lodemenage;
> (I [A], 401–403)

i.e., he navigated by soundings and landmarks and currents, around Western Europe from Hull to Carthage, from Gootland to Finistere, and would have been lost if out of sight of land.

Coleridge's nameless seaman on a nameless ship from a nameless port becomes the narrator through whom the reader observes vivid scenes of mast-high emerald icebergs or the tropical ocean burning green and blue and white. Such details induce imaginative identification, and yet we know perfectly well that the ship could not literally have been storm-driven as far as the Antarctic and then homeward across the Pacific. We are left to invent what might have been the actual events during his delirium. We summon up our geographical knowledge. Perhaps the ship encountered icebergs off Newfoundland and then drifted down to the Sargasso Sea. Even the mariner's later life is full of enigmas. How does he actually travel "from land to land"? How did he acquire his "strange powers of speech" (presumably, foreign languages)? We draw upon such legends as the Flying Dutchman and the Wandering Jew.

For many reasons, the most remarkable phenomenon of Coleridge's poetry is *Kubla Khan,* and it is strange that Professor Kroeber should mention it in his book, since it tells no story at all. One is reminded of the old anecdote about a mad painter (a sort of super-Haydon) who exhibited a huge blank canvas as "The Passage of the Israelites," explaining that the Red Sea has just been driven back and the Israelites are about to arrive. In *Kubla Khan* the process of constructing the pleasure gardens has ended when the poem begins, and any adventures of Kubla Khan are yet to occur. Kroeber remarks that "an evanescent narrative" is "a disturbing element" in the poem. The fantastic landscape is so vivid that the reader feels impelled to populate it with characters and action, and therefore seizes on the "ancestral voices prophesying war" to create some episode of dire destruction, compounded out of Macpherson's gloomy soothsayers and the penalties for hubris in Greek tragedy.

In an attempt to forestall complaints about the non-narrative, Coleridge gave it the subtitle "a vision in a dream," and provided the circumstantial preface in which he declares he "has frequently purposed to finish what had been originally, as it were, given to him" to the extent of "two or three hundred lines." As with *Christabel*, one must feel that any such extension, presumably recounting Kubla Khan's downfall, would have destroyed the unique magic of the poem, which, as Lamb wrote to Wordsworth, "he repeats [*i.e.*, recites] so enchantingly that it irradiates and brings heaven and elysian bowers into my parlour when he sings or says it; but," Lamb goes on, "I fear lest it should be discovered by the lantern of typography and clear reducing to letters no better than nonsense or no sense." Like its author's other two truly Romantic poems, *Kubla Khan* avoids this disaster less by any inherent logic than by the reader's spontaneous provision of the missing data.

The second generation of Romantic poets displays the same sharp difference between imaginatively suggestive narratives and literally informative ones. Only in Byron's first oriental tale, *The Giaour*, does he leave much for the reader to infer, and so he attached the apologetic subtitle, "a fragment." A summary is required if we are to perceive the peculiar obliqueness of the narrative. After a long description of Aegean scenery in Byron's own voice, the point of view abruptly shifts to an unidentified onlooker, who understands nothing about what he observes and asks frequent questions, presumably addressed to a listener even less informed than himself. From a few hints we guess that he is a local fisherman, who catches a glimpse of a young Venetian galloping past. There follows a description of Hassan's deserted palace, contrasting its desolation with its former splendid luxury; and then occurs a brief episode in which the narrator's boat is commandeered by an emir for sinking an unidentified bundle in the sea. Only after one has read the whole poem can one infer that this episode must have preceded the glimpse of the agonized giaour and that both events occurred long before the devastation of Hassan's mansion. A narrator (perhaps not the same one) next mentions some conflicting rumors about Leila's disappearance from the harem. After an extended rhapsody over Leila's beauty, another specific episode suddenly begins: when Hassan and his henchmen are setting out on a journey—reportedly to find a new bride—they are waylaid by a robber band and Hassan is gorily slain, after which a survivor delivers his severed head to his mother (not previously mentioned in the tale). Though told with an observer's immediacy, these scenes can scarcely be accepted as reported by the fisherman who was present at the first events. Another interlude invokes hideous curses on the slayer without indication as to whether they are uttered by the bereaved mother or by someone else. Then a snatch of conversation indicates that many years have passed and that the scene has shifted to a Christian monastery (Mount Athos?). The Moslem who at the beginning saw the giaour riding by is now visiting the monastery and recognizes him among the cowled figures. One of the monks takes up the narrative (if so it may be designated), and the poem ends with an incoherent dying confession of the nameless giaour, which reveals a few clues to the story before he lapses into hallucinations.

This medley of uncoordinated glimpses, with abrupt flashbacks in time and shifts in point of view, in some respects foreshadows experimental techniques of the twentieth century. One might expect it to have been totally baffling to the reading public in the era that could not understand Wordsworth and Coleridge; but the violent emotions of revenge and remorse, the barbaric bloodshed and the sentimental rhapsodies, combined to achieve a sensational success.

Nevertheless, Byron did not continue to use the implicative technique. A trace of it remains in the abrupt transitions between scenes in *The Bride of Abydos*, but the point of view is consistently impersonal and the chronology is straightforward. *The Corsair*, though it begins *in medias res*, promptly cuts back to a factual chronicle of Conrad's previous life and an analysis of his character, after which the narrative advances smoothly. Only in *Manfred* is there any strong element of implication, since Manfred's unpardonable sin has to be left to the reader's imagination. It is in *The Giaour* and *Manfred*, then, that we find the quintessence of Byronic Romanticism; the other narratives move in the direction of *Beppo* and *Don Juan*, which are realistic (except for comic exaggeration) and explicit (except for sly innuendoes).

While Scott and Byron fall short of the subtle technique of imaginative suggestion, Shelley goes too far in the opposite direction. Dedicated to allegory and symbolism, he so overtly requires his readers to perceive esoteric meanings that his narratives lose much of their evocative power. In *Alastor* the young poet's frenetic roving through Europe, Asia, and North Africa is insistently a parable of the platonic search for ideal beauty, compounded with the death-wish. When compared with other accounts of wanderings, it lacks either the factual solidity of *Childe Harold's Pilgrimage* or the weird intensity of *The*

Ancient Mariner. There are improbabilities aplenty: how can the shallop, whose sides "gaped wide with many a rift," sail on a stormy sea without leaking? how can the maelstrom act like an elevator to raise the boat several hundred feet upward? But we merely accept these unnatural phenomena passively as part of Shelley's dream world. The crucial mystery in the poem is the identity of the veiled maiden. Shelley indicates that she is no mere figment of an erotic dream, but an apparition of the spirit of solitude, or the creative imagination, or the muse of poetry, or the poet's inmost identity. To modern readers the vision has fascinating Freudian and Jungian implications, but this sort of analysis is totally different from imaginative response. Even the simple question as to whether the veiled maiden is to be regarded as good or evil is an abstract problem, unlike the imaginative one posed by Geraldine.

Similarly, *The Witch of Atlas* does not stimulate us to continue the story beyond the abrupt conclusion. The furniture of the cave, charmingly sensuous though it is, remains allegorical and therefore does not draw the reader into an illusion of actuality, as Tennyson, for example, does in his story of a similar magic tapestry-weaver, *The Lady of Shalott*. Shelley apparently abandoned the poem before beginning to invent any adventures for the witch when she emerged from her cavern. *The Revolt of Islam* is a more elaborately developed narrative, but the exploits of Laon and Cythna are impenetrably enwrapped in cosmic personifications and revolutionary transports. In *Julian and Maddalo,* the cryptic story of the maniac breaks off just when it ought to provide a few tangible clues, and is terminated with a perfunctory and ambiguous summary. Undeniably, Shelley himself is a highly Romantic figure, but he never mastered the elusive technique of Romantic narrative. We enjoy his poems by submerging our imagination in his rather than by proceeding to imagine anything for ourselves.

Between Byron, with his rationalistic bent for explicitness, and Shelley, with his ethereal obscurity, Keats stands as the paragon of Romantic narrative poets, rivaling Coleridge in his mastery of imaginative stimulation. *Endymion* is in some respects as elusive as *Alastor*, which it resembles in much of its story; but Keats has the advantage of using familiar classical myths, so that his reader is able to rely on a few firm identifications. In this 'prentice work, however, Keats is so addicted to sensuous description for its own sake that the reader's imagination becomes cloyed by the sluggish flow of verbal honey. By the time Keats was ready to send *Endymion* to press, he was already outgrowing what he termed "a space of life . . . in which the soul is in a ferment, the character undecided, the way of life uncertain, the ambition thick-sighted; thence proceeds mawkishness." So far as narrative verse was concerned, the maturing experience was the writing of *Isabella*, which is so unlike Keats's other poems that it is unduly scorned by some critics. Under the wholesome influence of the unromantic Boccaccio, Keats tells a straightforward story with realistic thoroughness, building up to a gruesome climax enhanced by its explicitness.

In his subsequent narratives he was firmly in control of the Romantic evocation. In writing *La Belle Dame Sans Merci* he submitted to the condensation and allusiveness of the folk ballad. One may profitably compare it with Coleridge's poem on the same theme, which is usually overlooked because the poet inexplicably imbedded it in another narrative under the title of *Love*. The story of the narrator and his Genevieve is so sentimental that one scarcely recognizes the very different ballad hidden in the middle of it. When freed of its encumbrances, it becomes a minor masterpiece:

> I told her of the Knight that wore
> Upon his shield a burning brand;
> And that for ten long years he wooed
> The Lady of the Land. . . .
>
> But when I told the cruel scorn
> That crazed that bold and lovely Knight,
> And that he crossed the mountain-woods,
> Nor rested day nor night;
>
> That sometimes from the savage den,
> And sometimes from the darksome shade
> And sometimes starting up at once
> In green and sunny glade,—
>
> There came and looked him in the face
> An angel beautiful and bright;
> And that he knew it was a Fiend,
> This miserable Knight!
>
> And that unknowing what he did,
> He leaped amid a murderous band,
> And saved from outrage worse than death
> The Lady of the Land!

> And how she wept, and clasped his knees;
> And how she tended him in vain—
> And ever strove to expiate
> The scorn that crazed his brain;—
>
> And that she nursed him in a cave;
> And how his madness went away,
> When on the yellow forest-leaves
> A dying man he lay . . . .

(ll. 29-64)

There can be little doubt that Keats was familiar with this poem: the frame situation shows close resemblance to the episode in *The Eve of St. Agnes* when Porphyro plays "an ancient ditty, long since mute, / In Provence call'd 'La belle dame sans mercy'" (ll. 291-292). In Coleridge's poem it is described as "an old and moving story— / An old rude song."

In *La Belle Dame*, even the metrical adaptation of ballad stanza, with the foreshortened last line, echoes Coleridge's. The shared elements are obvious—the crazed knight, the weeping lady, the cave, even the autumn leaves; but Keats has revised and tightened the story with consummate skill. The abrupt, violent fight with the murderous band is eliminated, the hard-hearted lady and the ambiguous angel-fiend of the wilderness are combined into a single female being; and instead of the pedestrian chronological order, the story is told retrospectively by the question-and-answer method—devices that Coleridge had used adeptly in *The Ancient Mariner*. As a result, the reader of the Keats poem employs his own resources—stories of chivalric quests and fairy tales of nature-spirits striving for union with mortals—to flesh out the episode of the knight and the merciless lady. Acquaintance with the particular folk ballad of *Thomas the Rymer* may contribute, but it is not essential.

The Eve of St. Agnes is the very archetype of Romantic narrative, in that the story is conveyed almost wholly through setting and mood. The entire situation is little more than that of Coleridge's *Love*, as noted above—the moonlight, the Gothic setting of ruined tower and "statue of the armed knight," the eager lover and shy but compliant maiden. Regarded in terms of conventional narrative method, *The Eve of St. Agnes* flouts the basic rules. Suspense is built up meretriciously and then flagrantly disappointed. Angela's warnings lead us to expect a confrontation between Porphyro and his enemies, and the elaborate preparation of the supper seems like a foolhardy gesture that will ensure discovery. Instead, the lovers tiptoe out of the castle and escape unsuspected.

As peculiar as this anticlimax is the total absence of explicit beginning or conclusion. We have no information as to why Madeline's family hates Porphyro; there may have been a family feud or he may be of inferior birth. In view of the hatred, however, we must wonder how the lovers ever met each other. At the end, too, we are told only that "these lovers fled away into the storm." Some readers may put together the emphasis upon intense cold, the absence of any reference to warm clothing, even the problem of transportation (did Porphyro have a horse tethered conveniently nearby?) to infer that they soon perished of exposure, though happy in each other's arms. The morbid details in the last stanza reinforce this assumption. Sentimentalists, on the other hand, will insist that "they lived happy ever after" in the proper manner of fairy tales such as *The Sleeping Beauty, Rapunzel,* and many others with the same theme of a secluded heroine rescued by a venturesome lover.

The lack of substantive information in *The Eve of St. Agnes* can be made obvious by comparing it with *Romeo and Juliet,* which it resembles closely in situation and characters. Writing for the objective medium of the stage, Shakespeare could leave nothing to be guessed at. We are fully informed as to the Montague-Capulet enmity and we witness the misdelivery of the invitation, which results in Romeo's first glimpse of Juliet. Romeo fights the inevitable duel with Paris, and at the end we are spared no pang of the lovers' deaths. Keats, in his poem, concentrates on Act III, scenes ii and v, of Shakespeare's play, and loads every rift with the ore of erotic suggestion through sense impressions.

After this high point, *Lamia* seems relatively informative; but the key issue is left ambiguous, to the confounding of critics ever since. Like Geraldine, and Shelley's veiled maiden, and La Belle Dame, Lamia seems to be a malicious enchantress who is nevertheless inwardly tormented. Remembering the Wyf of Bathe's tale and other variants of the "loathly lady" theme, we tend to sympathize with her and condemn the heartlessness of her dismissal. On the other hand, Apollonius is the very embodiment of the wise and loyal mentor who so often protects rash youths from disaster. We are left to choose whichever interpretation suits our taste.

When we move on to the Victorian age, the matter of Romantic narrative technique retains its significance, as the Victorian poets were strongly affected by the Romantics and yet began to drift away from their exclusive influence. Various poems therefore fall distinctly into one or other of the two unlike categories.

Tennyson at the outset of his career proved himself to be adept in the Romantic mode; *Mariana* is an exemplary specimen. The quotation in the epigraph is misleading, as the line in *Measure for Measure* merely triggered Tennyson's imagination with a fortuitous suggestion of a Lincolnshire landscape; otherwise Shakespeare's heroine has little if any relationship to Tennyson's obsessed recluse. The reader's inventive faculty accordingly enjoys full freedom. Nothing in the poem determines the woman's age or circumstances. It is solely our background of legends that induces us to believe that she is a beautiful girl and that the unnamed "he" is her lover. She could be an old woman and he her son; she could be middle-aged and he her husband; he could be no more than a figment of her disordered fancy; if we choose to be facetious we may suggest that he is the errand-boy bringing groceries. Certainly, in the light of practicality it is impossible that Mariana can survive indefinitely without food supplies or human contact or even any physical action apart from going to bed each night and (apparently) winding the clock. We are obliged to resort to the fairy-tale motif of enchantment; but the poem does not mention a spell and offers no explanation for Mariana's certainty that "he will not come." Such is the vividness of the scene and the unity of the mood that we invent a whole past and future of action for a situation which as presented is totally static.

The Lady of Shalott moves only a short step toward clearer information. We do know here that the physically impossible isolation is the result of a spell, and we do have an account of the lady's punishment when she defies it; but there is still no evidence as to who imposed the curse, or when, or why, or how the lady knows about it. The identification of the "he" as Lancelot links the episode to the Arthurian cycle, but Tennyson is careful to avoid denominating "the fairy Lady of Shalott" as the Elaine of the tradition, who suffered from no enchantment beyond the universal one of falling in love. When he retold the story in *The Idylls of the King,* the Romantic allusiveness is wholly dispelled; we have a perfectly practical reason for the girl's embroidery work, and a plausible one for her broken-hearted death.

The Romantic technique of imaginative suggestion bears a

distinct but ambiguous relationship to the most original poetic genre of the Victorian period, the dramatic monologue. Developed simultaneously by Tennyson and Browning, it has unmistakable affinities with *The Thorn, The Ancient Mariner,* and even *La Belle Dame Sans Merci,* insofar as those poems are spoken by a fictitious character and addressed to a listener. Certainly, too, Victorian dramatic monologues enlist the reader's cooperation in reconstructing the full background of the episode. Nevertheless, there are basic differences between the two modes.

When the first-personal point of view is used in a Romantic poem, it is simply a device to give readers a sense of closer contact with a past event. The narrative itself is what matters, and the speaker merely transmits it. In the dramatic monologue, on the other hand, the emphasis is on the present situation, to which the antecedents led up, and attention is focused largely on the speaker's personality and motives.

This intention vitally modifies the communication between the text and the reader. Instead of being lulled into an involuntary use of his imagination, he is challenged to a battle of wits, like that entered upon nowadays in reading a detective story. The reader is expected to pick up clues, to evaluate them in terms of the speaker's temperament and prejudices, and to establish not only past events but also future probabilities on the basis of the evidence. In *The Bishop Orders His Tomb,* for instance, we feel fully informed as to the record of the bishop's rivalry with Gandolf for power and women, and we savor the irony of the inevitable future when the sons will prove as venal as their parents and the tomb will remain unbuilt. At the same time, we anatomize the bishop as a laboratory specimen of Renaissance paradoxes, with his sensuality and aesthetic taste, his unscrupulousness and his gross lack of spiritual perception. Sometimes, indeed, the analysis may be debatable, as is illustrated by recent disputes among competent critics as to the nobility of Tennyson's Ulysses, the intelligence of Browning's Duke of Ferrara, or the purity of the lady in *Count Gismond.* Obviously, however, the questions remain in the realm of ratiocination, not in that of imaginative creation.

In general, then, Browning's poems are objective and intellectual rather than subjective and imaginative. His first one, *Pauline,* leaves many unanswered questions, but it is so utterly devoid of specific clues that the reader's imagination finds no launching pad for an independent flight. We can make no guess as to the speaker's identity, or his relationship with Pauline, or why he is dying. In his mature work, Browning offers us only one distinct example of purely Romantic narrative, and he himself was well aware of its strange unlikeness to his other poems. Of *Childe Roland to the Dark Tower Came* he reported that it "came to me as a kind of dream. I had to write it, then and there, and I finished it the same day, I believe . . . . I did not know then what I meant beyond that, and I'm sure I don't know now." This statement remarkably resembles Coleridge's account of his writing *Kubla Khan*; and the genesis of Browning's poem also bears a fortuitous affinity with *Mariana,* in that its starting point is an evocative line in a Shakespearian play. Following the authentic Romantic mystique, we are left to guess why Roland undertook the quest and how his predecessors failed. Especially, of course, the abrupt ending is a bravura specimen of evocative evasion. The psychological purpose of the poem has been fulfilled when Roland conquers his fears and sounds the horn, and the reader is compelled to invent the sequel. We expect an evil knight, or a giant, or an enchanter to emerge and engage Roland in battle, resulting in either his triumph or his heroic death. It is just as possible, however, that he will be greeted by a hospitable host. If the reader prefers irony, he can assume that no one responds to the summons—that the tower is an abandoned shell. Each reader's background of fairy tales and romances of chivalry will determine his choice among the alternatives.

It would be easy to apply the same criterion to the Pre-Raphaelite poets, who were the mid-Victorian inheritors of the Romantic tradition. As may be expected, Rossetti emerges as a master of evocation in *The Blessed Damozel* and *Sister Helen.* Morris shows touches of it in a few poems in his first published volume; but his essentially objective imagination and his preference for physical energy were more at home with the straightforward epic manner.

It is interesting to discover that the foregoing method of analysis applies equally well to prose fiction. Readers are always aware that *Wuthering Heights,* uniquely among Victorian novels, conveys the very spirit of Romanticism. I suggest that this quality is not due wholly to the violent passions of the characters and their isolation in a wild natural landscape, but also to the technical use of imaginative stimulus. The narrative begins near the end of the action and is reported by one fictional character to another, just as in *The Ancient Mariner* and *La Belle Dame Sans Merci.* Because of Nelly Dean's limited knowledge of events, we cannot know the facts about Heathcliff's origin and Mr. Earnshaw's adoption of him; one is tempted to guess that he is a bastard son and hence Catherine's half-brother. Similarly, we can only speculate as to what happened during the years of his absence, when the illiterate brat somehow acquired money and culture. The final scene, with Heathcliff's corpse beside the open window, harks back to the initial episode of Lockwood's dream to compel us to infer a spiritual reunion with Catherine, which is reinforced by the peasants' superstitions but is never explicitly stated.

Now that an array of evidence has been offered, it is possible to draw several conclusions about Romantic narrative. One is that, although many ultra-Romantic stories contain elements of the supernatural, their distinctiveness does not reside primarily in their remoteness from the material plane. The *Idylls of the King* are permeated with magic of many varieties, but it is treated in the matter-of-fact tone of epic exposition: the enslavement of Merlin by Vivien is utterly different in effect from that of Lycius or the Knight at Arms. The technique of imaginative suggestion simply happens to function particularly well when applied to paranormal themes.

In a further respect, the poems I have discussed are particularly characteristic of the Romantic attitude. This is the minimizing of dramatic action, with its essential element of conflict, in favor of passive surrender. Christabel is helplessly mesmerized by Geraldine; the Knight at Arms offers no resistance to La Belle Dame; Lycius is totally in the power of Lamia until the intervention of the rationalistic Apollonius; Mariana fatalistically accepts her solitude; even Roland seems to be almost an automaton as he traverses the sinister plain. The situations are suspended in a timeless void, unrelated to any wider context of human relationships or decisive action. Thus, they conform closely with the profound Romantic conviction of inwardness and isolation.

In conclusion, I wish to emphasize that my discussion is not intended to contribute to the current vogue of concern with symbolism and archetypal myths in poetry. The poems that I have mentioned may or may not convey transcendental significance. I have dealt solely with a matter of technique: the Romantic poets in some of their best narratives discovered a way of enhancing their readers' aesthetic satisfaction by enlisting a spontaneous imaginative participation.

SOME DANGERS OF DIALECTIC THINKING, WITH ILLUSTRATIONS FROM BLAKE AND HIS CRITICS

Peter L. Thorslev, Jr.

Anyone should hesitate before adding one more to the plethora of definitions of Romanticism, but doing so can perhaps be excused and even justified by the rule of Ockham's Razor, if the new definition succeeds in reducing other definitions to a common denominator, or at least in demonstrating previously unperceived relationships among them. I believe one can make such a case for defining Romanticism as consisting in large part of a resurgence of dialectic thinking, and its application in fields—especially in the sciences of psychology and physiology, in aesthetics and criticism, and in theology and the philosophy of history—in which it had not been dominant before.

The term "dialectics" is admittedly imprecise: it has had a long history, and its meanings have varied with the dominant philosophical schools of the period. For the Socrates of the Platonic dialogues, who is generally credited with having popularized the term, it referred to the method of debating and learning through question and answer: the famous "midwifery." For Plato himself dialectics was the copestone of the sciences in that it dispensed with hypotheses and dealt with first principles immediately and intuitively apprehended—the innate truths which Socrates attempted to draw out in his question-and-answer dialogues. For Aristotle, on the other hand—and this is the meaning of the term which became dominant in the revival of Aristotelian rhetoric and remained current through most of the Renaissance—"dialectics" referred to the method of reasoning from commonly received opinions, as opposed to "demonstrative" reasoning, which proceeded syllogistically from demonstrable truths. Kant, in the *Critique of Pure Reason,* used "dialectic" in a very special sense to refer to his method of critical

apprehension of those antinomies and paralogisms (arguments
which proceed from premises commonly assumed, but which
involve one in contradiction) eventuating when one attempts to
apply the forms of Sensibility or of the Understanding (*e.g.,*
space, time, and causation) to the realm of things-in-themselves
(*e.g.,* God, the immortal Soul, the Free Will).

There is perhaps a common denominator in all of these definitions, an emphasis on thinking as process, and on isolating, defining, and perhaps reconciling conflicting or contradictory premises or opinions. These aspects of dialectic were picked up by
the German Romantic idealists, by Fichte and Schelling, but
especially by Hegel, who systematized them and made them
characteristic of what he called "speculative" or "philosophical"
reasoning, as distinct from the "mere analytic understanding"
characteristic of the sciences and of the empirical philosophical
tradition which he and his fellow Romantics so vigorously opposed. It is with what we might call Hegelian and post-Hegelian
dialectic in its broadest sense that we must be concerned, because
it is this dialectic thinking which characterized so much of Romanticism. I prefer to use the term dialectic "thinking" rather
than "reason," because for most of us—and certainly for most
of the Romantics—the term "reason" has become firmly associated with traditional logic and with scientific method. Coleridge
does, it is true, use "Reason" to refer to an intuitive faculty
which transcends the mere "Understanding" (somewhat on
the analogy of the German distinction between *Verstand* and
Vernunft), but for most of the English Romantics—for Blake,
Wordsworth, Shelley, and Byron, for instance—"reason" and
the logical and empirical understanding were synonymous.

Dialectic thinking, in this Romantic and post-Romantic sense
of the term, can be characterized most clearly by contrasting it
with analytic reason, as of course the Romantics did.[1] In the
first place, dialectic thinking is concerned with quality rather
than quantity, and, moreover, qualitative differences which the
dialectician insists cannot be reduced to quantitative differences,
as the analytic reasoner attempts to reduce them. Second—and
all of these characteristics are closely related—dialectics is concerned primarily with evolutionary or historical process, and
process which can produce qualitative change or genuine novelty.
To borrow a term from the structuralists, dialectic thinking is
persistently diachronic rather than synchronic, *i.e.,* it is concerned
with developments which occur over a period of time, not merely

with present events and their constellations of present conditions. The dialectician's complaint about traditional logic has always been that it cannot account for time or for qualitative change, and Hegel did indeed claim that he had created in his dialectics a new "temporalized" logic which both included and transcended Aristotelian or formal logic. For these reasons, the key science for the dialectician is history and perhaps evolutionary biology, just as the key or model science for the analytic reasoner is physics and perhaps inorganic chemistry. There is no necessary connection, but frequently there is an element of teleology in dialectic thinking; *i.e.*, the "Process" is considered as directed toward some end, whether that end be Hegel's World-Spirit self-consciously realized, Blake's Eden, Shelley's Prometheus Unbound, or Spengler's *Sonnenuntergang*. In any case, the dialectical process is usually seen as inevitable and irreversible, even if it is left "open-ended," *i.e.*, if the end-goal is unforeseen or even unforeseeable. In the term used by Karl Popper, dialecticians are typically "historicists": they see the dialectical process as an organic development proceeding to a preordained end, sometimes in concurrence with, but often in spite of anything philosophers or historians attempt to do about it.[2] As Hegel put it, "speculative" philosophy can only be a bringing to consciousness of processes already concluded: "The owl of Minerva takes flight only at twilight."[3] The analytic reasoner, on the other hand, is usually a determinist, in his insistence that every event must have necessary and sufficient causes, but he is not a historicist or a teleologist: he can be satisfied with probabilities or even with an element of chance and uncertainty in the events he studies, either because of imperfections in his methods of observation, or because there may be some basic uncertainty or fortuity in the very nature of things.

Finally, and most characteristically, the dialectician seems always to conceive of the Process he is describing as consisting in the conflict of opposites. As Coleridge confidently asserts (in a free translation from Schelling), "Grant me a nature having two contrary forces . . . and I will cause the world of intelligences with the whole system of their representations to rise up before you."[4]

Thinking in terms of polar opposites is at least as old as philosophy—indeed, Claude Lévi-Strauss has suggested that it is basically characteristic of all human thinking whatever, and that it is this which we moderns have in common with the savage mind.[5] The Pythagorean Decalogue of Contraries—having mostly to do with number, but including light and darkness, male and female—was in standard reference through most of the Middle Ages and beyond. Heraclitus opposed Stasis and Flux, Parmenides the One and the Many, Plato the World of Forms and the World of (ephemeral) Things. For the most part, however, these oppositions were static rather than dynamic, and they were resolved by making the one contrary real, the other illusory.[6] So for Heraclitus only the Flux is real, for Parmenides only the One. Even for Plato the Forms are the only true reality, and the world of evanescent things is merely apparent and ultimately illusory (at least incapable of being the object of "real" knowledge). For the Romantic dialectician, on the other hand, the Contraries are dynamic, not static, because they are given ontological status as irreducible forces rather than intellectual concepts or categories; they are equal and sometimes even coeval, and all of reality consists in their conflict. The sophisticated argument of the analytic reasoner has been that dialectic process as consisting in the conflict of opposites and their reconciliation or transcendence is perhaps characteristic of the operations of mind—as in the dialectic progression of philosophical opinion illustrated in the Platonic dialogues—but that one cannot therefore assume that it is characteristic also of the objects of mind, of the world of things or outside reality. This is an argument, however, which would be unacceptable to any of the major Romantic dialecticians—to Blake and Coleridge as well as to Schelling or Hegel. For the Romantic dialectician the world of reality *is* the world of mind: the world of matter and of the senses is dependent and derivative, even illusory. So for Blake and Coleridge as well as for Hegel, all history is the dialectical progress of universal mind, and metaphysical reality is ideal. The restless movement of mind from thesis to antithesis, from contrary to contrary, and perhaps to synthesis, is not only a mirror of, but is identical with, the movement and development of the suns and stars and of all sublunary bodies whatever. Mind is the ultimate creator; the creative process is dialectical; and ultimately creator and created are one.

Opposition exists for the analytic reasoner as well, as perhaps the simplest and most fundamental of all systems of classification.[7] But for the analytic reasoner binary opposition is a mental construction only; he attempts wherever possible to redefine opposites in terms of relative degrees and serial or hierarchical order. So the traditional categories of heat and cold, light and darkness, conceived by the dialectician as opposing and independent forces, are reduced to relative measurements of heat or light or their absence, degrees on thermometers or on photometers. One remembers that David Hartley, Bentham, and the Utilitarians attempted to reduce even the psychological contraries of pleasure and pain, desire and aversion, to a calculus, a pleasure-pain thermometer.[8] For the dialectician, on the other hand, opposites are not static categories but positive conflicts; the contraries are not relative, but absolute, not mental constructs but metaphysical principles.

Dialectic thinking in this Romantic sense had its most obvious origins, I believe, in what is called the "perennial philosophy": in neo-Platonism and in gnostic heresies; in the alchemy of Paracelsus and in the organic pantheism of Giordano Bruno; above all, perhaps, in the mystic theology represented by Jakob Boehme and his followers (William Law in England, especially).[9] Schelling pays Boehme tribute and shows a deep influence. Coleridge also records his debt, in the *Biographia Literaria,* to one whom he considers a predecessor in the "Dynamic Philosophy." Hegel goes so far as to call Boehme the "Father of modern philosophy"—"modern" meaning of course Romantic idealism. Indeed, the most fundamental of the triads in Hegelian dialectic—Being (thesis) versus Non-Being (antithesis) to Becoming (synthesis)—has its counterpart already in Boehme's mystic theology, if in a rather more poetic terminology. And certainly dialectic thinking is fundamental to a great deal if not all of Romantic literature and art.

Take for example René Wellek's defining principles of Romanticism: organicism in art, history, and metaphysics; imagination in esthetics; symbolism in the arts.[10] Dialectic thinking is implicit or explicit in any organicist metaphysics, perhaps because the most intimate and originative of all theses and antitheses is that of the contraries of male and female, with the "synthesis" of offspring—and certainly the sexual analogy seems never far below the surface, even in the speculations of mystics and theologians like Boehme (it is of course omnipresent in Blake). Coleridge is at the center of Romantic tradition when he defines imagination as the capacity for the dialectic "reconciliation" of opposites. Finally, it is also distinctive of Romantic criticism, in Coleridge and in his German predecessors, to define the symbol, as the product of the creative imagination, in terms of the synthesizing of such opposites as unity and multeity, the finite and the infinite, the concrete and the universal.

Romantic dialectics dominated later nineteenth-century philosophy and even made inroads in science—as when evolution was conceived of in dialectic terms by Herbert Spencer—but it is surely fair to say that no aspect of Romanticism has suffered such a critical eclipse in the twentieth century, in the hard sciences and in the academy, with the triumph of scientific method and logical empiricism and philosophical or linguistic analysis. Hegel has still his defenders—indeed, he seems to be enjoying something of a minor Renaissance, especially in France—but it is generally his critical and political treatises which are defended, and not his logic.[11] In most departments of philosophy Romantic dialectic is taught as an interesting aberration in the history of logic, and the venerable Hegelian triads are trotted out in class as useful conundrums for students to try their analytic teeth on. Even Marxist dialectic, which with its materialist rather than idealist base might seem to be more congenial in a scientific age, has fairly well lost its intellectual respectability (witness the disastrous reign of Lysenko in the Soviet scientific academy), and for the most part it seems to survive largely as a kind of rationalization for political reform or for a revised and neo-Romantic nationalism.[12] The older Santayana was no militant logical empiricist, but in his comment on the dialectic thinking still dominant in his student days at Harvard he sums up the modern attitude: "dialectic is merely verbal or ideal, and its application to facts, even to the evolution of ideas, entirely hypothetical and distorting . . . . Dialectic merely throws a verbal net into the sea, to draw a pattern over the fishes without catching any of them. It is an optical illusion."[13]

Yet in various attenuated forms dialectical thinking is still very influential in the lives of all of us—in the theologies of Paul Tillich and of Teilhard de Chardin; in Freudian psychoanalysis and in any of the myth-and-symbol psychologies; the peculiar synthesis of Freud and Marx in Herbert Marcuse's works and in New Left ideology in general would be impossible without it; and above all it survives in the arts and in criticism, with our tensions and paradoxes and concrete universals—in short, in most of those areas of our "Other Culture" which have not been deeply affected by philosophical analysis or by the mathematical ordering of scientific method. In this respect, at least, we are still very much heirs of the Romantic Age.

This would not be the place nor would a mere literary historian be the person to offer a general critique of dialectic thinking.[14] Moreover, even if one were as convinced as Santayana was of its invalidity, for a literary critic to stand Canute-like on positivist shores and defy its persistent tide would not only be futile, but self-defeating. If such time-honored contraries as those of a Rage for Order versus a Rage for Chaos, of Appearance versus Reality, of Science versus Poetry, and even of Life against Death (to paraphrase the titles of some well-known works by some of our foremost literary dialecticians) were somehow to be analyzed out of existence, most of us would be, if not out of business, at least left with our business severely curtailed. Scholarly and critical works on Romantic literature seem especially inclined to the use of dialectic thinking—perhaps by contagion from their subject matter. One would expect this to be the case with Blake scholars, and more generally with scholars such as Kathleen Raine and G. Wilson Knight, who have acknowledged their debts to Boehmenism and the *philosophia perennis*, but in truth the practice extends also to those critics whom Miss Raine has recently condemned as having been contaminated with "positivist" or "materialist" reasoning.[15] The typical G. Wilson Knight essay begins by the positing of some variation on his favored contraries—masculine versus feminine, aggressive and intellectual versus passive and imaginative, light versus dark eternities—but I believe there are few works of Romantic scholarship written in the last decade (including some of my own) which could not be reduced to some variation of those most basic of Romantic contraries: Ego (self, consciousness) versus Non-Ego (Nature, unconsciousness); Science (Reason, analysis) versus Poetry (Imagination, synthesis); the Lust for Experience (directly emotional and chaotic) versus the Compulsion for Artistic Creation (ordered, aesthetically distanced). And surely these conflicts are real, in life and in art, whether the "contraries" are metaphysical (or psychological) absolutes in the nature of things, or mere mental constructs capable of analytic reduction. But if we cannot reverse the tide of dialectic thinking, we can at least chart a few of the shoals and reefs, so that when we do launch once more into that sea so measureless to man we can be more sure of our polar bearings.

In this spirit, then, and—paradoxically enough, for a Romantic scholar—in the spirit quite frankly of analytic reason, I would like to discuss three of the most prominent dangers of dialectics. Adapting a term from Kant, we might call them the antinomies of dialectic reason. Blake was the most consistently and explicitly dialectic of all the English Romantics, and so I have drawn most of my illustrations from his works and from their explication by his critics, but I believe that once the dangers are defined, their application very broadly to Romanticism and Romantic scholarship becomes readily apparent. I have invented names for these three broad classes of dangers, names which I hope will seem apt, and which are not technical. The first danger is characterized by the Either-Or Syndrome, or the tendency to confuse contraries with contradictories, and to see both where they do not in fact exist. The second is the Absolutizing of Abstractions—parallel in a way to what Whitehead calls the Fallacy of Misplaced Concreteness in scientific thinking. The third is characterized by the Both-And Syndrome, or the yearning for apocalypse and for the transcendence of the laws of logic, especially the law of contradiction.

The first of these dangers, characterized by the Either-Or Syndrome, is one which Blake himself warned against in *The Marriage of Heaven and Hell:* the confusion of contraries with contradictories, or the tendency of dialectic thinking to treat contrary forces in the world of things as if they were logical propositions in contradiction. There is, in other words, really a double confusion here: first, a confusion of the logical categories of propositions, and second, the application of these logical relationships between propositions to the world of things. The distinction between contrary and contradictory propositions in formal logic is clear enough, and has been traditional ever since Aristotle discussed it in the seventh chapter of his *De Interpretatione.*[16] Contradictory propositions cannot both be true, and they cannot both be false: they are exclusive, and between them they exhaust the field of discourse. Contraries, on the other hand, cannot both be true, but they may both be false; they are exclusive but not exhaustive. The contrary of the proposition that all poets are prophets is the proposition that no poets are prophets. Both propositions cannot be true, and both may be (and demonstrably are) false: there is a middle ground, so to speak, in the possibility that some poets are prophets, and some are not. The contradictory or negation of the proposition that all poets are prophets, however, is the proposition that some poets are not prophets. Between these propositions there is no middle ground: they cannot both be true, and they cannot both be false.

Strictly speaking, of course, these logical relationships apply only to propositions, to statements or thoughts about things, rather than to the things themselves, but of course this argument cannot be applied to Romantic dialecticians—to Blake or Coleridge or Hegel—because, as I pointed out above, for them reality is ultimately ideal or mental, and therefore intrinsically logical or dialectical. The logic (of whatever kind, Aristotelian or Hegelian) is not a mental construction or a program which we impose upon some outside reality; it is inherent in the reality itself. Not only is it true that what cannot be thought cannot be real ("Nor is it possible to Thought / A greater than itself to know," as Blake puts it in *A Little Boy Lost*), but thought is the *only* real.

To define oneself or one's personal moral imperatives purely in terms of contradiction or negation rather than in terms of contraries is of course self-defeating. One can make this point clear in the contrast between what one might call the Satanic dilemma and the Promethean alternative, a contrast which Shelley draws in his Preface to *Prometheus Unbound*, if not in these terms, and one which is implicit in Blake's reinterpretation of *Paradise Lost* in *The Marriage of Heaven and Hell*. When Satan in *Paradise Lost* declares that henceforth evil will be his good, he defines his purposes and therefore his reason for being solely in terms of the contradiction or negation of God's purposes, and thereby makes himself in Hell as dependent upon God, although in an inverse relationship, as ever he was in Heaven.[17] Prometheus, on the other hand, defines his purposes independently—the furtherance of human culture and the alleviation of man's suffering—and not merely in terms of contradiction. When these purposes come in conflict with those of Olympus he declares himself in opposition to Zeus (whereas he had previously, of course, been Zeus's chief ally). But he defines his opposition in terms of his contrary purposes, not his purposes in terms of his opposition. Blake, in his reinterpretation of Milton's account, implies that Milton was quite unfair in defining Satan purely in terms of negation. Blake's Satan, in *The Marriage*, stands for passionate energy and has thus a clear and creative purpose of his own (a purpose later divided between Orc and Los). Indeed, Blake almost goes so far as to define the Messiah as pure analytic and "devouring" reason, in terms of the negation of hellish energy and creativity.[18]

But if it is self-defeating to define oneself in terms of contradiction or negation, it is a common polemic device so to define

one's opposition: "He who is not for me is against me, and
he who gathereth not up, scattereth abroad." Blake's complaint
against the priesthood, the believers in a "cloven fiction," is
that they take upon themselves this divine prerogative—much as
John Foster Dulles is reported to have done in American foreign policy, so that whatever nation was not for us was *ipso
facto* against us. The "priests" (fathers, beadles, magistrates,
and authority figures in general, in *Songs of Experience* and
after) set up a finite and limited good—the negative prohibitions
of the Ten Commandments, for instance, quite narrowly interpreted—and then define all opposition solely in terms of negation. To do so, Blake insists, is to set up a false dichotomy, to
make contradictories out of what should rightly be contraries.[19]

It is nevertheless a favored polemic device, and the painful
truth seems to be that Blake himself employed it. I cannot otherwise see how one can account for Blake's amazingly heterogeneous collection of opponents of "imaginative vision": Bacon,
Locke, Newton, Voltaire, Hume, Gibbon, and Rousseau, among
scientists, historians, and "natural philosophers," and all legalistic moralists, all priests, all Druids, and all prudes. Here is the
Either-Or Syndrome with a vengeance; it seems to me that the
only factor common to all of these groups and individuals is
that they are not poet-prophets (and even in that, surely Rousseau could lay some claim to being both). There is a parochial
intellectual arrogance in operation here, not unlike the Greek
classification of all humanity into the two contradictory (mutually
exclusive and exhaustive) classifications of Greeks and "bar-
barians," *i.e.*, non-Greeks. It is of course true that all who are
not Greek are non-Greeks, but in a broader ethnographic perspective the latter category seems hardly of defining significance.

Moreover, because Greeks are civilized, it does not follow
that all non-Greeks are uncivilized—but this was of course the
implication of the dichotomy. In other words, the Either-Or
Syndrome can be carried a step farther, to imply not merely a
virtual but an actual identification of the motives and methods
of the heterogeneous individuals who make up the opposition.
In the Introduction to Chapter 3 of *Jerusalem* Blake quite explicitly names Voltaire and Gibbon—and what they represent—
as responsible for "all wars whatsoever." Harold Bloom in
his comment on this passage concedes that Blake is "being somewhat outrageous," but defends Blake as a poet and a polemicist,
and therefore as not obliged to be fair: "His critics can be

fair for him."[20] Certainly Blake is unfair, but it is more important to note that he is wrong. Pope is also unfair to Theobald and Colly Cibber, but he is not in the same sense wrong. Whatever Theobald and Cibber may have been in life, in *The Dunciad* they are made to represent precisely those qualities of mind and motive which do indeed lead to dullness and insipidity. In *Jerusalem*, on the other hand, Voltaire and Gibbon are rightly made to stand for analytic reason—and surely analytic reason causes no wars. (In this century, as C. P. Snow was so unfortunate as to point out, our most prominent scientists—whatever the horrifying uses to which their discoveries have been put—have been quite consistently on the side of peace and understanding. One cannot make the same claim for our most prominent poets.) In this respect dialectic thinking, with the attendant oversimplifications of the Either-Or Syndrome, has far more to account for (one recalls that Blake's Christ comes not to bring peace but the sword). Simplistic and sloganized dichotomies of the Either-Or variety, whether religious, racial, nationalistic, or more vaguely philosophical—the Chosen People versus the pagans, the true church versus the heretics, Aryan versus non-Aryan, Free Enterprise versus Communism—have surely been behind many of the wars of Western history, and it is precisely such simple-minded dichotomies which the careful analysis of motives and interests by a Voltaire or a Gibbon does much to dissolve.

The manifestation of the Either-Or Syndrome which leads Blake to associate warmongers and analytic reasoning is, however, relatively peripheral to his "system," and the injustice of the association is fairly apparent even to the most dedicated of his apologists. There is another identification which is much more fundamental, and which causes great difficulty for the beginning Blake scholar, that is, for one not so habituated to dialectic thinking as to take such paradoxes in stride. I refer to Blake's insistence upon the identity of motive and method in scientific generalization and in repressive and legalistic morality. This identification is perhaps implicit in the *Songs of Experience*; it is surely implicit in *The Marriage* and in *The Visions of the Daughters of Albion*, and it becomes explicit and permanent doctrine with the appearance of *The Book of Urizen* and in all of the prophecies which follow. Urizen (and later the "Female Will") is the only begetter both of the Ten Commandments and of Newton's *Principia*: the motives and method of reasoning are identical in both—or so Blake implies. This identification is especially difficult for the modern student to realize: if it is difficult to see what eighteenth-century empiricists and skeptics had in common with pietists or Evangelicals, it is perhaps even more difficult to see what the W.C.T.U. has in common with the National Academy of Sciences. The philosopher's shears which clip an angel's wings may have something in common with the legalist's razor which emasculates him, but the analogy seems more metaphorical than real.

The usual apology for Blake's thinking here has been to point to the brief and ultimately unfruitful alliance between Newtonian physics and the established church, via the doctrines of "natural religion," in Blake's eighteenth-century England. That some such loose alliance did exist is of course a fact, but it was surely more of a historical accident than a sign of doctrinal agreement. The latitudinarian theologians who preached "natural religion" were hardly narrow-minded legalists (as Methodists and enthusiasts frequently were), and if Bishops Clarke and Wollaston shared an enthusiasm for Newtonian physics and a somewhat misunderstood experimental method, so also did Voltaire and David Hume. It was perfectly apparent to the youthful Wordsworth in 1791 (the date of Blake's *Marriage*), as he records his feelings in *The Prelude* (especially Book X), that "naked" reason and scientific analysis were behind the ferment of emancipation which eventuated in the French Revolution, and that they were if anything directly subversive both of established religion and of any restrictive and legalistic morality. Yet Blake's assertion of an alliance, even an identification, is one of his most persistent doctrines, fundamental both in his psychology and in his view of history.

I believe the only Blake scholar who faces this difficulty squarely is Northrop Frye, in a passage of close argument in *Fearful Symmetry*.[21] Blake is perhaps unfair to Bacon, Locke, and Newton, Frye concedes, and yet he insists that there is a basic identity in the methods and to a certain extent in the motives of the legalistic moralizer and the scientific generalizer. Both are intent upon the formulation of rules or laws, he insists, and in doing so both depend upon a deadening and stultifying abstraction.[22] Furthermore, just as the scientist becomes irritated with exceptions to his laws and "prefers" to deal with dead or inanimate and predictable matter, so the moralist "prefers" to deal with invariable and uniform conditions, and becomes irritated with the "uniqueness" of historical events and with mitigating circumstances.

There does indeed appear to be some basic similarity here, but again a little further analysis shows it to be superficial, and shows the dissimilarities to be of far greater significance. All knowledge, indeed all discursive thinking depends upon generalization (Blake's dialectic thinking is no exception), and all generalization implies some degree of abstraction. If things, events, persons—or even poems, for that matter—were in every respect "unique," then any generalization would be impossible, and scientific, moral, or even poetic assertion would be meaningless. All that one could assert of a thing would be perhaps that it exists, and communication would be reduced to pointing. (There are of course degrees of abstraction. Physics is more abstract than botany, and the Ten Commandments are more abstract than a municipal code—but that point is not really at issue.)

Both science and morality depend upon abstraction, then, but there the similarity ends. The legalistic moralist accepts his rules as given and does not test them in experience; he applies them deductively to a series of particular sets of circumstances; he is interested in moral judgment, not in disinterested prediction, and qua legalist, he is not concerned with consequence. The analytic reasoner, on the other hand, accepts no rules as given and must continually test his hypotheses in experience; he induces his laws from a series of events and particular sets of circumstances; he is interested not in judgment but in prediction, and, qua scientist, he must always be concerned with actual (as distinct from legal) consequences.

When so considered, it becomes apparent that what we have here, far from an identity of motive and method, is as perfect a set of "contraries" as any in Blake's system. As Wordsworth pointed out in *The Prelude*, "The freedom of the individual mind," which "magisterially adopts / One guide, the light of circumstances, flash'd / Upon an independent intellect" (1805 version, Book X, 826-830) can indeed be subversive of all moral rules and regulations. The point becomes even clearer when one considers the one of Blake's contemporaries most closely identified with analytic reason, William Godwin. Whether or not Wordsworth had Godwin in mind in the famous passage of *The Prelude* just quoted, it is an apt description of Godwin's method.[23] In *Political Justice* he attempted to bring all things to the bar of analytic reason or the "independent intellect," and in doing so he was surely as subversive of moral and legal rules as any twentieth-century "situational ethicist"—and fully as much so as Blake. Godwin would admit the legitimacy of some moral precepts, but only as "temporary resting-places" for the mind, and in his fervor for particularity and for the consideration of practical consequences he would allow no immutable rules or binding contracts—not even marriage. It is this kind of analytic and scientific reason, with its attention to fact and to cause and effect, and therefore to the prediction of actual as distinct from legal consequences, which has done more to break down the abstract and simplistic codes of the moralists than ever dialectic prophecy has. Moreover, it is not mere historical hindsight which makes this fact apparent; it was quite clear to such of Blake's predecessors or contemporaries as Rousseau, Hume, Godwin, Priestley, and the younger Wordsworth. Indeed, the reaction of the older Wordsworth and Coleridge against the analytic eighteenth-century *philosophes*—the reaction which Wordsworth chronicles in Books VIII-XI of *The Prelude* and which Coleridge describes in the *Biographia* ("Such men need discipline, not argument; they must be made better men, before they can become wiser," he says in an uncharacteristically uncharitable aside[24])—this reaction is certainly based in part on the realization that a reliance on analytic reason alone is very much subversive of those traditional moral principles which the older Wordsworth and Coleridge had come to respect. But Blake is led into this fundamental inconsistency in his system by the Either-Or Syndrome: both analytic reason and legalistic morality are in some sense opposed to a more free-wheeling poetic prophecy, and since they are, they must be basically alike.[25]

The use of abstraction and generalization is not a particularly significant common denominator for science and morality, since they are so totally unlike in motive (disinterested prediction versus moral judgment) and method (hypothesis and experiment versus the application of intuitive or revealed precepts). It might nevertheless seem to provide an important distinction between science and morality on the one hand, and poetry on the other—and of course it has frequently been so applied, in this century particularly. Most poetry is more "concrete" than most science—than relativity theory, for instance, although not an anthropologist's field reports. The distinction is not very fruitful, however, as is shown by the demise of the old simplistic dichotomy between (good) concrete and (bad) abstract poetic diction. In any case, it is not a distinction which can be applied to scientific reason versus dialectic thinking, and the poetry dependent upon it. And that brings us to the second pitfall of dialectic: the Absolutizing of Abstractions, or the hypostatization of contrary qualities.

It has always seemed to me one of the more obvious ironies in Blake—and one of which he seems unaware—that he does indeed condemn theologians, moralists, and above all scientists such as Newton, of stultifying abstraction; and yet there is surely nowhere in the *Principia* such a portentous parade of abstractions as those which march across the pages of *The Four Zoas, Milton,* and *Jerusalem.* Blake's abstractions are of course disguised; they are clothed in the concreteness of the poetic imagination, and so the Female Will and Analytic Reason are transformed into Giant Forms which go howling about the walls of Golgonooza, breathing fire and destruction. Abstractions they nevertheless remain; with Blake one cannot take the poetry and let the allegory go, because he was not willing that his poems should be appreciated for their poetic "surface" alone, which, in the later prophecies at least, is rather thin. As Northrop Frye puts it:

> The disadvantage of demonstrating a total form of vision from Homer or Shakespeare is that they give so much for so little effort, and it is easy for their commentators to incur the charge of needless over-subtlety. The advantage of demonstrating it from Blake's Prophecies is that without it, except to the rare and lucky possessor of a set of the original engravings, they give almost nothing. Homer and Shakespeare are not superficial, but they do possess a surface, and reward superficial reading more than it deserves.[26]

Blake has indeed a message, and it is this message which gives the later prophecies their structure and most of their interest. Moreover, his message and theories—about the human psyche or universal history or the relationships between imagination and reason—can to some extent be paraphrased in non-poetic terms, and this has been done not only by interpreters such as Frye, but indeed by Blake himself, with his talk of Reason and Energy, Emanations and Spectres, Selfhood and Self-Annihilation, Female Wills and Imaginative Visions.

Furthermore, Blake's mythopoeic presentation in his texts and in his illuminations, the transformation of the abstractions into

"Giant Forms," is not the result of poetic or artistic necessity alone; it is a tendency inherent in dialectic thinking as such, and is not less evident in mystic tradition generally, especially in the theologies of Boehme and Swedenborg. Opposition exists for everyone, of course, but for the analytic reasoner it is only a mental construction, a convenient system of classification, and often only a first step in an analysis which shows the opposition to be a matter of relative degree or measurement. For the dialectic thinker, on the other hand, the opposites are reified, they are made independent and dynamic forces, and they therefore take on the qualities of physical, even metaphysical things. Human "Energy," for instance, analytically considered, is always motive force, actual or potential, directed toward some object, good or bad, beautiful or ugly, and usually defined in terms of its object. "Reason" is not a force at all, but a method of disciplined thinking, a neutral tool moved and directed by human energies toward various and indifferent ends. As David Hume, that most rigorous of analytic reasoners, pointed out: "Reason is, and ought only to be the slave of the passions, and can never pretend to any other office than to serve and obey them."[27] In Blakean dialectic, on the other hand, Reason and Energy are reified, both are made dynamic, and they are pointed toward rather arbitrary ends—in Blake's scheme those of Reason being generally evil, those of Energy generally good. They become Urizen and Orc. (With the introduction of Los, in the prophecies, things become more complicated, and the contraries of Reason versus Energy are of course replaced by the Female Will, including both repressive and analytic reason versus Creative and Prophetic Imagination.)

Blake's Reason versus Energy is of course a variation on the venerable Romantic opposition between Head and Heart. Indeed, Hawthorne, in an off moment, once suggested that the placing of head before heart might be Original Sin, and a similar notion is surely at the basis of much of the incipient anti-intellectualism so widespread in Romantic poetry and criticism. Yet clearly this is a case of difference rather than of opposition: All conflicts between head and heart turn out, on analysis, to be within the heart itself. A passion for intellectual order and system is as much a matter of the heart as is a passion for charity or social reform, and both stand about equally in need of the ministrations of mind. (As "naked reason" Godwin pointed out, mindless compassion has probably done more dam-

age, in the long run, than has the discompassionate mind.)
"Head versus Heart" may be only a kind of poetic shorthand
for "passion for scientific order versus a passionate sympathy
for others"—but when it is so spelled out, of course, it becomes
obvious that "Reason" is not a force at all, and the neat symmetry of the contraries disappears, along with the metaphysical
mystique. As Hawthorne himself described it, in his tales, a
passion for artistic creation (Owen Warfield in "The Artist as
the Soul of the Beautiful") or even for philanthropy and reform
(Hollingsworth in *The Blithedale Romance*) can be fully as
destructive or as "heartless" as the scientific mind. It is interesting to note that Blake seems never to have been aware of the
possibility of a conflict between a passion for artistic creation
and a compassion for one's weaker and less imaginative fellow
men—or perhaps he was aware of the possibility, and was only
very sure of his priorities. "The cut worm forgives the plow,"
as he puts it in one of the "Proverbs of Hell" in *The Marriage*;
and however much in the right Los may be in *Jerusalem,* he
does sometimes seem less than charitable to the weaker and
rather fearful Enitharmon.

Reason and Passion (or Energy), Attraction and Repulsion
(or Love and Wrath, in Boehme's more poetic terms), Imagination and the (Female) Will, are not of course things, they are
mere abstract terms for potentialities, relationships, states of
mind—*i.e.*, for the properties of things—and one can make no
judgments about them until they are defined in terms of objects
and ends. There is no such "thing" as Attraction and Repulsion;
there are only things being attracted or repelled, just as there
is no such "thing" as Being, there are only existent things. It
is characteristic of dialectic thinking, however, first to abstract,
and capitalize, a relationship or a state of mind, then to reify
and hypostatize, and finally to personify and even mythicize.
Newton's concepts of gravity and of the ether were also very
highly abstract, and they were also in a sense absolute, since
Newton was forced to concede that they could not be further
analyzed or reduced in the state of scientific investigation of the
early eighteenth century. They were nevertheless quite clearly
and precisely defined in terms of their objects or functions—and
the same cannot be said of Blake's concepts of Reason, Energy,
the Female Will, or of Selfhood. Urizen ("Your Reason") can
be held equally responsible for Newton's *Principia* and for the
Ten Commandments only because the concept of reason has

become considerably confused in relation to methods and ends. This is not to say that the same degree of logical clarity or precision is possible or desirable in dealing with the psychologically or metaphysically abstract concepts with which Blake deals in his prophecies. On the other hand, one cannot say that such relative imprecision is characteristic of poetry or myth as such. It is, however, characteristic of dialectic thinking—and it is even more in evidence in Boehme and Swedenborg than in Blake.

Nevertheless, Enitharmon is allowed a promise of salvation at the close of Blake's last prophecy—along with those English arch villains, Bacon, Locke, and Newton (not, I believe, Voltaire or Rousseau)—and the prospect of this ultimate reconciliation leads us to the last of our three dangers of dialectic thinking: the longing for apocalypse characterized by the Both-And Syndrome, or the Over-Emphasis on Synthesis.[28] In dialectic thinking all reality consists in the conflict of contraries; as Blake puts it in the famous apothegm from *The Marriage*: "Attraction and Repulsion, Reason and Energy, Love and Hate, are necessary to Human existence."[29] Indeed, in dialectic thinking they are necessary for all existence whatever; as Jakob Boehme insisted, God himself literally has no existence, He is not merely the *Urgrund*, He is the *Ungrund*, until He splits into the primary contraries of Wrath and Love.[30] Nevertheless, there is also in dialectic thinking a hope, a yearning—even more pronounced in Coleridge than in Blake, I believe—somehow to transcend the conflict of contraries, to return to the primal unity as the ultimate good. From this follows the curious fact that for Blake as for Boehme, and for the Catharic and Manichaean heretics before them, the creation of the finite universe itself is the first Fall from which all other falls proceed, in dialectical recession. The ultimate conflict of contraries is that between the Force which separates into Many, and the Force which unites into One; the first being Primary Evil, and the second Primary Good. Indeed, some early heretics for this reason ascribed the creation of the universe to Satan rather than to God, and attempted to frustrate any further generation in various bizarre symbolic ways.[31] For Blake the Separative Force is named the Female Will, perhaps indicating again the origins of dialectic thinking in the sexual contraries of male (thesis) and female (antithesis). In any case, Blake's identification of the Separative Force and the world of material generation with the Female has plenty of tradition behind it, and cannot be accounted for merely by his perhaps having had a somewhat "Turkish attitude toward women" (as Johnson said of Milton). In mystic interpretations of the Biblical texts on creation, Adam's weakness and lack of self-sufficiency accounts for the separate (and dependent) creation of Eve; Eve's assertion of a separate and independent will, even in Milton's more orthodox account of the story, precedes her fall. The female principle, then—variously personified in Blake's prophecies as Enitharmon, Vala, Tirzah, or Rahab, or in abstract terms as Nature—comes to stand symbol for the assertion of self as a separate reality, independent of the male or of the creator. Man's ultimate fall comes when he concedes this independence, conceives of the female principle as truly creative, and comes even to worship the generative "Mother" Nature.[32] For Blake, Female-worship constitutes the origin of "natural" religion, and, as he makes plain in *Jerusalem*, of all the institutionalized religions which followed.

The creation of particular and finite things is then a fall from Grace, and yet it is also the act which causes the infinite variety of the world we live in, and even our separate selves. The apocalypse, the ultimate synthesis, is in a sense impossible without the annihilation of our separate selves, and yet it exists as an impossible hope for each of us. It is this basic ambivalence of attitude inherent in Romantic dialectic, I believe, which causes many of the major difficulties in Blake criticism. On the question of the possibility of escape from the otherwise endless wheel of generation, for instance: Some critics, such as Karl Kiralis, insist on the necessity of the conflict of contraries for continued existence, and therefore on the necessity of eternal and cyclic recurrence, and profess to see indications of it even at the seemingly apocalyptic close of *Jerusalem*: "Having reached full maturity, man, precisely because he is free, will again fall into error, but with his freedom (Jerusalem) and with the help of the poet he will renew the cycle from earthly to eternal life." In a note, he asserts that "the inevitability of the cycle is made clear" in the last lines of the poem:

All Human Forms identified, even Tree Metal Earth & Stone. all Human Forms identified, living going forth & returning wearied Into the Planetary lives of Years Months Days & Hours reposing, And then Awaking into his Bosom in the Life of Immortality.[33]

Northrop Frye, on the whole, inclines toward apocalypse, but he wisely declines any precise definition, and confines his dis-

cussion of it to a modest appendix on Blake's "Mysticism." Of
the apocalypse he writes: "When we have taken this short and
inevitable step beyond *Jerusalem*, the struggles of the mystics to
describe the divine One who is all things, yet no thing, and
yet not nothing . . . to make it clear how the creaturely aspect
of man does not exist at all and yet is a usually victorious
enemy of the soul, begin to have more relevance to Blake. . . ."
He continues: "This effort of vision, so called, is . . . the realization in total experience of the identity of God and Man in
which both the human creature and the superhuman Creator
disappear. Blake's conception of art as creation designed to
destroy *the* Creation is the most readily comprehensible expression of this effort of vision I know. . . ."[34] Not, of course,
comprehensible to the analytic understanding. Harold Bloom,
finally, seems to opt for a kind of oscillation between the last
two stages in man's redemption, in which those fortunate enough
to have achieved Eden, or the Apocalypse, retire periodically,
for rest and recuperation, to the less strenuous land of Beulah,
where contraries are still discrete and in generative interaction.
In commenting on the closing lines of *Jerusalem*, he writes: "This
is not our cycle of Innocence and Experience that is being
described, but the eternal alternation of contrary states, the living
and going forth of Eden, and the returning wearied and reposing of Beulah."[35] I would not presume to judge between
these various and conflicting views—although there is probably
a connection between Bloom's interpretation and his insistence
on Blake's "humanist" rejection of the mystical and the occult[36]
—yet they are certainly important. The apocalyptic vision
climaxes Blake's most ambitious work, and yet his most distinguished critics are unable to agree as to whether that vision
is permanent or temporary, the object of a genuine aspiration
or merely an ideal impossible of realization.

The Both-And Syndrome also accounts for—or perhaps one
should say is expressed in—the very equivocal attitude toward
sex and the body all through this dialectical tradition. In this
tradition the "creation" of the body and the division of the
sexes (symbolized of course in the creation of Eve from Adam's
rib) are inescapable signs of man's Fall from Grace. Some kind
of reunion of the sexes and of body with spirit seems a necessary
prelude to any ultimate synthesis or apocalypse. Such a sexual
reunion, however, involves a double paradox: In the first place,
it seems to imply that the only way for the spirit to transcend

the body or matter is to give way to the most sensual and firmly physical of compulsions. Second—and this is the difficulty implicit in the Both-And Syndrome—the ultimate synthesis of these polar contraries always seems to imply the subordination, even the extinction, of one or both of the contraries, or, to put it another way, the synthesizing of sexual opposites seems to abolish sex.

The ambivalence of attitude becomes immediately apparent to the reader of Blake. In the *Songs of Experience* and in the early prophecies, especially in *The Visions of the Daughters of Albion*, Blake celebrates sex and the body, and seems to come very near suggesting not only that all suppression of sexual energy is evil, but that its uninhibited indulgence is an ultimate good:

Take thy bliss O Man!
And sweet shall be thy taste & sweet thy infant joys renew!
Infancy, fearless, lustful, happy! nestling for delight
In laps of pleasure . . . .[37]

Some scholars, therefore, have followed the early lead of Wicksteed, who in his 1928 edition gave a highly sexual reading of the *Songs*, both text and illumination, and have seen Blake as the proto-Freudian *par excellence*. Or perhaps one should rather say, since Freud never suggested that the uninhibited indulgence of the polymorphously perverse instincts of infancy was any kind of ideal, they have seen Blake as the forerunner of such latter-day neo-Freudian saints as Erich Fromm, Norman O. Brown, and Herbert Marcuse, all of whom have in different ways attempted some kind of synthesis of the Freudian contraries of Eros and Thanatos, or at least a transcendence of what was for Freud the irreconcilable conflict between Reality Principle and Pleasure Principle: the former implying inhibitions which for him were prerequisite for any civilization, the latter aiming at an unlimited indulgence.

In the later prophecies, on the other hand, and especially in the vision of the apocalypse in *Jerusalem*, Blake makes it clear that there is no marrying or giving in marriage in the ultimate Eden, and although Enitharmon, Los's bride and symbolic representative of womankind, may be allowed redemption, it is only upon her unequivocal renunciation of her "female" and separate will.[38] In the Fall, Enitharmon had become "separated" from Los:

She separated stood before him a lovely Female weeping
Even Enitharmon separated outside . . .
Two Wills they had; Two Intellects: & not as in times of old.[39]

This separation, and the consequent "Woman's Pride" in her
own individuality and independence is, as Los makes plain, the
source of all the evils of "Generation," for "when the Male
and Female, / Appropriate Individuality, they become an
Eternal Death."[40] In the last chapter of *Jerusalem*, especially,
Blake seems to imply that the veneration for chastity and
modesty, the analytic reason, natural religion, and all wars can
be attributed to woman's will to dominate man. This is not
mere anti-feminism on Blake's part, however: the Female Will,
in an expression of the Either-Or Syndrome, as I suggested, has
by this time become representative very broadly of the Force
which Separates into Many, the ultimate motive behind all the
evils of generation. Enitharmon's only salvation must be to
accept Los's "Fibres of Dominion," as Los suggests, and when
Enitharmon demurs, fearing that in so doing she will "annihilate
vanish for ever," Los replies that in the Apocalypse "Sexes
must vanish and cease / To be, when Albion arises from his
dread repose," for only so will the evils of Generation cease,
so that one "may foresee and Avoid / The terrors of Creation
and Redemption and Judgment."[41]

This particularly sexual aspect of the ambivalence inherent
in the Both-And Syndrome is perhaps even more clearly apparent
in what we might call the theme of the Angelic Androgyne
versus the Hellish Hermaphrodite. Most modern dictionaries
list the terms as synonyms, although there is perhaps a vague
distinction in contemporary usage, the term "androgyne" referring more broadly to a case of shared psychological characteristics of both sexes, and the term "hermaphrodite"—perhaps
because of its use in biology—referring more narrowly to the
sharing of physical and functional characteristics. But there is no
ground for this distinction in etymology or in myth: Hermaphroditus, the androgynous son of Hermes and Aphrodite,
shared the beauties of both parents, and was indissolubly united
with a nymph whose love he had rejected, thereby becoming
the first physical hermaphrodite.[42]

Blake does not, so far as I know, use the term "androgyne"
in his writings, but he follows a very long Judeo-Christian
mystic tradition—having an origin, perhaps, in Aristophanes'

myth in Plato's *Symposium*, but evident especially in gnostic heresies, in alchemy, and in the theologies of Boehme and Swedenborg—in making the unfallen Los and Albion quite unmistakably androgynous.[43] Adam Kadmon, Albion's nearest progenitor in Cabbalist tradition, was of course androgynous, and as such the image of prelapsarian integrity and purity. So also is Albion before his separation from Jerusalem and his fall into the sleep of Ulro, and so is Los before his separation from Enitharmon.[44]

Nevertheless, the "Hermaphrodite"—a term which Blake does use frequently in the later prophecies—is invariably allied with "Selfhood" and the Spectres which interfere with or frustrate man's redemption, symbolizing not the heavenly union of the sexes of the androgynous and prelapsarian Adam or Los, but a "self-doubting" and "self-contradictory" state, identified at different times with Satan and Ulro, and with Tirzah and Rahab, who between them represent the physical, sensual, and mysterious world of external and female Nature. Satan in his as yet "unformed" state, representing the war and chaos fomented by Urizen, is spoken of as "a Shadowy hermaphrodite black & opake . . . hiding the Male / Within as in a Tabernacle," and later, as a "Vast Hermaphroditic form / . . . hiding the shadowy female Vala as in an ark & Curtains."[45] In *Milton* the temptresses Rahab and Tirzah appear before the poet as "The Twofold form Hermaphroditic: and the Double-sexed; / The Female-male & the Male-female, self-dividing stood / Before him in their beauty, & in cruelties of holiness!"[46]

It becomes apparent that for Blake androgyne and hermaphrodite represent not merely contrary, but indeed contradictory states: the latter the true "negation" of the first, the androgyne in Eden and the hermaphrodite in Ulro. Yet both terms denote quite simply the union of the two sexes in one body, and it is difficult to see precisely where the distinction lies. Blake nowhere specifically defines it, and there is no basis for it in etymology or myth, or in his most probable sources—Plato, Boehme, and Swedenborg—all of whom use the terms interchangeably, and only to apply to an ideal union such as that of Blake's prelapsarian Albion.[47]

Yet there is of course an ambivalence inherent in the very concept of the androgynous man; he may on the one hand be considered admirably self-sufficient, or on the other he may be considered sterile and narcissistic. He can therefore stand symbol for the basic paradox of the Both-And Syndrome of dialectic thinking: The primal unity, of creator and created, of subject and object, of spirit and matter, of male and female, which the androgyne represents, is the ultimate good, and the division of this unity is a Fall from Grace. Yet the whole world we know —indeed, the only world we can conceive, as Boehme pointed out—depends upon this separation of the one into many and frequently conflicting entities, and in this view the androgyne comes to represent the concepts of creator without creation, of subject without object, of male without female—in short, a string of concepts which are either empty or evidently self-contradictory. At most he represents solipsism (which the dialectician Fichte called a logical necessity and a moral impossibility), sterility, the void.[48] Blake attempts to separate these symbolic significances, to call one androgynous, the other hermaphroditic, and to conclude the second to be the "negation" of the first. But the concepts of absolute self-sufficiency and of sterility and solipsism do not seem contradictory: if anything they seem concomitant. And there, of course, lies the difficulty.

This basic paradox of the Both-And Syndrome has broader and more directly aesthetic consequences than merely to cause difficulties for Blake scholars. In his yearning for a new unity and synthesis the Romantic poet deprecates the separation into many, the force of the Female Will. On the other hand, as any great poet knows and as Blake repeatedly insists, the artistic imagination must deal in "minute particulars." In many passages of their most intensely felt poetry the Romantic poets came down on the side of synthesis, in an emphasis on the unity and simplicity rather than the fecundity and variety of the universe around them.[49] The difficulty becomes clearly apparent in their attempts to describe apocalypse—in Blake's later prophecies, for instance, and in passages of *The Prelude* and of the fourth act of *Prometheus Unbound*. In the final unity, when all conflicting contraries are transcended, when subject and object, self and not-self, become One, there can be no "minute particulars." When distinctions apparent to and binding upon the sensuous eye and the analytic understanding are transcended, the poetry, too, insofar as it is sensuous and concrete, and insofar as it is logical, grammatical, or even merely verbal discourse, must fall silent, or risk incoherence. "Without contraries is no progression," the younger Blake said, and he might have added, "nor poetry, either." It becomes apparent in the last analysis that the dialectician exhibiting the Both-And Syndrome is denying the limits imposed on thought by the law of contradiction.

There have been few critics and scholars in the last decades—with certain brave exceptions like John Crowe Ransom and the late Yvor Winters—who have been willing to defend the hegemony of the laws of logic in the field of literature, even that most basic of all of them, the law of contradiction. (Indeed, in a recent discussion with one of my colleagues I learned a new vituperative term when he called the critics of Norman O. Brown "mere syllogists.") Norman O. Brown, still, I suppose, the most popular of neo-Freudian literary dialecticians, in the last chapter of *Life Against Death* goes so far as to suggest that the law of contradiction is only the ultimate inhibition, the last repressive influence, which must be overcome before one can find salvation. He also suggests that Freud himself might have been spared his tragic vision had he been able to share this final truth.[50] In a sense Brown is right, of course; what kept Freud hung on the horns of his tragic dilemma between Eros and Thanatos (or, earlier, between the Pleasure Principle and the Reality Principle) was probably a rather old-fashioned respect for the laws of contradiction. (I suggest that this respect might also account in part for the difference in outlook between, say, Blake's *Jerusalem* and Byron's *Cain* or *Don Juan*.) Freud was of course a dialectic thinker, but he belonged to that relatively small minority of dialecticians—Empedocles was also one of them, among the ancients—who did not exhibit the Both-And Syndrome. Eros and Thanatos—Love and Wrath, in Empedocles' terms—the Reality and the Pleasure Principles, are in eternal conflict, and between these opposites there can be no ultimate synthesis or reconciliation. For the dialectician the temptation to "transcend" the law of contradiction is always great, however, because it is the one sure way to avoid the tragic vision and to achieve apocalypse.

It is a temptation which has its dangers, as we have seen. As logicians tell us, once one allows a single contradiction into a language system, it becomes literally possible to prove anything whatever—and that, of course, means the end of logical discourse.[51] But poetry and prophecy are not logical discourse, we are told, and just as Blake, as a polemicist, is not obliged to be fair, so, as poet-prophet, he is not obliged to be logical. This is an appealing argument, but it seems to me too easy a way out. Poetry is not mere logical discourse; it is much more than that. But I believe it must in some sense *also* be that. And the laws of contradiction are not analogous to the axioms of Euclidian geometry, arbitrary assumptions upon which one bases a closed system which has no necessary reference outside itself. The laws of contradiction are far more basic, and apply not only to any conceivable geometry or mathematics, but indeed to any conceivable discourse or system of symbols to which one applies a criterion of inner consistency. And that must surely include both poetry and prophecy.

Moreover, one cannot assume that the Both-And Syndrome of dialectic mysticism appears only at the fringes of the poetry, a "short and inevitable step beyond *Jerusalem*," as Northrop Frye puts it; that the laws of consistency can apply until one crosses over some boundary of vision. Once one allows an element of the trans-logical into one's "total vision," the Both-And Syndrome will appear in quite unexpected and mundane places: not only in the discussion of the apocalypse or of creation, but in discussion of sex and generation, of androgynes and hermaphrodites, and even in the ambiguity of such a concept as Blake's of the "Selfhood," where one seems at first urged to self-assertion and independent creativity, and then told that the only way to salvation is through self-annihilation.

In the Fourth Memorable Fancy of *The Marriage of Heaven and Hell* Blake gives a final reply to the analytic angel: "We impose upon one another," he says, "and it is but lost time to converse with you whose works are only Analytics." Perhaps our defense might be that, like Aristotle, author of the *Prior* and *Posterior Analytics*, we are neither poets nor prophets, but scholars and critics, and although the scholar-critic may at times find dialectic thinking a useful tool, surely his first job is properly analysis.

The three dangers of dialectic thinking which I have been discussing are by no means of equal importance, nor are they equally dangerous. The Either-Or Syndrome is perhaps the most pernicious, but also the most avoidable. Perhaps to be truly consistent, if we are to criticize John Foster Dulles or HUAC for using it as a polemic device, we should also criticize Blake. In any case, it is a polemic device, and the first job of the critic should be to explicate it as such, not to justify it, much less to treat it as a privileged piece of gospel or prophecy. The Absolutizing of Abstractions is another matter, and here surely we as critics are as guilty as the poets, and perhaps more so.

How many critics have applauded the perceptiveness of White-head's description of the Fallacy of Misplaced Concreteness, as applied to scientists, without seeing the beam in their own eyes, and then have gone on to talk of an irreconcilable conflict between "scientific method" and "poetic creativity," without much analysis of either abstraction? One has said very little indeed about a work of art, for instance, when one says that its theme is the conflict between Appearance and Reality, unless one has a clear conception of Reality, and of how and why it should take the trouble to disguise itself in deceptive Appearance. The positing of a pair of contraries or opposites should not be the last step in an analysis, but the first.

The Both-And Syndrome is another and more difficult matter. It seems to me unavoidable in any dialectic vision of apocalypse —and, since apocalyptic visions are most often dialectic, perhaps in all apocalyptic visions whatever. On the other hand—and remembering the fate of Blake's Little Boy Lost, whom the priest overheard "setting reason up for judge / Of our most holy Mystery"—few would want to be so bold as to deny these visions all authority whatever. To contradict the boy, it *may* be "possible to Thought / A greater than itself to know." In any case, and even if it is, I believe it behooves us as scholars and critics to leave such heavenly and paralogical dis-course to poets and prophets. For a critic to assert a string of self-contradictory abstractions—the unity of self and not-self, creator and created, subject and object—surely serves little de-scriptive purpose. To stand mute before these mysteries is for us —as it would have been for the Little Boy Lost—the wiser, certainly the more politic course.

NOTES

1. See, for instance, Coleridge's contrast in *Hints Towards the Formation of a more Comprehensive Theory of Life* (London, 1848): "The Mechanic system knows only of distance and nearness . . . in short, the relations of unproductive particles to each other; so that in every instance the result is the exact sum of the component qualities, as in arithmetical addition . . . . In life . . . the two component counterpowers actually interpenetrate each other, and generate a higher third, including both the former" (p. 63). One should of course recognize Col-eridge's polemic purpose—and the fact that much of the essay is a loose paraphrase of his notes from his German studies.

2. See *The Poverty of Historicism*, 2nd ed. (London, 1960); also *The Open Society and Its Enemies*, rev. ed. (Princeton, 1963).

3. The entire sentence reads: "Wenn die Philosophie ihr Grau in Grau mahlt, dann ist eine Gestalt des Lebens alt geworden, and mit Grau in Grau lässt sie sich nicht verjüngen, sondern nur erkennen; die Eule der Minerva beginnt erst mit der einbrechenden Dämmerung ihren Flug." As in *Grundlinien der Philosophie des Rechts*, vol. 7 of *Sämtliche Werke*, ed. Hermann Glock, *et al.* (Stuttgart, 1952), 36–37.

4. *Biographia Literaria*, ed. J. Shawcross (Oxford, 1907), I, 196, and notes. The loose translation is from Schelling's *Transcendental Idealism*, as Shawcross points out.

5. See especially the first chapter of *The Savage Mind* (Chicago, 1966).

6. For Empedocles, on the other hand, the contraries (Love and Wrath) were equal, irreconcilable, and alternating—or at least so most scholars contend, from the evidence available.

7. The only work I know of specifically on the subject of opposition is the little monograph by C. K. Ogden entitled *Opposition: A Linguistic and Psychological Analysis* (London, 1932), reissued with an introduction by I. A. Richards (Bloomington, Indiana, 1967). Ogden notes that it is a subject which logicians have tended to avoid.

8. And this is surely the ultimate origin of Keats's figure in *Endymion*. Hartley attempted in a speculative way to reduce pleasure and pain to a matter of the relative intensity and/or frequency of his "vibrations and vibratiuncles" in the "white medullary substance" of the brain and spinal cord, in his *Observations on Man* (1749). In the preface to his work he confesses that he was attempting to reduce psychology and physiology to measurement and certainty, on the model of Newton's physics.

9. The best introduction to this tradition for the literary scholar is, I believe, Desirée Hirst's *Hidden Riches: Traditional Symbolism from the Renaissance to Blake* (London, 1964). See also Kathleen Raine's *Blake and Tradition* (Princeton, 1968), 2 vols. I do not mean to suggest that either of these scholars discusses dialectic reason as such, however.

10. See "The Concept of 'Romanticism' in Literary History," *Comparative Literature*, I (1949), 1–23, 147–172; reprinted in *Concepts of Criticism* (New Haven, 1963).

11. The French apologists include André Kojève and Eric Weil; the most thorough recent English apology, including the dialectic, is J. N. Findlay's *Hegel: A Re-Examination* (London, 1958).

12. Popper's famous attack on Hegel, Marx, and Historicism in *The Open Society and Its Enemies* (note 2 above) did call forth a reply from the English Marxist Maurice Cornforth: *The Open Philosophy and the Open Society* (New York, 1968). Jean-Paul Sartre has also defended Marxian dialectic in his *Critique de la raison dialectique* (Paris, 1960), although his is a rather peculiar existentialist reading of it. (See Lévi-Strauss's reply to Sartre in the essay "History and Dialectic" in *The Savage Mind* [note 5 above].)

13. In "College Studies," in *Persons and Places* (New York, 1944), p. 247.

14. Most of the philosophical critiques of dialectic refer specifically to Hegel or to Marx, rather than to dialectic thinking in general. But see Karl R. Popper's essay "What is Dialectic?" pp. 312–335 in *Conjectures and Refutations* (London, 1963).

15. See *Defending Ancient Springs* (London, 1967), in which she names almost all of her contemporaries, in Cambridge and Oxford.

16. For a discussion of Aristotle's distinctions, also as it relates to the logic of categories, I have depended upon William and Martha Kneale, *The Development of Logic* (Oxford, 1962). As Coleridge observes (*Biog. Lit.*, note 4 above), Kant discussed a distinction between "logical" opposition (mere negation), and "real" opposition (dynamic contraries) in *Versuch, den Begriff der negativen Grössen in die Weltweisheit einzuführen* (1763). I suppose one might say that the confusion of Kant's distinction had a determining influence on the next half-century of the history of philosophy.

17. Sartre has recently made this dilemma the basis of his redaction of Goethe's *Götz von Berlichingen* in his *Le diable et le bon Dieu* (Paris, 1951). The dilemma seems simple enough, in analytic terms, but of course it is susceptible of a great deal of existentialist and dialectic complication.

18. As Martin Price complains, "It is difficult for Blake to make order [*i.e.*, "Reason"] seem more than negative . . . . As soon as the idea of rational order appears, it is reduced to 'the cunning of weak and tame minds which have the power to resist energy' . . . it is hardly a contrary with its own purpose." (*To the Palace of Wisdom* [New York, 1964], p. 424).

19. It is sometimes suggested that when Blake writes in *The Marriage* that good and evil are "contraries" rather than contradictories and that both are necessary for man's existence, he is presenting a version of the rather simple-minded "contrast" or "chiaroscuro" theodicy, *i.e.*, that in speaking of "Evil" he is referring to the genuine evil of the suffering of innocence, and is suggesting that evil and suffering are necessary in order to enable one to recognize good and happiness, as shadows in painting are "necessary" to enable one to recognize light. I do not—indeed, I would rather not—believe that this is Blake's intention. He means that the terms "good" and "evil" have been badly misused by the opposition, the priesthood, and that what the priests refer to by these terms—restrictive, and especially rational order, versus creative and passionate energy—are neither of them good or evil *per se*, but that if he (Blake) had indeed to choose between them, he would choose the second, "evil."

20. *Blake's Apocalypse* (Garden City, N. Y., 1963), p. 403.

21. (Princeton, 1947), Chap. 7, especially pp. 187–191, 197–201.

22. The confusion between prescriptive and moral "natural laws," and descriptive and scientific "laws of nature," a confusion even more common in the eighteenth century than in our own, Frye concedes to be an "illegitimate pun" (p. 189), but he suggests that it has its origins in this similarity between moralist and scientist.

23. It was Émile Legouis, in his *Early Life of Wordsworth*, trans. J. W. Matthews (London, 1897), who first pointed out the similarity and suggested the influence. Most recent scholars dispute it, however, at least insofar as direct influence is concerned.

24. (Note 4 above), I, 85.

25. In an interesting modern example of the Either-Or Syndrome, Northrop Frye insists that in making common cause with analytic reason, one also allies oneself with those who perpetrate "human sacrifice." As he puts it, in the close of his chapter on *Jerusalem*: "Every attempt to minimize or ridicule the free use of the imagination in the name of common sense is a little murder of human life, and is related to human sacrifice." He continues, "All we need to do is to persist

in *natural* and *reasonable* tendencies, and in a very short time we shall get the society we want: the society of the Roman Empire which crucified Jesus all over again, only much more so. We shall get a church-state ruled by a divine Caesar; a religion which is a tyranny of custom as pervasive as atmospheric pressure; a government organized for imperial war without any real purpose beyond waging it, and an increasingly obvious desire for the extermination of all human life within reach" (pp. 399–400, italics mine). Writing as he was in the years just after the war, Frye must have had Nazi Germany in mind. But whereas the Nazi vision of the hegemony of the Teutonic race and of the millennial Reich may not have been particularly "imaginative," by what stretch of poetic hyperbole could it be called "natural," "reasonable," or "commonsensical?" Reasonable or sensible it certainly was not, and it could be considered "natural" only if one subscribes to a very Hobbesian view of nature in which compassion becomes "unnatural." One begins to feel that what is taking place here is a kind of juggling with abstract terms for a forensic purpose—but then that is, I believe, very much in the tradition of dialectic thinking.

26. Frye, p. 421. This seems to me the implication of Frye's assertions about these poets, although I am not sure he would concur in my wording of the implication.

27. In Bk. II, Part III, Sect. III of *A Treatise of Human Nature,* ed. L. A. Selby-Bigge (Oxford, 1968 [1888]), p. 415.

28. The best treatment—and a sympathetic treatment—of what I call the Both-And Syndrome is in E. D. Hirsch, Jr., *Wordsworth and Schelling* (New Haven, 1960), especially Chapter 7, "Both-And Logic in the Immortality Ode."

29. Plate 3; in *The Poetry and Prose of William Blake,* ed. David V. Erdman (Garden City, N. Y., 1965), p. 34.

30. Not, of course, a temporal event. See Howard H. Brinton, *The Mystic Will* (New York, 1930), the best general introduction to Boehme's thought.

31. Pierre Bayle, in his *Dictionary,* art. "Manichees," tells of eucharistic rituals among the Manichaean heretics in which semen was consumed with the wafers, thereby frustrating generation and helping to purify or "spiritualize" degenerate matter. Sexual abstinence (or *coitus interruptus*) was of course a more common way of frustrating generation, and was practised among many heretical and utopian sects, including our own American Shaker community.

32. Northrop Frye speaks of the salvation of the "beloved object" (represented by Enitharmon) as being possible only when "it surrenders its 'female' or independent quality and takes its form from the will as well as the desire of its creator. The refusal of the beloved object to surrender this independence, which of course is really man's inability to make it do so, is the 'female will,' or belief in an ultimate externality, which blocks our final vision" (pp. 262–263). See also pp. 75 and 336, where he draws the parallel between the Female Will and all of generative "Mother" Nature, and with nature worship.

33. "The Theme and Structure of William Blake's *Jerusalem,*" ELH, XXIII (1956), 135–136. The passage from *Jerusalem* quoted is on Plate 99, in Erdman ed., p. 256.

34. Frye, p. 431.

35. (Note 20 above), p. 433. In support of his contention Bloom quotes the passage cited by Kiralis.

36. In comment on the passage of *Jerusalem* in which Blake makes scornful reference to the Smaragdine Table of Hermes, Bloom writes, "Blake is rejecting

all Hermeticism here even as he rejected Swedenborg, Behmen, and Paracelsus in *The Marriage of Heaven and Hell*. No amount of insistence on this point is likely to stop the continuous flow of writings on Blake's relation to arcane traditions .... A lunatic fringe of enthusiastic occult Blakeans is likely to abide as the left wing of Blake studies until the veritable apocalypse, and all one can do is to counsel students and readers to ignore them." This "lunatic fringe" evidently includes a great many Blake scholars: Ellis and Yeats, S. Foster Damon, Desireé Hirst, Jean Hagstrum, and Kathleen Raine, to name only a few of the more eminent. Perhaps one must distinguish among occultists: it is true that Blake seems to reject Hermes Trismegistus' Smaragdine Table in the passage Bloom alludes to in *Jerusalem*, and that he paid only a backhanded compliment to Paracelsus and "Behmen" in *The Marriage,* but as late as 1825 he told Crabb Robinson that Boehme was "a divinely inspired man," and that Swedenborg was "a divine teacher" (*Henry Crabb Robinson on Books and Their Writers,* ed. Edith J. Morley [London, 1938], I, 327). For good summaries of the influence on Blake's "system" of Paracelsus, Boehme, and Swedenborg, see the articles in S. Foster Damon's *A Blake Dictionary* (Providence, 1965) ; the influence of the whole tradition has recently been massively catalogued by Kathleen Raine (note 9 above).

37. Plate 6, lines 2–5; Erdman ed., p. 48.

38. The only Blake scholar who acknowledges a clear and important transformation in Blake's expressed attitudes toward sex and the body is, I believe, E. D. Hirsch, Jr., in his *Innocence and Experience* (New Haven, 1964). He dates it from the poem *Tirzah,* which he sees as appended in 1804–1805 as a kind of palinode to later editions of *Experience* (see especially pp. 281 f.). He does not, of course, discuss *Jerusalem* in any detail.

39. Plate 86, lines 57–61; Erdman ed., p. 243.

40. Plate 90, lines 53–54; Erdman ed., p. 248.

41. Plate 92, lines 12–20; Erdman ed., p. 250. I take this to mean that this is the way to avoid cyclic recurrence, but of course this may refer only to an ideal incapable of realization, and, in any case, it would not necessarily imply that one could also avoid the comparatively minor lapse into Beulah, which Bloom suggests is an alternative state to Eden (note 35 above).

42. There is nevertheless some ambiguity in the legend itself: Hermaphroditus' union with the nymph may be considered a judgment upon him for his self-centered rejection of the nymph's love. Tiresias was not of course a hermaphrodite, although he is sometimes so represented in art and literature, because he existed alternately as male and female. Yet his alterations were indisputably a curse or a judgment.

43. I am not aware that any scholar discusses Blake's androgyne at any length, but see the close of the article "Hermaphrodite" in Damon's *Dictionary* (note 36 above). For the widespread use of the theme, and for a summary account of its origins, see A. J. L. Busst, "The Image of the Androgyne in the Nineteenth Century," in *Romantic Mythologies,* ed. Ian Fletcher (London, 1967), pp. 1–96. Except for Novalis, Busst is concerned almost solely with the French, and does not mention Blake or any of the English Romantics. He also points out, however, that among many mystics—he cites gnostics generally, and Boehme and Mme. Blavatsky—Christ was also, as unfallen man and the second Adam, androgynous (p. 7).

44. In a summary of one of his conversations with Blake, Crabb Robinson

mentions Blake's confusing him with his doctrines about Adam and the Fall: "he replied that the Fall produced only generation of death and then he went off upon a rambling state [-ment?] of a union of sexes in man as in God—an androgynous state in which I could not follow him" (note 36 above, I, 330).

45. *The Four Zoas*, Night the Eighth, p. 101 (2nd portion), lines 34–37, and p. 104 (2nd portion), lines 20–27; in Erdman ed., pp. 359, 363.

46. Book the First, plate 19, lines 32–34; in Erdman, p. 112. In *Jerusalem* the term is associated especially with the "Spectres" of Albion, Luvah, and Los: see plates 58, line 20, and 64, lines 25–31.

47. See Busst, note 43 above.

48. It is interesting to note that, according to Busst, the image of the androgyne did indeed come to have such irreconcilable connotations in later nineteenth-century literature: on the one hand, the "optimistic" androgyne, connected especially with mystic visions of human history and of man's ultimate transcendence of all distinctions of matter and spirit, sense and soul, etc., and the "pessimistic" androgyne—appearing most frequently in the *fin de siècle* French decadence—who was associated with incest, homosexuality, sadism, masochism, onanism, what Busst calls "cerebral lechery," and a general "confusion of good and evil." But of course none of the writers Busst discusses used the image with *both* sets of connotations.

49. See Richard Harter Fogle, "A Note on Romantic Oppositions and Reconciliations," in *The Major English Romantic Poets*, ed. Clarence D. Thorpe, *et al.* (Carbondale, Ill., 1957), pp. 17–23.

50. Modern Library edition (New York, 1959). Brown specifically defines "dialectical" as "an activity of consciousness struggling to circumvent the limitations imposed by the formal-logical law of contradiction," and asserts that Freud, because of his commitment to common sense, to logic, and to "scientism," is "trapped because he is not sufficiently 'dialectical.'" We must therefore go beyond Freud; we must "entertain the hypothesis that formal logic and the law of contradiction are the rules whereby the mind submits to operate under general conditions of repression" (pp. 318–320).

51. As Karl Popper puts it (note 14 above, p. 317): *"if two contradictory statements are admitted, any statement whatever must be admitted*; for from a couple of contradictory statements any statement whatever can be validly inferred.... This . . . is one of the few facts of elementary logic which are not quite trivial, and deserve to be known and understood by every thinking man" (Popper's italics).

THE HERETIC IN THE SACRED WOOD; OR, THE NAKED MAN, THE TIRED MAN, AND THE ROMANTIC ARISTOCRAT: WILLIAM BLAKE, T. S. ELIOT, AND GEORGE WYNDHAM

Ernest J. Lovell, Jr.

T. S. Eliot's lack of enthusiasm for the English Romantic poets of the early nineteenth century is well known—if not yet wholly understood—and his shocking inadequacy as a critic of Blake has been pointed out repeatedly if briefly by Northrop Frye. The contradictory nature of Eliot's remarks on Blake, however, has not been analyzed at any length, nor are their personal origins generally known. It was in 1920, fifty years ago, that Eliot (with his romantic features of clerical cut and a neatly analytical mind playing upon the surface of his missionary zeal) chose Blake, first of the great English Romantic poets, as the object of his first public attack upon any one of those poets. Then, it may be recalled, Eliot proceeded in orderly fashion to deal in chronological succession with Wordsworth and Coleridge, Shelley and Keats. The disreputable Byron he could not bring himself to attack until 1937, although he seems to admit a Byronic influence on one of his juvenile poems.[1]

On 6 July 1921, however, suffering from exhaustion four months before going to Lausanne for psychiatric treatment, he confessed (once again), in a letter to Richard Aldington, to a deliberately conceived campaign to convert critical judgment to his own view of the Romantic poets.[2] This view almost certainly stemmed in most important part from the lectures of Irving Babbitt on "Literary Criticism in France, with special Reference to the Nineteenth Century," which Eliot had heard at Harvard in 1909-1910, when he was also listening to the much less stimulating lectures of William Allan Neilson on the English "Poets of the Romantic Period." Babbitt's *Rousseau*

75

and Romanticism would appear in 1919, early enough, if need be, for Eliot to read the remarks there on Blake, before writing his own essay. But Blake, clearly, had already been prejudged by Eliot, however little of Blake's poetry he may have read at the time. In an early letter to Richard Aldington, unpublished, he wrote (on ruled paper), "In re philosophy—anyway I agree and applaud everything you say about Wm Blake. Blake is a chapter in the History of Heresy (my great unwritten work in 15 vols. 4to)."[3] The tone of this should not be allowed to obscure its intent. As early as 1917 Eliot had lamented "the decline of orthodox theology and its admirable theory of the soul."[4]

Eliot's attitude toward English Romanticism, it may be recalled, had been publicly established well before the date of *The Sacred Wood*, most of the essays in which had been written and separately published as reviews between 1917 and 1920, when the book appeared. Because the volume contains some of Eliot's most influential concepts and judgments, all the more influential because published early, reprinted eight times or more, and still in print, its importance may be again recognized here. In considering a book which set forth repeatedly and, as the author later admitted, pontifically an impersonal theory of art, it is proper to glance tentatively at least, here at the beginning, at one aspect of the personal basis of the impersonal theory, for it has been said to be clearly and belligerently anti-Romantic.[5] I shall return to this. It may be noted, however, that between 1917 and 1920, the period of *The Sacred Wood*, in which the essay on Blake appears in the penultimate position, Eliot while working full time as a clerk in Lloyd's Bank of London[6] produced eighty contributions to periodicals and five books or pamphlets. In addition, between 1917 and 1919 he was assistant editor of the *Egoist*, which appeared monthly. The astonishing quantity of this activity suggests that much of the prose of this period is mere journalism, produced to be sure by a most remarkable mind, of brilliant if often perverse or limited insights. In the Bel Esprit circular of 1922, attempting to raise money for Eliot, Pound stated that Eliot "tried some years ago to live by journalism," referred to "hackwork" interfering "with his good writing," and concluded that "his prose has grown tired." Eliot, earning between £500 and £600 a year at the bank, ground out these reviews and essays for money.

That this haste often left somewhat less than adequate time

for thought is suggested further by an examination of the most famous paragraph in *The Sacred Wood*, that on the objective correlative,[7] central to Eliot's anti-Romantic theory of an impersonal poetry. It is significant and understandable that Eliot chose to omit the essay on "Hamlet and His Problems," in which the paragraph appears, from his paperback volume of *Essays on Elizabethan Drama* (1956). In this famous paragraph, then, which sets forth in typically Eliotic and pseudo-scientific language ("correlative," "formula," "equivalent," "objective") the *"only* way of expressing emotion,"[8] we are told that "Hamlet (the *man*) is dominated by an emotion which is inexpressible, because it is in excess of the facts as they appear." The facts as they appear in fact are that Hamlet has seen the Ghost of his father, who has told him what he has told him. If Eliot's statement refers also to the Hamlet of Act V, and it seems clearly so intended, Hamlet has become aware of a great many more "facts," quite sufficient to evoke the emotion in question. Here we may pause to notice, as others have done, the confusion of playwright, dramatic character, and audience in the paragraph, bristling with difficulties which have been discussed by Leonard Unger, René Wellek, Ivor Winters, and Eliseo Vivas.

We are next told, more specifically, that the problem resides in the fact that "Hamlet is up against the difficulty that his disgust is occasioned by his mother, but that his mother is not an adequate equivalent for it." Now this is remarkable, coming from Eliot, a man who has written elsewhere, "the love of man and woman is only explained and made *reasonable* by the higher [divine] love, or else is simply the coupling of animals."[9] This is precisely the situation of the bored typist and the young man carbuncular in *The Waste Land*, and one would have thought that Eliot could have understood very well a character whose mother had engaged in a hasty and incestuous marriage to Claudius, whom Hamlet from the beginning neither loves nor respects. It is this very coupling of animals which disgusts both Hamlet and Eliot. The famous first soliloquy cries out against it:

> O God! a beast, that lacks discourse of reason,
> Would have mourned longer.

Eliot explains, "it is just because her character is so negative and insignificant that she arouses in Hamlet the feeling which she is incapable of representing." Now this represents such a failure of understanding of a basic human relationship (to say no more) as to be truly astonishing. Hamlet has been wildly disillusioned; he was not always so; he has only *recently* discovered that his mother has a character "negative and insignificant." Anyone except Mr. Eliot at this time would have understood that such a discovery, such a "fact," is quite enough to explain Hamlet's revulsion and to function as an adequate objective equivalent or dramatic cause of it.

Finally, this same paragraph tells us that Hamlet's "disgust" with his mother "obstruct[s] action." Here we have the ghost of the Coleridgean Hamlet, in this very essay deplored by Eliot, and I will not waste much time explaining the obvious: that Hamlet is a most remarkable, indeed impetuous man of action, and that the plot must come to an inevitable end whenever Hamlet takes effective action against the King, a character who has a curious lack of interest for Eliot.

This is all that need be said at this time of Eliot on the Romantic poet Shakespeare, but Eliot's misunderstanding of his greatest play, said to be "most certainly an artistic failure," may give us pause when we consider Eliot on the Romantic poets of the early nineteenth century, specifically Blake.

In April 1918 and July 1919, shortly before publishing the essay on Blake entitled "The Naked Man," 13 February 1920, to be reprinted in *The Sacred Wood, Selected Essays*, and elsewhere, Eliot made two significant statements[10] which would lead one to believe him to be a fervent admirer of Blake, whose poetry revealed to him a "continuous syntactic variety" equal to that of Gautier. Such variety is a mark of "professionalism in art." This is interesting, in view of Eliot's later assertion that Blake was an "amateur." More significantly, if perversely, Eliot asserted in July 1919, "Crabbe, Blake, Landor, and Jane Austen are precisely the spirits who should have guided and informed the period of transition from the eighteenth century; they all preserved the best formal or intellectual tradition of that century, and they are not only original but unique." Aside from the wild incongruity of this grouping of Blake with Crabbe, Landor, and Jane Austen, suggesting how little Eliot could have known about Blake at this time, the latter part of the statement is an interesting contradiction of the position taken seven months later in "The Naked Man," where Blake is damned for the very reason that he lacked "a framework of accepted and traditional ideas." But it would seem at the earlier date that Blake and Eliot had much in common, for Eliot went on to deplore the influence of Wordsworth upon the development of English poetry. Blake and Eliot even knew the same kind of hell. For Eliot, thinking of Dante's Francesca, "it is a part of damnation to experience desires that we can no longer gratify."[11] For Blake, "hell is the being shut up in the possession of corporeal desires which shortly weary the man."[12]

In *The Sacred Wood*, the essay on Blake, now entitled simply "Blake," is followed by an essay on Dante, the last and climactic essay in the slim volume, and the author without question wished the reader to compare the two, which I shall do. Eliot himself compared the two poets briefly at the end of his essay on Blake: "Dante is a classic, and Blake only a poet of genius."[13] The important word here of course, in this somewhat elusive distinction, is the word "only." The same essay, however, seems to tell us at its opening that Blake wrote "great poetry," or at the very least that his poetry has qualities shared by all great poetry: a peculiarity, a peculiar honesty and unpleasantness which Eliot finds in Homer, Aeschylus, and Shakespeare. This is a great deal to concede, and it appears even more if we consider Eliot on "What Is a Classic?" (1944), where we learn that "There is no classic in English"; "great authors, like Chaucer . . . cannot be regarded in my sense as classics of English literature."[14] The grand example here is Virgil, melancholy, derivative, humorless, his hero the pious and dutiful Aeneas, the superbly dedicated stoic fearful of the passionate and disorderly Dido, and above all, Virgil the apostle of the chosen-people concept, the Roman or Latin, also Eliot's chosen people. Considered in these terms, it may be well for English literature that "there is no classic in English" and well for Blake that he is "only a poet of genius." But Eliot did not explain to us what a classic is until two decades after he denied the name to Blake, and from 1920 to 1944 the clear implication was that it was somehow better immeasurably to be a classic than a mere poet of genius.

Even so, as I have said, early in his essay on Blake, Eliot makes a good many remarkable concessions to Blake's greatness, considering the conclusions of the essay. "His peculiarity is the peculiarity of all great poetry," shared with Dante. "It is merely a peculiar honesty, which, in a world too frightened to be honest, is peculiarly terrifying." This would seem to be very high praise indeed, for in 1918, Eliot, discussing Joyce's *Ulysses* and Wyndham Lewis's *Tarr*, had written: "Both are terrifying. This is the test of a new work of art. When a work of art no longer terrifies us we may know that we were mistaken, or that our senses are dulled . . . . But this attractive terror repels the majority of men."[15] Although it appears that Eliot was not always thus eager to be terrified, his high praise of Blake at the beginning of the essay continues: "Blake's poetry has the unpleasantness of great poetry," ". . . which, by some extraordinary labor of simplification, exhibit[s] the essential sickness or strength of the human soul. And this honesty never exists without great technical accomplishment." Further, his philosophy is more "interesting" than that of Lucretius or Dante, and finally "Blake was endowed with a capacity for considerable understanding of human nature, with a remarkable and original sense of language and the music of language, and a gift of hallucinated vision." It would seem that Blake could ask for no more, especially when we recall Eliot's high praise elsewhere of simplification, by which he meant at this time some kind of universalization: "The essential thing is . . . this precise statement of life which is at the same time a point of view, a world —a world which the author's mind has subjected to a complete process of simplification."[16] If there is a gain for Blake here, there is a loss in what first appears to be Eliot's praise of Blake's philosophy, said to be more "interesting" than that of Dante or Lucretius, for in Eliot's view the quality of being "interesting" is not of primary importance in judging "artistic success."[17] "*Coriolanus* may be not as 'interesting' as *Hamlet,* but it is . . . Shakespeare's most assured artistic success."[18] Even Byron's romantic verse tales are said to be "interesting,"[19] so it cannot be a virtue of any great magnitude.

The unimportance of being interesting does not emerge with force, however, from the essay on Blake. Eliot attacks on other grounds. "But the weakness of the long poems is certainly not that they are too visionary. . . . It is that Blake did not see enough, became too much occupied with ideas." We are all aware of the dangers of the intentional fallacy, but even so we may recall that Blake wrote, "To Generalize is to be an Idiot. To Particularize is the Alone Distinction of Merit." Or, "To Me This World is all One continued Vision of Fancy or Imagination."[20] Blake of course falls outside Eliot's golden age of English poetry, "when the intellect was immediately at the tip of the senses," a period ending with Donne. Afterwards, "Sensation became word and word was sensation." Milton followed, and "the decay of the senses."[21] But Eliot nowhere finds room to observe that it was Blake who wrote, "Imagination . . . is Spiritual Sensation" or "that call'd Body is a portion of Soul discern'd by the five Senses" or "my senses discover'd the infinite in every thing."[22] Blake would not have recognized himself as one who suffered from Eliot's "dissociation of sensibility," but he would have agreed with Eliot that "men ripen best through experiences which are at once sensuous and intellectual; certainly many men will admit that their keenest ideas have come to them with the quality of a sense-perception; and that their keenest sensuous experience has been 'as if the body thought.' "[23] It is significant that Eliot refers by name to only one of Blake's longer works, *The Marriage of Heaven and Hell*. We may wonder how much of Blake Eliot had in fact read at the time that he wrote "The Naked Man," the last man in the world that Eliot would risk being. There is rather clear evidence in his review of Blake in 1927 that he had not, before that year, read or read seriously the "prophetic books." There he wrote (using the editorial "we"), "Our chief interest . . . is that we want to make up our minds about the[ir] value, as poetry." I shall discuss this review below.

In 1920 Blake's philosophy was said to be "home-made," that is, insufficiently impersonal and thus without "the advantages of [European, that is, Latin or Roman] culture." A "certain meanness of culture," evident in Blake's poetry, "frequently affects writers outside of the Latin traditions." The "meanness" of Blake's culture is flatly disproved by the several studies of his sources, but even a casual skimming of a portion of his prose reveals that he had read and made thoughtful or penetrating comments on such writers as Homer, Plato, the authors of the Bible, Virgil, Ovid, Cicero, Dante, Chaucer, Mallory, Shakespeare, Milton, Bacon, Locke, Newton, Voltaire, Rousseau, Gibbon, Hume, Gray, Prior, Pope, Swedenborg, Reynolds, Burke, Byron, and Wordsworth.

The central criticism of Blake would seem to be that his poetry is not impersonal enough: "You cannot create a very large poem without introducing a more impersonal point of view, or splitting it up into various personalities." One may recall here what Eliot seemingly did not know at the time: that in his long poems, peopled by such archetypal characters as Orc,

Los, and Urizen, Blake created a vast cosmic myth, moving from the time of Creation to the French Revolution and functioning on several levels, most interestingly on the psychological level, perhaps, and that such a myth must be called a form of impersonal art—unless such art is defined to include only those poetic works written within the Roman Catholic tradition. Eliot very nearly does so define it. Finally, we are told, had Blake's poetry "been controlled by a respect for impersonal reason, for common sense, for the objectivity of science, it would have been better for him." Surely, this is the most startling remark ever made about or even by William Blake. And just as surely Eliot had not read Blake's lines, "May God us keep / From Single vision & Newton's sleep!" or "What is the Life of Man but Art & Science! . . . What are the Pains of Hell but Ignorance."[24]

In short, if Blake had had a better philosophy, he would have been a better poet. "What his genius required, and what it sadly lacked, was a framework of accepted and traditional ideas," a "framework of mythology and theology and philosophy" such as Dante had, it is implied. I submit that it is impossible to misunderstand any poet more completely. Organized religion Blake regarded as an ancient and tyrannous fraud; traditional concepts of the Christian deity, especially those of the Old Testament Jehovah, he found abhorrent; Christ he worshiped after his own fashion and understanding. Lamely, Eliot's last sentence concedes, "perhaps the circumstances compelled him to fabricate, perhaps the poet required the philosopher and mythologist."

When we turn to the essay on Dante, immediately following, and read it in light of (or in the darkness of) the essay on Blake, we see how much Eliot has omitted to say about the English visionary and how much he could have said if he had applied the same principles to both poets.

Dante's great three-part poem has two chief virtues, according to Eliot; the first is a Coleridgean unity and the second a philosophy which is perceived, that is, highly visual. Eliot says, "the philosophy is essential to the structure and . . . the structure is essential to the poetic beauty of the parts." If it is permissible to hear Blake on the essential nature of unity, he wrote, "Every Poem must necessarily be a perfect Unity," and further, "Poetry admits not a Letter that is Insignificant."[25] It may be said that this is Blake the critic and not the poet, but the unity of Blake's great cosmic myth is now one of the accepted facts of life: that unity depends upon recurrent imagery, poems clearly linked with one another, recurrent characters who also develop and sometimes fade into one another in cyclical fashion, and the doctrine of the contraries permeating the whole. It is perhaps the artistic expression of this doctrine that displeased Eliot, as when Los takes on some of the characteristics of Urizen or when Orc grows into Urizen and is then reborn. In Dante's characters, Eliot informs us, there is none of "that ambiguity which affects Milton's Lucifer." Dante's Satan is of course a much simpler dramatic character than Milton's, and Dante's "framework" is more arithmetical or, as Eliot calls it, more "mechanical" than Blake's. This we are intended to accept as a virtue. And the scheme is of course thoroughly mechanical. *The Divine Comedy,* one may recall, is a poem of three parts, the last two parts with 33 cantos each, the first part with 33 cantos plus one, the total 100 cantos comprising *one* single poem, reflecting the threefold deity in one. Further, 100 is the square of 10, and 10 is the perfect number, for it equals the square of the trinity plus one. Hell is divided into three parts according to the three main types of sins, but geographically it is divided into four parts (three plus one). By means of the interlocking terza rima form, Dante places every sinner with exact precision at some level in the Inferno. And there at his proper level each character is made to react emotionally according to his level in the scheme and is given speeches appropriate to it. So it is that Eliot can write of the poem, the "structure is an ordered scale of human emotions . . . the most . . . ordered presentation of emotions that has ever been made." Yes, Dante's world is neater, less vital, and insofar as I understand it, less ambiguous than Blake's, but I do not know either that these qualities must be said to be major literary virtues, although they have a clear appeal for any reader with the tastes of a medieval schoolman.

The crowning glory of Dante, however, is a quality Blake possesses in abundance. "Dante, more than any other poet, has succeeded in dealing with his philosophy, not as a theory . . . but in terms of something perceived." The next sentence makes clear that Eliot is referring to the visual element in the poem, the expression of Dante's "impersonal" medieval Roman Catholic vision (which allowed him, one recalls, to place his very personal enemies in the fires of hell). Herein lies the difference, Eliot tells us, between poems that employ philosophy successfully and unsuccessfully. An important source of the success is that the philosophy be dealt with *not* as the poet's "own comment or reflection." Dante's traditional or derivative philosophy is thus upheld, while Blake's is condemned for being "home-made." And yet the quality of newness or originality is repeatedly enunciated in *The Sacred Wood* (echoing Pound) as a principle of critical evaluation: a work which is not "new" is "therefore not . . . a work of art" at all. Or, "the language which is more important to us is that which is struggling to digest and express new objects . . . new feelings, new aspects, as, for instance, the prose of Mr. James Joyce."[26] Blake was most certainly struggling to express "aspects" so new, it may be said, that no man had ever before tried to express them, in the form that he gave to them.

Finally, it may be observed, Eliot has damned Blake on grounds directly contradicting the first critical principle announced in the 1928 Preface to *The Sacred Wood,* hopefully said to unify the essays there collected: "when we are considering poetry we must consider it primarily as poetry and not another thing." Or as he put it in "The Perfect Critic," "the 'historical' and the 'philosophical' critics had better be called historians and philosophers quite simply," not literary critics at all.[27] To the extent then that Eliot damns Blake for his philosophy, he is "quite simply" not functioning as literary critic, but as something else.

And it is quite clear that a number of Blake's ideas Eliot found most distasteful, although he did not specify any one of them, and that this distaste for the ideas determined the final judgment of the poetry. As he confessed in 1929, "I cannot, in practice, wholly separate my poetic appreciation from my personal beliefs . . . . Actually, one probably has more pleasure in the poetry when one shares the beliefs of the poet."[28] Beliefs which Eliot would find repugnant at this time would include some of Blake's most central assumptions, beginning with the revolutionary cast of most of Blake's thought, such as his attacks upon sexual restraint and other inhibiting traditions or rules enforced by church and state, all mind-forged manacles to bind and blind man. One need not omit here either Blake's tone of seemingly total confidence, the absence in him of any felt need to assume a tentative or hesitant manner, his genius for singing the simplicity and purity of joy, the latter, I believe, never expressed in any poem written by T. S. Eliot. The gulf

separating Blake and Eliot, effectively excluding him from the
company of understanding critics of Blake, may be pointed up
by the opinion the two men held of Virgil. For Eliot, Virgil is
the great example of a classic, with all the virtues attributed to
such a work; for Blake, Virgil is the apostle of war and empire,
and these are the enemies of art. In support of his view, Blake
quotes from the *Aeneid*, VI: "Let others study Art: Rome has
somewhat better to do, namely War & Dominion."[29]

One of the most interesting qualities of Eliot's essay on
Blake is his use of the word "terrifying," which appears twice
at separate intervals in reference to Blake. The word is never
used to refer to Dante, nor, I believe, does Eliot use it to
refer to any other poet discussed in *The Sacred Wood*. The
reasons why Blake is "terrifying" are curiously revealing of
Eliot, although he did not, I think, intend them to be. Blake's
"peculiar honesty . . . in a world too frightened to be honest,
is peculiarly terrifying." This statement takes the form of an
objective and inclusive generalization, without restriction. It
is not, however, the world which finds the poetry of Blake
terrifying: it is Eliot. And it is not so much the world that is
"too frightened to be honest," that is, to reveal itself fully as
Blake the naked man had done; it is Eliot, the least naked critic
who ever wrote, Ole Possum, with "his conversation, so nicely
/ Restricted to What Precisely / And If and Perhaps and But."
"Do I dare / Disturb the universe?" "*Datta*: what have we
given? / My friend, blood shaking my heart / The awful daring
of a *moment's* surrender / Which an age of prudence can never
retract." Blake, by contrast, says, "Damn braces. Bless relaxes."
To use Eliot's own words, Blake "was not distracted, or frightened . . . . He was naked, and saw man naked"; that is, he
felt no need to prepare a face to meet the faces that you meet.
Eliot's paragraph closes, "He approached everything with a
mind unclouded by current opinions. There was nothing of the
superior person about him. This makes him terrifying." And
this is the second time that Eliot has said he found Blake terrifying. Blake had looked as deeply into the horrors of existence
as Eliot had, and Blake had done so with tremendous, sometimes overwhelming originality and honesty, "with a mind unclouded by current opinions" and with "nothing of the [tradi-
tionally educated] superior person about him." Eliot, in short,
knew nobody in literature or outside it who was like Blake, and
I submit that he was therefore frightened by him and thus had

to find a way to deal with him, a way to cancel out some of the unpleasantness. Blake, I suggest, spoke much more personally to Eliot at this time than Dante did. Eliot prefers the poetry of Dante, he says, to that of Shakespeare because it expresses "a saner attitude towards the mystery of life." This is from the 1928 Preface to *The Sacred Wood,* but if the preference may be moved back to 1920, we may see how very important to Eliot, for the most personal reasons, a "sane" poetry was. He was at this time much concerned about his own mental and emotional state. In letters written to Aldington on 16 September and 6 November 1921, Eliot used two technical terms to refer to his psychological condition, which I do not have permission to quote.[30] The first term is defined in *The American College Dictionary* as referring to one who suffers from a "nervous debility or exhaustion, as from overwork or prolonged mental strain, characterized by vague complaints of a physical nature in the absence of objectively present causes or lesions." There is no indication in Eliot's letter that this condition is one of recent origin. The second term is used by Eliot to describe a condition which he says has afflicted him all his life. It is defined in the same dictionary as "a form of mental derangement in which volition is impaired or lost." These would seem to be biographical facts which the history of literary criticism cannot afford to ignore.

A rather remarkable number of personal details may be deduced from *The Sacred Wood,* which called so insistently for an impersonal art. The Eliot of these years denounced emotion, or the direct expression of it, too repeatedly to be a man without fear of emotion within himself. Thus, more than once the ideal in both poetry and criticism emerges as the cool, detached, objective, impersonal ideal of science (scientists are said to have a higher "level of intelligence" than literary men). "But a literary critic should have no emotions," he tells us, "except those immediately provoked by a work of art—and these . . . are, when valid, perhaps not to be called emotions at all." Coleridge's "metaphysical interest was . . . like most metaphysical interest, an affair of his emotions" and had an adverse effect on his criticism, "one more instance of the pernicious effect of emotion."[31] As with criticism, so also with poetry: "It is in this depersonalization that art may be said to approach the condition of science."[32] In the famous words, "Poetry is not a turning loose of emotion, but an escape from emotion; it is not the expression of personality, but an escape from personality."[33] The sentence which immediately follows is less famous: "But, of course, only those who have personality and emotions know what it means to want to escape from these things." The doctrine here is clear: poetry is an escape for the psychoneurotic personality from that which is personally painful to contemplate, specifically, one's own "personality and emotions." The personal origins of Eliot's impersonal theory seem quite evident, and such a critic cannot be expected to do justice to any poetry of personality and emotion, especially such visionary poetry as that of Blake, who was temperamentally biased against the forces of Urizen despite the doctrine of contraries, which asserted that "Reason is the bound or outward circumference of Energy" and, of course, essential to it.[34] We are now in a better position to understand why Eliot preferred the ordered scale of emotions in Dante to the swirling dialectic of Blake.

The personal origin of much of Eliot's criticism is further suggested by two startling admissions made some years after "The Naked Man," one in 1932 and the other in 1961. The perfect critic is now no longer a poet, as he was in 1920: "When the critics are themselves poets, it may be suspected that they have formed their critical statements with a view of justifying their poetic practice."[35] Even more damaging is the confession made in 1961: "It is that in my earlier criticism, both in my general affirmations about poetry and in writing about authors who had influenced me, I was implicitly defending the sort of poetry that I and my friends wrote."[36] But almost as much may be gleaned from *The Sacred Wood*, despite its pose of objectivity. The epigraph attached to "The Perfect Critic" is a sentence from Remy de Gourmont, much admired by Eliot: "Eriger en lois ses impressions personnelles, c'est le grand effort d'un homme s'il est sincère." One may in fact doubt the sincerity of such a critic. It is true that the critic has nothing but his personal impressions to begin with, which he then attempts to reduce to some kind of order and to justify, but if he pretends to a scientific precision and objectivity and adopts a pontifical or ex cathedra tone when delivering his judgments, he may well deceive the unwary, which, I propose, is exactly what Eliot has done when discussing Blake. This is propaganda, not criticism. The degree of self-deception that may have been involved is a separate question. Eliot wrote in 1919 of Ben Jonson, "A writer of power and intelligence, Jonson endeavoured to promulgate, as a formula and programme of reform, what he chose to do himself; and he *not unnaturally* laid down in abstract theory what is in reality a personal point of view."[37]

It is undoubtedly true that a wholly dedicated, greatly suffering poet-critic can entertain emotional prejudice toward a literary tradition or view of life, as genuine in its way as racial or religious prejudice harbored by others, usually less literary. It is also undoubtedly true that such prejudice toward a particular literary tradition will tend to prejudge individual writers within it, just as prejudice against an entire race tends to prejudge individual members of that race. This, I submit, was true of the early Eliot's views of the Romantic tradition, which emerge with startlingly personal emotion in a review of a now obscure book, George Wyndham's *Essays in Romantic Literature* (1919), published after the death of the author and edited with a complimentary biographical introduction by Eliot's Tory friend Charles Whibley, to whose memory Eliot dedicated *The Use of Poetry and the Use of Criticism*. Eliot's review, reprinted in *The Sacred Wood*, is as much an outraged essay on the author as a discussion of the book. The first thing wrong, Eliot complains, is "the unity of Wyndham's mind, the identity of his mind as it engaged in apparently unrelated occupations."[38] This is shocking, when we recall Eliot's most famous statement about the mind of Donne. "A thought to Donne was an experience; it modified his sensibility. When a poet's mind is perfectly equipped for its work, it is constantly amalgamating disparate experience; the ordinary man's experience is chaotic, irregular, fragmentary. The latter falls in love, or reads Spinoza, and these two experiences have nothing to do with each other, or with the noise of the typewriter or the smell of cooking; in the mind of the poet these experiences are always forming new wholes . . . . The poets of the seventeenth century . . . possessed a mechanism of sensibility which could devour any kind of experience."[39] This, of course, is Coleridge's great esemplastic power at work, achieving unity by means of the reconciliation or fusion of "opposite or discordant qualities," and it is the highest praise Eliot has for the Metaphysical poets. But, as Eliot points out, "Wyndham was a Romantic," and "the romantic fusion allured Wyndham," and this Eliot finds most deplorable. "His literature and his politics and his country life are one and the same thing. They are not in separate compartments, they are one career. Together they made up his world; literature, politics, riding to hounds.

In the real world these things have nothing to do with each other." (Three years earlier Eliot had written, ". . . our interest in art cannot be isolated from the other interests of life, among them interests of philosophy and religion.")[40] In other words (this contradiction aside), unity in the art work is essential; but the unity of a human life, when achieved, is a falsification of the "real world" in some way not explained. Poets may be allowed to devour all kinds of experiences and form a new whole or unity from them, but other men must compartmentalize their lives. Literature must be "detach[ed] . . . from ourselves," we are told elsewhere; it is a "collection of valuable porcelain."[41]

The key to this problem is perhaps to be found in Eliot's use of the word "real," misleading because much simpler and more naïve than one would anticipate. Elsewhere, in justifying Dante's use of literary characters representing men he actually knew in life and others such as "legendary and Biblical figures," Eliot writes, "the real and the unreal are all representative of types of sin."[42] Here the term "real" clearly refers to men who once lived, the term "unreal" to literary characters. The unreal world is the world then of art, the real world the nonaesthetic world. "But," Eliot says, "we cannot believe that George Wyndham lived in the real world." And the reason is given in the form of a quotation from the editor's Preface to Wyndham's book: "George Wyndham was by character and training a romantic. He looked with wonder upon the world as upon a fairyland." T. S. Eliot of the waste land of course had lost this ability, if ever he had it as a mature man. Wyndham in fact was everything that Eliot was not. He was undeniably English; he was a product of Eton, upon whose playing fields England's wars were won; he was a soldier, serving in Egypt and South Africa, a man of action married to the life of the mind, reading Virgil in his tent; he was a member of Parliament and prominent otherwise in his country's government; and he was a landowner with 2400 inherited acres. All these facts Eliot summarizes, with some bitterness. The last paragraph tells us where Wyndham had gone wrong, and of course where Eliot had gone right. "The Arts insist that a man shall dispose of all that he has, even of his family tree, and follow art alone. For they require that a man be not a member of a family or of a caste . . . but simply and solely himself." This sounds like dangerously Romantic doctrine. As Blake expressed it, "You must leave Fathers & Mothers & Houses & Lands if they stand in the way of Art."[43] Wyndham had not done this; he had lived his Romanticism, finding high romance also in the books that he wrote about. Eliot, by contrast, was disillusioned, poor, struggling, still obscure, working at an uncongenial job in a bank in order to write in the evenings, totally dedicated to his view of art. At the date of the review of Wyndham, 2 May 1919, Eliot's *Prufrock* volume had been published in an edition of 500 copies only, which did not sell out until 1921, and his *Poems* of 1919 (13 pp., 200 copies) had not yet been published. He had not seen his mother, sister, brother, or native country for four years; and his mother, who could not understand his poetry and wanted him to be a professor, contributed nothing to his financial support.[44]

Eliot in "A Romantic Aristocrat" feels constrained finally to admit Wyndham into the company of the many-sided men but compares him in this regard to Leonardo da Vinci; and we are solemnly told that "George Wyndham was not a man on the scale of Leonardo." Eliot always uses Wyndham's last or full name, but he is on a first-name basis with Leonardo, and the reason is not far to seek: Eliot and Leonardo are surprisingly similar men. Like Eliot, Leonardo "had no father to speak of, he was hardly a citizen, and he had no stake in the community. He lived in no fairyland." (Eliot's father, now dead, had begun his career as a clerk for a wholesale grocer and had gone on to become president of the St. Louis Hydraulic-Press Brick Co.)[45] Perhaps Wyndham's greatest error, however, was to be "enthusiastic." He was "a good critic, within the range allowed him by his enthusiasms," but he lacked both "balance" and "critical profundity," as one would expect of such a fellow. "Wyndham likes the best, but he likes a good deal," and from his book we do not learn, as we do from Eliot, that Shakespeare's *Phoenix and Turtle* is a "great poem, far finer than *Venus and Adonis*," said by Eliot to be "second-rate." What Eliot does not say is that the shorter poem is a threnody singing the constancy and the "married chastity" of the two birds of the title and that the longer poem is distinctly erotic, but what Eliot omits to say is often as important as what he does not omit to say.

The conclusion is that "Romanticism is a short cut to the strangeness [of life] without the reality, and it leads its disciples only back upon themselves," the worst of all possible places to be, according to Eliot, although he has already said that "any life, if accurately and profoundly penetrated, is interesting and always strange." Wyndham, Eliot continued, "had curiosity, but he employed it romantically, not to penetrate the real world, but to complete the varied features of the world he had made." In 1918, by contrast, Eliot could praise Sacheverell Sitwell's *The People's Palace* for its "distinguished aridity . . . . The defense for his imagination is that he does . . . create his own world, and when this happens there is no more to be said."[46] It would seem, then, that Wyndham had in fact made a work of art of his life, not allowed by Eliot, whose private or personal life at this time was in fragments, a chaos. To make a world of one's own, I suggest, unified and simplified, is no small achievement. Blake as poet, painter, and maker of his own illuminated books, moralist, patriot, and reformer, had done this. He did not understand that poetry must be "detach[ed] . . . from ourselves" or that the "real" world was the nonaesthetic world, the unreal world that of art. Blake wrote, "Mental Things are alone Real," meaning the things of his imagination or vision. " 'What,' it will be Question'd, 'When the Sun rises, do you not see a round disk of fire somewhat like a Guinea?' O no, no, I see an Innumerable company of the Heavenly host crying, 'Holy, Holy, Holy is the Lord God Almighty.' "[47] This cry is a far cry from Eliot's mute "collection of valuable porcelain," existing to allow us "to reach a state of pure contemplation" of aesthetic form,[48] divorced from all emotion.

When Eliot returned for the last time, in 1927, to make a major statement about Blake,[49] he repeated some of the old charges: "his visions have a certain illiteracy about them, like those of Swedenborg," whom Blake parodied and satirized. He was not "a great philosopher . . . . He did not know enough." The true or great poet "must have education," a concept then redefined in such a way as to cancel out the earlier statements about Blake's ignorance: it is not "erudition but a kind of mental and moral discipline" which Blake lacked, who sang the demanding law of the contraries. But this is merely Eliot's way of saying that Blake is a Romantic and so will not do. We are told of Dante's *Vita Nuova*, "There is also a practical sense of realities behind it, which is antiromantic: not to expect more from life than it can give or more from human beings than they can give; to look to death for what life cannot give."[50] Eliot the exhausted man, throughout much of his early life in London carefully conserving his energies so as to direct them into selected channels, could hardly understand the poet who wrote, "Energy is the only life, and is from the Body . . . . Energy is Eternal Delight."[51] For Eliot, Blake's poems remain "terrible," a term I take to be nearly synonymous with his earlier "terrifying."

Blake "made a Universe," but this is no longer enough for a poet; it is even improper: "It is not any one man's business to make a Universe . . . ." Presumably, it is the business of Sacheverell Sitwell and the accumulated wisdom of the Church to do this, for Blake is judged by Eliot, now a convert, to be "theologically a heretic." He also suffered from "Isolation . . . not conducive to *correct* thinking" and from "Pride (or lack of Humility) . . . one of the chief theological sins." (Presumably, Eliot had not read Blake's address "To the Christians," where he wrote, "He who despises & mocks a Mental Gift in another, calling it pride & selfishness & sin, mocks Jesus the giver of every Mental Gift.")[52] This, again, is hardly judging poetry as poetry. After solemnly informing the reader that "The poet also knows [what Blake did not know] that it is no good, in writing poetry, to try to be anything but a poet," Eliot proceeds to praise the last canto of the *Paradiso,* where Dante described "with economy and felicity of words, a mystical experience" and where he was obviously being something more than a poet, in Eliot's artificially limited sense of the word. The comparison of the two poets illustrates again the distressing duality of Eliot's critical standards. But Blake was merely a "visionary," not a mystic, Eliot is pleased to point out, here agreeing with Helen C. White, whose book on Blake he was reviewing.

This was in 1927, the year of Blake's centenary and of Eliot's conversion to Anglo-Catholicism. We may hope, but without much conviction or certainty, that Eliot was later caught up in the rising tide of Blakean enthusiasm; if so, it would have been more generous of him to admit it. Instead, he kept the 1920 essay on Blake in print in *The Sacred Wood,* his *Selected Essays,* and *Points of View,* permitting it to be translated into four foreign languages and thereby giving to it great circulation and continued influence. In 1950, when he wrote a preface for Leone Vivante's *English Poetry and its contribution to the knowledge of a creative principle,* which contains chapters on Blake, Coleridge, and Shelley, Eliot commented on the latter two but remained silent upon Blake. We must assume, I believe, that he had not changed his mind on the subject in the thirty years since writing "The Naked Man."

NOTES

1. "Byron," *On Poetry and Poets* (New York, 1961), pp. 223–224.

2. The autograph letter is in the Academic Center Library of The University of Texas at Austin.

3. In the Academic Center Library of The University of Texas at Austin; quoted with the permission of Mrs. T. S. Eliot.

4. "Eeldrop and Appleplex," *The Little Review*, IV (May 1917), 9.

5. See W. K. Wimsatt and Cleanth Brooks, *Literary Criticism, A Short History* (New York, 1957), p. 665.

6. In an autograph letter in the Academic Center Library of The University of Texas at Austin, 29 March 1917, Eliot indicated that he began work at Lloyd's on 19 March 1917.

7. "Hamlet and His Problems," *The Sacred Wood, Essays on Poetry and Criticism* (New York and London, 1966), pp. 100–101; hereafter referred to as *SW*. In the preface to the Harvest paperback edition of his *Essays on Elizabethan Drama* (New York, 1956), pp. vii-viii, Eliot wrote that the essay on *Hamlet*, with two others on aspects of Elizabethan drama, now in 1955 "embarrassed me by their callowness, and by a facility of unqualified assertion which verges, here and there, on impudence." At the time of writing "Hamlet and His Problems," he stated, he was "a very young man, or an immature youngish man." It is pertinent here to observe that he was only five months older when he wrote the essay on Blake.

8. Italics throughout are mine unless identified as Eliot's.

9. "Dante," *Selected Essays* (New York, 1951), pp. 234–235; hereafter referred to as *SE*.

10. "Professional, Or . . . ," *Egoist*, V (April 1918), 61; "The Romantic Generation, If It Existed," *Athenaeum*, 18 July 1919, p. 616.

11. "Dante," *SW*, p. 166.

12. *The Complete Writings of William Blake, with Variant Readings*, ed. Geoffrey Keynes (London, 1966), p. 74; hereafter referred to as *Blake*.

13. *SW*, p. 158; quotations from the *SW* essay on Blake, pp. 151–158, will not hereafter be footnoted. For Blake on Dante, see *Blake*, p. 785.

14. *On Poetry and Poets*, pp. 61, 67.

15. "Contemporanea," *Egoist*, V (June/July 1918), 84.

16. "The Possibility of a Poetic Drama," *SW*, p. 68.

17. "Hamlet and His Problems," *SW*, p. 99.

18. *SW*, p. 99.

19. "Byron," *On Poetry and Poets*, p. 227. Contrast Eliot on Frost, whose "verse . . . is uninteresting, and what is uninteresting is unreadable, and what is unreadable is not read" ("London Letter," *Dial*, LXXII [May 1922], 513).

20. *Blake*, pp. 451, 793.

21. "Phillip Massinger," *SW*, p. 129.

22. *Blake*, pp. 149, 153, 794.

23. "A Sceptical Patrician," *Athenaeum*, 23 May 1919, p. 362.

24. *Blake*, pp. 717, 818.

25. "Dante," *SW*, p. 160 (quotations from the *SW* essay on Dante, pp. 159–171, will not hereafter be footnoted) ; *Blake*, pp. 611, 778.

26. "Tradition and the Individual Talent," *SW*, p. 50; "Swinburne as Poet," *SW*, p. 150. See also "London Letter," *Dial*, LXXII (May 1922), 511: "But a truly

independent way of looking at things, a point of view which cannot be sorted under any known religious or political title; in fact, the having the only thing which gives a work pretending to literary art its justification . . . : this is always detested" by the general public and, presumably, admired by Eliot.

27. *SW,* pp. viii, 16.

28. *SE,* p. 231.

29. *Blake,* p. 778, where one reads also, "The Classics! it is the Classics, & not Goths nor Monks, that Desolate Europe with Wars."

30. The autograph letters are in the Academic Center Library of The University of Texas at Austin. For T. S. Eliot's account of the way in which these letters came to Austin, see *Richard Aldington: An Intimate Portrait,* ed. Alister Kershaw and Frédéric-Jacques Temple (Carbondale, Illinois, 1965), p. 25.

31. "The Perfect Critic," *SW,* pp. 12–13.

32. "Tradition and the Individual Talent," *SW,* p. 53.

33. *Ibid.,* p. 58.

34. *Blake,* p. 149.

35. *The Use of Poetry and the Use of Criticism* (London, 1933), p. 29.

36. "To Criticize the Critic," *To Criticize the Critic* (New York, 1965), p. 16.

37. "Ben Jonson," *SW,* p. 117.

38. "A Romantic Aristocrat," *SW,* p. 25, one of a group of five essays collectively entitled "Imperfect Critics." References to the essay on Wyndham will not hereafter be footnoted. It may be noted that in 1927 unity was permitted to the Greeks and applauded: "This is merely a particular case of the amazing unity of Greek, the unity of concrete and abstract in philosophy, the unity of thought and feeling, action and speculation, in life" ("Seneca in Elizabethan Translation," *Essays on Elizabethan Drama* [New York, 1956], p. 7).

39. *SE,* p. 247.

40. A review of A. J. Balfour, *Theism and Humanism,* in *IJE,* XXVI (January 1916), 285.

41. "A Note on the American Critic," *SW,* p. 40.

42. *SE,* p. 209.

43. *Blake,* p. 776.

44. Autograph letter from Eliot to Aldington, 23 June 1921; journal of Sir Osbert Sitwell, both in the Academic Center Library of The University of Texas at Austin.

45. Herbert Howarth, *Notes on Some Figures Behind T. S. Eliot* (Boston, 1964), pp. 19–20.

46. "Contemporanea," *Egoist,* V (June/July 1918), 84.

47. *Blake,* p. 617.

48. "A Note on the American Critic," *SW,* p. 40.

49. "The Mysticism of Blake," *The Nation & Athenaeum,* XLI (17 September 1927), 779. Eliot's statement in this review that Blake "did not know enough" is a precise echo of Matthew Arnold's statement, quoted by Eliot in his 1920 Introduction to *The Sacred Wood,* p. xii, that the poetry of the first quarter of the nineteenth century "did not know enough."

50. "Dante," *SE,* p. 235.

51. *Blake,* p. 149.

52. *Blake,* p. 717.

THE MODE OF ARGUMENT IN
WORDSWORTH'S POETRY

Michael G. Cooke

In his lecture "On the Living Poets" Hazlitt proffers a couple
of seminal, if cryptic, insights into a problem arising within the
very structure of Romanticism, and affecting both the content
and the formulation of its poetry. He observes (1) that Romantic poetry in principle deals with what is at once "natural and
new," and (2) that the Romantic poet "sees nothing but himself
and the universe."[1] On the surface these could be taken as positively fruitful and just remarks; but in actuality they come from
Hazlitt with a challenging air of complaint. As Lascelles Abercrombie says, Hazlitt "meant it maliciously."[2]

It may be well to recall that, in his essay on "Mr. Wordsworth" in *The Spirit of the Age,* Hazlitt speaks admiringly of
this same Wordsworth, whose "genius is a pure emanation of
the Spirit of the Age" (*Works,* XI, 86); he who had seen fit
to query has come to praise:

> As the lark ascends from its low bed on fluttering wing, and salutes
> the morning skies; so Mr. Wordsworth's unpretending Muse, in russet
> guise, scales the summits of reflection, while it makes the round earth its
> footstool, and its home! Possibly a good deal of this may be regarded as
> the effect of disappointed views and an inverted ambition. Prevented by
> native pride and indolence from climbing the ascent of learning or great-
> ness, taught by political opinions to say to the vain pomp and glory of
> the world, "I hate ye," seeing the path of classical and artificial poetry
> blocked up by the cumbrous ornaments of style and turgid *commonplaces,*
> so that nothing more could be achieved in that direction but by the most
> ridiculous bombast or the tamest servility; he has turned back partly
> from the bias of his mind, partly from a judicious policy.

The idea of the morning "lark" choosing his song essentially
as the arch-practitioner of the artificial style had done, with a
view to the "one way left of excelling," has a pungency all its

own; this by the way. The main point of the essay, at least in connection with Wordsworth's early "productions," is to show the poet who "has given a new view or aspect of nature" (p. 89), thus implicitly reconciling the natural and the new. But the charm and authority of Hazlitt's change of disposition do not quite yield a critical solution to the problem he originally posed. A new principle, rather than an altered disposition, would be in order here.

The source of Hazlitt's complaint is not far to seek; both his statements, separately and together, suggest problematical polarities and obscurities which, one is led to infer, the poetry can neither expel nor explain. The oxymoronic joining of the natural and the new sets up a quizzical perspective, with the state of something general, permanent, and necessary falling in danger of being confused with or usurped by the busy vividness of something lately seen, accidental, and unproved. In like manner the self and the universe, though presented as coordinate, verge on becoming identities in an implicitly solipsistic scheme, where the universe is too huge and indefinite to bear any independent relation to the self. One can, without straining, sense in the poet's tendency to see nothing but himself and the universe an imminent threat of seeing himself *as* the universe or, like Oswald in *The Borderers,* compulsively reproducing himself there. Two problems then develop with real moment for practical Romanticism: how to convey the propriety and in fact the agelessness of what to consciousness appears like mere innovation, and how to set forth the complementary oneness of "personality and infinity."[3]

Certainly, though, these problems did not beset the poets without their full consciousness. The Preface to *Lyrical Ballads* plainly recognizes them, as does the *Essay Supplementary to the Preface of 1815* with its exposition of the "true difficulty" inherent in the poet's need to "call forth and communicate *power*" or, alternatively, to "call forth and bestow power." The problematical relation with the reader repeatedly attracts Coleridge's attention in the *Biographia Literaria,* and Byron's (if on different grounds) in the *Letters and Journals* as well as in *Don Juan.* There is room for arguing that in the Major Prophecies Blake pays scant courtesy to the reader in the way of honoring the difficulties of the literature of power.[4] But Blake himself bears witness to the diversified portfolio of rhetorical resources which the Romantic poet can boast. The style of the *Songs of Innocence and Experience* is markedly dramatic, that of *Auguries of Innocence* declamatory or assertive, that of *To Tirzah* abstract and analytical; and none of these quite sorts with the compacted style of the Major Prophecies.

In short, the Romantic poets give little warrant for supposing they did not seek to impose order, as any work of art must do, not only on their subject matter but also on the mind of the reader. This is, of course, the period which saw Coleridge enunciate the principle of "poetic faith" and Macaulay, in his *Life of Dryden,* aver that "poetry requires not an examining but a believing frame of mind." But such remarks intend to free poetry of the ultimate requirements of expository rigor, not to license it for arbitrary propositions. It is obvious, too, that the latter gets no countenance from any of the poets in question.

The issue, as it boils down, becomes not whether but how any Romantic poet copes with the true difficulty of communicating power. It possesses a peculiar interest in the case of Wordsworth, because he gives the appearance of bluntly ignoring in practice the problem he so sensitively defines in principle, and arriving at that sort of *dixit* in communicating which succeeds through a predisposition or cowed submission in the reader. We call him a poet of statement and—amply supported by his reading style, which counted so much on "an animated and impassioned recitation"—sum up his work as the poetry of assertion.[5] But at least as late as 1838, in the *Valedictory Sonnet* to the volume published that year, Wordsworth announces another ideal. He wants Truth and Fancy to agree, and would win "a passage" to the reader's heart by "simple Nature *trained by careful Art*" (italics mine).[6] This is hardly the sexagenarian Yeats avowing the ageless energy of his heart and imagination, but it does confess a continuing artistic conscience and aspiration. We may deny that Wordsworth wins us (especially with the late poetry), but we still need to consider the nature of the attempts he made. On this ground something valuable stands to be learned about the cast of his poetry, and indeed the cast of his mind, in that the former continually reflects scruples about the accuracy or clarity of what is being said, and further a lively sense of the problem of meeting potential doubts and objections from a neutral, or perhaps antagonistic, mind. Between the claims of accuracy and the claims of persuasion, Wordsworth gets into his poetry something worthy of being considered a mode of argument.[7]

This will not resemble good neoclassical practice any more

than the summary prefacing *Descriptive Sketches* or *An Evening Walk* resembles the argument of *Dunciad IV*—indeed, what Wordsworth calls the argument of *The Prelude* (I.643, XIV.277) is really its subject matter or "theme," and not a thing of rhetorical disposition. But a variety of features, ranging from the habitual use of litotes to the use of Coleridge in *The Prelude,* sufficiently attests to the point that "the poetic imagination cannot hope to shake itself free from scepticism . . . . It is impossible to claim that the imagination can give us what can be known for truth, or what may, in all strictness, be called knowledge."[8]

The skepticism of Wordsworth as poet is salient in *The Prelude.* Wordsworth reveals a more than conventional anxiety over his worthiness and fitness for his task—an anxiety over himself as subject, as artist, and as seeker of an unprecedented Muse with the paradoxical trick of "vexing its own creation" (I.38). In relation to Coleridge, as of his first major appearance at the end of Book I (ll.612 ff.), this anxiety takes a specifically argumentative turn. Coleridge, when the lines are scrutinized, simply is made to burst out of the role of auditor and dedicatee, and to assume the functions of a devil's advocate (whose understanding can be assumed but still must be cultivated), of a father confessor or, perhaps, sounding board, and of a lightning-rod for skepticism, in a complex utterance of self-deprecation and vindication on Wordsworth's part.

The self-deprecation is easy enough to see:

> I began
> My story early—not misled, I trust,
> By an infirmity of love for days
> Disowned by memory—ere the breath of spring
> Planting my snowdrops among winter snows:
> Nor will it seem to thee, O Friend! so prompt
> In sympathy, that I have lengthened out
> With fond and feeble tongue a tedious tale.
> (ll. 612–619)

In short, both good sense, which would overcome doting nostalgia (ll. 613-615), and good taste, which should renounce "a tedious tale," stand to challenge the present undertaking. But the lines actually have built into them a correction of attitude which protects Wordsworth from their seemingly fatal weight and aim. Two rhetorical features may be glanced at here: the

litotes of "not misled," and the image of the snowdrops. Both
tend to reverse the negative bearing of the lines. Substantially
the rest of the poem is to answer the question whether Wordsworth is misled, but here the effect is to open the issue and relieve
its pressure, as a safety-valve might do. The negative possibility,
"misled," is explicit, but gets blocked and negated itself by the
assurance (partially qualified by "I trust") that he is "not."
The poem thus admits, as it denies, the negative possibility; it
incorporates potential resistance and rejection in a controlled,
innocuous form. This is the rhetorical work of the litotes, to
staunch the flow of objections, if not to establish validity.

The image of the snowdrops, linked to the question of being
misled, supports the litotes by giving a positive dimension to
the state of which a negative version has been denied. It brings
up the earliest flower of spring in, and out of, the apparently
inhospitable context of snow, and develops substance and familiarity for the faith which, in the litotes, must seem abstract,
or even cryptic.

It is important to see that Coleridge, who now enters as one
"prompt / In sympathy" with Wordsworth, takes a part in a
process of deliberation and confirmation that is already under-
way. The process does not depend on him and his sympathy. He
extends it into a new area.[9] Beyond the concretization brought
about by the snowdrop image, he allows for the incarnation and
personalizing of the problematical relation between Wordsworth
and his material. Clearly he provides a likely audience for an
ample statement by Wordsworth, in assessing his stage of
progress, of his hope and object in the poem (ll. 620-625)—
that the hope is of psychological and philosophical stability,
and the object honorable toil, can but work in Wordsworth's
favor. Furthermore, in his role as recipient of the poem, Coleridge comes to stand for and function as *the reader*, the fit
audience, and thereby curtails and controls the play of skepticism
around the working of *The Prelude*.

This is not to suggest any sort of sinister or artificial maneuver-
ing on Wordsworth's part. Rather, there comes to the surface
here a deep pressure of inquietude to which the poem, or the
poet, responds in keeping with characteristic rhetorical resources
(litotes, imagery, as agents of affirmation); also here we see
emerging the nature of an implied contract with the audience
(Coleridge as a conscious, independently sympathetic participant
in the issues and causes of the poem). In a sense the poet not

only creates the taste by which he is to be relished, as Wordsworth maintained, but also, as Milton resignedly saw, he *presupposes* a fit audience. Alessandro Manzoni, the Italian Romantic, enunciates this latter view as a law, which Lascelles
Abercrombie renders thus: "Every poem . . . contains within
itself the principles by which it should be judged" (p. 32).
Modern aesthetics subscribes to this view, of course, without
allowing Darwin or Duck, or Blackmore or Proctor, to step
over a high threshold of regard; that is to say, the principle of
judgment in the poem is neutral as to value. For present purposes, it needs to be observed that, with Coleridge, Wordsworth
effectively sketches in some of the necessary features of the poem's
audience and, hence, some of the factors involved in judging it.

The resurgent force of doubt in Wordsworth's mind becomes
apparent as each difficulty met yields to another seen. The problem thus far has had to do with the past: the dwelling on
bygone days, and staying with a poem upon them. The shift of
attention to the future, as stated hope, produces a candid fear
for the future:

> Yet should these hopes
> Prove vain and thus should neither I be taught
> To understand myself, nor thou to know
> With better knowledge how the heart was framed
> Of him thou lovest. . . .
> (ll. 625–629)

What follows, in the implied "no" to the possible incurring of
"harsh judgments," at one and the same time checks the negative
impetus and positively capitalizes on Coleridge's favorable position in the poem. For if doubt presses up from a considerable
depth in the poem, its ultimate depth is occupied by the affirmation that gains strength from the very act of sustaining doubt
and rendering it harmless; here is Wordsworth's "power growing under weight" (VIII.555). We can recognize in these lines
(629-635) a complex rhetorical recapitulation: the submerged
litotes of "[no] harsh judgments" transfers to another mind
the double negative of Wordsworth's "not misled," paralleling
the way the basic activity shifts from Wordsworth's telling his
tale to Coleridge's evaluating it; the protective depreciation of
memory's function seen in "an infirmity of love for days / Dis-
owned by memory" reappears in "Those recollected hours that
have the charm / Of visionary things"; and above all, the suasive

use of an image comes back, not as the all-but-wintry snowdrop, but as the scene of infancy in full sun (ll. 616 and 634-635). A subtle mastery over skepticism is effected through the latter image, which in context deserves patient attention.

The effect of the sunlight image is both slow in building up, and dramatically abrupt when it comes at the end of an accretive sentence:

> . . . need I dread from thee
> Harsh judgments, if the *song* be loth to quit
> Those recollected hours that have the charm
> Of visionary things, those lovely forms
> And sweet sensations that throw back our life,
> And almost make remotest infancy
> A visible scene, on which the sun is shining?
>   (ll. 629-635)

An indulgence toward self-avowed nostalgia is as much as the opening lines invite; the evocative power of "visionary things" can hardly come into play with the notion of "charm" calling up fancy and romance, instead of transcendence. But this statement, seeming to continue on parallel ground (those. . . , those), smoothly carries itself upward into universal philosophy. While the grammatical construction equates "those recollected hours" with "those lovely forms," the equation entails a major revaluation of our understanding of the first term. Lovely forms, of course, have the strongest roots in the Platonic system, but they show a radical mutation, being contained in the past and in actual experience, as are the "beauteous forms" of *Tintern Abbey* (and as against the pre-existence posited in the *Intimations* ode). With this instance of concrete idealism, it becomes apparent that Wordsworth remembers, not out of an infirmity of love or owing to any charm, but because what he remembers as belonging to him belongs also in a timeless and perfect domain, and leads him there. How surely it leads him, and *us* (for "our life" in l. 633 suggests a common experience), can be gathered from the final lines: "And almost make remotest infancy / A visible scene, on which the sun is shining."

It is a metaphor, but so close to its subject as to seem literal: a visible scene, including everything short of remotest infancy. The rational uncertainties of the situation stand resolved, and assurance is made doubly sure by the shining sun, which affords the best light for what we see. The sun also subtly dispels the mist of spiritual uncertainty in the passage, insofar as the phrase "on which the sun is shining" not only bespeaks clarity but betokens blessedness. Hence, for the immediate purposes of the poem, Wordsworth's mind is "revived" and he enters a "genial mood," his spirit filled with vitality and fruitfulness. The spirit of the entire complex of lines is delicately reflected in one of the last details we see, Wordsworth's "certain hopes." The qualifier, "certain," at first may seem tentative in tone, with the sense of something not explicitly fixed and named; but it reverberates powerfully with the other sense of "certain," something beyond doubt or the possibility of failure. The fusion of these two senses confirms, but also grows out of, the temper of poised argument Wordsworth is expressing.

As a whole, the passage checks the course of the poem only to release it with increased impetus and definition. The "end" of the poem (l. 636) is in a sense as mysterious as its beginning, and yet its knowledge of where it might go, and whence—the gist of the lines under analysis—has undeniable authority. From the way the poem's "hopes" and roots become explicit in a context of argument, oblique but precise, one is encouraged to see such argument as material, even intrinsic, to the work.

Perhaps *The Prelude* does not become in any handy sense "a rigorous inquisition" (I.148), but early and late it gives evidence of an informal argumentative impulse and skill. The use of litotes, with its argument-bracing effect, can be abundantly illustrated.[10] In like manner, a current of images continually advances the poem's propositions. These may be given a brief examination.

Helen Darbishire has spoken of the apt directness and simplicity of Wordsworth's images (pp. 163 ff.), with particular stress on their naturalistic aesthetic appeal. They also do distinctive intellectual work, especially in relation to Wordsworth's conception of organically developing time. This conception, recognizable at once in the planting of snowdrops, emerges twice again in the opening books. Wordsworth speaks of himself as "gathering . . . / Through every hair-breadth in that field of light, / New pleasure like a bee among the flowers" (I.578-580); and he asks who can know when "His habits were first sown, even as a seed" (II.207). Without going into questions of activity-passivity or spontaneity-inscrutability in the two images, we can see that they create a lively awareness of a rich productivity resulting from the accumulation of the minutest elements (the bee) or from the irresistible articulation of a single small thing (the seed). Both the inherent power and the ultimate wholeness of Wordsworth's experiences take on a substantiating concreteness from the images. Furthermore, the long process of the poem's development (that is, the correlation between the character of Wordsworth's experience and the formation of the work) is given tacit reception in the reader's mind. The reader is conditioned to watch and to allow for the slow, partitive way of the poem.

Progressively through *The Prelude* the references to beginnings and ends, to sources, birth, infancy, dawn, and spring, cluster to reinforce the bee and seed images. How they do so would warrant a separate study; here, a couple of special reminiscences of these images will help to show the intricate connections of the poem. The allusion to "Divine Comates" (XI.443-448) adds a life-giving and redemptive function to the richness of the bee image. Where before the image had enabled Wordsworth to look forward with clarity and comprehension, now it enables him to look back with assurance, out of a time of crisis. As regards the seed image, reinforcement comes from a piece of literal description:

> Thus long I mused,
> Nor e'er lost sight of what I mused upon,
> Save when, amid the stately grove of oaks,
> Now here, now there, an acorn, from its cup
> Dislodged, through sere leaves rustled.
> (I.80–84)

Here the setting so happily fits the context—Wordsworth is meditating "some work / Of glory"—that a symbolic resonance comes straightway to mind. It is nature now, spontaneously, and not Wordsworth, deliberately, saying that the seed of something great is there; the "startling" acorn (l. 85) intimates the stately oak. A like effect occurs when Wordsworth describes himself as "harassed with the toil of verse" and getting little done, when "at once / Some lovely image in the song rose up / Full-formed, like Venus rising from the sea" (IV.110-114).

The foregoing discussion represents major, but not exclusive, ways in which *The Prelude* explicitly certifies the mind of Wordsworth and works on the reader's. The poem displays a continuing pressure toward accuracy, as in the revision of "peace" to "ease and undisturbed delight" (I.24-27), a continual "tenta-

tive note"[11] and yet a strong sense of necessary logical cause;
a tendentious organization, as in the juxtaposition of the Bar-
tholomew and Helvellyn Fairs, with the description bringing
home an unmistakable pro-rural thesis, or in the contrasted opening lines of Books III and IV which show the same bias; and
above all a confidence-winning candor (*e.g.*, IV.612 ff., V.293
ff. and 510 ff., XIV.321 ff. and 336).

Inevitably, this helps to determine the light in which we see
the poem; it is not a thing of argument, with a systematic
assemblage of topics disposed in keeping with proper rhetorical
principles, but neither is it a thing ignorant or innocent of
argument. Rather, it incorporates argument in its own lyrical-
epical system, to confess and contend with its inherent difficulties
of understanding and statement, to meet and answer the difficulties conceivable in the reader's situation.

A certain sententious and moralistic strain ominously marks
Wordsworth's earliest poems, like the *Lines Left upon a Seat
in a Yew-tree* or *Descriptive Sketches*. But here again an under-
voice of Wordsworthian position-taking and position-making
can be readily discerned. The very opening of *Lines Left upon
a Seat in a Yew-tree* bespeaks confrontation and hoped-for resolution of a difficulty: "Nay, Traveller! rest." The speaker is
trying to overcome the aversion of the "stranger"—the silent
partner in a tacit dialogue—to a desolate place. The poem is
not really focused on the "favoured Being" who became a mis-
anthropic solitary, though it dwells on him so. His story serves
as an illustrative anecdote in a course of instruction which, given
the context of the stranger's resistance and ignorance, becomes
an act of implied argument. Working on an amplifying and
incorporating definition of humanity, the poem seeks to show
and sympathize with humanity existing "far from all human
dwelling." The "what if" constructions of the opening lines
explicitly counter the stranger's prejudices, just as the "if" that
introduces the second verse paragraph, the second stage of the
poem's movement, engages him to promote the poem's terms
or confess himself corrupt.

Even the final lines of the poem, which seem most blatantly
sermonistic, contain an argumentative thrust, in the phrases,
"true knowledge" and "true dignity." Milton uses this locution
to good effect in *Paradise Lost* to invoke and combat "false"
examples, and Wordsworth may be given credit for doing as
much. *Lines Left upon a Seat in a Yew-tree* may ultimately ask

for direct assent or for conversion, but first it seeks a thinking-through of the propositions it makes concerning the definition of humanity. Not that its argument is orderly and analytical; the dramatic situation makes for an emotional heightening from the outset, and what is argumentative works in complement with this emotion, purposely seeking to attach it to particular, if unfamiliar, objects.

A brief quotation from *Descriptive Sketches*, also a solemn and didactic piece, will serve to show the engagement of the reader's mind in argumentative terms:

> Think not the peasant aloft has gazed
> And heard with heart unmoved, with soul unraised:
> Nor is his spirit less enrapt, nor less
> Alive to independent happiness,
> Then, when he lies, out-stretched, at even-tide
> Upon the fragrant mountain's purple side:
> For as the pleasures of his simple day
> Beyond his native valley seldom stray,
> Nought round its darling precincts can he find
> But brings some past enjoyment to his mind;
> While Hope, reclining upon Pleasure's urn,
> Binds her wild wreaths, and whispers his return.
>   (ll. 421–432)

These lines casually incorporate the overcoming of denial ("not . . . unmoved") and the recognition of logic ("for") which more obviously argumentative poems of the early years, such as *Expostulation and Reply* and *The Tables Turned*, more formally exploit. Perhaps *Tintern Abbey*, the auspicial poem of the first volume, best indicates how naturally Wordsworth's work curves into an area of confronting negative possibilities and actively, logically, confirming its dominant positions.[12] The mode of progression in the poem—with "therefore" and "for," "thus," "but," "and so," "if," and "nor . . . if" continually before our eyes—is as much logical as chronological. John Jones calls these "words of modest function," but they are vital at last; as Jones himself acknowledges, the poem develops "a logical, knitted quality" (p. 207).

Recognizing the presence and the peculiar ways of argument in Wordsworth's poetry leads to valuable modifications of our sense of him as assertive, and of our conviction that in his work truth "is its own testimony" and "a direct revelation of reality."[13] But more than this is involved. *She Dwelt among the Untrodden*

Ways, as soon as we recognize that the middle stanza is using the images of violet and star[14] to provide information to ignorant men and thus *to redefine their common standards of value*, moves upon us with striking breadth and power, and ceases to look like an interpretation "of human experience . . . too personal to be sympathetically received or readily shared by most readers."[15] Rather, it puts personal experience over against common assumptions and, with the image serving as a counter of understanding and a pivot, implicitly argues the superiority of personal to common judgment in terms of lucidly observant knowledge and sensitive appreciation. Indeed, the relation exactly images the relation of the subject of judgment (Lucy) to the implied others in the poem; as the images suggest, she is unique; they, merely members of the multitude. The poem, then, is arguing a typical point of view; to wit, that uniqueness is precious, though it advances unrecognized cases. Or again, without implying a philosophical treatise, we may recognize the logical under-voice of the *Intimations* ode becoming exquisitely audible in the final couplet of stanza VII: "As if his whole vocation / Were endless imitation." The poem, as G. Wilson Knight declares, catches Wordsworth in an ecstasy,[16] but it is a peculiarly reflective and critical one; and that reflection gives the strongest claims of the poem, if not sanction, a more respectful hearing than Coleridge set the pattern for.

What the strain of argument manifests in the poetry is a vigorous combination of immediacy and comprehensiveness of view, of definiteness and openness of mind. These features, more than incidentally perhaps, reappear in the more impressive of the later poems: *To a Skylark*, *The Wishing-Gate*, parts of *On the Power of Sound*, assorted sonnets, and of course *The Prelude*. Contrariwise, a poem such as *The Excursion*, though Wordsworth adopted "something of a dramatic form," fails in taking its own statements, and its immediate and effective audience, too much for granted. It is Wordsworth talking to himself, not to Coleridge or someone else definite and substantial.[17] As Geoffrey Hartman says, "we do not wish to ask what the heart understands, or how, etc. . . . But the poet has put it into an argumentative context, so that we are forced to ask questions about 'relations,' . . . and so, finally, to disparage."[18]

But even failures of argument, as in the *Sonnets on the Punishment of Death* or in the strange moment when Wordsworth praises "penniless poverty" for sparing him the contamination of luxury (*The Prelude*, ll. 78-84), indicate something like a settled habit of argument, early formed and long continued. *Nutting* itself—the poem we see as a record of swarming, rapacious passion—proves cool, inquisitive in writing, with its scrupulous pursuit of accuracy in description and analysis ("or," "perhaps," "unless"); in fact it fosters a sense of detachment and generality through the use of phrases like "such suppression . . . / As joy delights in," "a temper known to those who . . . ," "that sweet mood when pleasure loves to pay / Tribute to ease. . . ."

It bears repeating that the situation of the Romantic poet entails primary problems of definition and value, and that these problems are alive in the poet's own mind as well as in the construction of his relation to his audience. An exacting but pervasive sense of the need for redefinitions appears in the treatment of key conceptual terms (such as dream, pleasure, imagination) and of key literary conventions (such as the ballad, the pastoral, and the epic). It is a situation which presupposes and summons argument. The mode of argument adopted by Wordsworth helps to convey while it also copes with the situation. In fine, it need not be because he was "betrayed by the ineradicable weakness of civilized men" that Wordsworth was inclined "to explain, to rationalize."[19] Nor need his doing so prove a disability. It is at best part of a vital dialogue with himself and his audience.

NOTES

1. *Complete Works,* ed. P. P. Howe, after the ed. of A. R. Waller and Arnold Glover, vol. V (London, 1930), 161, 163.

2. *The Art of Wordsworth* (Hamden, Ct., 1965), p. 131.

3. Samuel Taylor Coleridge, *Biographia Literaria,* ed. with his aesthetical essays by J. Shawcross (Oxford, 1907), I, 134.

4. For Wordsworth clearly assumes what De Quincey later enunciated, the dichotomy between the literature of knowledge and the literature of power.

5. This point of view resides in "the fourth class of defects" drawn up against Wordsworth's poetry in the *Biographia Literaria,* where Coleridge criticizes "an intensity of feeling disproportionate to *such* knowledge and value of the objects described, as can be fairly anticipated of men in general . . . and with which therefore few only, and those few particularly circumstanced can be supposed to sympathize" (II, 109). It occurs ubiquitously now, as in Raymond Dexter Havens, *The Mind of a Poet: A Study of Wordsworth's Thought* (Balti-

more, 1941), I, 4; G. Wilson Knight, *The Starlit Dome: Studies in the Poetry of Vision* (Oxford, 1941), pp. 22, 36; Norman Lacey, *Wordsworth's View of Nature and Its Ethical Consequences* (Cambridge, 1948), pp. 122, 126; Goeffrey H. Hartman, *The Unmediated Vision: An Interpretation of Wordsworth* . . . (New Haven, 1954), pp. 4, 6, 8; John Jones, *The Egotistical Sublime: A History of Wordsworth's Imagination* (London, 1954), pp. 2, 15, 35; M. H. Abrams, "Wordsworth and Coleridge on Diction and Figures," *English Institute Essays, 1952,* ed. Alan S. Downer (New York, 1954), pp. 171–172; Donald Davie, *Articulate Energy: An Enquiry into the Syntax of English Poetry* (New York, 1955), p. 107; Josephine Miles, *Eras and Modes in English Poetry* (Berkeley and Los Angeles, Calif., 1957), pp. 125, 131–136; R. A. Foakes, *The Romantic Assertion: A Study in the Language of Nineteenth-Century Poetry* (London, 1958), pp. 80, 115; Anthony E. M. Conran, "The Dialectic of Experience: A Study of Wordsworth's *Resolution and Independence*," *PMLA,* LXXV (1960), 70; David Perkins, *The Quest for Permanence: The Symbolism of Wordsworth, Shelley and Keats* (Cambridge, Mass., 1959), pp. 91, 100; Edward E. Bostetter, *The Romantic Ventriloquists: Wordsworth, Coleridge, Keats, Shelley, Byron* (Seattle, Wash., 1963), p. 5; Harold Bloom, *The Visionary Company: A Reading of English Romantic Poetry* (New York, 1963), p. 141. Perhaps the most sweeping presentation of the charge of "assertion-making" comes from a non-Wordsworthian, R. L. Drain, who writes: "It was Wordsworth . . . who smuggled over the stormy borderline between the centuries just those conceptions ['law of nature,' 'right reason,' 'the moral sense,' 'natural rectitude'] Bentham worked so hard to destroy. He did so in a way that it baffled even Benthamite analysis to stop. A comprehensive intellectual refutation of materialistic fallacies . . . had no part in it. The day was won not by intellectual strength but by intellectual weakness. . . . The message . . . slipped by [the reader's] logical defenses not by overcoming the critical intellect, but by offering it no hold" (*Tradition and D. H. Lawrence* [Groningen, 1960], p. 6).

6. Quotations of Wordsworth's poetry are taken from the *Poetical Works,* ed. with intro. and notes by Thomas Hutchinson, new ed. rev. by Ernest De Selincourt (New York, Oxford U. Press, 1959). Concerning this question of "art," Helen Darbishire sees in Wordsworth an opposition between "impulse and intuition" and "careful art" (*The Poet Wordsworth* [Oxford, 1950], p. 4). This conjures up the image of Wordsworth warbling his native woodnotes wild, and denies what Wordsworth knows: namely, that careful art is the handmaiden of impulse and intuition. Miss Darbishire later appraises Wordsworth's art at a higher rate, especially when contending against the treatment of him as a doctrinaire poet (pp. 65–66, 193).

7. The word *dialectic* occurs widely in criticism of Wordsworth and of Romanticism (see, *e.g.,* Bloom, *The Visionary Company,* p. 143; Conran, "The Dialectic of Experience: A Study of Wordsworth's *Resolution and Independence,*" *passim*; Colin Clarke, *Romantic Paradox: An Essay on the Poetry of Wordsworth* (London, 1962), p. 12; and Geoffrey Hartman, "Romanticism and 'Anti-Self Consciousness,'" *Centennial Review,* VI (1962), 556). It is used to describe perhaps the sort of life situation or process or structure that would give occasion for argument, a situation marked by contraries and working toward an equipoise or resolution. It has not heretofore been carried to the point of identifying the rhetorical procedures or strategies whereby, in portraying the dialectical situation, the poets convey and earn distinctive philosophical posi-

tions, except negatively by F. R. Leavis when he says, "Wordsworth's verse . . . goes on and on, without dialectical suspense and crisis or rise and fall" (*Revaluation: Tradition and Development in English Poetry* [New York, 1947], p. 162), quoted by Davie, *Articulate Energy*, p. 112.

8. D. G. James, *Scepticism and Poetry: An Essay on the Poetic Imagination* (London, 1937), p. 273.

9. The chronology of the poem's composition fairly bears out this point (see Darbishire, pp. 87–88, 90–91); the toning down of intimacy in the revised references to Coleridge (pp. 121–122), if anything, promotes this effect.

10. As in I.14–15, 329–330, 404, 445, 475, 550, 554–558, 591, and further selectively in II.140, 306, 312; III.157, 158, 169–170, 193; XIV.308, 358, 414. In *The Egotistical Sublime* John Jones says that "Wordsworth carries his delight in negatives to the point of tiresome mannerism: there are too many double negatives." (p. 204). I. A. Richards, in turn, calls the double negatives in Wordsworth "opacities" (*The Portable Coleridge* [New York, 1961], p. 36). It needs to be recognized that with his double negatives, as with the less common "not . . . but" constructions, Wordsworth adds general definition, not just idiosyncratic delight, to what he says.

11. Robert Langbaum, "The Evolution of Soul in Wordsworth's Poetry," *PMLA*, LXXXII (1967), 268.

12. The use of argument in this poem is touched on by this writer in *The Blind Man Traces the Circle* (Princeton, 1969), pp. 62–63.

13. Carlos Baker, ed., *The Prelude, with a Selection from the Shorter Poems* . . . , Rinehart ed., rev. and enlarged (New York, 1954), p. xii.

14. "When only one is shining in the sky" must of course be read as *limiting* the function of the image exclusively to that time. It goes outside the compass of the poem, and counter to the restricted applicability of the image as image, to fill the heavens with stars and depreciate Wordsworth's subject. If anything, we should imagine a second sky elsewhere, full of undistinguished stars. The same limiting use of the conditional "when" occurs in *The White Doe of Rylstone*, ll. 60–62.

15. Perkins, p. 91.

16. *The Starlit Dome*, p. 38.

17. One can observe two further instances of an intellectual falling-back which costs Wordsworth's poetry some of its vibrancy, some of its special power to be both natural and new. In the poem *Suggested by a Picture of the Bird of Paradise*, which indeed reaches for argument tardily and lamely after giving vent to a quasi-Puritanical bile, concrete idealism becomes a conventional idealism, or Platonism (ll. 33 ff.). More striking yet, the second of the *Miscellaneous Sonnets*, Pt. II, shows Wordsworth taking fright and shrinking from a wood wherein "thoughts, link by link / Enter through ears and eyesight, with [a] gleam / Of all things. . . ." This is not just the "avoidance of apocalypse" that Hartman posits in *Wordsworth Poetry: 1787–1814* (New Haven and London, 1964, pp. 17–18, 45 ff., *passim*); it is avoidance of experience itself, and of experience which has constituted the anchor and nurse of apocalypse for Wordsworth.

18. *The Unmediated Vision*, p. 38.

19. Darbishire, p. 133.

THE *ANCIENT MARINER* AND COLERIDGE'S THEORY OF POETIC ART

Charles Richard Sanders

It has been generally assumed that if ever a volume of verse grew out of a matrix of conscious literary theory the *Lyrical Ballads* of Wordsworth and Coleridge, first published in 1798, did so. The long walks and talks among the Quantock Hills in which the two young poets delighted when they were composing the poems, the testimony which they both give in letters written during this period, the statements which Wordsworth made in his Preface to the second edition of the volume, and the long critique on Wordsworth and his theories of poetic art which Coleridge wrote later for the *Biographia Literaria*, all testify to the fact. That they agreed in accepting some principles and disagreed in dealing with others, as Coleridge was careful to make clear in the *Biographia*, merely reflects the stimulus which each received from their discussions, the intensity of their thought about what was to them an extremely exciting subject, and the seriousness with which each attempted to develop, clarify, and validate conceptions through his own individual thinking and writing of verse. The recognition which each displayed of differences of temperament, character, and cast of mind in the other did little if anything to diminish at the time the pleasure they found in one another's company and the gratification they experienced in being able to discuss, on what both considered a very high level, a subject so dear to the hearts of both.

Certainly it was in such an atmosphere that *The Ancient Mariner* was written. Coleridge the poet had been a theorist and experimenter for some years before he met Wordsworth, and he continued to theorize and experiment with verse as long as he lived, long after the best years of his friendship with Wordsworth; but his close association with Wordsworth at the time he was writing *The Ancient Mariner* intensified his thinking about the true nature of poetry and encouraged him to test his theories in the poem he was writing, a poem markedly different from any of its type that had been written before. Unfortunately, Coleridge did not at the time draw up a systematic statement of his ideas about poetry as Wordsworth soon did in his famous Preface of 1800; but Coleridge did say as early as the autumn of 1800, "The Preface contains our joint opinions on Poetry."[1] A little later, July 1802, he wrote, "It is most certain that that P[reface arose from] the heads of our mutual Conversations &c—& the f[irst pass]ages were indeed partly taken from notes of mine / for it was at first intended, that the Preface should be written by me."[2] During the same month he wrote Southey that the Preface was "half a child of my own Brain."[3] And although at this time, as well as years later in the *Biographia*, Coleridge took exception to some of the things Wordsworth said about the nature of poetry, it is easy to recognize in the Preface much that is clearly Coleridgean.

The point is that the basis of poetic theory which Coleridge had in mind when he wrote *The Ancient Mariner* was much broader and more complex than that indicated in his well-known statement in the *Biographia*: "My endeavours should be to persons and characters supernatural, or at least romantic; yet so as to transfer from our inward nature a human interest and a semblance of truth sufficient to procure for these shadows of imagination that willing suspension of disbelief for the moment, which constitutes poetic faith."[4] This is of course a wonderful statement which fits the poem perfectly; but it is very general and falls far short of being an adequate summary of all the ideas about the true nature of poetry with which Coleridge experimented in this poem.

The question naturally arises, "How do we know what ideas belonging to Coleridge's theory of poetic art as explicitly stated later in his lectures, the *Biographia*, his other published writings, his notebooks, and his marginalia were already in his mind when he wrote *The Ancient Mariner*? The answer is not simple, but most assuredly, once we are thoroughly and clearly familiar with his favorite ideas about poetry, repeated many times in his later works and not difficult to grasp or remember, we are in a position to recognize them in writings roughly contemporaneous with *The Ancient Mariner*: Wordsworth's Preface, his other poems, significantly including *The Prelude* written about this time, and Coleridge's other poems belonging to this period. Then, too, nothing is more Coleridgean than his belief that ideas, both philosophical and aesthetic, were often prefigured in his mind long before he found them expressed by others or rendered them articulate himself. The letters, too, provide much help. But the best evidence is provided by Coleridge's practice in *The Ancient Mariner* itself, a poem which, though revised from time to time, never underwent radical revision in terms of artistic principles. It may therefore be valid to set up as a working hypothesis the assumption that most of the ideas about poetic art which Coleridge made articulate later were in his mind (or in his instincts as an artist) when he wrote the poem, to summarize these as clearly and briefly as possible, and then to ascertain the extent to which Coleridge was governed by them in writing the poem. If the ideas fit, they may be said to belong to the poem as surely as Cinderella's slipper belonged to her. So far as this method succeeds it may complement Lowes[5] in a modest but useful way, since he worked forward from Coleridge's sources to the fusion they underwent in the artistic unity of the poem, while the present method, by concentrating on Coleridge's artistic principles, may throw new light on just how that fusion took place.

Fundamental to Coleridge's thinking is his definition of a poem in a well-known passage in the *Biographia Literaria*: "A poem is that species of composition, which is opposed to works of science, by proposing for its *immediate* object pleasure, not truth; and from all other species (having *this* object in common with it) it is discriminated by proposing to itself such delight from the *whole*, as is compatible with a distinct gratification from each component *part*. . . . The reader should be carried forward, not merely or chiefly by the mechanical impulse of curiosity, or by a restless desire to arrive at the final solution; but by the pleasurable activity of mind excited by the attractions of the journey itself."[6] Further, the poet "diffuses a tone and spirit of unity that blends, and (as it were) *fuses*, each into each, by that synthetic and magical power, to which we have exclusively appropriated the name of imagination," a power revealing itself through many functions, among which two of the most important are the balancing or reconciling of opposite or discordant qualities and of sameness with difference.[7] Poetry is among the imitative arts, and "imitation, as opposed to copying, consists either in the interfusion of the SAME throughout the radically DIFFERENT, or of the different throughout a base radically the same."[8] In this last function, as in some of the others, poetic art may reflect the workings of Nature herself: "The requisite and only serviceable fiction, therefore, is the representation of CHAOS as one vast homogeneous drop! In this sense it may be even justified, as an appropriate symbol of the great fundamental truth that all things spring from, and subsist in, the endless strife between indifference and difference. . . . The symbol only is fictitious: the thing signified is not only grounded in truth—it is the law and actuating principle of all other truths, whether physical or intellectual."[9] Coleridge insists further: "Perhaps the most important of our intellectual operations are those of detecting the difference in similar, and the identity in dissimilar, things. Out of the latter operation it is that wit arises. . . . The true comic is the blossom of the nettle."[10]

Coleridge feels that as a poet, critic, and philosopher he is working in the tradition of Pythagoras and Plato. He asserts that his "Dynamic Philosophy scientifically arranged" will be when completed "no other than the system of Pythagoras and of Plato revived and purified from impure mixtures."[11] He accepts Pythagoras' definition of the Beautiful as "multeity in unity." "The safest definition, then, of Beauty, as well as the oldest, is that of Pythagoras: THE REDUCTION OF MANY TO ONE. . . . *The sense of beauty subsists in simultaneous intuition of the relation of parts, each to each, and of all to a whole: exciting an immediate and absolute complacency, without intervenence, therefore, of any interest, sensual or intellectual.*"[12] "To perceive and feel the Beautiful, the Pathetic, and the Sublime in Nature, in Thought, or in Action—this combined with the power of conveying such Perceptions and Feelings to the minds and hearts of others under the most pleasurable Forms of Eye and Ear—this is poetic Genius. . . . To counteract this Disease [the loss of poetic power and perception] of long-civilized Societies, and to establish not only the identity of the Essence under the greatest variety of Forms, but the congruity and even the necessity of that variety" is one of Coleridge's own principal aims.[13] He disagrees with John Locke's assertion that simple ideas are adequate: "A simple Idea, as a simple Idea, cannot refer to any external Substance, representatively: for as Pythagoras said, nothing *exists* but in complexity."[14] Fond of the words *homogeneous* and *hetero-*

geneous, he draws a distinction between the poetry of Greek drama and that of his day in terms of them: the great rule of Greek drama was the "separation, or the removal, of the Heterogeneous—even as the Spirit of the Romantic Poetry, is modification, or the blending of the Heterogeneous into an Whole by the Unity of the Effect."[15]

But fully as important, Pythagoras and Plato discovered ways to free the mind from the dominance of the senses and to make possible a mode of thought upon a high level of abstraction, which becomes one of the glories of human experience. Coleridge declares:

> To emancipate the mind from the despotism of the eye is the first step towards its emancipation from the influences and intrusions of the senses, sensations and passions generally. Thus most effectually is the power of abstraction to be called forth, strengthened and familiarized, and it is this power of abstraction that chiefly distinguishes the human understanding from that of the higher animals—and in the different degrees in which this power is developed, the superiority of man over man mainly consists. Hence we are to account for the preference which the divine Plato gives to expressions taken from the objects of the ear, as terms of Music and Harmony, and in part at least for the numerical symbols, in which Pythagoras clothed his philosophy.[16]

Pythagoras, he also says, included music and rhythm as a preparatory discipline "to the study and contents of mathematics," through which his pupils were to pass "on their road to wisdom or the knowledge of the immediate."[17] And he links up this principle with the understanding and appreciation of poetry. "Some persons have contended that mathematics ought to be taught by making the illustrations obvious to the senses. Nothing can be more absurd or injurious: it ought to be our never-ceasing effort to make people think, not feel; and it is very much owing to this mistake that, to those who do not think, and have not been made to think, Shakespeare has been found so difficult of comprehension."[18] Aristotle likewise affirms this principle, Coleridge says in a highly illuminating passage:

> I adopt with full faith the principle of Aristotle, that poetry as poetry is essentially *ideal,* that it avoids and excludes all *accident.* [Coleridge then adds this note quoted from *The Friend*:] Paradoxical as it may sound, one of the essential properties of Geometry is not less essential to dramatic excellence; and Aristotle has accordingly required of the poet an involution of the universal in the individual. The chief differences are, that in Geometry it is the universal truth which is uppermost in

the consciousness; in poetry the individual form, in which the truth is clothed . . . . [The ancients were not mere realists copying what they perceived through their physical senses.] Their tragic scenes were meant to *affect* us indeed; but yet within the bounds of pleasure, and in union with the activity both of our understanding and imagination. They wished to transport the mind to a sense of its possible greatness, and to implant the germs of that greatness, during the temporary oblivion of the worthless "thing we are," and of the peculiar state in which each man happens to be, suspending our individual recollections and lulling them to sleep amid the music of nobler thoughts.[19]

It follows that the writing of great poetry is a very exacting art. In a frequently quoted passage from the *Biographia*, Coleridge expresses his gratitude to his old schoolmaster James Bowyer for teaching him this lesson: "I learnt from him that Poetry, even that of the loftiest and, seemingly, that of the wildest odes, had a logic of its own, as severe as that of science; and more difficult, because more subtle, more complex, and dependent on more, and more fugitive causes."[20] Possibly Bowyer pushed his point too hard for the tender young Coleridge in his formative period. Throughout life he expresses some doubts about his own qualifications as a poet;[21] and, even though he was proud of *The Ancient Mariner*, he did not consider it a perfect poem. The perfect balance between philosopher and creative artist is very difficult to achieve. "There is no profession on earth," he says, "which requires an attention so early, so long, or so unintermitting as that of poetry; and indeed as that of literary composition in general, if it be such as at all satisfies the demands both of taste and of sound logic."[22] And he also says: "No man was ever yet a great poet, without being at the same time a profound philosopher. For poetry is the blossom and fragrancy of all human knowledge, human thoughts, human passions, emotions, language. In Shakespeare's *poems* the creative power and the intellectual energy wrestle as in a war embrace. Each in its excess of strength seems to threaten the extinction of the other."[23] John Frere reports that he heard Coleridge say,

The depravity of the spirit of the times is marked by the absence of poetry. For it is a great mistake to suppose that thought is not necessary for poetry; true, at the time of composition there is that starlight, a dim and holy twilight; but is not light necessary before?

Poetry is the highest effort of the mind; all the powers are in a state of equilibrium and equally energetic, the knowledge of individual existence is forgotten, the man is out of himself and exists in all things . . . .[24]

De Quincey, who we know was not always generous in his comments on Coleridge, testifies: "I can assert, upon my long and intimate knowledge of Coleridge's mind, that logic the most severe was as inalienable from his modes of thinking as grammar from his language."[25] Yet Coleridge always remembers Bowyer's teaching that poetry has a logic "of its own," distinct from ordinary logic; and he insists that it must use both kinds: "Poetry must be *more* than good sense, or it is not poetry; but it dare not be less, or discrepant. Good sense is not, indeed, the superstructure; but it is the rock, not only on which the edifice is raised, but likewise the rock-quarry *from* which all its stones have been, by patient toil, dug out."[26] Finally, however profound the thought of the poem may be, its tone must not be dogmatic. The tone of a poem should be dictated by the ways of the imagination, which "hovers between images" and, remaining on the wing, refuses to commit itself to "fixities and definites" as the mere fancy does, but manifests its life in its power to suggest multiple and at times ambiguous entities vital to the unity of the poem.[27] This is what Coleridge had in mind in replying to Mrs. Barbauld's objection that *The Ancient Mariner* had no moral by saying that the moral sentiment of the poem obtruded too openly on the reader for "a work of such pure imagination."[28]

Most if not all of these principles are followed in the composition of *The Ancient Mariner*. They do much to determine the quality of its artistic texture and aesthetic dynamics. In their operations they are interwoven with amazing dexterity in order to give to the reader both maximum pleasure and a deep and unforgettable sense of the theme or "truth" of the poem. This theme is not a mere "notion" of Coleridge's but a lifelong conviction which had roots deep in his own nature. It is a sense of the mysterious unity which binds together creation in all its vastness and complexity and of the infinite power which love has to vitalize and make healthy all relationships. To Coleridge this is a universal law with which the human will may place itself in harmony and thereby work toward good; but fundamentally it is independent of the human will. In the poem neither the shooting of the albatross nor the blessing of the water snakes is an act of will. There is no more forethought in the shooting of the albatross than there is in the act of a trigger-happy twelve-year-old boy who shoots a friendly robin; but there is cruelty in it just the same, as Coleridge says in his prose gloss, and the mariner has violated a fundamental relation among God's creatures which cannot, regardless of motive, be violated with impunity. Likewise he blesses the water snakes "unaware" rather than through conscious act of will; yet the dead albatross falls from his neck just the same. Furthermore, Coleridge provides as the motto of the poem a Latin quotation from T. Burnet's *Archaeologiae Philosophiae* (1692), which has been translated as follows:

> I readily believe that there are more invisible beings in the universe than visible. But who shall explain to us the nature, the rank and kinship, the distinguishing marks and graces of each? What do they do? Where do they dwell? The human mind has circled round this knowledge, but never attained to it. Yet there is profit, I do not doubt, in sometimes contemplating in the mind, as in a picture, the image of a greater and better world: lest the intellect, habituated to the petty details of daily life, should be contracted within too narrow limits and settle down wholly on trifles. But, meanwhile, a watchful eye must be kept on truth, and proportion observed, that we may distinguish the certain from the uncertain, day from night.[29]

Hence in the poem most of the action is controlled by the "Storm-Blast," "the good south wind," "the lonesome Spirit from the "south-pole," "guardian saints," "angelic spirits" which enter the bodies of the dead crew, the gambling of Death with Life-in-Death, and the mysterious influence and potencies of the sun and moon. All these operate in accordance with the universal law.

And to Coleridge, although this law is fixed, it is also benign. God was to him essentially and primarily a God of Love, not a God of wrath and punishment.[30] The power of love and the need for it, as many passages in his writings attest, were among the things most deeply rooted in his own nature.[31] His nature was social, and there were times when he suffered, almost as much as the Ancient Mariner on the wide, wide sea, from loneliness, whether it derived from incompatibility with his wife, misunderstandings with his friends Charles Lloyd and Wordsworth, or from many other incidents involving his relationships with other people.

Coleridge's extension of the principle of love to the lower animals was not a mere passing fancy, limited to the albatross and the water snakes in this poem. The jack-ass, which he hales as a brother in his much derided poem of 1794—even though the poem is amusing in its ineptness, has its place in Coleridge's

affections near that of the albatross of *The Ancient Mariner.*
Also in 1794, in a passage which is jocular only in part, Coleridge writes to Francis Wrangham: "I call even my Cat Sister
in the Fraternity of universal Nature. Owls I respect & Jack
Asses I love: for Aldermen & Hogs, Bishops & Royston Crows
I have not particular partiality."[32] In 1796 he writes in another
letter: "I mean to raise vegetables & corn enough for myself
& Wife, and feed a couple of snouted & grunting Cousins from
the refuse."[33] In *This Lime-Tree Bower My Prison* (1797),
he addresses Lamb significantly:

> My gentle-hearted Charles! when the last rook
> Beat its straight path along the dusky air
> Homewards, I blest it! deeming its black wing
> (Now a dim speck, now vanishing in light)
> Had cross'd the mighty Orb's dilated glory,
> While thou stood'st gazing; or, when all was still,
> Flew creeking o'er thy head, and had a charm
> For thee, my gentle-hearted Charles, to whom
> No sound is dissonant which tells of Life.
> (ll. 70–78)

His delight in real nightingales, which sing joyful songs and
not the sad ones of the traditional Philomela, is expressed in
a poem of April 1798.[34] Coleridge read and admired William
Cowper; no doubt he shared his affection for the lower animals
and feeling of intimacy with them. His albatross is not a mere
symbol; Coleridge belongs to the tradition of St. Francis of
Assisi and Androcles.[35]

Given, then, this theme which to Coleridge relates to "truth,"
that is, to the way in which the universe actually does operate,
and given also an albatross which Wordsworth had found in
his reading, together with a dream about a spectre ship which
a Somerset neighbor, John Cruikshank, had related to him,[36]
Coleridge proceeds to draw upon the riches of his own mind
and compose a poem which will intensify the activity of the
imagination by uniting the "real" with the supernatural. His
problem at the beginning is to elicit from the reader "that willing
suspension of disbelief for the moment" which he calls "poetic
faith." This he does skillfully by starting with the usual (though
highly interesting and joyful), a wedding feast; proceeding to
the unusual, as the guest, who is next of kin, is stopped at the
door; going then to the strange, as the mysterious-looking
Mariner holds the guest first with his skinny hand and then

with his glittering eye; and then to the improbable and the supernatural as the Mariner gets into his tale, which more and more as he goes along carries the listener away from the world of ordinary reality. At the end of the poem the transition back to this world uses abnormal psychology similarly in the behavior of the Hermit, the Pilot, and the Pilot's Boy as they observe the Mariner.[37] Other details in the poem also appeal to "our inward nature" and help produce that "semblance of truth" which Coleridge believes is necessary. He not only exploits the paradoxical truth that we may find our humanity in our affection for the lower animals (here a friendly, playful albatross and water snakes beautifully alive), but he also comforts and delights us with other details in which human beings and their institutions are represented in a favorable light: the wedding guest, who is thoroughly human in all his responses to the Mariner's amazing story; the benign, sweet-natured old Hermit; the merry minstrelsy of the wedding feast, with the bride and her bridesmaids singing together in the garden-bower (very appropriate in a poem which has much to teach us about broadening the basis of love); and the "goodly company" of "Old men, and babes, and loving friends / And youths and maidens gay" (ll. 608-609) joyfully walking together to the church, each blessed by the great Father as He bends over them. There is much that is deeply Coleridgean in the human side of *The Ancient Mariner,* clearly related to the thought which he gives later to the high potentialities of man's nature, of his institutions, and of social relationships.

But the immediate object of a poem, Coleridge insists, is pleasure, not truth; and in this respect it is one of the fine arts. It differs from the other fine arts in that it seeks to derive as much pleasure from the parts as the central purpose of producing maximum pleasure from the whole will permit. The imagination is the vitalizing as well as the unifying power, and in *The Ancient Mariner* every detail, every image, every motion, every sound has a life of its own, whether it is the painted ship upon the painted ocean, the death-fires dancing at night, slimy things crawling with legs upon a slimy sea, the grotesque Nightmare LIFE-IN-DEATH, the souls of the other mariners, now dead, whizzing like arrows from a cross-bow past the Ancient Mariner, the serenely beautiful moon softly going up the sky, the pyrotechnics in the nighttime sky as it bursts into life and a hundred shining fire-flags hurry about, while "to and fro, and

in and out / The wan stars danced between" (ll. 316-317), or
the home port with the light-house top, the kirk with its steady
weathercock, or the bay, clear as glass, white with the silent light
of the moon. Images often move forward, become intensely
vivid, and for the moment perform the function of musical
instruments in a symphony as, one by one, they emerge from
the writhing mass of sound, play their solo parts, and then re-
cede. An excellent example of this is the passage beginning with
line 352 ("Sweet sounds rose slowly through their mouths")
and ending with line 372 ("Singeth a quiet tune") which,
describing all sorts of sounds in lovely music, contains what might
almost be called a nature lyric of the first water, with a skylark,
"all little birds that are" filling the sea and air with "their sweet
jargoning," and "A noise like of a hidden brook / In the leafy
month of June, / That to the sleeping woods all night / Singeth
a quiet tune." The principle, which Coleridge knows very well
must not violate Horace's dictum and merely provide a sequence
of "purple patches," is not a new one but is as old as epic poetry,
in which the Homeric or extended simile behaves very much the
same way and performs the double function of delighting the
reader with its own life and injecting new life into the poem as
a whole. Coleridge uses it in many of his other poems, the best-
known example being "The one red leaf, the last of its clan, /
That dances as often as dance it can" in *Christabel* (ll. 49-50).
Other examples are "the thin blue flame" called a *"stranger"*
fluttering on the grate in *Frost at Midnight* (ll. 13 ff.) and the
"tiny cone of sand" with "its soundless dance, / Which at the
bottom, like a Fairy's Page, / As merry and no taller, dances
still" in *Inscription for a Fountain on a Heath* (ll. 9-11).

The aesthetic dynamics of the poem are further intensified and
the unity further strengthened by the full use of the principle
achieving the reconciliation of opposites, which Coleridge believes is one of the most important functions of the imagination.
The poem literally swarms with dichotomies, most of which
could be classified as polarities: joy and sadness, solitude and
sociality, the old and the young, the archaic and the modern (in
language particularly), the wet and the dry, darkness and light,
stillness and motion, the right and the left, the south and the
north, the fast and the slow, the serenely beautiful and the
grotesque, the natural and the supernatural, the living and the
dead, the rotting and the vital, growing, healthy, the high
heavens and the deep ocean, the fiery, hostile masculine sun and

the cool, kindly feminine moon, the far and the near, diffusion and concentration,[38] vastness with its long vistas and intimacy with its sharp focus and concern for details, silence and sound, simplicity and complexity, the cold and the hot, cruelty and kindness, the human and the inhuman, the perpendicular and the horizontal. These are interwoven in a complex but unified pattern in which they are related to two other principles which Coleridge delights in theorizing about, multeity in unity, and sameness in difference. Lowes's *The Road to Xanadu* is really a massive and monumental study of how Coleridge brings together odds and ends of raw materials gathered through his reading from the four corners of the earth in accordance with the principle of multeity in unity.[39] Combined with polarity and with what Wordsworth calls the perception of "similitude in dissimilitude, and dissimilitude in similitude," this principle produces amazing results. Often one of the entities will fan out like a peacock's tail and as a multeity display itself in various forms. Darkness tends to be homogeneous, but light assumes many shades and appearances as the sun, the moon, and the stars manifest themselves under various circumstances. Against the vast whiteness of the Antarctic ice, Coleridge gives us what is almost a complete spectrum of colors, appearing in all sorts of unexpected places throughout the poem. The dryness is intensified and is very dry indeed, while the wet assumes many forms, whether it is the thousands of acres of ice, the salt water of the sea, the pleasant dew, the blood the Mariner sucks from his arm, or the refreshing rain falling in great abundance. When the ship is becalmed, the stillness is almost unbearable and provides us with an unforgettable image of a painted ship upon a painted ocean; but against this we have an almost infinite number of expressions suggesting motion in great variety. The Storm-Blast chases the ship southward; the south wind springs up behind; the white foam flies; the furrow follows free; in reel and rout the death-fires dance at night; the spectre ship in the distance dodges a water-sprite as it plunges and tacks and veers; its strange shape drives suddenly between the mariners and the sun; "The Sun's rim dips; the stars rush out: / At one stride comes the dark" (ll. 199-200) ; and the spectre ship shoots off over the sea; the water snakes flash their colors and coil as they swim; the upper air bursts into life, and the stars dance among the shining fire-flags; in lines 324-326, "Like waters shot from some high crag, / The lightning fell with never a jag, / A

River steep and wide" (a delightful polarity in which the perpendicular lighting bisects not merely a horizontal line but a
whole plain); the spirit slides under the boat, and the ship for a
time moves backward and forward in "a short uneasy motion"
and then "like a pawing horse let go, / She made a sudden
bound" (ll. 389-390) and begins to move swiftly toward the
home country; it spins round and round before it sinks; and
the Pilot shrieks and falls down in a fit. The differentiation of
sounds is even more multifarious and ranges all the way from
the cacophonous cracking, growling, roaring, and howling of the
ice to the music of the wedding feast and the divine sounds of
the angelic spirits which animate the bodies of the dead mariners. In its heterogeneous appeal to the ear, the poem deserves
its reputation as one of the most musical poems in the English
language, reflecting Coleridge's own profound love of music.[40]

There are other very important ways in which similitude
in dissimilitude appears. The combination of the verse narrative
with a prose gloss is an application of the principle. The poem
is primarily a ballad, but it is also a travel tale and a tall tale.
All three have definite conventions well established throughout
the centuries. These Coleridge retains as his norms or dominants.
But *The Ancient Mariner* is certainly a ballad with a difference.
Not only is it much longer than most ballads, but underneath its
ostensible simplicity appropriate to the ballad form is an astonishing richness and complexity. It keeps the ballad stanza as
its dominant, but from time to time provides many ingenious
variations in its length and pattern. It makes much of dramatic
situations, as the ballad does, but not just a few as is usual with
the ballad; instead it develops its story through a long, heterogeneous sequence of them. It reflects the taste of its age and imposes elements of Gothic terror on the ballad form. Most daring
of all, perhaps, it imposes philosophy on it. Although like many
other travel tales it manifests an affinity for the tall tale, there
is not another travel tale just like it. To compare it with the
Odyssey, More's *Utopia, Gulliver's Travels,* or Goldsmith's *The
Traveller* is immediately to sense its difference. In its compact-
ness, which always seems unlabored, relaxed, and easy, in the
magic which runs through it, and in the spell which it weaves
round a succession of unforgettable images, it stands by itself.
No other poem has used repetition more variously or ingeniously,
and repetition is a sameness. Not merely the conventional repetitions of prosody, such as rhyme, alliteration, assonance, and

so on, which are used with countless variations of form and pattern, but words, phrases, clauses, and whole lines and sentences appear and reappear without losing their identity, in fresh attire, in a new light, with a change of context, accent, or rhythm. Here again Coleridge's method is very much like that by which great music is composed. In sharing the delight in variety characteristic of Romanticism, he generously provides many of the "tiny breezelets of surprise" which he maintains poetry should have.[41]

Although at first glance a comparison of *The Ancient Mariner* with *King Lear* may seem far-fetched, in certain important respects Coleridge's poem suggests Shakespeare's great tragedy in miniature. His admiration for the play was practically unlimited. "Lear is the most tremendous effort of Shakespeare as a poet," he writes; "Hamlet as a philosopher or mediator; and Othello is the union of the two." Despite the fact that the fables with which the two work are radically different, the themes have much in common, and we discover many striking similarities of method as we go from the play to the poem. Both works deal with the compelling power of love, the necessity for broadening its basis, the contrast between compassion and inhuman cruelty, the penalty which must be paid when the great, universal law of love is violated, and the possibilities of redemption through the operation of the same law. Lear discovers that he has thought too little of this and in the midst of the storm feels deep compassion for poor naked wretches, wherever they may be; the Ancient Mariner blesses the water snakes. Both works use animal symbolism in developing the theme, though in different ways.

It is significant that Coleridge chooses the ballad, one of the most dramatic forms of narrative poetry, for his work. He writes: "There is the epic imagination, the perfection of which is Milton; and the dramatic, of which Shakespeare is the absolute master. The first gives unity by throwing back into the distance . . . . The dramatic imagination does not throw back, but brings close; it stamps all nature with one, and that its own, meaning, as in *Lear* throughout."[42] For such a tremendous theme as these two works have, a colossal stage is required; and both works use concepts which seem to reach out into almost infinite space. But even though in them the imagination provides immeasurable vistas and the possibility of apprehending the abstract and the ideal which Coleridge says that Plato and Pythagoras attempted to achieve, they do so in accordance with the dramatic method as Coleridge describes it. Nothing could be more intimate than many of the scenes in *King Lear,* the most wonderfully intimate being that of the King's awakening and reunion with Cordelia. And the Ancient Mariner, whether he is talking to the Wedding Guest, or in the region of Antarctic ice, or in the Atlantic, or in the Pacific, is always near to the reader of a poem that never loses the sharp focus of things close to the observer.

Both works have major problems concerning probability to deal with. We have already taken note of the way in which Coleridge deals with improbability related to the extensive use of the supernatural in his poem. But he also has to deal with another improbability which, on a greatly reduced scale, reminds us of that in *King Lear* when the King, with a curse in the first act, violently disowns Cordelia, the one daughter who loved him deeply; and the whole later development of the play is made to hinge on this. Coleridge discusses this improbability in a passage beginning: "It is well worthy notice, that *Lear* is the only serious performance of Shakespeare the interest and situations of which are derived from the assumption of a gross improbability"; and he proceeds to show the soundness of Shakespeare's methods in dealing with the problem.[43] The foolish action of Coleridge's Mariner in shooting the Albatross, a creature that loves him, is analogous, as is the fact that the whole later development of the tale derives from this. It is a minor point but an interesting one that both works make use of the curse as a literary device, *King Lear* very extensively; but Coleridge instead of using the violent language of Shakespeare's King places the curse in the eyes of the protagonist's fellow mariners.

It is not difficult to find examples of similitude in dissimilitude in *King Lear.* It is woven into the texture of the language; it appears in the various forms which evil assumes in Goneril, Regan, Cornwall, and Edmund, and the various forms which love and loyalty assume in Cordelia, Edgar, and Kent; and it also appears in the various ways in which the King and Gloucester are alike but different. Perhaps the most striking use of it is in the relation of the main plot to the subplot, each basically the same story dealing with the same questions as the other, but stated in different dimensions and terms.

King Lear also makes extensive use of the principle which assumes that it is one of the chief functions of the imagination to reconcile opposites. In it the central conflict, both internally and externally, is vitalized, intensified, and diversified by numerous closely related polarities: the old and the young, the human and the bestial, loyalty and treachery, the natural and the unnatural, the selfish and the unselfish, fate and free-will, the healthy and the diseased, the civilized and the primitive, blunt, brief, honest speech and florid, insincere speech, the calm and the stormy, the near and the far, physical suffering and suffering in the mind and spirit, unity and disintegration, order and chaos, fear and suspicion and trust, rashness and slow deliberation, cruelty and kindness, patience and impatience, the dreadful "pudder" of a horrible storm and the healing power of sweet music and soft, kind human speech.

King Lear is a classic example of multeity in unity. Coleridge describes it as such, with "its soul-scorching flashes, its ear-cleaving thunder-claps, its meteoric splendors, . . . the contagion and fearful sympathies of nature, the Fates, the Furies, the frenzied elements dancing in and out, now breaking thro' and scattering, now hand in hand with, the fierce or fantastic group of human passions, crimes, and anguishes, reeling on the unsteady ground in a wild harmony to the swell and sink of the earthquake."[44] And he describes Act III, Scene iv, thus: "What a world's *convention* of agonies! Surely, never was such a scene conceived before or since. Take it but as a picture for the eye only, it is more terrific than any a Michael Angelo inspired by a Dante could have conceived, and which none but a Michael Angelo could have executed. Or let it have been uttered to the blind, the howlings of convulsed nature would seem converted into the voice of conscious humanity."[45] The dynamic action of *The Ancient Mariner* is strongly suggested in both these descriptions, emphasizing both heterogeneity and the important role which nature, the weather, the heavens, and other things beyond the control of the human will may play in the action.

This kinship with Shakespeare's great work, his most tremendous effort "as a poet," if we are willing to accept Coleridge's opinion, may, when we relate it to the fact that in *The Ancient Mariner* Coleridge embodies most of the principles which he associates with what he calls "ideal" poetry, lead us to accept the high praise which Leigh Hunt bestowed upon Coleridge, almost in Hunt's own terms: "Of pure poetry, strictly so called, that is to say, consisting of nothing but its essential self, without conventional and perishable helps, he was the greatest master of his time. If you could see it in a phial, like a distillation of roses, . . . it would be found without a speck."[46] The phial is an appropriate symbol with which to represent the poet Coleridge, suggesting as it does his marked power of condensation. Equally appropriate, however, is the ocean symbol; and Coleridge's ocean in *The Ancient Mariner* is one in which the bright waters on the surface as they sparkle like champagne are delightful to behold but in which also there are almost immeasurable depths where swim the shadowy, elusive fish of meaning, for which Mr. Warren[47] and others like to cast their lures.

NOTES

1. *Collected Letters of Samuel Taylor Coleridge,* ed. E. L. Griggs (Oxford, 1956, 1959), I, 627. Hereafter referred to as *Letters.*

2. *Ibid.,* II, 811.

3. *Ibid.,* II, 830.

4. *Biographia Literaria,* ed. J. Shawcross (Oxford, 1907), II, 6.

5. J. L. Lowes, *The Road to Xanadu* (Boston and New York, 1927).

6. II, 10–11. Cf. Humphry House, *Coleridge* (London, 1953), p. 149, quoting from Notebook 18: poetry is "the Art of representing Objects in relation to the *excitability* of the human mind . . . for the purpose of immediate pleasure, the most pleasure from each part that is compatible with the largest sum of pleasure from the whole."

7. *Biographia Literaria,* II, 12.

8. *Ibid.,* II, 56.

9. Roberta Florence Brinkley, *Coleridge and the Seventeenth Century* (Durham, N. C., 1955), p. 589. The word *homogeneity* was to Coleridge particularly applicable to Wordsworth. See *Letters,* II, 811.

10. Brinkley, p. 615.

11. *Biographia Literaria,* I, 180.

12. "On the Principles of Genial Criticism concerning the Fine Arts," printed with the *Biographia Literaria,* II, 238. Coleridge also writes in this essay: "Thus the Philosopher of the later Platonic, or Alexandrine school, named the triangle the first-born of beauty, it being the first and simplest symbol of *multeity in unity*" (p. 230; see also p. 232). Using a grotesque figure of which he was fond, he says on one occasion: "I envy dear Southey's power of saying one thing at a time, in short and close sentences, whereas my thoughts bustle along like a Surinam toad, with little toads sprouting out of back, side, and belly, vegetating while it crawls." From R. W. Armour and R. F. Howes, *Coleridge the Talker* (Ithaca, N. Y., and London, 1940), p. 32.

13. *Inquiring Spirit: A Coleridge Reader,* ed. Kathleen Coburn (New York, 1951), 151–152.

14. *Letters,* II, 691. This is from a letter dated 24 February 1801.

15. *Inquiring Spirit,* p. 152. See also p. 106 and *Coleridge the Talker,* p. 134.

Lowes, *passim*, makes much of the aurora borealis as a useful symbol to Coleridge.

16. Alice D. Snyder, *Coleridge on Logic and Learning* (New Haven and London, 1929), pp. 126–127. In quoting, as we like to do, Coleridge's "I love Plato–his dear *gorgeous* Nonsense!" we should note that the letter in which he says it is very early, 31 December 1796 (*Letters*, I, 295).

17. Snyder, pp. 107–108.

18. From Lecture II, 1811–1812, quoted in *Samuel Taylor Coleridge: Selected Poetry and Prose*, ed. Elisabeth Schneider (New York and London, 1951), p. 393. Sir John Taylor Coleridge heard Coleridge say that he wished some portion of mathematics was more essential to a degree at Oxford, as he thought a gentleman's education incomplete without it, and had himself found the necessity of getting up a little, when he could ill spare the time (*Coleridge the Talker*, p. 157). For Coleridge's delight in playing with the number three, see *ibid.*, pp. 173–174.

19. *Biographia Literaria*, II, 33.

20. *Ibid.*, I, 4.

21. See W. J. Bate, *Coleridge* (New York and London, 1965), pp. 41–42, 46.

22. *Biographia Literaria*, I, 32. Coleridge writes of Southey in 1796: "I think that an admirable Poet might be made by *amalgamating him & me*. I *think* too much for a *Poet*; he too little for a *great Poet*" (*Letters*, I, 294).

23. *Biographia Literaria*, II, 19.

24. *Coleridge the Talker*, pp. 213–214.

25. *Ibid.*, p. 193.

26. *Letters*, III, 470.

27. Lecture VII, 1811–1812, in Schneider, *Selected Poetry and Prose*, pp. 419–420. "The deeply shaken Mariner is no philosopher, no prophet, no leader of men. He has learned a profound and simple truth. But he is not able–he is not even pretending–to explicate the entire mystery of what he has encountered. That continues to elude him . . . . It is left for the reader as well to infer or guess at them [meanings] from the greatest and certainly the most dramatic of Coleridge's poems" (Bate, p. 65).

28. From *Table-Talk*, quoted in Schneider, p. 462.

29. The translation is from G. B. Woods, *English Poetry and Prose of the Romantic Movement* (Chicago and New York, 1916, 1929), p. 1236.

30. See C. R. Sanders, *Coleridge and the Broad Church Movement* (Durham, N. C., 1942), pp. 78, 184.

31. "To be beloved is all I need,/And whom I love, I love indeed." From *The Pains of Sleep*, ll. 51–52. Cf. Coleridge's letter to Southey, 10 [11] September 1803, in *Letters*, II, 982–984.

32. *Ibid.*, I, 121.

33. *Ibid.*, I, 277.

34. The emphasis on joy appears very early in Coleridge. "When a man is unhappy, he writes damn bad poetry, I find." To Southey, 21 October 1794, in *Letters*, I, 116. The delight in "happy living things" is vitally related to the joy theme in all of Coleridge's poetry, coming out with great strength in *Dejection: An Ode*, lines 69–75. See House, pp. 102, 138. His insistence that nightingales sing joyful songs, we know, influenced Keats, whose nightingale is not a sad Philomela but a happy bird. It may even be possible to leap forward and link Coleridge and Keats with another great Romantic, Yeats, in whom the gaity theme is a vital part of his philosophy of life and whose golden bird of Byzantium singing in ecstasy becomes the symbol of highest value in the art of living. For Coleridge

and nightingales, see not only his two poems on the subject but *Coleridge the Talker*, pp. 283–284, and *Letters*, II, 797, and IV, 942.

35. With all his love for the lower animals, Coleridge cannot stomach Swift's reasoning horses, which to him are highly abnormal and inconsistent in their behavior. He writes: "Critics in general complain of the Yahoos; I complain of the Houyhnhnms" (*Coleridge's Miscellaneous Criticism*, ed. T.M. Raysor [Cambridge, Mass., 1936], pp. 128–130).

36. See Lowes, pp. 222–224.

37. For Coleridge on animal magnetism or hypnotism, see *Inquiring Spirit*, pp. 45–51. Cf. also his use of hypnotism in *Christabel*.

38. For Colderidge's marked power of compression, which suggests comparison with Yeats, see *Letters*, I, 351, and *Coleridge the Talker*, p. 134.

39. In a letter of 1818 Coleridge clarifies this principle in terms of his reading of Kant, whose chief merit, he says, was that he proved, as Leibnitz and Plato were unable to, that Space and Time are "the pure a priori forms of the intuitive faculty . . . the Acts of the perceptive Power." Time, he adds, equals "unity, the point, resistance"; Space equals "Multeity, area, absence of resistance." "In the circle all possible Truths are symbolized" (*Letters*, IV, 852). In *The Ancient Mariner* the almost unlimited space does much to make possible the free movement and multeity of the poem. Coleridge preserves the time sense by references to darkness and light, day and night, and thus helps to achieve point and focus. But he does not subject Time to measurement by indicating the length of the whole or the parts of the story. Thus he draws the parts of the poem together in a closer unity by ignoring duration in a sense and suggesting timelessness in time just as he suggests space concepts in infinite space. The Mariner also, like the Wandering Jew, suggests the same thing. One of the functions of the imagination, Coleridge says, is to reduce "succession to an instant" (*Biographia Literaria*, II, 16). Thus he makes use of space and time without being confined by them. Cf. Shakespeare's similar use of space and time in *Othello* and *King Lear*.

40. Like Tennyson and Yeats, Coleridge had no ear for music proper. Yet he enjoyed it very much, delighted in Mozart and the "dithyrambic movement of Beethoven." See *Coleridge the Talker*, pp. 434–435. Late in life (6 July 1833) he wrote: "I could write as good verses now as ever I did, if I were perfectly free from vexations, and were in the *ad libitum* hearing of fine music, which has a sensible effect in harmonising my thoughts, and in animating and, as it were, lubricating my inventive faculty" (*Miscellaneous Criticism*, p. 424).

41. See Schneider, *Selected Poetry and Prose*, p. 476; and *Biographia Literaria*, II, 5. Cf. Wordsworth's delight in the sudden scene or vision and Keats's praise of "fine suddenness" in poetic art.

42. *Miscellaneous Criticism*, p. 436. Lionel Stevenson has been able to show that the poem may be classified as a dramatic monologue. See " 'The Ancient Mariner' as a Dramatic Monologue," *The Personalist*, XXX (Winter 1948), 34–44.

43. *Coleridge's Shakespearean Criticism*, ed. T. M. Raysor (Cambridge, Mass., 1930), I, 59–60.

44. *Ibid.*, I, 109.

45. *Ibid.*, I, 66.

46. From *Imagination and Fancy* (1844), quoted by George Watson in *Coleridge the Poet* (London, 1966), p. 132.

47. R. P. Warren, "A Poem of Pure Imagination: an Experiment in Reading," in *Selected Essays* (New York, 1945–1946, 1958), pp. 198–305.

BYRON: ARTISTRY AND STYLE
Brian Wilkie

Difficile est proprie communia dicere.
—Horace, *Ars Poetica*, l. 128; epigraph for *Don Juan*

'Tis hard to venture where our betters fail,
Or lend fresh interest to a twice-told tale;
And yet, perchance, 'tis wiser to prefer
A hackneyed plot, than choose a new, and err;
Yet copy not too closely, but record,
More justly, thought for thought than word for word;
Nor trace your Prototype through narrow ways . . . .
—Byron, *Hints from Horace*, ll. 183–189

For a long time men interested in Byron have aired a question that would seem appallingly silly if it were asked about virtually any other established poet: Was he an artist? The question seems slanderous; one thinks of Blake's observation that the man who inquires modestly into the truth of a self-evident proposition is a knave. T. S. Eliot might seem to have incurred such an indictment when (along with a certain amount of backhanded praise of Byron, of the kind that Eliot meted out grudgingly to Romantic poets) he wrote this in 1937: "[Of the major Romantics] Byron . . . would seem the most nearly remote from the sympathies of every living critic: it would be interesting, therefore, if we could have half a dozen essays about him, to see what agreement could be reached. The present article is an attempt to start that ball rolling."[1] It is not true that the ball had been lying inert before 1937, but most of the true literary criticism of Byron has in fact been done since the mid-thirties, with Calvert's important study serving as a milestone.[2] And the criticism makes it clear that the question whether or not Byron was an artist is not, to speak exactly, a silly one. It is just vague; its terms are not so clear as they should be.

No longer is it true that Byron is "remote from the sympa-

thies of every living critic"; an age which admires Sartre and
Beckett has no trouble taking seriously Byron's absurdism,
whether expressed in the ottava-rima romps or through the melodramatic grotesques who collectively make up the "Byronic
hero." Men who once agreed blithely with Goethe's condescending dismissal of Byron's thought as childish have been refuted
by events and by works like Bertrand Russell's *History of
Western Philosophy* (1945), where Byron is taken quite seriously, at least as a historical phenomenon. And I can testify as
a teacher that students today take Byron's attitudes very solemnly.

But to say that Byron's world-view is worth taking seriously
is not to say that he was an artist, any more than, say, Napoleon
was, and it is in more strictly aesthetic criticism that things become muddled. Many critics have defended Byron's craftsman-
ship, but too often their apologia depend on critical assumptions
that in my opinion are seldom appropriate to him. As Eliot
pointed out, "We have come to expect poetry to be something
very concentrated, something distilled; but if Byron had distilled
his verse, there would have been nothing whatever left" (p.
224). The second half of this sentence is not true, but the first
half is, and Eliot's remark about Byron's lack of density, whatever the intended implications may have been, is on the right
track. For, however embarrassedly we may disclaim the un-
fashionable label, most of us still are "New Critics," at least
when we talk about artistry. Our distinctive criteria are two: a
Flaubertian economy of diction and thematic, structurally coherent imagery such as Ridenour finds in *Don Juan*.[3] We also
respect metrical virtuosity, as almost every school of criticism
has done, in every age. For some of us New-Critical scrupulo-
sity has been reinforced by the accident of our profession as
teachers; we prefer good "teaching" poems like Keats's odes
or Donne's lyrics or Eliot's own *Waste Land* to less "well made"
poems like the lyrics of Herrick or of Burns or Jonson's epistles,
since these latter, being less amenable to the laws of analytic
evidence which we have been trained in, provide us with a less
solid platform for inculcating our methods, or at least our
methodicalness.

Defenses of Byron's metrical virtuosity have generally been
convincing and are no more than his due, though often they
lean too heavily on onomatopoetic effects, which are as close as
prosodic analysis can come to showing that a poet is systematic.

Furthermore, Byron did produce a few truly "well made" poems. From the standpoint of imagistic coherence a good case can be made for *The Bride of Abydos,* and an even better one can be made for *The Prisoner of Chillon.*[4] Lines like "vacancy absorbing space, / And fixedness—without a place" (ll. 243-244) have density and metaphysical paradox worthy of Marvell, and the parallel between mental and physical duress is pursued through the poem with almost relentless consistency of diction and image, from the opening explanation of the prisoner's white hairs and stigmata through lines like "Among the stones I stood a stone" (l. 236) to the final confirmation of the prisoner's enslavement after his release: "It was at length the same to me, / Fettered or fetterless to be, / . . . So much a long communion tends / To make us what we are." (ll. 372-373, 390-391).[5]

But these works are exceptions. Though Byron has more than one style, as he once remarked himself,[6] his most typical effects are extended ones done with long strokes on a large canvas; he is an "action-painter" and not a methodical *pointilliste.* As Paul West points out, he does not rely on "clever shades."[7] My argument here is not wholly new, of course. More than once, for example, it has been said of Byron that he is a master of narrative and that digression is a key to his success. But the technique of narrative poetry is one that twentieth-century criticism has given us almost no tools to analyze, and in any case this point and others that imply Byron's need for extendedness are usually made in passing, by critics mainly concerned with other issues. I should like to treat the matter in a more sustained way. And I should like to argue that extendedness can itself be the vehicle of a true kind of artistry, a kind inadequately recognized by critics today.

The length of Byron's unit of utterance can be illustrated on a number of different scales. Take, for example, the "Ocean" passage near the end of *Childe Harold's Pilgrimage:*

> Roll on, thou deep and dark blue Ocean—roll!
> Ten thousand fleets sweep over thee in vain;

—and so on through the six familiar stanzas. Encountered out of context this passage may be powerful, but in itself it seems to some readers a faded and shrill anthology piece. To meet it after reading *Harold* straight through is a very different experience, however, one that can be moving and even frightening.

To account for its power one might look back to the beginning, where Harold had embarked on this same ocean to begin his travels. Thus the ocean would be the alpha and omega of the poem, a symbol used neatly for structural, here cyclic, purposes in the way to which modern criticism has acclimated us. Doubtless this kind of analysis would have persuasiveness, and even some truth. But it would not, I think, account for the distinctively Byronic power in the passage, power that made it popular in an age when people really did read *Harold* complete and without condescension. For the ocean stanzas are less a re-sounding for thematic purposes of a motif introduced earlier than a sweeping away of the whole matter, a gesture of exhaustion of the poem and of what it is about, a grand dismissal of human thought, history, and art. We are not being asked to make intricate connections; we are being asked to see that all the immensely dappled stuff of man's experience which this poem has pictured is nothing compared to the Eternity which the ocean suggests and indeed to the literal ocean itself. Yet—and this is what I want to stress—our sense of human futility (along with some sense of accompanying relief, since Eternity and the ocean limit the destructiveness of man) depends on our having been exposed, without design on us in the way of calculated thematic manipulation, to the world's bemusing variety: the filthiness of Lisbon, Beckford's pleasure palace, bullfights in Spain, English sabbaths, the Parthenon, the cape where Sappho committed suicide, Waterloo, meditations during Alpine storms, castles on the Rhine, the writings of Gibbon and Rousseau, Byron's own domestic tragedy, the Bridge of Sighs, Tasso's imprisonment, shining Soracte, schoolboy drudgery in translating Horace's ode about Soracte, the Colosseum. All this awesome or precious or trivial particularity will disappear; Eternity and the ocean devour everything. An astounding thought, but there is nothing meretricious about it. And its power depends not on thematic manipulation, not on the deft repetition of an image used earlier, but on *everything* that has happened since the beginning of the poem—in other words, on sheer, undirected accumulation.

Here the scale is that of an entire poem, but a similar effect can often be observed in passages of, say, five to a hundred lines. The following speech from *Marino Faliero,* like the whole of *Childe Harold,* accumulates images at almost dangerous length, then dismisses the scene they comprise:

The music, and the banquet, and the wine,
The garlands, the rose odours, and the flowers,
The sparkling eyes, and flashing ornaments,
The white arms and the raven hair, the braids
And bracelets; swanlike bosoms, and the necklace,
An India in itself, yet dazzling not
The eye like what it circled; the thin robes,
Floating like light clouds 'twixt our gaze and heaven;
The many-twinkling feet so small and sylphlike,
Suggesting the more secret symmetry
Of the fair forms which terminate so well—
All the delusion of the dizzy scene,
Its false and true enchantments—Art and Nature,
Which swam before my giddy eyes, that drank
The sight of beauty as the parched pilgrim's
On Arab sands the false mirage, which offers
A lucid lake to his eluded thirst,
Are gone.

(IV. i. 51–68)

This is certainly not Byron at his best, but it is close to his most typical; the effect of the climax depends on the amassing of details along the way. The technique, incidentally, is especially useful in the most horrific of Byron's maledictions—the curse on Manfred (I. i. 192-261), for example, or Marino Faliero's prophetic denunciation of Venice (V. iii. 26-101), or Eve's curse on Cain (III. i. 421-443). Eve's speech is a particularly apt example here, since its conclusion was an addendum which Byron communicated to Murray in a letter, along with a significant remark. To the catalogue of agonies Eve invokes on her son the following lines were to be added, according to Byron's directions:

> May the Grass wither from thy foot! the Woods
> Deny thee shelter! Earth a home! the Dust
> A Grave! the Sun his light! and Heaven her God!

Byron then wrote: "There's as pretty a piece of Imprecation for you, *when joined to the lines already sent* [my emphasis], as you may wish to meet with in the course of your business. But don't forget the addition of the above three lines, which are clinchers to Eve's speech."[8] It is clear how Byron's mind was working: the effect of the curse was to depend on a long arc of sustained rhetoric ending climactically with the equivalent of a high C at the curtain in Donizetti.

Byron's habits of cataloguing and "accretion" and his stylistic penchant for anaphora are well known,[9] but we need to distinguish extendedness from mere swollen repetition. Sometimes a particular message or point is involved; thus, the five stanzas of rejected heroes at the beginning of *Don Juan* are both a reminder of Milton's and Tasso's discrimination in choosing an epic hero and a wry dismissal of recent heroes as a stanza a dozen. Usually there is at least a crescendo of tone and feeling. When Byron is flatly repetitious he usually recognizes that he is being so and often consciously mocks himself for it:

> And she bent o'er him, and he lay beneath,
>   Hush'd as the babe upon its mother's breast,
> Droop'd as the willow when no winds can breathe,
>   Lull'd like the depth of ocean when at rest,
> Fair as the crowning rose of the whole wreath,
>   Soft as the callow cygnet in its nest;
> In short, he was a very pretty fellow,
> Although his woes had turn'd him rather yellow.
>   (*Don Juan*, II, 148)

The mindlessly similar images make fun of themselves apart even from the cynical couplet. Except when he wants to achieve some such bathetic effect as this one, Byron's repetitions are seldom static; instead, rhetorical units overlap to produce a sense of slowly but irresistibly expanding meaning. Or else they produce a crescendo of magniloquence, as in these lines from *The Prisoner of Chillon:*

> I burst my chain with one strong bound,
> And rushed to him:—I found him not,
> *I* only stirred in this black spot,
> *I* only lived, *I* only drew
> The accursed breath of dungeon-dew . . . .
>   (ll. 210–214)

The three clauses beginning with the emphatic *I* not only reflect the rapid stages in the prisoner's recognition of his loneness but also, and perhaps more important, provide emotional and rhetorical heightening for this critical incident in the poem. Yet the three clauses *mean* exactly the same thing; the dictional variation from *stirred* to *lived* to *drew breath* is wholly irrelevant.

To say so may seem paradoxical, but even at his pithiest

Byron sometimes relies on this kind of breadth of rhetorical gesture. Consider his scatological epigram on Castlereagh:

> Posterity will ne'er survey
> A nobler grave than this;
> Here lie the bones of Castlereagh:
> Stop, traveller,   *   *

Obviously the force is in the shock effect of the ending, but, without the gravely platitudinous, conventionally inflated words which go before, the shock effect would not come about. The slightest touch of wit or originality before the end would spoil the poem.

It may seem perverse to claim that Byron's artistry lies in his avoidance of economy and well-made-ness, but there is good reason to believe that for Byron himself the long rhetorical unit, along with conventionality of diction and imagery, was part of a pugnaciously deliberate policy. Consider these passages from his letters:

> When Mr. Hare prattles about the "Economy," etc., he sinks sadly;— all such expressions are the mere cant of a schoolboy hovering round the Skirts of Criticism.

> In yesterday's paper, immediately under an advertisement on "Strictures in the Urethra," I see—most appropriately consequent—a poem with "*strictures* on Ld B., Mr. Southey and others," though I am afraid neither "Mr. S.'s" poetical distemper, nor "mine," nor "others," is of the suppressive or stranguary kind. You may read me the prescription of this kill or cure physician.

> I can't correct; I can't, and I won't. Nobody ever succeeds in it, great or small . . . . Pope *added* to the "*Rape of the Lock*," but did not reduce it . . . . I would rather give [my poems] away than hack and hew them.[10]

The following comment on *The Two Foscari* makes the opposite boast, but here Byron is claiming to renounce his earlier and presumably more typical manner:

> The Simplicity of plot is intentional, and the avoidance of *rant* also, as also the compression of the Speeches in the more severe situations. What I seek to show . . . is the *suppressed* passion, rather than the rant

of the present day. For that matter—"Nay, if thou'lt mouth, / I'll rant as well as thou"—would not be difficult, as I think I have shown in my younger productions.[11]

During the controversy with Bowles, Byron adduced Johnson's praise of a passage from Congreve's *The Mourning Bride* as "the most poetical paragraph" in English poetry and quoted Johnson's words:

> He who reads those lines enjoys for a moment the powers of a poet; he feels what he remembers to have felt before, but he feels it with great increase of Sensibility: he recognizes a *familiar image*, but meets it again amplified and expanded, embellished with beauty and enlarged with majesty.[12]

Although at this point in the controversy Byron was mainly interested in showing that artifacts (which are what the Congreve passage describes) are more poetical than external nature, there is another good reason why he should have cited Johnson's words. They happen to be perfectly applicable to Byron's own poetry.

Much of Byron's disgust with his fellow Romantics, and with himself when he wrote like them, arises from the same policy. His antagonism toward the Lakists is largely political, and some of his contempt for "Cockneys" like Keats is social snobbery. But Byron's grounds are not mere rationalizations from these motives, they are genuine aesthetic convictions (though sometimes they overlap with less literary impulses, especially the social class-consciousness). There has been much discussion of Byron's professed contempt for poetry and of the question whether that sentiment was a pose or was not. However we answer this question in general, we need to see that Byron's basic impatience is not with poetry generically but rather with a particular approach to it which he finds characteristic of his age and sometimes of himself. Though they are poets, he never finds fault with Pope or Gifford, and rarely with Moore or Rogers or Scott. What he dislikes in Keats and Wordsworth and Coleridge and Hunt as artists is that they are systematic and concentrated, and claim to be so. They are too intensive and too intense. Melody, prosody, truthfulness of fact—these were areas of art that Byron could respect, but intricacy of aesthetic effect, achieved through subtleties of diction and imagery, was alien to his taste, socially because it seemed to him a kind of pedantry beneath the level of gentlemen, and aesthetically because he himself gravitated toward a more broadly rhetorical tradition in poetry which tends, perhaps accidentally, to be associated with patrician values. (I shall say more about this tradition presently.) When in the Preface to *Prometheus Unbound* Shelley defined what "distinguishes the modern literature of England" as its "peculiar style of intense and comprehensive imagery" he was saying much about Romanticism and putting his finger accurately on what made Byron restive. Shelley would only have had to mention intensiveness of *diction* for the formula to be complete. Byron's attitude toward the distinctive qualities of his contemporaries is dismal critical short-sightedness, but it is only what we ought to have come to expect in criticism which is written by important poets who are at least unconsciously justifying their own literary ways. Jonson and Milton were short-sighted about medieval literature, Wordsworth about Gray, Eliot about Tennyson. As with these poet-critics, the sensible thing for us to do is to use Byron's short-sightedness as a gloss on his poetry.

Again Byron's letters are helpful. For example, we find him (in a relatively gentle mood) chiding Leigh Hunt for dictional fussiness:

. . . I must turn to the faults [in *The Story of Rimini,* apparently], or what appear to be such to me: these are not many, nor such as may not be easily altered, being almost all *verbal;* . . . viz., occasional quaintness and obscurity, and a kind of a harsh and yet colloquial compounding of epithets, as if to avoid saying common things in a common way; *difficile est propriè communia dicere* seems at times to have met with in you a literal translator.[13]

The same distaste for what he considered "quaint" is reflected in the architectural metaphors Byron used in order to contrast Pope with other poets. Pope is a "Greek Temple," "the Temple of Theseus," "the Parthenon"; Shakespeare and Milton may be "pyramids" (a dubious compliment), but other poets and their work, especially Byron's contemporaries and sometimes he himself, are a "Gothic Cathedral," "a Turkish Mosque," "fantastic pagodas and conventicles," builders of a "grotesque edifice," of a "Babel, attended by a confusion of tongues."[14]

It seems possible also that Byron's use of the word "system" (a particularly contemptuous one for him, like "school" of poetry) reflects the same attitude. He wrote to Moore about

Hunt: "When I saw *Rimini* in MS., I told him that I deemed it good poetry at bottom, disfigured only by a strange style. His answer was, that his style was a system, or *upon system,* or some such cant; and, when a man talks of system, his case is hopeless."[15] On another occasion he wrote, "*all* of us—Scott, Southey, Wordsworth, Moore, Campbell, I,—are all in the wrong, one as much as another; . . . we are upon a wrong revolutionary poetical system, or systems . . . from which none but Rogers and Crabbe are free."[16] And on still another occasion: "The great cause of the present deplorable state of English poetry is to be attributed to that absurd and systematic depreciation of Pope, in which, for the last few years, there has been a kind of epidemical concurrence."[17] In these passages the words "system," "systems," and "systematic" refer to "philosophies" of poetry, but in view of Byron's hatred for the words they may also refer to the quality of *being* systematic which these systems have in common. Byron so contemned the legitimation of Romantic poetry as a category that a trend on the Continent to contrast "Romantic" and "Classical" elicited from him a contemptuous sniff: the "terms . . . were not subjects of classification in England, at least when I left it four or five years ago . . . . [Then] nobody thought [the new writers] worth making a sect of."[18]

Byron sometimes showed the same disdain for the most talismanic of Romantic terms: "imagination." He lumped it with "invention," presumably in contrast to the ability *communia dicere* which ought to be the poet's peculiar talent. "It is the fashion of the day to lay great stress upon what they call 'imagination' and 'invention,' the two commonest of qualities: an Irish peasant with a little whisky in his head will imagine and invent more than would furnish forth a modern poem."[19] And of rereading Pope: "I was really astonished . . . and mortified at the ineffable distance in point of sense, harmony, effect, and even *Imagination,* passion, and *Invention,* between the little Queen Anne's man, and us of the Lower Empire."[20] Much of Byron's point lies in the italics and the word "even"; Pope surpasses the Romantics even by the petty criteria they cared most about; he can beat them at their own silly little game.

It is hard to say how much Byron felt the force of the root "image" in "imagination"; I am inclined to think he felt it strongly, for he uses exactly the same forensic strategy which we have just observed in his attempt to prove that Pope was a great imagist. "I will show more *imagery*"—i.e., *even that—*

"in twenty lines of Pope than in any equal length of quotation in English poesy, and that in places where they least expect it." He goes on to list in a column twenty-three images from the character of Sporus in the *Epistle to Dr. Arbuthnot:* "1. The thing of *Silk.* 2. *Curd* of *Ass's* milk. 3. The *Butterfly.* 4. The *Wheel,*" and so on to the end, each image doggedly numbered. What is most interesting about this enumeration, though, is that it is just that—not an attempt to find the kind of thematic system in imagery that the Romantics and twentieth-century critics have both prized (Shelley's "peculiar style of intense and comprehensive imagery") but a rhetorical effect, much like Byron's own effects, achieved through the accumulation of more or less unrelated comparisons, leading to a virile and climactic cadence. In fact, at the end of his table of laconic excerpts Byron cannot resist writing out Pope's final couplet, with the flourish of Byron's own gleeful emphasis:

> Beauty that shocks you, parts that none will trust,
> Wit that can creep, and *Pride* that *licks* the *dust.*[21]

One can easily sense his excited delight in the explosion of contempt at the end of this swelling train of insults. I don't believe it would have occurred to Byron to praise Pope for the intricacy that Cleanth Brooks, rightly or not, finds in *The Rape of the Lock*[22] and that Ridenour finds in Byron's own *Don Juan.*

Another source of Byron's revulsion against the Romantics comes out especially clearly during the Bowles controversy in his comments on the "Cockney" poets, whom he brands with vulgarity. His reasons are instructive. In this context even Wordsworth and "the higher of the Lake school" are not vulgar, "though they treat of low life in all its branches" (one suspects that this concession is made temporarily and casually, in order to clear ground for the attack).

> The grand distinction of the under forms of the new school of poets is their *vulgarity.* By this I do not mean that they are *coarse,* but 'shabby-genteel,' as it is termed. A man may be *coarse* and yet not *vulgar,* and the reverse. . . . It is in their *finery* that the new under school are *most* vulgar, and they may be known by this at once; as what we called at Harrow 'a Sunday blood' might be easily distinguished from a gentleman, although his cloathes might be the better cut, and his boots the best blackened, of the two:—probably because he made the one, or cleaned the other, with his own hands.

"In the present case, I speak of writing, not of persons," Byron continued, and if this is true he was probably thinking not only of the barbaric neologisms which he held against Hunt's disciples but also of a kind of fussy and ignoble originality or invention or "imagination" which is the literary equivalent of making one's own clothes. At any rate, Byron seems to have felt that the passage was excessively snobbish (even for him). A few sentences later he wrote, "Far be it from me to presume that there ever was, or can be, such a thing as an *aristocracy of poets;* but there *is* a nobility of thought and of style, open to all stations, and derived partly from talent, and partly from education,—which is to be found in Shakespeare, and Pope, and Burns, no less than in Dante and Alfieri, but which is nowhere to be perceived in the mock birds and bards of Mr. Hunt's little chorus." Even this corrective was apparently not enough to satisfy him, for a subsequent letter to Murray directed him to make an insertion after the words *aristocracy of poets:* "I do not mean that they should write in the Style of the Song by a person of Quality, or *parle Euphuism."* The original passage continues with an attempt by Byron to define nobility of thought and of style, which he can do only through examples: military men have it more often than naval, men of rank more often than lawyers, and so on. His letter to Murray ordered that this whole sentence be deleted as "not much to the purpose." In the original version his final example of nobility is Fielding, "the man of education, the gentleman, and the scholar, sporting with his subject,—its master, not its slave." But the correcting letter to Murray leaves him and his advisers the option of striking out the entire two-paragraph discussion of vulgarity and nobility. The incident shows Byron struggling, though uncertainly and with indifferent success, to isolate the issue as a literary rather than a social one.[23]

What we have, then, is not mere class prejudice on Byron's part but allegiance to a poetic tradition. For Byron the symbol of this tradition was Pope, but it would be a mistake to identify it too closely with him or solely with the Augustans or indeed too closely with any particular period or group of poets. The tradition is the perennial Horatian one of *communia* and *publica materies* and includes not only the more doctrinaire exponents of poetic generality like Jonson and Pope but also the Cavalier poets (though there is little evidence that Byron knew them well), Caroline wits, Gray, the Burns of the lyrics, the Wordsworth of the more ringing sonnets, A. E. Housman, and Yeats when he is not writing about gyres or phases of the moon but making poems like "An Irish Airman Foresees His Death." In this tradition words are used—like Byron's favorite "clay" or Yeats's "meet my fate"—with offhand, aristocratic negligence, like beloved old garments better loved for being worn, and images either are avoided, as in the Yeats poem, or are developed, often at facile length, from simple objects like the cup of wine and the cut roses in Jonson's "Drink to Me Only With Thine Eyes." Intricacy, except of rhythm and cadence, are beneath one's dignity. At its worst this tradition can degenerate into pompousness, as it sometimes does in Housman, or in Gray's "Eton College" ode, or in Byron. But then every poetic manner goes bad, when it does, in its own distinctive way; pomp must sometimes risk being pompous as "imaginativeness" risks being precious.

It is this tradition which in *English Bards and Scotch Reviewers* is the implicit criterion for Byron's praise of Crabbe and denunciation of Romantic over-inventiveness (significantly, the passage was one of the addenda to the poem, a case of "accretion") :

> There be who say, in these enlightened days,
> That splendid lies are all the poet's praise;
> That strained Invention, ever on the wing,
> Alone impels the modern Bard to sing:
> 'Tis true, that all who rhyme—nay, all who write,
> Shrink from that fatal word to Genius—Trite;
> Yet Truth sometimes will lend her noblest fires,
> And decorate the verse herself inspires . . . .
> (ll. 849-856)

The essentially favorable review of Wordsworth's 1807 edition which Byron wrote at the age of nineteen is a similar key to his tastes. Byron praises Wordsworth for "a native elegance, natural and unaffected, totally devoid of the tinsel embellishments and abstract hyperboles of several contemporary sonneteers," though he disapproves of the vein of puerility and "namby-pamby." What he likes best is the sonnet "Another year! another deadly overthrow!" (he quotes it in full)—a poem in the vein of Wordsworth's public rhetoric and one which, I might add, contains two excellent examples of Byronic anaphora. His parting advice to Wordsworth is "Paulo majora canamus."[24]

Byron's poetic tradition has several distinctive aesthetic

virtues. One is the sheer sonority of amplitude, the advantage of even the simplest organ over the most expressively played oboe or piano. Another merit is what Byron called nobility, a dignity of subject matter which is above intricacy as the nude in Titian's *Sacred and Profane Love* is above wearing clothes. Byron identified this nobility with truth ("Yet Truth sometimes will lend her noblest fires"). Pope excelled in ethical poetry, Byron wrote, "and, in my mind, the latter is the highest of all poetry, because it does that in *verse*, which the greatest of men have wished to accomplish in prose. If the essence of poetry must be a *lie*, throw it to the dogs."[25] The aristocratic scorn for equivocating indirection blends with the candor of the moralist who scorns casuistry and the honesty of the poet who scorns intricacy.

But perhaps the greatest virtue of Byron's rhetorical tradition of poetry serves truth on a humbler level, that of sheer clarity. Byron was constantly charging his contemporaries with obscurity; Wordsworth, for example, was the "arch-apostle of mystery and mysticism."[26] (This was a charge Byron shamefacedly brought against himself too when, as in *Manfred* and *Cain*, he believed he had forsaken the true faith and obscured the Old Light. *Manfred* was "wild," "metaphysical," "inexplicable," a "piece of phantasy," a "sort of mad Drama," a "Bedlam tragedy"; *Cain* was "in the *Manfred* metaphysical style" and entitled a "Mystery" in accordance with "the former Christian custom, and in honour of what it probably will remain to the reader."[27]) To understand what Byron means we have to discount his half-symbolic emphasis on Pope as an individual; it seems unlikely that many readers would prefer Pope to Wordsworth mainly because Pope is clearer. We also have to rethink our twentieth-century bias that, because verbosity is so often fuzzy, economy is clear. To say something twice or three times is in fact clearer than to say it once with dense weightedness. This is especially true of words which are directed to the mind's *ear* rather than to the mind's *eye*, and by this aural appeal I do not mean melody so much as an apprehension of *meaning* that works as our minds do when we hear speech.

Byron's verse communicates in this manner; that is why, for example, he likes to use italics. The same appeal to a kind of interior aural sense is characteristic of the whole rhetorical tradition I have been discussing. The opening lines of Housman's "Epitaph on an Army of Mercenaries,"

>These, in the day when heaven was falling,
>The hour when earth's foundations fled,

do more than achieve Winston Churchillian orotundity of phrase; the lines have a clarity together which they do not have singly, and this despite the fact that the literal, lexical differences between terms of the antitheses—day and hour, heaven and earth, falling and fled—can be largely ignored. What happens is that our minds have extra time to play over and absorb the sense.

Everyone who literally communicates to the ear knows this —conversationalists, auctioneers, lecturers, and especially orators. When Lincoln spoke the words "government of the people, by the people, for the people" he was going beyond an orator's license; the variation of meaning from one phrase to the next is too subtle to be understood by auditors, especially since the variation depends on abstract prepositions. On the other hand, when he said "we cannot dedicate, we cannot consecrate, we cannot hallow this ground" he was observing the rules, for the increments in meaning from verb to verb are slight, barely enough to keep the series from being absolutely repetitious.

Byron too was an orator, literally, and an avid student of the art. His letters and journals contain a good deal of comment on the subject, from his boasts of success at Harrow and in the House of Lords through his mature years, when he once recorded in "Detached Thoughts" a critique of some twenty eminent speakers.[28] Many connoisseurs thought highly of Byron's gifts as an orator—his headmaster at Harrow (who, Byron stated, praised "my fluency, my turbulence, my voice, my copiousness of declamation, and my action"—significant nouns), his fellow peers ("my periods are very like Burke's!!"), Moore, Sheridan.[29] Sheridan's praise of Byron's oratorical potential was based partly on *English Bards and Scotch Reviewers*, and in the same passage from his journal where he records this fact Byron himself seems to imply that for him his careers as orator and poet were alternative channels of the same talent, for he suggests that one of the reasons he gave up his career as orator was the publication of *Childe Harold*; "nobody ever thought about my *prose* afterwards: nor indeed did I; it became to me a secondary and neglected object, though I sometimes wonder to myself *if* I should have succeeded?" Framing this statement, but from the earlier part of Byron's life, is another and more explicit equation of public speaking and poetry; when he was nineteen he wrote to John Hanson:

> I coincide with you in opinion that the *Poet* yields to the *orator*; but as nothing can be done in the latter capacity till the Expiration of my *Minority*, the former occupies my present attention, and both *ancients* and *moderns* have declared that the two pursuits are so nearly similar as to require in a great measure the same Talents, and he who excels in the one, would on application succeed in the other.[30]

Whether or not the "ancients and moderns" were right, the affinity between poet and orator seems to hold good for Byron. Students of his style can learn a good deal about his method from his three parliamentary efforts. Here are two passages from his speech on the Frame-work bill:

> How will you carry [the death-penalty provision of the bill] into effect? Can you commit a whole country to their own prisons? Will you erect a gibbet in every field, and hang up men like scarecrows? or will you proceed (as you must to bring this measure into effect) by decimation? place the country under martial law? depopulate and lay waste all around you? . . . Are these the remedies for a starving and desperate populace? Will the famished wretch who has braved your bayonets be appalled by your gibbets? When death is a relief, and the only relief it appears that you will afford him, will he be dragooned into tranquillity? Will that which could not be effected by your grenadiers be accomplished by your executioners?

> But suppose it passed; suppose one of these men, as I have seen them, —meagre with famine, sullen with despair, careless of a life which your Lordships are perhaps about to value at something less than the price of a stocking-frame;—suppose this man surrounded by the children for whom he is unable to procure bread at the hazard of his existence, about to be torn for ever from a family which he lately supported in peaceful industry, and which it is not his fault that he can no longer so support;—suppose this man—and there are ten thousand such from whom you may select your victims—dragged into court, to be tried for this new offence, by this new law; still, there are two things wanting to convict and condemn him; and these are, in my opinion,—twelve butchers for a jury, and a Jeffreys for a judge![31]

From the rhetorical arc of these passages to that of *Childe Harold* is not a long step, and in the second passage one can also find the rhythm of the *Don Juan* stanza and method, as well as some of that poem's acid. But the main point is not that Byron the poet and Byron the orator are alike. Even more than this we need to see that the technique of patrician oratory displayed in this speech and in hundreds of others like it, *by* others, helps define a general tradition that Byron asserted in his poetry and cast in the teeth of his contemporary Romantics.

NOTES

1. T. S. Eliot, "Byron" (publ. 1937), in *On Poetry and Poets* (New York, 1957), p. 223.

2. William J. Calvert, *Byron: Romantic Paradox* (Chapel Hill, 1935).

3. George M. Ridenour, *The Style of "Don Juan"* (New Haven, 1960). Although this is one of the best books on Byron, I agree with Paul West that *Don Juan* is more relativistic and less organized than Ridenour believes it is; see West's Introduction to *Byron: A Collection of Critical Essays* (Englewood Cliffs, N. J., 1963), p. 10.

4. On both these poems see Robert F. Gleckner, *Byron and the Ruins of Paradise* (Baltimore, 1967), pp. 121–138, 191–199.

5. Even in this poem, however, the prefatory sonnet contradicts flatly what the poem proper says. The latter asserts the vulnerability of man's mind, the sonnet declares it to be unconquerable. Cf. Byron's "mobility," his insouciant inconsistency.

Except when I am quoting directly from a letter, or from *Don Juan*, for which I use the *Variorum* edition of Truman Guy Steffan and Willis W. Pratt (Austin, 1957), my text for the poems is *The Works of Lord Byron: Poetry*, ed. Ernest Hartley Coleridge (London, 1898–1905).

6. Letter to John Murray, 22 July 1821, from *The Works of Lord Byron: Letters and Journals* (hereafter *L & J*), ed. Rowland E. Prothero (London, 1898–1901), V, 324.

7. West, Introduction, p. 1. A number of points in my essay are parallel to points West makes there and in *Byron and the Spoiler's Art* (New York, 1960), and also to *some* of what G. Wilson Knight says in "The Two Eternities," in *The Burning Oracle* (New York, 1939), pp. 197–215.

8. 12 September 1821, *L & J*, V, 361. The lines are quoted as they appear in the letter.

9. See Steffan, *Byron's "Don Juan,"* Vol. I: *The Making of a Masterpiece* (Austin, 1957); West, *Byron and the Spoiler's Art*, pp. 112–113, 115–116.

10. To Webster, 31 August 1811, *L & J*, II, 15; to Murray, 12 June 1813, *L & J*, II, 216–217; to Murray, 18 November 1820, *L & J*, V, 120.

11. To Murray, 20 September 1821, *L & J*, V, 371–372.

12. *L & J*, V, 563–564.

13. 22 October 1815, *L & J*, III, 226.

14. To Moore, 3 May 1821, *L & J*, V, 274; Bowles controversy, *L & J*, V, 559.

15. 1 June 1818, *L & J*, IV, 237.

16. To Murray, 15 September 1817, *L & J*, IV, 169.

17. "Reply to Blackwood's *Edinburgh Magazine*," 15 March 1820, *L & J*, IV, 485.

18. To Murray, 14 October 1820, *L & J*, V, 104.

19. Bowles controversy, *L & J*, V, 554.

20. To Murray, 15 September 1817, *L & J*, IV, 169.

21. March 1821, *L & J*, V, 259–260.

22. *The Well-Wrought Urn: Studies in the Structure of Poetry* (New York, 1947).

23. Bowles controversy, *L & J*, V, 591–592 (this part of the debate was not published until after Byron's death) ; to Murray, March 1821, *L & J*, V, 258–259.

24. *L & J*, I, 341–343.

25. Bowles controversy, *L & J*, V, 559.

26. To Hunt, 30 October 1815, *L & J*, III, 239.

27. To Murray, 15 February 1817, *L & J*, IV, 54–55; to Moore, 25 March 1817, *L & J*, IV, 80; to Moore, 19 September 1821, *L & J*, V, 368.

28. *L & J*, V, 410–413.

29. "Detached Thoughts," *L & J*, V, 453; to Hodgson, 5 March 1812, *L & J*, II, 104–105; to Moore, 16 February 1814, *L & J*, III, 40, and note; "Detached Thoughts," *L & J*, V, 414–415.

30. 2 April 1807, *L & J*, I, 126.

31. 27 February 1812, *L & J*, II, 429, 430.

NATURE, ART, REASON, AND
IMAGINATION IN *CHILDE HAROLD*
Carl Woodring

Childe Harold's Pilgrimage, although not highly valued of late, will endure. The English language contains no greater triumph of the commonplace. Stanza after stanza affords the reader acknowledged sentiments in a combination of new and familiar phrases. Even if the reader is fully alert—and it is a mistake to suppose that the reader of poetry should be always in a state of cerebration—there is a strength of suspense in the expectancy of further commonplace. Readers of the first fifteen or twenty editions found novelty in the vital injection of personal feeling into journalistic observation, but Byronic force of feeling has itself become a commonplace for readers of poetry. The first avid readers were surprised by the aptness and force of the familiar no less than by the novelty. They were surprised also because the directness that Dryden and Pope had perfected in antithetical half-lines of the heroic couplet was here extended to nine lines of picture-making by *camera obscura* in the Spenserian stanza. Much as travelers in pursuit of the picturesque sought vistas fitted to the *camera obscura*, Byron sought sublime historical vistas suitable to the Spenserian stanza.

When Byron thinks aloud, if not a child, he is childlike in the simplicity of his terms. *Childe Harold* is simple, wavering, and human, but Cantos III and IV catch up the themes of Cantos I and II, and the whole treats seriously questions that teased all the English romantics into and out of thought. As he confesses in dedicating Canto IV to his fellow-traveler Hobhouse, this is a "poetical work which is the longest, the most thoughtful and comprehensive of my compositions."[1] *Don Juan* was yet to come, but the interweaving of themes in *Childe Harold* is intricate enough to deserve some of the attention accorded in recent years to *Don Juan*.[2]

147

Prominent among the themes interwoven are Nature and Art, Reason and Imagination. Harold is sent on a pilgrimage through nature and civilization in southern Europe. Surveying the ruins of human endeavor at the edges of the sea and the Alps, the poet finds that Nature is greater than Art, but there are qualifications to be made. Wordsworth and Shelley have not seduced him altogether away from Pope.

Of *Childe Harold* as a unified imaginative poem, most of the remarks built into the work itself are depreciatory. The Preface to Cantos I and II declares that Harold is "the child of imagination." That is, "a fictitious character is introduced for the sake of giving some connection to the piece" (EHC, II, 3). *Imagination* carries here a pejorative connotation. Similarly, in Canto II, the poet claims to proceed, by "pensive Sadness, not by Fiction, led," through "Climes, fair withal as ever mortal head / Imagined in its little schemes of thought" (II.36). Justified by the practice of Ariosto, Thomson, and particularly Beattie, the minstrel of the piece oscillates—in Beattie's own terms—"droll or pathetic, descriptive or sentimental, tender or satirical, as the humour strikes me" (EHC, II, 5). At the beginning of Canto III, Byron renounces any other claim for the poem, "So that it wean me from the weary dream / Of selfish grief or gladness" (III.4). He writes to escape the self: so at least his disclaimers of more serious purpose. But it is to be noted that *dream* is used here in a restricted sense to mean divorce from reality in his actual life.

For the stuff of the poem itself, he claims a union of the actual and the real, free of inventive dream. All his life, like other poets and poetical spirits, he has dreamed of Parnassus. Now he addresses the very mountain from the foot of its slopes,

> Not in the phrensy of a dreamer's eye,
> Not in the fabled landscape of a lay,
> But soaring snow-clad through thy native sky . . . .
> (I.60)

He reflects that some of the mightiest bards have lacked the happiness to see this actualization of a dream carried through life.

By *dreams* in the sense of his most frequent usage in this poem, Byron means hope for improvement, accomplishment, and self-realization. As such, dreams belong to youth. Dreams are of love, fame, ambition achieved, with the addition in Canto IV of rewarded avarice. To age belongs disillusionment, for "Love, Fame, Ambition, Avarice . . . all are meteors with a different name" (IV.124). Most readers have marked in *Childe Harold* its melancholy acknowledgment of universal vanity: every man's life is the same tale of sin and death. This, as stanzas yet to be noted make even clearer, is the gnomic wisdom of a prophetic rather than cynical voice. A poet who distrusts dreams and imagination can still believe in much.

Writers whom Byron admires—some of them, like Words-worth, in spite of warnings from Apollo—have claimed for imagination the creation of a reality, an embodiment of more than dream. Since man feels more of sublimity than he can reasonably express (IV.158), belief in an imaginative creation or imaginative grasp of reality would meet a seriously felt need. This poet preeminently, and particularly in 1816-1818, would like to concentrate his thought, like Nature, into lightning (III.97). If life courses toward disillusionment, we may rescue, refine, and preserve our dreams through art:

> 'Tis to create, and in creating live
> A being more intense that we endow
> With form our fancy, gaining as we give
> The life we image . . . .
>
> (III.6)

This is to claim a higher purpose than claimed two stanzas earlier for the escape from self. E. H. Coleridge, as editor, laughs at the pretense of seriousness in this passage, and the poet quickly shakes off such "Platonizing": "Yet I must think less wildly," must avoid a "whirling gulf of phantasy and flame" (III.7). The thought will not down that imagination can create a kind of reality, but reason cannot approve what reason cannot find in nature.

> Of its own beauty is the mind diseased,
> And fevers into false creation:—where,
> Where are the forms the sculptor's soul hath seized?
> In him alone. Can Nature show so fair?
>
> (IV.122)

If Nature cannot, only disillusionment can come from the realization in art of dreams that cannot be realized in life. Particularly the idealizations of Canova, more unnatural to us than to Byron in their smoothed-out, characterless classicism, raised the question of "false creation"; but these lines are a thematic return to the stanzas on the Venus de' Medici earlier in Canto IV.

The two passages build upon the same observation—that the woman conceived by the sculptor is more beautiful than anything Nature can provide for man's experience—but the earlier passage had noted the transcendent mental power implied in the observation:

> We stand, and in that form and face behold
> What Mind can make, when Nature's self would fail . . . .
>   (IV.49)

It was not only because this Venus, discovered in the recent past, had just been freed from Paris and returned to Florence that Byron awarded it the longest tribute, and the highest, of all he saw in Florence. Venus shows what mind can do. The "ambrosial aspect" instils in the beholder part of its immortality, and the veil of heaven itself "is half undrawn" (IV.49). From the metaphor of transcendent imagination, the stanzas turn to one of imperial triumph. "Chained to the chariot of triumphal Art, / We stand as captives, and would not depart" (IV.50). The difference between Byron's metaphor and the captivity to Life avoided only by the sacred few in Shelley's last great fragment lies in the consent of Byron's captive—which was supplied almost automatically by the traditional metaphor of captivity to an alluring dream. Later, in two stanzas on the Apollo Belvidere, Byron notes a similar visitation of immortality in ideal beauty; there he makes his usual reservation concerning the ecstasy of vision, but does not reject it: The ideal beauty of this enduring work was expressed after "a dream of Love" by some solitary Nymph, "maddened in that vision" (IV.162). Like Rousseau, the sculptors of the Venus and the Apollo were inspired by Love.

Nevertheless, the ingredient of fear remains in Byron's awe of the human imagination. At the simplest level of response, he distrusts poetry that has no anchor in fact. This distrust, along with most of his other attitudes toward nature and art, is present in the stanzas on the "dying Glory" of Venice that open Canto IV. Praising glamorous Venice, he acknowledges as always the power of historical reminiscence to enhance the beauty of place. Yet in these stanzas his highest praise goes to characters associated with Venice but created by the imagination of playwrights—Shylock, Othello, and Pierre in Otway's *Venice Preserved*. These are free of the trammels that degrade our actual lives. Writing to Murray about four months before he composed the stanzas on Venice, Byron made a distinction not apparent in the verse: "I hate things *all fiction;* and therefore the *Merchant* and *Othello* have no great associations to me: but *Pierre* has. There should always be some foundation of fact for the most airy fabric, and pure invention is but the talent of a liar."[3] In the poem Pierre as well as Shylock and the Moor is taken as a purely invented character in a recreated past.

> The Beings of the Mind are not of clay:
> Essentially immortal, they create
> And multiply in us a brighter ray
> And more beloved existence.
> (IV.5)

This is the splendid fairyland of the imagination, not susceptible, as dreams are, to disillusionment.

Man is capable, at least in youth, of even stronger idealization: ". . . there are things whose strong reality / Outshines our fairy-land" (IV.6). This stronger idealization is greater than the imagining of personalities in a recreated past, because it purports to prepare the subjective being of the individual for the realization of his potential in the actuality of the future.

> I saw or dreamed of such,—but let them go,—
> They came like Truth—and disappeared like dreams.
> (IV.7)

The moral force of such lines is made clearer by the similar assertions of Manfred:

> I have had those earthly visions,
> And noble aspirations in my youth,
> To make my own the mind of other men,
> The enlightener of nations . . . .[4]

The poet in *Childe Harold* could replace the vanished idealizations with new ones, but the realities of life make such elevation of the future above the present inadvisable: "Let these too go—for waking Reason deems / Such over-weening phantasies unsound" (IV.7). He has made a distinction similar to one of those made by Keats in *The Fall of Hyperion*, between the self-enclosed dreamer and the poet who serves mankind, but Byron lets the distinction go on the plea that reason must be the final judge of human conduct and experience.

Like Keats, he is assaying the reality of imaginative creation. Does the imagination tell us true? The author of *Childe Harold* has no trouble believing that poetry can have a practical effect on civilized man. On this question the poem has a ready answer. Poets, like conquerors, kings, orators and other statesmen, and philosophers ("Sophists"), are subject to the madness of the overreacher, a fever that "makes the madmen who have made men mad" by "their contagion" (III.43). Rousseau, who knew how "to make Madness beautiful," was inspired to love of Ideal Beauty, but he was inspired also to issue those "oracles which set the world in flame," and "good with ill they also overthrew" (III.77-82). It is precisely because the imagination has a practical effect on mankind that it is especially dangerous. Byron's fear of imagination is far more socially conscious than Keats's fears for imagination. More variable as a poet than Southey, Byron is scarcely less moral.

Imagination becomes dangerous to others, and not merely to the possessor, most often because of the overreacher's desire for fame. As described in *Childe Harold,* the overreacher, whether sculptor, dramatist, pirate, monarch, or "Imperial Anarch," seeks fame for his exploits rather than power. Bull-fighters are repaid by "all that kings or chiefs e'er gain" (I.73). Chieftains "barter breath for fame" (I.44). The warring barons on the Rhine had the misfortune to be mute, inglorious Napoleons; they had accomplishment without fame (III.48). All such strife and striving is vanity, and the poet of this gnomic travelogue repeatedly advises against it. In response to ballads about Roderick's violation of Count Julian's daughter and the consequent invasion of Spain by the Moors, he exclaims, "See how the Mighty shrink into a song!" (I.36). So much, always, for "Ambition's honoured fools" (I.42).

Fate plays a special role in the lives of the overreachers. Byron's fatalism, with its conventional and frequent appeals to Nemesis, is usually ascribed to his need to excuse his own faults. For the overreachers, however, fate is to provide the same ministry of fear that Wordsworth took from Nature. The moral force that Deists had found in natural law is available to Byron in the idea of preventive fate. Napoleon could not "curb the lust of War, / Nor learn that tempted Fate will leave the loftiest Star" (III.38). When Byron summarizes, "There is the moral of all human tales," he means all tales of interest, both of individuals and of political states in the classic cycle of civilizations:

> 'Tis but the same rehearsal of the past,
> First Freedom, and then Glory—when that fails,
> Wealth—Vice—Corruption,—Barbarism at last . . . .
> (IV.108)

He had summarized in the previous stanza: " 'tis thus the Mighty falls."

Yet in the stanza addressed to his friend John Wingfield of the Guards, who had died of a fever at Coimbra, he laments Wingfield's failure to achieve equality with "the mighty low" who had fallen by the sword,

> While Glory crowns so many a meaner crest!
> What hadst thou done to sink so peacefully to rest?
> (I.91)

Here and in other stanzas Byron honors as other than fools those like the Maid of Zaragoza who led "in Glory's fearful chase" (I.55). The explanation is that true glory can be had in fighting for freedom; the highest glory can be had in expelling a foreign tyrant, to begin the upward arc in the fatal cycle of a nation. Morat and Marathon were "true Glory's stainless victories," won by a civic band of "unbought champions" (III.64). Although Harold loathed "the bravo's trade," even mercenaries, in the cause of national self-determination, can "strike, blest hirelings! for their country's good" (II.40; I.44). It is moral and natural to fight for freedom; it is immoral and unnatural to serve ambition.

All readers observe that the poet of *Childe Harold's Pilgrimage* appeals to the Titanic elements of Nature as analogous to the forces of his own mind. At several points he strengthens the analogy with structural parallels in the verse. "Sky—Mountains—River—Winds—Lake—Lightnings!," for example, at Stanza 96 in Canto III, is echoed in the next stanza by "soul—heart—mind—passions—feelings"—the energies of one who wished to express them all in lightning. Thus Nature provides an analogy for the power of imagination; in a function closely akin, its dread might enforces the moral imperative of Byron's fatalism: Nature's strength shows the vanity of man's aspirations. The Alps "leave vain man below" (III.62). The sea, mightier than man, will never be tamed by him (IV.179-183). Nature crumbles man's most pretentious monuments. Nature also humbles the overreacher in art. "Art, Glory, Freedom fail, but Nature still is fair" (II.87). It seems barely just; the poet praises Nature when she outlasts beauty created by man, but he condemns the sculptor who creates a beauty not to be found in nature. The injustice derives from Byron's insistence on fact in his pursuit of reality.

The poem passes in contrast from the tempests of dread nature to calm waters, from the roar of the cascade at Terni to an iris at the edge of "the infernal surge," from placid Lake Leman to "torn Ocean's roar" and on to the chirping of a grass-hopper (IV.63-72; III.85-86). All Nature is a harmony. At Rousseau's Clarens, the perfect harmony speaks the presence of Love as god of all (III.99-103).

Byron takes the opportunity to insist further that Nature here provided Rousseau with the reality for art.

> 'Twas not for fiction chose Rousseau this spot,
> Peopling it with affections; but he found
> It was the scene which Passion must allot
> To the Mind's purified beings . . . .
> (III.104)

Love was there for Rousseau to find. Once more, as with Otway's Pierre, reality has provided a sanative check to the imagination. For *Venice Preserved* it was the actuality of history; for the *Nouvelle Héloïse*, and even for Rousseau's *Confessions*, it was the deeper reality of Nature that saved their author from the vortex of the imagination.

Like the other Romantics, Byron uses the word *Nature* in various ways, nearly all derived from the meaning of Nature as the underlying principle of each thing or of all. In claiming strength for Harold's solitude, he opposes Nature against Art. But Byron is closer than the other English Romantics to Alexander Pope's emphasis on Nature as the basis of human nature expressed in art, where Nature and Homer can be the same. It therefore need not be altogether a pose of Titanism in the final stanzas when the poet avers, "I love not Man the less, but Nature more" (IV.178; cf. III.69). Even when his language includes the contrast of Art and Nature, he describes a melding of the two in the grandeur of Greece, Rome, and Venice. He walks among ruins, but the grandeur in Greece and

Italy is not fallen: it is submerged and must arise. Italy is "the Garden of the World, the Home / Of all Art yields, and Nature can decree" (IV.26). Nature as a principle is inevitably inherent in civilization. Freedom as the face of Nature is obvious in all great civilizations. This pattern of thought informs the perplexed stanza of rhetorical questions that plead for a return of natural freedom to Italy and Greece:

> Can tyrants but by tyrants conquered be,
> And Freedom find no Champion and no Child
> Such as Columbia saw arise when she
> Sprung forth a Pallas, armed and undefiled?
> Or must such minds be nourished in the wild,
> Deep in the unpruned forest, 'midst the roar
> Of cataracts, where nursing Nature smiled
> On infant Washington? Has Earth no more
> Such seeds within her breast, or Europe no such shore?
> (IV.96)

Nature in America brought forth a Pallas, armed goddess of wisdom from Greece, ideal land of freedom and proportion. George Washington's dream in youth, free of personal ambition, was a dream fulfilled in the new birth of Pallas. Although Byron finds dangers in the unwatched imagination, he enters hellenic myth as passionately as did Shelley or Keats.

We have not described a circle, for we are not back where we began. Dreams and imagination do not require madness for fulfillment. The inspired poet need not become his near ally, the overreacher who drives others to a madness like his own. In the reflections in Canto III on Napoleon and others who surpass or subdue mankind, Byron's language was careless enough to deserve chastisement from Francis Jeffrey for implying that the average man is ungrateful to the point of hatred for all who surpass or benefit him. Jeffrey also rejected Byron's moral simplification in prophesying agitation, sorrow, and supineness for all overreachers.[5] Byron merely comes to the commonplace conclusion—which seemed no commonplace in the context of his rebellious, melancholic Titanism—that those like himself tempted to become overreachers should learn like the creator of Harold to honor Pallas Athene:

> Away with these! true Wisdom's world will be
> Within its own creation, or in thine,
> Maternal Nature!
> (III.46)

The blending of all beauties, in Nature or in Art, accepts the rule of reason. From trances of the imagination, the dionysiac poet must return to "waking Reason" (IV.7).

"Our life is a false nature"; the "uneradicable taint of Sin" (IV.126) keeps us out of harmony. But critics of late have taken this full look at the worst without acknowledging what Byron goes on immediately to say:

> Yet let us ponder boldly—'tis a base
> Abandonment of reason to resign
> Our right of thought—our last and only place
> Of refuge; this, at least, shall still be mine.
> (IV.127)

In a footnote Byron quotes Sir William Drummond's *Academical Questions* to the same effect as his stanzas: "Philosophy, wisdom, and liberty support each other: he, who will not reason, is a bigot; he, who cannot, is a fool; and he, who dares not, is a slave" (EHC, II, 423).

The four cantos of *Childe Harold* trace a holy pilgrimage to Athens and Rome. When the poet declares near the end of Canto III that Rome is the fount at which "the panting Mind assuages / Her thirst of knowledge" (110), the metaphor accounts for most of the restlessness; aspiration for a rebirth of Italy accounts for the remainder. Greece, ancient Rome, and less obviously Venice are the touchstones for a division, not between Nature and Art, but between the presence and absence of worth in all the civilizing arts. All those who strive must be judged by the test of worth left by Greece and the Roman Republic. Art contains Nature where there is worth, and nature in Greece and Italy has been made more beautiful by the human history imprinted there. Emphasis has been given to the wrong words in the famous line, "Fair Greece! sad relic of departed Worth!" (II.73). A later stanza rejects all "empires with a just decay" because there exists the contrasting immortality of "the high, the mountain-majesty of Worth" (III.67). The Pantheon in Rome is "Relic of nobler days, and noblest arts!" (IV.147). In *Don Juan* the tone changes, but the distinction remains. By the standard of Greece and Rome the poet judges England,

> that spot of earth,
> Which holds what *might have been* the noblest nation;
> But though I owe it little but my birth,

I feel a mixed regret and veneration
For its decaying fame and former worth.
                                    (*Don Juan*, X.66)

The protagonist of *Childe Harold* is sent

                    to track
Fall'n states and buried greatness, o'er a land
Which *was* the mightiest in its old command,
And *is* the loveliest, and must ever be
The master-mould of Nature's heavenly hand;
Wherein were cast the heroic and the free,—
The beautiful—the brave—the Lords of earth and sea,

The Commonwealth of Kings—the Men of Rome!
                                    (IV.25–26)

Childe Harold's Pilgrimage is a hornbook of scholastic commonplaces from a teacher for whom the glory and grandeur of Greece and Rome mean worth, an amplitude of life that affords amplitude to others. The bad Lord Byron could not observe this fallen worth without an effort at restoration. The Byronic irony and Byronic energy do not make for sweet reasonableness, but the Byronic insistence upon worth is the realization of a youthful dream endorsed by reason and approved by nature from the Swiss Alps to the Greek and Italian seas.

NOTES

1. Lord Byron, *Works: Poetry*, ed. Ernest Hartley Coleridge, 2nd ed. (London, 1922), II, 321. Unless otherwise noted, all quotations come from this Volume II, indicated as III.4, etc., for canto and stanza of *Childe Harold*, and as EHC, II, 321, etc., for other matter.

2. An exception is the splendid survey by Ward Pafford, "Byron and the Mind of Man: *Childe Harold III–IV* and *Manfred*," Studies in Romanticism, I (1962) 105-127. If I differ it is in considering the four cantos as one poem.

3. *Works: Letters and Journals*, ed. Rowland E. Prothero (London, 1904), IV, 93.

4. *Manfred* III.i.104–107. EHC, IV, 124, reads "early visions" for "earthly visions."

5. Quoted in *Childe Harold's Pilgrimage: A Romaunt* (London, 1842), p. 156 n., from the review in *Edinburgh Review*, XXVII (December 1816), 277–310.

THE ISLAND AND THE EVOLUTION OF BYRON'S "TALES"

Robert D. Hume

Within the last decade there has been a remarkable upsurge of interest in Byron's "tales." *The Giaour, The Bride of Abydos,* and *The Corsair* are being treated with a new respect; *Parisina* is dealt with as a serious psychological study; *The Prisoner of Chillon* is now hailed as a great dramatic monologue. Many critical issues are still far from settled—how to read *Mazeppa,* for instance—though presumably they will be thrashed out in the next decade. But there are already several stimulating readings of most of the "tales," and now that these works are again the source of interest and lively debate it seems time to attempt an overview.

To my knowledge there has never been a serious attempt to define the canon of the "tales" or to consider what *kind* of works they are. In recent explications and analyses *The Corsair* and *The Prisoner of Chillon* are lumped together under the general rubric of "tales." Does this make sense, and if so, why? What makes the "tales" distinct—if they are—from Byron's other works? What can be learned from studying them as a special group, and what perspectives on them can the critic most usefully adopt?

To answer such questions is my object in this essay. For a number of reasons I will devote particular attention to *The Island:* in comparison with the others it is still relatively little studied; it is clearly related to the earlier tales but represents interesting development and departure from them; it seems to offer significant evidence of the direction in which Byron's thought was moving. Overall, I am going to suggest that some useful distinctions in kind can be made among the tales and that chronologically there are some clear patterns of change.

158

i

Any general study of "the tales" must start with a question:
what works are properly considered "tales?" By common usage
The Giaour, The Bride of Abydos, and *The Corsair* (all of
1813) are termed the "early" or "oriental" tales, and *Lara,* a
kind of sequel to *The Corsair* written a year later, is generally
categorized with them. Only these four works are dubbed "A
Tale" in the title or subtitle, and beyond them there are problems. *The Siege of Corinth* and *Parisina* (written in 1815) are
usually called "tales" and discussed with the first four, though
they display some very obvious differences. *The Prisoner of
Chillon* (1816) and *Mazeppa* (1818) are discussed both as
monologues and—in some sense—as tales. *The Island* (1823),
when mentioned at all, is most often viewed as a throwback to
an earlier style—though to precisely *what* style is not clear.[1]
What constitutes the "tale" category within the Byron canon?
Apparently operating on the principle that a tale's a tale, critics
have tended to discuss first and think later. The result is a series
of disconnected explications in which at least two sorts of categorical criteria are apparent. When tested, however, neither appears
at all satisfactory. 1) Subject and handling: the early tales are
often described as "oriental," and *Mazeppa* and *The Island,*
set respectively in Russia and the South Seas, do concern relatively remote subjects. Are the "tales" "verse-novelettes"
which stress exaggerated action and exotic scenery? The first
four, *The Siege of Corinth,* and arguably *Mazeppa* could be described this way, but such a description fits *The Island* poorly and
Parisina and *The Prisoner of Chillon* not at all. The last two do
have rather lurid subjects, but in both the emphasis is placed on
character and psychology rather than action: despite the subjects,
both seem a long way removed from the intoxicating blood and
thunder of *The Corsair.* Insofar as these works are to be considered adventure stories, a distant setting might be considered
an attempt to escape ordinary standards of probability—as frequently seems to be the case in Gothic novels. But *The Island*
is in no way improbable, and *Parisina* and *The Prisoner of
Chillon* both have historical European subjects and so would be
excluded if a distant setting is accepted as a defining characteristic.[2] There would be some logic to such an exclusion, since both
these works are clearly different from those which precede them.
On the other hand many of Byron's other works possess equally

"remote" settings. 2) Theme: exile, the hero's "crime," illicit
love, and lost love are common in all of these works. Unhap-
pily, they can be found just as easily in most of Byron's other
productions, which makes "theme" a poor categorical criterion.

Granting, then, that the first four and perhaps *The Siege of
Corinth* are pretty much of a type—"verse-novelettes . . . in the
main line of eighteenth-century Gothico-orientalism," as M. K.
Joseph puts it[3]—it seems evident that we need no close analysis
to tell us that *The Corsair* and *The Prisoner of Chillon* represent very different sorts of endeavors on Byron's part. A critic
who wants to discuss both as "tales" must justify the connection.
More broadly, recent trends in Byron criticism make justification
of *any* kind of categorization necessary, since critics are no
longer willing to accept the radical polarities and compartmental-
izations which were once assumed to fragment Byron's thought
and work. M. K. Joseph draws parallels between the earlier and
later portions of *Childe Harold* and the earlier and later tales.
Robert F. Gleckner and Jerome J. McGann include the tales in
general surveys of Byron's development, as W. Paul Elledge
does in a study of his poetic techniques.[4] Plainly, this is a healthy
trend: it helps us see Byron "whole" and it contributes to the revaluation of works long dismissed as negligible and unrelated
to the poet's "serious" works. *Is* there a meaningfully definable
group of "tales" distinguishable from Byron's other works?

I think so. Of course, no such category can be absolute: it has
already proved profitable to compare lyrics and dramas, tales
and satires, as productions of what Gleckner calls a unified and
coherent poetic outlook. But this does not mean that careful categorization cannot prove helpful. To stress the parallels between
the tales and *Childe Harold* is laudable, but there remain real
differences between the narrative fashion of the former and the
"meditative-topographical manner" of the latter. The principal
object of categorization is to help us see similarities and differences with the hope of better understanding single works.

I want to suggest that the "tales" are best conceived as Byron's nonsatiric, nondramatic, *narratives* and *monologues* in
which *the events and emotions are demonstrably not those of the
author*. And with the exception of *The Island*, it can be added
that there is relatively little commentary from the author or a
detached narrator-persona. These criteria differentiate "tales"
from lyrics and dramas as well as from *Childe Harold*, which is

explicitly a projection of Byron's own feelings, and from *Don Juan*, whose persona-narrator comments extensively on the story and frequently seems to reflect the personality of the actual author. Relative to these other works, the "tales" seem more objective and impersonal.

Obviously, I intend this definition to include *Parisina* and *The Prisoner of Chillon*, and I want to add *The Lament of Tasso* and *The Prophecy of Dante* as well, works which seem to me very similar to the former pair in a variety of ways.[5] These later works are generally classified as "Italian poems," presumably on the basis of time and place of composition, as well as subject, by which standard *Parisina* is equally Italian. But in kind *The Lament of Tasso* and *The Prophecy of Dante* are of the variety of *The Prisoner of Chillon*: dramatic monologues by exiled or imprisoned men who have loved and lost and who are struggling to control and comprehend their experiences.[6] *Mazeppa* is more problematical, but broadly it fits this description: it is a framed monologue by a man in serious straits recounting his experiences in an earlier predicament.

In this essay, then, I want to consider the "tales" as comprising Byron's nonsatiric narratives and dramatic monologues, works which, like the dramas, seem distinctly more "impersonal" than Byron's most famous productions. Plainly, the early narratives are quite different from the later "monologues": two distinct phases are involved. In the next section I will try to show that they are organically related through *The Siege of Corinth* and *Parisina*, and that the two types can properly be dealt with as part of a continuum. I would like to suggest in addition, though I lack the space to go into it here, that the dramas represent a further attempt at an "objective" working out of some of the same problems and materials. Except for *Manfred* (which is unique and more related to *Childe Harold* than to the "plays"), the dramas postdate all of the tales except *The Island*, a work in which Byron explores some of the central problems raised in the dramas from a different perspective. Very generally, I would claim that tales and dramas together constitute a relatively "objective" attempt on Byron's part to deal with subjects and problems which throughout his career we see paralleled in his more directly "personal" expressions. My immediate object, however, is to survey the evolution of the tales from verse-novelette to dramatic monologue.

ii

How best to view the tales remains a problem, for their "kind" and value have not yet been firmly established. Until very recently, neglect and contempt were their usual lot. Andrew Rutherford's comments reflect long-standard opinion. The tales, he says, are casually written melodramatic entertainments which cannot be taken seriously. He praises *The Prisoner of Chillon,* but condemns the rest of the tales as overwritten adolescent day-dreams lacking psychological insight.[7] It is a measure of the rapid change in Byron criticism that these judgments, which seemed commonplace a decade ago, now appear wholly out of line with current opinion. Marshall,[8] Gleckner, and McGann all treat the early tales as serious poetic endeavors worthy of careful explication and comparison to other works. Marshall emphasizes the psychological subtlety of these works—particularly the monologues; McGann offers essentially allegorical readings, sometimes in explicitly Blakean terms.

Welcome as this serious attention is, I think it likely that in time there will be a reaction against such dead-serious readings of the "oriental" tales, for such an approach must inevitably ignore or belittle the obvious character of these works. Appeals to Byron's view of them are little help, for the evidence of the *Letters and Journals* is treacherous—one can find signs both of contempt and of some real artistic effort. In the works themselves both haste and care seem apparent, and undeniably they contain serious themes and problems which quickly take Byron into another mode of tale. But—perhaps because the tales seem less a personal expression than other works—there is a persistent tendency to over-allegorize them. Works so full of Love and Death are easy to cast in allegorical patterns, and such an approach has the added virtue, for many critics, of seeming to add profundity and "meaning" to stories which can appear all too simple if complexity is one's standard of excellence. We must beware of manufacturing universal significance where there is none. The tales are not abstruse, and though they have some serious import, all of them are designed to be pleasant reading. Byron is never intellectually pretentious, and his critics should avoid becoming so.

What is the "obvious character" of the oriental tales? Exaggeratedly "romantic" in the worst sense of that term, I would say. Their effect depends on extremes of passion, lurid action, and exotic scenery. Their resemblance to *Vathek* is noted by several critics (M. K. Joseph makes the most of the parallels); and the comparison is apt, for like Beckford's overblown romp the tales have scarcely any *real* passion at all. The characters are shadowy, superficial, and type-cast; the sentiments, inflated. Are Selim and Zuleika Byron's Hamlet and Ophelia, as Gleckner suggests?[9] I would say rather that *The Bride of Abydos* is a penny-novelette whose pseudo-heroics we can enjoy but which is without the power to seize and hold our attention and concern. The first four tales exist for their thrill-value, and they should be read—and enjoyed—primarily as exuberant exercises of Fancy. The reader's concern is not much engaged; despite the bloody conclusions of *The Giaour, The Bride,* and *Lara,* all three seem less essentially pessimistic than the peaceful ending of *The Prisoner of Chillon.* As in such early Gothic efforts as *Vathek* and *The Castle of Otranto,* there remains an essential lightheartedness despite the presence of potentially serious themes.

The Giaour is the most ambitious and complicated of the first four tales. How to judge it is a major problem. The basic plot is contained in the first "sketch" of 407 lines, but by the seventh edition additions had blown it up to 1334 lines. Marshall attacked these additions as "accretive" and inorganic, arguing that they merely confuse and dilute the story. Gleckner, in a long and detailed analysis, has replied that the additions *are* related to the substance of the poem, which he considers not the action but the view which is taken of it.[10] In this reading the poem emerges—rightly, I think—not as a glorification of the outlaw, but as a kind of vision of the chaos into which man's passions drive him. It must be said, however, that this does not emerge at all clearly from the poem. Gleckner brilliantly demonstrates what Byron was evidently *trying* to add to his narrative, but, for me at least, the poem as it stands conveys more confusion and mystery than coherent vision. The connections between tale and commentary (the opening passage on Greece, for example) simply do not come across to the reader. In one of the best of the recent studies of the poet, M. G. Cooke suggests that "Byron is evidently feeling or blindly expanding his way in *The Giaour* toward a more than narrative statement."[11] I think this states the case well: onto a brisk and simple story are piled impossibly complex explanations and digressions-by-association, and so what actually comes through in the final version is a muddled extravaganza.

The extreme simplicity and narrative clarity of *The Bride of Abydos* may indicate Byron's awareness that his aspiration had outrun his technique. *The Bride* has scarcely any commentary and *The Corsair* only a little more. Whatever Byron was trying to do in *The Giaour*, there is little evidence of divided purpose in the next two tales. It is with *Lara* that greater complexity appears again. *Lara's* reputation is not high: it lacks the surging energy of its predecessors and so fails to compensate as well for its large share of mysterious sensationalism. Such episodes as the unexplained midnight attack on Lara (I.xii) and Byron's most unbridled display of Gothic trappings fall slightly flat without more dash in the telling. But the rebellion of serfs which Lara instigates (for selfish purposes) introduces more serious social questions (II.viii) than are explicitly raised in the first three tales. Here too there is much more outright analysis of character:

> His early dreams of good outstripped the truth,
> And troubled Manhood followed baffled Youth;
> With thought of years in phantom chase misspent,
> And wasted powers for better purpose lent;
> And fiery passions that had poured their wrath
> In hurried desolation o'er his path . . . .
> . . . .
> But haughty still, and loth himself to blame,
> He called on Nature's self to share the shame,
> And charged all faults upon the fleshly form
> She gave to clog the soul, and feast the worm;
> Till he at last confounded good and ill,
> And *half mistook for fate the acts of will* . . . . [my italics]
> . . . .
> And this same impulse would, in tempting time,
> Mislead his spirit equally to crime;
> So much he soared beyond, or sunk beneath,
> The men with whom he felt condemned to breathe,
> And longed by good or ill to separate
> Himself from all who shared his mortal state . . . . (I.xviii)

More striking still is the direct narrative commentary that Byron permits himself:

> What boots the oft-repeated tale of strife,
> The feast of vultures, and the waste of life?
> The varying fortune of each separate field,
> The fierce that vanquish, and the faint that yield?

The smoking ruin, and the crumbled wall?
In this the struggle was the same with all;
Save that distempered passions lent their force
In bitterness that banished all remorse.
None sued, for Mercy knew her cry was vain,
The captive died upon the battle-plain:
In either cause, one rage alone possessed
The empire of the alternate victor's breast;
And they that smote for freedom or for sway,
Deemed few were slain, while more remained to slay.
It was too late to check the wasting brand,
And Desolation reaped the famished land;
The torch was lighted, and the flame was spread,
And Carnage smiled upon her daily dead.

                                        (II.x)

Here the gloomy power of the comment undercuts the heroic
side of the tale: for the first time Byron makes it unmistakably
plain that he is not presenting outlaws to be admired, and this
should reinforce Gleckner's interpretation of *The Giaour*.

In the past it was commonly assumed that Byron reveled uncritically in these outlaw-heroes. Reveled, yes—hence the riotous
energy of *The Bride* and *The Corsair*—but uncritically, no. Replying to Jeffrey's denunciation of these heroes' "voluptuous-
ness" and "misanthropy," M. G. Cooke says,

> It seems doubtful that Byron meant them as exemplary persons or was
> unaware of what Jeffrey called their "morbid exaltation." Rather he
> illustrates . . . morbidity of will . . . . The sublimity of characters
> such as Alp and Conrad, instead of embodying a state of transcendence,
> resembles a sort of defection from humanity . . . .[12]

Let there be no mistake: Byron is depicting egregiously flawed
characters and he knows it. Extravagant these works are,
but in 1813-1814 Byron was no daydreaming adolescent. The
evidence of *The Giaour* and *Lara*, combined with the more explicit treatment of imperfect characters in the later tales, should
tell us that the ruin to which the early heroes are brought is
more than a tidy way of concluding their stories. In the balance
the early tales seem neither utterly serious nor utterly frivolous,
and we can see in them the beginnings of more disciplined endeavors.

The Siege of Corinth and *Parisina* (written in 1815) clearly
represent a transitional phase between the early narratives and
the later monologues. To link these two works may seem odd,

since the reputation of the former stands very low while that
of the latter is by far the highest of the first six tales. But despite
some very obvious differences, both of them exhibit characteristics of an intermediate stage. Both works are prefaced by historical quotations: like the later monologues and dramas they are
imaginative departures from historical situations rather than
fanciful flights begotten upon Scott's methods by Byron's early
travels. This grounding in fact is of little importance in *The
Siege* and little more in *Parisina,* but their departure from the
freewheeling practice of the oriental stories leads into the method
of *The Lament of Tasso* and *The Prophecy of Dante.*

The Siege displays much of the extravagance and bombast
characteristic of the earlier tales, and it is even less redeemed
than *Lara* by a compensatory exuberance. Gleckner calls it "Byron's most slipshod production" but rightly notes that the work
is interesting for its experimentation with a narrator-participant
(the first since *The Giaour*) and its use of hallucinatory description (ll. 454 ff.).[13] In *The Bride, The Corsair,* and *Lara*
we are given little objective judgment of the heroes, nor do we
ever really get inside their minds. The picture we are given is
extrinsic but one-dimensional. Here Alp's mind becomes the
central object of attention. Like his predecessors he is alienated,
outlawed, and separated from his lady-love, but here we are
taken more into his feelings and psychology as he struggles with
a moral dilemma. In Selim, Conrad, and Lara we see little
psychology and less dilemma. With Alp we again begin to move
(as at the end of *The Giaour*) into the inside of one of Byron's
mysterious heroes, and as the brief commentary on Lara should
warn us, what we find is anything but favorable. Alp is a Coriolanus too perverse and stubborn to yield, and the end of the
tale, theatrical as it is, presents an utter ruin and desolation
which is damning commentary on Alp and his kind. *The Siege*
awkwardly combines psychology with the extravagant action of
the preceding tales, and it is an easy work to criticize. Its importance in Byron's development lies in its move toward the primacy
of character rather than action.

The Siege of Corinth and *Parisina* were published together,
but to move from the one to the other is to enter a wholly different world. *Parisina* is utterly without extravagance or padding; it
is more understated than overwritten—a change which critics
welcome. It is a story of illicit love, trial, and execution, but it is
quite without elaborate descriptions, and the action remains

strictly secondary. The crux of the tale is the psychological interplay among the three principals. Hugo and Azo are allowed to
put their contradictory positions clearly, but the reader must
realize that there is much beneath the surface here. None of the
participants fully understands his own feelings and actions, and
each justifies himself as best he can. Here character has full
precedence over action, complicated by the complex of feelings
attendant on illegitimacy, adultery, revenge, and "incest."[14] The
narrative standpoint is of particular importance in *Parisina*.[15] It
is extrinsic to the characters (though Hugo is allowed to speak
directly at length), but it does not fix our attitude; instead we
are left to realize that the contradictions are irreconcilable,
that none of the participants is "right." This suspension of
explicit narrative judgment is a change from *Lara* and *The
Siege:* it presages the technique of the monologues, in which we
are given no external help at all in judging the accuracy and consistency of the speakers' claims.

To move directly from the "oriental" tales to the monologues
is something like looking first through one end of a telescope and
then through the other: it is hard to believe that two such
different perspectives are directly connected. The parallel is not
exact, for in the later works we do not enter the mind of the
same sort of character that appears in the earlier ones. Bonnivard, Tasso, and Dante are vastly more sympathetic and de-
fensible characters than Conrad or Alp: in these later characters
the nobility is more than that of the outlaw thundering defiance
at the world. Imprisonment and exile are not, in these cases,
the deserved result of a perverse outlawry. Rather, all three
men speak from circumstances in which they have to try to come
to terms with their experience of persecution. Each monologue
is a study in self-knowledge. The speaker tries to make sense of
what has happened to him against a background of larger issues
—in Dante's case the whole condition and future of Italy. The
relation to Hugo's situation in *Parisina* is obvious: each speaker
justifies himself while at the same time betraying much that he
does not fully understand or control.

Bonnivard understands the least of the three. Recent critics
are agreed that the story which to its speaker appears to be a
triumph of fortitude over adversity is actually anything but
that.[16] There is no triumph: rather there is enforced adaptation
to circumstance. Bonnivard endures, but at the cost of acquiescence to the intolerable. As Cooke observes, the poem seems un-

derlaid by a profound pessimism—not only does Bonnivard break down under captivity, but he largely fails to understand the import of his admission that prison becomes "a second home" (1. 380) and that "I / Regained my freedom with a sigh" (1. 392).

Tasso, by contrast, is looking at present rather than past circumstances. At the outset of the poem he denies fiercely that he is mad, but that he verges on it becomes apparent, and he later admits this, though insisting that it is the result, not the cause, of his incarceration. Throughout his monologue Tasso tries to picture himself as heroically impervious to circumstances, but as Marshall comments on the concluding stanza, "despite his many promises never to upbraid, to hate, or to surrender, the speaker has, to some extent, done all."[17] Tasso's excessive protestations make it plain that he half-understands his own disturbance: far more than Bonnivard he is grappling actively and consciously with emotional chaos.

In *The Prophecy of Dante* this trend is carried much further: Dante is struggling to justify himself and his world view, but he understands his own feelings to a vastly greater extent than either Bonnivard or Tasso. In the two preceding poems the reader should not accept the interpretations and valuations of the speaker; here he may do so to a much greater extent. Dante can recognize and admit his own weakness and pain in a way that the others cannot, and he struggles with more success to control his feelings and maintain an objective view of himself and others. At times he burns "with evil feelings hot and harsh," but he refuses to succumb to them:

> Revenge,
> Who sleeps to dream of blood, and waking glows
> With the oft-baffled, slakeless thirst of change,
> When we shall mount again, and they that trod
> Be trampled on, while Death and Até range
> O'er humbled heads and severed necks—Great God!
> Take these thoughts from me—to thy hands I yield . . . .
> (I.113–119)

Unlike Alp he will not avenge his wrongs on his own city:

> My own Beatricē, I would hardly take
> Vengeance upon the land which once was mine,
> And still is hallowed by thy dust's return . . . .
> (I.99–101)

Dante's struggle with his feelings is successful: he is able to surmount injustice, "penury and pain," and devote himself to the fruitful and prophetic function of his art. Even here, though, we must not accept the speaker wholly at his word. The prophecy is, *in part,* a device which permits Dante to assert his superiority over his enemies. In this respect it is as much a response to his own emotional needs in poverty and exile as it is an objective statement. Dante's struggles with his feelings tell us that he is *not* cool and rational; what Byron finally gives us is a subtle account of a complex but honest mind in an emotionally difficult situation.

In the context of these monologues *Mazeppa* (1818) seems problematical. In time of composition it falls squarely between *Tasso* (1817) and *Dante* (1819). It is a monologue, but set within a narrative frame. At present there is no agreement at all on what should be made of it. The story of Mazeppa's wild ride is exciting in its own right—it is easy to see why Liszt wrote a symphonic poem on the subject. But one's assessment of the work depends on whether one stresses the story or the frame. McGann does the former; Marshall the latter.[18] In energy and emphasis on action the story is reminiscent of the early tales. Is the frame merely the vehicle of a feeble and obvious joke? Or does it constitute, as Marshall argues, an ironic commentary which utterly undercuts the "providential" interpretation which Mazeppa places on his rescue? On internal evidence there is no conclusive answer. Marshall believes that Mazeppa is denigrated and Charles XII implicitly glorified; McGann rightly notes that Byron's "Advertisement" quotes from a history of Charles by Voltaire which treats him as the epitome of the power-mad ruler who overreaches himself. With Charles's lust for conquest and Mazeppa's emphasis on revenge, both men seem similar to heroes in the early tales. Given the cumulative impact of the disapproval of such men, which mounts throughout the tales, it is hard to see how Byron could mean to glorify either man. Charles has overextended himself and been brought to defeat; the self-control Mazeppa has learned has been turned to revenge and self-aggrandizement. Hence, it seems unlikely that we are expected to take Mazeppa's interpretation at face value, any more than we are meant to take Alp (whom he resembles) as ideal: both men hold fiercely to self-induced delusions. That Charles falls asleep during the story I interpret partly as the obvious joke and partly as an indication of the complete isolation from humanity which Mazeppa—like Lara and Alp—has arrogantly imposed upon himself. The construction Mazeppa places on his story is meaningful only to him, and he is not at all bothered by the others' indifference:

> And if ye marvel Charles forgot
> To thank his tale, *he* wondered not,—
> The king had been an hour asleep.
>
> (xx)

The excitement of the story aside, *Mazeppa* seems primarily a monologue devoted to the revelation of the speaker's character.

As we survey what I am defining as tales up to this point, both changes and constants are evident. Thematically, exile, alienation, and lost love are pervasive, but from the action-orientation of the first four tales there is evolution into increasing concern with psychology and revelation of character. Blood and thunder give way to serious portrayal of individuals struggling to understand and control themselves. Dante's efforts seem largely successful; the claims of Bonnivard and Mazeppa appear mostly self-delusory. After *The Giaour's* unsuccessful experiment in narrative standpoint, refuge is sought in extrinsic and factual narration, but the idea behind *The Giaour* is picked up again in the use of a participant-narrator in *The Siege of Corinth,* and from there it evolves naturally into dramatic monologue. Byron's later move into drama should come as no surprise, for in many respects the plays represent an extension of the interests and problems of the later tales. But this development is beyond the scope of the present essay: my immediate concern is to show how Byron adapts tale-form to new purposes in *The Island.*

iii

The Island (1823) is contemporaneous with cantos XV and XVI of *Don Juan.* There is nothing quite like it in all of Byron's writings. Like the middle and later tales it builds from a historical foundation (though the headnote does no more than cite the source),[19] and like the tales as a group it is a nonsatiric narrative with a strong crime/exile theme. But despite the usual critical assertion that the tale represents a return to an earlier manner, there are some surprising departures from Byron's earlier methods.

1) Not only does Byron abandon monologue form and interior perspective in favor of a return to extrinsic narration, but for the first time he gives authorial commentary a prominent place in the poem. Though there are hints of this in *Lara* (quoted above), we may guess that the immediate impetus for it came from the manner of *Don Juan*. 2) In the early tales and the monologues it is frequently anything but evident how the reader should respond to outlawed or exiled protagonists; careful reading and judgment are required, and some critics still believe that Conrad and others are intended as admirable characters—fierce, bold, independent, and chivalrous. No such construction could be placed on the mutineers in *The Island*, for they are condemned both by the narrator and out of Christian's own mouth. 3) Generally, there is a more obvious moral bent than is evident in any of the earlier tales. Several of them are implicitly stories of crime and punishment, but *The Island* is explicitly so.

All this is surprising: in some ways it may appear that Byron is retrogressing to a more simpleminded style and outlook. What, we must enquire, was he trying to do?

Andrew Rutherford, representative of an older school of Byron criticism, is openly contemptuous of what he terms "a belated verse tale with a most unskilful mixture of romance and humour"; he calls it a "rag-bag of old Byronic themes" and denounces the poem's "absolute opposition of Nature and Civilization."[20] Recent critics have taken the tale more seriously. The idyllic state of the island and the happy ending for Torquil and Neuha have led several acute critics to believe that Byron "for once, allows himself to surrender to the charms of a utopia." Gleckner defends such a surrender (which fits the thesis of his book) as an effort to regain the pristine past, not "a surrender to sentiment" but rather "an extraordinary personal confession as well as the poet's last desperate articulation of hope for man." McGann says that *The Island* "lays out an unequivocal program for the possession of the earthly paradise" and "describes the term of man's furthest hopes."[21]

Does *The Island* present Byron's idea of utopia? Despite my real respect for the critics who say so, I cannot believe it. *Byron* succumb to *this* idea of perfection? That he could revel in the idyll seems evident from the work—just as he had been able to revel in the heroics of *The Corsair* a decade earlier. But he could write caustically to Leigh Hunt: "I will bet you a flask of Falernum that . . . the most pamby portions of the Toobonai Islanders, will be the most agreeable to the enlightened public."[22] So far as I can see, *The Island* is primarily a story of crime and retribution, and the "utopia" it presents, far from being an ideal, actually constitutes the temptation for the crime. In view of this radical divergence of opinion, I think it worthwhile to examine the work more closely than I have any of the others, in an attempt to see what goes on in it.

Any reader of the tale should be struck by the slightness of the story-connection between the mutineers and the islanders. The island serves as a backdrop and the innocence of its inhabitants as a contrast, but for the most part Byron keeps the two elements of the story discrete. At times one almost forgets the island; rather more of the time one tends to forget about the mutiny, which proves slightly awkward when it comes to trying to keep the story's theme in mind. The separation does preserve a contrast of guilt and innocence: for once Byron makes it quite impossible for us to become too wrapped up in a guilty hero to judge him properly. But the separation does make it too easy to forget that thematically the story (subtitled "Christian and His Comrades") rests on mutiny and its punishment.

The first canto opens with a brief description of the mutiny. Readers brought up on other recensions of the story will be too ready to sympathize with the mutineers. Byron is *not* recounting a rebellion against tyranny. Captain Bligh is called "gallant" at the outset; his behavior as he is forced into a small boat is such that "they who pitied not could yet admire"; the high heroism of his desperate voyage home is praised in the warmest terms (I. ix). Nowhere is there any suggestion that the mutineers rebelled against intolerable tyranny. As early as the second stanza Byron goes out of his way to make it plain that the mutiny is caused not by tyranny but by a lawless desire to be utterly without discipline:

> The wish—which ages have not yet subdued
> In man—to have no master save his mood . . . .

Byron stresses the uncivilized nature of the South Sea islands, and much of the brief first canto is devoted to explaining the attractions of "the happy shores without a law" (I.x) for the mutineers, who are drawn to throw off all restraint and eschew all endeavor in favor of a primitive but easy life.[23]

In the second canto Byron introduces Torquil and his wife

Neuha. The first seventeen stanzas depict the idyllic nature of their lives and surroundings. "Pleasant," "softest," "warbling," "sighing"—such are the terms of stanza one. Neuha "feared no ill, because she knew it not" (vii), and in these circumstances she can well afford to be "Rapt in the fond forgetfulness of life" (xiv). Time means nothing in these surroundings (xv, xvi); peace and serenity reign (xvii). Byron neither lets this idyll go on until it palls nor fractures it with theatrical abruptness. Four more stanzas will have the mutineers at bay, but he interrupts the idyllic mood not with melodrama but with a humorous digression. A pipe-smoking sailor approaches the native couple, and the narrator exclaims:

> Sublime Tobacco! which from East to West
> Cheers the tar's labour or the Turkman's rest;
> Which on the Moslem's ottoman divides
> His hours, and rivals opium and his brides;
> Magnificent in Stamboul, but less grand,
> Though not less loved, in Wapping or the Strand;
> Divine in hookas, glorious in a pipe,
> When tipped with amber, mellow, rich, and ripe;
> Like other charmers, wooing the caress,
> More dazzlingly when daring in full dress;
> Yet thy true lovers more admire by far
> Thy naked beauties—Give me a cigar!
> (II.xix)

This reminds us of *Don Juan,* and presumably it horrifies Mr. Rutherford, but it does serve the function of easing a tricky transition from the idyll back to the story of the mutineers: after many months a punitive expedition is at hand. Torquil has allied himself to Christian. Compare the whole of his farewell to Neuha with that of Conrad to Medora.

> "My Neuha! ah! and must my fate pursue
> Not me alone, but one so sweet and true?
> But whatsoe'er betide, ah, Neuha! now
> Unman me not: the hour will not allow
> A tear; I am thine whatever intervenes!"
> "Right," quoth Ben; "that will do for the marines."
> (II.xxi)
>
> One kiss—one more—another—Oh! Adieu!
> She rose—she sprung—she clung to his embrace,
> Till his heart heaved beneath her hidden face:
> He dared not raise to his that deep-blue eye,
> Which downcast drooped in tearless agony.

> Her long fair hair lay floating o'er his arms,
> In all the wildness of dishevelled charms;
> Scarce beat that bosom where his image dwelt
> So full—*that* feeling seem'd almost unfelt!
> Hark—peals the thunder of the signal gun!
> It told 'twas sunset, and he cursed that sun.
> Again—again—that form he madly pressed,
> Which mutely clasped, imploringly caressed!
> And tottering to the couch his bride he bore,
> One moment gazed—as if to gaze no more;
> Felt that for him Earth held but her alone,
> Kissed her cold forehead—turned—is Conrad gone?
>
> (*The Corsair*, I.xiv)

And this, it must be said, follows more than one hundred lines in the same vein and goes on for another twenty-five.

By 1823 Byron was losing little time over nonessentials. The principal battle is passed over in silence: "The fight was o'er . . . . The mutineers were crushed, dispersed, or ta'en" (III.i). Christian and two others remain briefly at large, but "their guilt-won Paradise" no longer shields them from "the vengeance of their country's law" (III.ii). Pursuit follows quickly, and they have to flee.

The "renegades" remain dauntless; Christian is "Obdurate as a portion of the rock / Whereon he stood"; but Byron cuts these heroics off short:

> They stood, the three, as the three hundred stood
> Who dyed Thermopylae with holy blood.
> But ah! how different! 'tis the *cause* makes all,
> Degrades or hallows courage in its fall . . . .
> .   .   .   .
> However boldly their warm blood was spilt,
> Their Life was shame, their Epitaph was guilt.
> And this they knew and felt, at least the one,
> The leader of the band he had undone . . . .
>
> (IV.xi)

The crew carries out its "duty"; the resistance is fierce but finally in vain; and Christian, defiant to the last, casts himself off a cliff. Byron's comment is pitying rather than admiring:

> The rest was nothing—save a life mis-spent,
> And soul—but who shall answer where it went?
> 'Tis ours to bear, not judge the dead; and they

> Who doom to Hell, themselves are on the way,
> Unless these bullies of eternal pains
> Are pardoned their bad hearts for their worse brains.
> (IV.xii)

The futility of such earlier heroes as Selim, Conrad, Lara, and Alp is implicit in their ends, but here Byron says it outright, though he resolutely mocks the self-righteous. Like the others, Christian has thrown off all restraints of law and social order and become a renegade; and he is hunted down like the wild beast he has made himself (III.i). Byron calls him *"this poor victim of self-will"* (IV.xii; my italics): Christian is deluded and fallen, not superhuman. Byron treats him with sympathy, and he retains some nobility (III.vi), but having cast off discipline Christian has made a "moral wreck" of himself as well as of the *Bounty*. His act was criminal folly, as is said at the outset:

> And now the self-elected Chief finds time
> To stun the first sensation of his crime,
> And raise it in his followers—"Ho! the bowl!"
> Lest passion should return to reason's shoal.
> (I.vi)

After the first defeat Christian proudly says,

> "For me, my lot is what I sought; to be,
> In life or death, the fearless and the free."
> (III.vi)

But this freedom, gained at the expense of duty, brings only chaos and ruin.

Critics have made a great deal of Torquil's escape, finding in it Byron's "solution" to human problems. This is a peculiar misreading of the tale. As I have shown, the poem is laden with explicit condemnations of the mutineers' attempt to escape from duty and responsibility; are we really to infer that the work betrays an unconscious "urge to regress to an infantile state of irresponsibility," as a recent critic puts it?[24] On the contrary, it seems to me that the whole point of the radical division made between civilization and nature is to reinforce the idea that natural innocence, once lost, cannot be regained. The tale is a conscious rejection of "infantile irresponsibility." Christian and his men have sought an escape which is not and cannot be open to them, for they seek a serenity and freedom from responsibility such "as *only* the *yet* infant world displays," as the poem's final line puts it (my italics).

M. K. Joseph correctly notes that Byron's attitude toward the island is ambiguous: it is a place of beauty, joy, and peace, *but* it is also the temptation which sets off the mutiny. Throughout the first canto Byron emphasizes this. The undeniable charm of the island and the complete freedom it offers constitute for civilized man a dangerous temptation to reject responsibility. Torquil can be spared because the island is his natural habitat and he is merely a friend of the mutineers, not one of them. The island is Byron's lotus, but he resolutely refuses to sanction "fond forgetfulness of life."

Ten years earlier Byron might have told this tale as a story of doomed rebellion against tyranny. Here his focus is on the moral wreck which comes from yielding to the temptation of "self-will" and on the retribution which follows. The island *is* beautiful, and even after the defeat Christian views Torquil and Neuha with "a gloomy joy" (III. ix), but there is no way for him to share the simplicity of their way of life. There is no sentimentalism here, and when Byron says that the public will stupidly prefer the "most pamby portions," we may guess that he is expressing his impatience at mooning over the unavailable. The totality of the division Byron draws between civilization and nature makes Torquil's way of life not an ideal but a dangerous temptation. Thematically, *The Island* rests on issues raised in the dramas. Self-indulgence in place of discipline in *The Deformed Transformed* and evasion of responsibility in *Werner* are clearly shown to be bad; here too Byron's vision is bluntly moral. Self-will cannot be indulged at the expense of social order. Among critics of *The Island* only Cooke has taken this view.[25] "Mutiny is abhorrent; so is its punishment"—but, though Byron feels the temptation of the island and can see a certain grandeur in the mutineers' defiance, he utterly rejects them.

The new firmness and clarity of this moral perspective are paralleled by a poetic economy utterly lacking in the earlier narrative tales, as the two farewell scenes quoted earlier show. Byron's relatively terse essays in monologue stand him in good stead. Almost every line in *The Island* can be read for its sense; far too often in the early tales Byron wallows in long descriptions which are more atmospheric than strictly meaningful, but in *The Island* even the idyllic descriptions are thematically as well as atmospherically relevant. The poem's humor is often criticized, and perhaps with some justice, for it does not always blend well with the predominating mood. Its inclusion is not, I think, mere self-indulgence, but rather a sign of Byron's difficulties in controlling the tone of the poem and guiding the reader's response. Here he refuses to let us become engrossed in the agonies of the outlaw-hero. Consequently, we do not enter Christian's mind, and Ben Bunting is made to serve as a foil to his gloomy leader, making the mutineers seem more human and ordinary, more pitiable than grand. The narrator's own occasional humorous interjections both lighten the severity of his tone and help hold us off from a story we are not to be allowed to revel in. For example:

> his pistols were
> Linked to his belt, a matrimonial pair
> (Let not this metaphor appear a scoff,
> Though one missed fire, the other would go off) . . . .
>
> (II.xx)

It is important to recognize that *The Island* is not a "throwback" or a "return" to an earlier style, but rather a new departure based on a synthesis of earlier endeavors. It is not a "culmination," but it does represent a definite step in a progression. The early tales are to a considerable degree escapist and frivolous, but they are for Byron the beginnings of a form which increasingly he makes the vehicle of a serious exploration of the psychology of exiled and alienated man. Through all of the tales and monologues runs the problem of self-knowledge. The early heroes are driven to outlawry and destruction by a "self-will" over which they have scarcely any control. With the monologue-speakers we enter the minds of men pushed into "exile" and follow their attempts to understand and control themselves. *The Island*—which breaks with the monologue form and interior perspective and returns to the earlier sort of hero— is a study of the sort of self-delusion whose results we see in the early tales but which is never analyzed there in any detail.

Studying the tales as a group lets us see how radically Byron's handling of the outlaw-hero changes. *The Island* starts with a deliberate act of self-will which places the mutineers outside the bounds of society. For the first time Byron explores the temptation and concentrates on the retribution which follows, explicitly rather than implicitly condemning "the Byronic hero." Admiration for gallantry remains, but we are given a far clearer and colder view of Christian than of any of his predecessors—the mysterious grandeur is gone. Gone too are the deliberate obscurities and Gothic trappings of the early tales; by 1823 Byron was satirizing such devices in *Don Juan*, XVI. Compared to *The Corsair* or *Lara*, with their emphasis on dark and night, *The Island* is sunny, though far more than they it is tinged by sadness and a serious sense of responsibility. Increasingly throughout the tales Byron deals with the conflict between self-will and responsibility: *The Island* stands as the furthest development of his growing insistence upon honest self-knowledge, restraint, and control. It is indeed curious that Byron, so often considered the most self-willed of men, came increasingly to affirm the necessity of self-discipline.[26]

NOTES

1. It is the nine works discussed in this paragraph which are generally printed under the heading of "tales" (for example, by Paul Elmer More, and in the Oxford Standard Authors edition) and commonly discussed as such. My references in this essay are to *The Works of Lord Byron: Poetry*, ed. E. H. Coleridge (London, 1898–1904), where the works are printed more by chronology than by type. It is only fair to note that Byron himself subsequently regretted his use of the term "tale." In a letter to Thomas Moore dated 25 March 1817 Byron says, "Talking of tail, I wish you had not called it [Moore's *Lalla Rookh*] a *'Persian Tale.'* Say a *'Poem,'* or *'Romance,'* but not 'Tale.' I am very sorry that I called some of my own things *'Tales,'* because I think that they are something better" (*The Works of Lord Byron: Letters and Journals*, ed. R. E. Prothero [London, 1898–1901], IV, 78). And on the same day he wrote to John Murray, *"tale* is a word of which it repents me to have nicknamed poesy. 'Fable' would be better" (*Letters and Journals*, IV, 85). The later "tales" bear no descriptive phrase, though we may note that *Mazeppa* concludes with "To thank his tale . . ." and *The Island* ends, "The tale was told; and then . . . ."

2. Of course distant settings are relative. To Mrs. Radcliffe and M. G. Lewis, Italy and Spain seemed quite reasonably remote; to Byron they were anything but that.

3. M. K. Joseph, *Byron the Poet* (London, 1964), p. 48.

4. Robert F. Gleckner, *Byron and the Ruins of Paradise* (Baltimore, Maryland, 1967); Jerome J. McGann, *Fiery Dust: Byron's Poetic Development* (Chicago, 1968); W. Paul Elledge, *Byron and the Dynamics of Metaphor* (Nashville, Tennessee, 1968).

5. M. K. Joseph comments that Hugo and Parisina have little in common with the earlier outlaw heroes, but rather belong to "the liberal martyrology" charac-

teristic of *Childe Harold* III and IV, "the later Tales," *The Lament of Tasso* and *The Prophecy of Dante* (p. 40). I heartily concur in seeing the resemblance, though my reading of the various works is considerably different.

6. Of the other "Italian poems," the "Ode on Venice" is neither a narrative nor a monologue; *Morgante Maggiore* and *Francesca da Rimini* are straight translations. *Beppo* is a narrative of sorts but is clearly transitional: Beppo's adventures —which are scarcely mentioned—might have been the subject of one of the early tales, but here ironic commentary in what was to become the final satiric manner completely displaces the narrative. M. K. Joseph comments that *Beppo* is "like one of the Turkish Tales turned inside-out" (p. 135).

7. Andrew Rutherford, *Byron: A Critical Study* (Stanford, California, 1961), pp. 35–47, 66–75.

8. William H. Marshall, *The Structure of Byron's Major Poems* (Philadelphia, Pennsylvania, 1962).

9. Gleckner, pp. 133–138.

10. William H. Marshall, "The Accretive Structure of Byron's *The Giaour*," *MLN*, LXXVI 1961), 502–509; cf. Gleckner, pp. 91–117.

11. M. G. Cooke, *The Blind Man Traces the Circle: On the Patterns and Philosophy of Byron's Poetry* (Princeton, 1969), p. 171.

12. Cooke, p. 74n.

13. Gleckner, pp. 164–175.

14. See William H. Marshall, "Byron's *Parisina* and the Function of Psychoanalytic Criticism," *The Personalist*, XLII (1961), 213–223, and *The Structure*, pp. 62–71; and Elledge's rebalancing of this interpretation (pp. 28–29).

15. See Gleckner's discussion, p. 178.

16. See particularly the analyses of Marshall (*The Structure*, pp. 111–120), Gleckner (pp. 190–199), McGann (pp. 165–173), and Cooke (pp. 87–88).

17. See Marshall, *The Structure*, p. 119.

18. See William H. Marshall, "A Reading of Byron's *Mazeppa*," *MLN*, LXXVI (1961), 120–124, and *The Structure*, also pp. 120–124; and McGann, pp. 174–185. (Rather surprisingly, McGann does not discuss Marshall's very different interpretation.)

19. "Advertisement": "The foundation of the following story will be found partly in Lieutenant Bligh's 'Narrative of the Mutiny and Seizure of the Bounty, in the South Seas, in 1789'; and partly in 'Mariner's Account of the Tonga Islands.' "

20. Rutherford, pp. 138–139; 202–203.

21. Joseph, p. 63; Gleckner, pp. 350–351; McGann, pp. 198, 201.

22. *Letters and Journals*, VI, 164–165 (25 January 1823).

23. E. H. Coleridge remarks in his introductory note (V, 581–584) that it is odd that Byron was apparently unaware of the actual fate of the mutineers. Pitcairn Island was visited as early as 1808 and an account of what was learned was published in the *Quarterly Review* in 1810. Leslie Marchand, in *Byron's Poetry* (Cambridge, Mass., 1968; orig. 1965), suggests that if Byron "had known all the facts he would undoubtedly, with his natural hatred of tyranny and his tendency to espouse the cause of the rebellious underdog, have taken the side of Christian and his comrades" (pp. 72–73). This is conceivable, but the whole nature of the work as we have it suggests that Byron was bent on rejecting sympathy for the mutineers, and further speculation seems idle. It is fair to say, though, that Byron still had some inclination to glorify the outlaw, as the letter to Leigh Hunt indi-

cates. Byron says he had to try "not to run counter to the reigning stupidity altogether, otherwise they will say that I am eulogizing *Mutiny*. This must produce tameness in some degree" (*Letters and Journals*, VI, 164).

24. Bernard Blackstone, *The Lost Travellers: A Romantic Theme with Variations* (London, 1962), p. 212.

25. Cooke, pp. 211–212. I would like to add that the view of Byron's outlook which I am presenting here is quite conformable, particularly in regard to the notion of "paradise," to the interpretation of E. D. Hirsch, Jr. See his essay, "Byron and the Terrestrial Paradise," in *From Sensibility to Romanticism: Essays Presented to Frederick A. Pottle,* ed. Frederick W. Hilles and Harold Bloom (New York, 1965), pp. 467–486.

26. I would like to record my debt to Maurice Johnson (University of Pennsylvania) for helpful criticism of this essay.

BYRON AND NATHANIEL HAWTHORNE
Richard Harter Fogle

Nathaniel Hawthorne tried hard to see life and literature comprehensively. Thus, there was no dominant emphasis in his reading and literary sources. There was of course his Puritan heritage: Spenser, Milton, John Bunyan, and his New England forebears. We have his library withdrawals from the Salem Athenaeum; these range widely, with a considerable representation of the English Augustans. He was conversant, too, with both eighteenth-century sentimentalism and rationalism, in English and in French. Of the English Romantics, his near-contemporaries, there is a substantial number of entries. He read the poetry of Coleridge, Shelley, and Keats in a well-known contemporary edition, and much of Coleridge's prose as it appeared. He checked out Byron's poems from time to time, Wordsworth's less frequently.[1] As a youth he is said to have been greatly smitten with Byron's *Childe Harold*.[2]

External evidence does not, then, indicate that the great English Romantic poets were constantly on Hawthorne's mind. One does not discern, either, an overwhelming interest in them from the internal evidence of his writings; Hawthorne had a very capacious imagination and intellect, which could handle a great deal without imbalance, and his fiction habitually assimilates and recreates its sources. It is nevertheless fair to say that the relationship between Hawthorne and the great English Romantics has been underrated in the past, and that it is important for a true estimate of his mind and his fiction.

There are specific allusions to the Romantics scattered throughout Hawthorne's *English* and *American Notebooks,* including a considerable proportion devoted to Byron, who in addition receives attention in the later *French and Italian Notebooks.*[3] To my eye there are hundreds of significant parallels to the Romantic poets in Hawthorne's tales and sketches, along

181

with some explicit references. These most frequently evoke Coleridge and Shelley, Keats somewhat less, and Wordsworth and Byron less discernibly but with large implications.[4] Their tracks are harder to trace in Hawthorne's novels, but, as we shall notice, there is at least one important relationship between Byron and *The Marble Faun.* In more detail, I have seemed to myself to observe about fifteen specific instances of Byronic influence in Hawthorne's canon of tales; starting from the other end with Byron's text, I find approximately forty passages from his poems that have general parallels in Hawthorne's thought, themes, and imagination. It is perhaps just as well to say herewith that I do not intend to take the reader fully into my confidence about these.

Of Hawthorne's acquaintance with Byron's life and works there can be no question. His most extensive reference to Byron occurs in a strange sketch, "P.'s Correspondence," published in 1845 in the *Democratic Review.* This sketch, it should be explained, is a grimly ingenious Hawthornean fancy. The correspondent, poor P., "has lost the thread of his life by the interposition of long intervals of partially disordered reason. The past and present are jumbled together in his mind in a manner often productive of curious results." P. is in fact confined to a New England lunatic asylum, but supposes himself to be in a London apartment, "writing beside the hearth, over which hangs a print of Queen Victoria, listening to the muffled roar of the world's metropolis, and with a window at but five paces distant, through which, whenever I please, I can gaze out on actual London."

P.'s central derangement is a reversal of time: the illustrious dead are to him alive and walking the London streets, while the living are dead. The sketch deals with most of the major English Romantics and some others, all of whom are viewed in this upside-down perspective. Wordsworth, for example, to P. "died only a week or two ago. Heaven rest his soul, and grant that he may not have completed The Excursion!" (By which it appears that unfeeling jokes about *The Excursion* were current in 1845, as they are now.) Conversely, Keats is still alive in London, an elusive, wistful shadow. "I have not seen him except across a crowded street, with coaches, drays, horsemen, cabs, omnibuses, foot passengers, and divers other sensual obstructions intervening betwixt his small and slender figure and my eager glance." As for Byron, P. is in constant contact with him.

Lord Byron, "his early tendency to obesity having increased
. . . is now enormously fat." This is a fair inference from
Byron's abnormal tendency to take on weight, and shows an
easy familiarity with Byron biography. As we well know, it is
not easy to fix on any central impression of the Protean Byron;
perhaps we end up with variability itself. His enormous prestige
and daemonic personality dazzled observers, who found it hard
to be objective about him. P., for his part, seems Hawthorneanly
disposed to moralize: "Were I disposed to be caustic," he says,
"I might consider this mass of earthly matter as the symbol, in
a material shape, of those evil habits and carnal vices which
unspiritualize man's nature and clog up his avenues of communication with the better life." This austere suggestion turns
out, however, to be a false trail that Hawthorne has deliberately laid down.

Byron, it would appear, has in his posthumous life become
a model of respectability and a pillar of conventional society.
He has been reconciled with Lady Byron, a circumstance of
which it is rather dubiously remarked that "They are said to
be, if not a happy, at least a contented, or at all events a quiet
couple." Under his wife's influence Byron "now combines the
most rigid tenets of Methodism with the ultra doctrines of the
Puseyites." "Much of whatever expenditure his increasing habits
of thrift [a hit at Byron's self-confessed avarice] continue to
allow him is bestowed in the reparation or beautifying of places
of worship." In politics he has become a conservative, "who
loses no opportunity, whether in the House of Lords or in private circles, of denouncing and repudiating the mischievous and
anarchical notions of his earlier day." His present bulk, as it
turns out, is a symbol not of his "evil habits and carnal vices"
but, instead, of his stultifying respectability. His vitality has
disappeared along with his outrageousness.

P. has failed not, he says, "to pay the meed of homage due
to a mighty poet, by allusions in Childe Harold, and Manfred,
and Don Juan, which have made so large a portion of the music
of my life." Now, however, he finds that Byron is preparing a
new edition of his complete works, which is "carefully corrected,
expurgated and amended, in accordance with his present creed
of taste, morals and religion." "The very passages of highest
inspiration" that P. has most admired are those that Byron is
most anxious to eradicate. "To whisper you the truth," says P.,
"it appears to me that his passions having burned out, the
extinction of their vivid and riotous flame has deprived Lord

Byron of the illumination by which he not merely wrote, but was enabled to feel and comprehend what he had written. Positively he no longer understands his own poetry."

Hawthorne's implied estimate of Byron is essentially sympathetic and Romantic. It treats him as a vital unity, in P.'s words a "vivid and riotous flame," and what have been taken to be his faults are in truth inseparable from the life and the identity of his achievement. Hawthorne's picture of Byron the man is at once shrewd and sympathetic, though lightly touched. Looking at Byron strictly from outside, it may be said that he was one of those unfortunate people whose lives are interesting and entertaining to almost everybody but themselves. He was intensely human and delightfully unregenerate: he heard the chimes at midnight with Tom Moore and Richard Brinsley Sheridan; titled ladies jumped in his windows to get at him; he got into all sorts of mischief and invariably blabbed about it; and he quarreled so fascinatingly with his wife that to this day we are arguing about the rights and wrongs of the famous separation. Recent research in hitherto unpublished material makes him look better than Lady Byron, as Hawthorne obliquely suggested of him in his 1845 "P.'s Correspondence."[5]

Like many others, Hawthorne was deeply interested in the separation. Years later in 1856, at a breakfast in London at Richard Monckton Milnes's, he fell into conversation with the mother of Florence Nightingale, a friend of Lady Byron's, who spoke of her "as a most excellent and exemplary person, high-principled, unselfish, and now devoting herself to the care of her two grandchildren." Hawthorne had his doubts: "Somehow or other, all this praise, and more of the same kind, gave me the idea of an intolerably irreproachable person." He asked Mrs. Nightingale "if Lady Byron was warm-hearted. With some hesitation, or mental reservation . . . she answered that she was."[6] Still later, Hawthorne speaks of "the cause (recently communicated to me) of the separation of Lady Byron from her husband." Consulting "a literary man about town" on the subject, he hears "another solution of the mystery, quite as discreditable to Byron. I hope neither is true."[7]

Byron, then, had some place in Hawthorne's thoughts for a good many years. He is said to have read *Childe Harold* with absorption as a youth, and the records of the Salem Athenaeum show withdrawals of Byron's poetry and his biography, the latter through Tom Moore and Leigh Hunt. I have noted the allusion to *Childe Harold, Manfred,* and *Don Juan* in "P.'s Correspondence," in addition to references in Hawthorne's American, English, and Italian *Notebooks.* Byron also appears explicitly in his fiction, not frequently but with assured familiarity. Thus in "The Seven Vagabonds" (*Twice-Told Tales*) the narrator comes upon "some of Byron's minor poems" (along with a Life of Franklin and Webster's Spelling-Book) on a casual book-stall of odds and ends. In "The Procession of Life" (*Mosses from an Old Manse*) Hawthorne seeks a proper ranking for mankind, deeper than accident or "the conventional distinctions of society." In his new and universal order "those whom the gifts of intellect have united in a noble brotherhood" will form an important class, in which Byron and Burns may join hands together. "Were Byron now alive, and Burns, the first would come from his ancestral abbey, flinging aside, though unwillingly, the inherited honors of a thousand years, to take the arm of the mighty peasant who grew immortal while he stooped behind his plough."

"Earth's Holocaust" (*Mosses*) casts all the past, including its literature, into a single bonfire. In this Byron's fate is equivocal, though he comes out better than Moore. "Speaking of the properties of flame, methought Shelley's poetry emitted a purer light than almost any other productions of his day, contrasting beautifully with the fitful and lurid gleams and gushes of black vapor that flashed and eddied from the volumes of Lord Byron. As for Tom Moore, some of his songs diffused an odor like a burning pastil." This glances at the tradition of Byron's diabolism, but like the "vivid and riotous flame" of "P.'s Correspondence" it pays implicit tribute to Byron's vitality.

"Passages from a Relinquished Work" (*Mosses*), like "The Seven Vagabonds," employs a wanderer as narrator and interpreter. Byron immediately comes to the wanderer's mind, although with a difference. He departs with joy from his guardian and his native village, "bade it a joyous farewell, and turned away to follow any path but that which might lead me back. Never was Childe Harold's sentiment adopted in a spirit more unlike his own." "A Virtuoso's Collection" (*Mosses*) contains two items that may well have been culled from Byron: "the spinning-wheel of Sardanapalus" and the lamp that "Hero set forth to the midnight breeze in the high tower of Abydos." The Virtuoso himself turns out to be The Wandering Jew, a figure far from un-Byronic.

I recollect only one direct and significant reference to Byron in Hawthorne's major romances, but this one is indicative of considerably more than itself with regard to Byron's influence on Hawthorne. At the same time it is thoroughly characteristic of Hawthorne's own imagination. The reference occurs in a description (chapter XVII) of the Coliseum by moonlight in *The Marble Faun*. "The splendour of the revelation took away that inestimable effect of dimness and mystery, by which the imagination might be assisted to build a grander structure than the Coliseum, and to shatter it with a more picturesque decay." Hawthorne, it should be remarked, is in his fiction "much possessed" by moonlight. At times it is the light of romance itself, the indispensable atmosphere of his art. Correspondingly, on occasion it comes close to symbolizing imaginative truth, the ultimate refinement of vision. He was, however, a cautious man: moonlight can represent mere fancy or even delusion and "lunacy," as in his tale "My Kinsman, Major Molineux." Further, though more a symbolist than Byron, like Byron he is unwilling to rest within his symbol; moonlight can have different meanings in different contexts, it can be limited by considerations of plot, of shading, and of plain verisimilitude. Here, for instance, it has been specified (chapter XVI, "A Moonlight Ramble") that we are dealing with *Roman* moonlight, "which seemed to have a delicate purple or crimson lustre, or at least some richer tinge than the cold, white moonshine of other skies."

To return to the later passage in *The Marble Faun*, "Byron's celebrated description is better than the reality. He beheld the scene in his mind's eye, through the witchery of many intervening years, and faintly illuminated it, as if with starlight, instead of this broad glow of moonshine." Hawthorne concludes by mentioning "a party of English or Americans, paying the inevitable visit by moonlight, and exalting themselves with raptures that were Byron's, not their own." It would seem that he is remembering rather than referring to *Childe Harold*, and that his memory plays him false, since Byron's medium *is* moonlight:

> Her Coliseum stands; the moonbeams shine
> As 'twere its natural torches—for divine
> Should be the light which streams here,—to illume
> This long-explored but still exhaustless mine
> Of Contemplation . . . .
>
> (IV.128)

Nevertheless, he catches the larger picture, with Byron's imaginative distancing through Time as its true medium; and in this he is at once influenced by Byron and thoroughly true to himself.

Hawthorne may also have been thinking of another famous description of the Coliseum by moonlight, as Manfred remembers it (III.iv.31-38):

> And thou didst shine, thou rolling Moon, upon
> All this, and cast a wide and tender light,
> Which softened down the hoar austerity
> Of rugged desolation, and filled up,
> As 'twere anew, the gaps of centuries;
> Leaving that beautiful which still was so,
> And making that which was not—till the place
> Became religion . . . .

This strongly suggests the idealizing effect of moonlight upon the Pyncheon garden, as in Byron an artistic triumph over time. "With the lapse of every moment, the garden grew more picturesque; the fruit trees, shrubbery, and flower bushes had a dark obscurity among them. The commonplace characteristics —which, at noontide, it seemed to have taken a century of sordid life to accumulate—were now transfigured by a charm of romance" (*The House of the Seven Gables,* chapter 14).

Childe Harold probably had a more powerful influence upon Hawthorne's imagination than any other work of Byron's. The reverberations of the Time-theme of Canto IV are too extensive to discuss here at length, in their effects upon *The House of the Seven Gables* and *The Marble Faun*. For Hawthorne, Byron's Time, which held within it both continuity and contrast, was a constant preoccupation. He inherited—and Byron was part of his heritage—an immense reverence for classical antiquity. His own ancestral past was more important to him, in the deep sense, than Byron's was to Byron, and correspondingly the problem of antique paganism more worrisome to him, yet his sense of history resembled Byron's. Greece and Rome were his symbols for human greatness, and the measure of human achievement. As with Byron, there was for Hawthorne a nonhistorical Paradise, long lost, of innocence, purity, and ideal beauty, and there had been the Fall that made human history a tragedy. Yet in both there was also at least a partial sense of the continuity of history; whatever the import of the past, it could not be dismissed.

Thus, no good could come from destroying the fabric of human institutions and beliefs. On the one hand radical reform was doomed to fail because of the fallen nature of man; on the other, because of the mysterious continuity of man's affairs, as they constitute history. The issue was simple neither to Byron nor Hawthorne. Byron was a Liberal and Hawthorne a Democrat; both believed that man's lot could be in some degree ameliorated. But in the end the past was inescapable. Byron is brilliantly paradoxical in his portraits of Rousseau, Voltaire, and Gibbon, those heaven-scaling rebels, in the third canto of *Childe Harold*. He admires—he is exhilarated by—their temerity, but is fearful of their destructiveness:

> They made themselves a fearful monument!
> The wreck of old opinions—things which grew,
> Breathed from the birth of Time: the veil they rent,
> And what behind it lay, all earth shall view.
> But good with ill they also overthrew,
> Leaving but ruins, wherewith to rebuild
> Upon the same foundation, and renew
> Dungeons and thrones, which the same hour refilled,
> As heretofore, because Ambition was self-willed.
>   (82)

Hawthorne draws the same conclusion in "Earth's Holocaust," earlier mentioned. "Once upon a time . . . this wide world had become so overburdened with an accumulation of wornout trumpery that the inhabitants determined to rid themselves of it by a general bonfire." Everything goes into the fire, including the Bible, the world's total stock of "spirituous and fermented liquors," and, as we have seen, the complete works of Byron. Reformers are delighted, while some, including reprobates, are deeply dismayed. A "dark-visaged stranger," however, clearly the Devil himself, laughs at the whole business. The human heart remains, " 'And, unless they hit upon some method of purifying that foul cavern, forth from it will reissue all the shapes of wrong and misery—the same old shapes or worse ones—which they have taken such a vast deal of trouble to consume to ashes . . . . Oh, take my word for it, it will be the old world yet!' "

So, too, in "The Celestial Railroad" (*Mosses*) the progressives have found a strictly modern way of getting to Heaven— a railroad train. John Bunyan's kind of transportation is completely superseded. "Instead of a lonely and ragged man with a huge burden on his back, plodding along sorrowfully on foot while the whole city hooted after him, here were parties of the first gentry and most respectable people in the neighborhood setting forth towards the Celestial City as cheerfully as if the pilgrimage were merely a summer tour." Especially remarkable is the fashion in which the new technology has disposed of Original Sin: "One great convenience of the new method of going on pilgrimage I must not forget to mention. Our enormous burdens, instead of being carried on our shoulders as had been the custom of old, were all snugly deposited in the baggage car, and, as I was assured, would be delivered to their respective owners at the journey's end." (A most heretical interpretation of the doctrine of Vicarious Atonement.) The whole affair turns out a dreadful cheat: the narrator's guide, Mr. Smooth-it-away, is an "impudent fiend" and Hell is the real destination, from which the narrator is rescued only by awakening. "Thank Heaven it was a Dream!"

Childe Harold presents more particular resemblances to Hawthorne, in passages that may have lain in Hawthorne's memory. The juxtaposition is startling, but the apostrophe to Ada at the end of Canto III could well have contributed to Pearl in *The Scarlet Letter*. Byron calls his daughter

> The child of Love, though born in bitterness,
> And nurtured in Convulsion! Of thy sire
> These were the elements,—and thine no less.
> As yet such are around thee,—but thy fire
> Shall be more tempered, and thy hope far higher!

So Pearl is the child of love—" 'What we did," says Hester to Dimmesdale, "had a consecration of its own' "—and she is most emphatically "born in bitterness, and nurtured in convulsion." Such, indeed, are Hester's sufferings on the scaffold that they impart themselves to the infant, "who, drawing its sustenance from the maternal bosom, seemed to have drank in with it all the turmoil, the anguish and despair, which pervaded the mother's system. It now writhed in convulsions of pain, and was a forcible type, in its little frame, of the moral agony which Hester Prynne had borne throughout the day" (chapter 4). Ada is the creature of her father's disharmonies, Pearl the product of Hester's. "The mother's impassioned state had been the medium through which were transmitted to the unborn infant the rays of its moral life; and, however white and clear originally, they had taken the deep stains of crimson and gold, the fiery lustre, the black shadow, and the untempered light of the intervening substance."

A single phrase in *Childe Harold* was echoed and reechoed in Hawthorne, "the electric chain." Byron is speaking of the psychic effects of suffering:

> But ever and anon of griefs subdued
> There comes a token like a Scorpion's sting,
> Scarce seen, but with fresh bitterness imbued;
> And slight withal may be the things which bring
> Back on the heart the weight which it would fling
> Aside for ever: it may be a sound—
> A tone of music—summer's eve—or spring—
> A flower—the wind—the Ocean—which shall wound,
> Striking the electric chain wherewith we are darkly bound . . . .
>
> (IV.23)

"The electric chain" is here the vital principle of the individual psyche; Hawthorne employs it for sympathy, the vital and indispensable relation of man to men, an emotional all-in-each.

The notion is central to *The Scarlet Letter,* redeeming as it does the isolation of the central three characters enforced by the original sin of Hester's and Dimmesdale's adultery. Thus, in "The Minister's Vigil" (chapter 12), the anguished Dimmesdale stands alone on the scaffold at night, where Hester and Pearl come upon him by accident. He asks them to join him. Hester "silently ascended the steps, and stood on the platform, holding little Pearl by the hand. The minister felt for the child's other hand, and took it. The moment that he did so, there came what seemed a tumultuous rush of new life, other life than his own, pouring like a torrent into his heart, and hurrying through all his veins, as if the mother and the child were communicating their vital warmth to his half-torpid system. The three formed an electric chain."

In itself this union is incomplete, and even to a degree false, since the minister refuses to accept its consequences. He will not avow it: " 'the daylight of this world shall not see our meeting!' " At the end, however, he wins redemption for all three by revealing the connection publicly on this same scaffold. The Puritan crowd, assembled on a great and symbolic holiday, "beheld the minister, leaning on Hester's shoulder, and supported by her arm around him, approach the scaffold, and ascend its steps; while still the little hand of the sin-born child was clasped in his." The electric chain of human sympathy, acknowledged, exerts its power.

Slightly varied, the phrase occurs again in "Ethan Brand," Hawthorne's most radical study of spiritual disharmony and alienation. Brand, originally "a simple and loving man," transforms himself into a remorseless analyst of the human heart; he perversely determines to discover the Unpardonable Sin. He finds it in himself, for the quest irrevocably separates his intellect from his feelings in a fatal division of head and heart. Intellectually he now stands "on a starlit eminence," but his heart has perished. "He has lost his hold of the magnetic chain of humanity. He was no longer a brother-man, opening the chains or the dungeons of our common nature by the key of holy sympathy, which gave him a right to share in all its secrets; he was now a cold observer, looking on mankind as the subject of his experiment."

"Ethan Brand" is Hawthorne's most extreme case, but it is generally agreed that, abstractly speaking, isolation is the principal theme of his fiction. It is the continual problem of his most interesting characters, the crux of his tensest situations, a noble malady suffered by all complex natures. As with Brand, it usually manifests itself in a separation of the "head" and "heart." Artists are subject to it: for example, the gifted painter of "The Prophetic Pictures" (*Twice-Told Tales*), and Owen Warland, "The Artist of the Beautiful" (*Mosses*). Scientists, such as Dr. Rappaccini or Aylmer of "The Birthmark" (*Mosses*) are even more susceptible. Philanthropists become monomaniacs in their zeal for the general good, as does Hollingsworth of *The Blithedale Romance*. Women of great talent and intelligence are forced into it by the situation of their sex, as happens with Hester Prynne, Zenobia of *Blithedale,* and Miriam in *The Marble Faun*. Victims are condemned to it, as with Ilbrahim of "The Gentle Boy," *The Marble Faun*'s Hilda, and *Blithedale*'s Priscilla. Some are imprisoned in isolation by some innate lack, like Wakefield, "The Outcast of the Universe" (*Twice-Told Tales*), or Gervayse Hastings ("The Christmas Banquet," *Mosses*).[8]

Positively isolation is spiritual pride, a disease for which the cure is humility, self-abnegation, and self-revelation. " 'Be true! Be true! Be true!' " says *The Scarlet Letter*. " 'Show freely to the world, if not your worst, yet some trait whereby the worst may be inferred!' " One notes the dark assumption that the truth is pretty bad. Poor Clifford Pyncheon, a victim, tries to rejoin the human race by an abortive attempt to throw himself down from a window of the House of the Seven Gables into a procession that is passing in the street. The acute Miles Coverdale (*Blithedale*) ends up as a male Sleeping Beauty never to be awakened, because he cannot forgo his spiritual privacy.

Hawthorne gives us redemptions, as with Dimmesdale, Hollingsworth, and perhaps Miriam, but never imaginatively portrays the redeemed man or woman, whether because the moment of salvation itself is ultimate, or perhaps that isolation is simply the human condition, and proper field of his fiction. At any rate, the disease is generally more interesting to the reader than the recovery. It is perhaps too simple to affirm, with *Childe Harold* and *Manfred* particularly in mind, that Hawthorne is writing a critique of the Byronic Hero. It is not, however, too much to say that his preoccupations bear strong resemblances to Byron's, and that, as in Byron's poems, it is the tragic dilemma that remains with us.

Byron's hero is fated to isolation from causes beyond his will. He is not fit for the normal intercourse of men:

> To fly from, need not be to hate, mankind:
> All are not fit with them to stir and toil,
> Nor is it discontent to keep the mind
> Deep in its fountain, lest it overboil
> In the hot throng, where we become the spoil
> Of our infection, till too late and long
> We may deplore and struggle with the coil,
> In wretched interchange of wrong for wrong
> Midst a contentious world, striving where none are strong.
>   (*Childe Harold*, III.69)

Human ties are disastrous ("There, in a moment we may plunge our years/In fatal penitence"). By his own nature the hero must flee them, and wander eternally.

> The race of life becomes a hopeless flight
> To those that walk in darkness: on the sea
> The boldest steer but where their ports invite—
> But there are wanderers o'er Eternity
> Whose bark drives on and on, and anchored ne'er shall be.
>   (III.70)

In his youth Hawthorne was "handsomer than Byron," in the opinion of his wife-to-be and some others. He had other resemblances to the Byronic hero. Upon graduating from college he "fled from mankind" for twelve years, hiding himself away in his chamber while he learned to write. Looking back upon this period of his life, he viewed it as a kind of evil dream, from which he was released by the love of Sophia Peabody. Yet, like Byron, he made an apologia for self-isolation. As Byron found advantages in keeping the mind "Deep in its fountain" and avoiding "the hot throng" of "a contentious world," so Hawthorne was inclined to think that his loneness had preserved him, in cool and friendly shadow,[9] from premature exposure to the heat and the dust of the broad thoroughfare of ordinary life. How literal this isolation was is open to argument,[10] but there can be no question of its symbolic importance in Hawthorne's own mind. It left a permanent mark. As to the "contentious world," he was fleeing the bustle and competition of American life, in which the young American male was expected to immerse himself. When Hawthorne emerged from his chamber, Longfellow, Franklin Pierce, and Horatio Bridge, his Bowdoin collegemates, were successful men of the world, and the realization was sore, though deeply no genuine alternative had existed for him.

Manfred, the greatest Byronic hero, bears the stigmata of Hawthornean solitude:

> The lamp must be replenished, but even then
> It will not burn so long as I must watch:
> My slumbers—if I slumber—are not sleep,
> But a continuance of enduring thought,
> Which then I can resist not: in my heart
> There is a vigil, and these eyes but close
> To look within; and yet I live, and bear
> The aspect and the form of breathing men.
> But Grief should be the Instructor of the wise;
> Sorrow is Knowledge: they who know the most
> Must mourn the deepest o'er the fatal truth,
> The Tree of Knowledge is not that of Life.
> (*Manfred*, I.i.1–12)

Of Manfred's own literary ancestry it must of course be specified that he is Faustian. So too are a number of Hawthorne characters. The associations surrounding Faust invoke the legendary pact with supernatural powers, in *Manfred* the nexus of the plot. Not to mention other instances, Hawthorne's Ethan Brand is possessed of an attendant fiend, whom like Manfred he finally repudiates as a spiritual inferior. The accompanying

theme of unholy and illicit knowledge, so attractive both to
Byron and Shelley, is frequent in Hawthorne, though less purely
Gothic and more medieval and Puritan, with Spenser's Archim-
ago perhaps its archetypal wizard.

In his sleeplessness, and in his hinted eternality, Manfred is
a son of the Wandering Jew, whom he also resembles in his
inability to die by suicide:

> I feel the impulse—yet I do not plunge;
> I see the peril—yet do not recede;
> And my brain reels—and yet my foot is firm:
> There is a power upon me which withholds,
> And makes it my fatality to live . . . .
> (I.ii.20–24)

In Hawthorne's "Ethan Brand" the presence of the Wandering
Jew is adumbrated in a traveling showman, who is carrying the
Unpardonable Sin in his pack. As has been mentioned, the Jew
is the virtuoso of Hawthorne's "Virtuoso's Collection." Along
with other references, a passage in the *American Notebooks*
gives striking evidence of his interest in the famous wanderer:
he sets down a suggestion for a sketch, "A disquisition—or a
discussion between two or more persons—on the manner in
which the Wandering Jew has spent his life. One period, perhaps, in wild carnal debauchery; then trying, over and over
again, to grasp domestic happiness; then a soldier; then a states-
man &c—at last, realizing some truth."

The Jew is a great symbol of spiritual isolation, and Hawthorne was almost obsessively concerned with the theme of
earthly immortality as isolation. For Shelley, we recollect, the
Wandering Jew is a people's hero, the victim of immortal op-
pression bravely endured. For Byron, as we observe in *Manfred*
and *Childe Harold,* he is a symbol of the Byronic hero. To
Hawthorne he represents spiritual pride and error, and the resulting misery. The Elixir of Life, recurrent in his fiction, is a
fatal and delusory draught. In "Dr. Heidegger's Experiment"
(*Twice-Told Tales*) it is a momentary intoxication which leaves
a bitter hangover. In "The Birthmark" the scientist Aylmer is
capable of producing it, but forbears, since it would bring about
"a discord in Nature which all the world, and chiefly the quaffer
of the immortal nostrum, would find cause to curse." In the
tortuous unfinished novels of Hawthorne's "last phase," especially *The Dolliver Romance* and *Septimius Felton,* earthly im-

mortality is a chief preoccupation. He was unable to work out his meaning, but presumably it was to be ironic. The Elixir of Life would turn out to be eternal death instead.

Most significant for Hawthorne, however, was Manfred's discovery that "Sorrow is knowledge," the fatal truth that "The Tree of Knowledge is not that of Life." This is his division of head and heart, the deadly separation. Thus Ethan Brand conceives the Unpardonable Sin and is led into it. I quote an oft-quoted passage, the *locus classicus* on this theme.

> Then ensued that vast intellectual development, which, in its progress, disturbed the counterpoise between his mind and heart. The Idea that possessed his life had operated as a means of education; it had gone on cultivaitng his powers to the highest point of which they were susceptible; it had raised him from the level of an unlettered laborer to stand on a star-lit eminence, whither the philosophers of the earth, laden with the lore of the universities, might vainly strive to clamber after him. So much for the intellect! But where was the heart? That, indeed, had withered,—had contracted,—had hardened,—had perished! It had ceased to partake of the universal throb.

There is not space here to consider Byron's imagery of withering, hardening, and barrenness in *Manfred,* present also in *Childe Harold.*[11] Suffice it to say that it has its counterparts in Hawthorne's lost ones. Of Hester Prynne we find that "All the light and graceful foliage of her character had been withered up" by the "red-hot brand" of the Scarlet Letter. Her emotions are crushed, but her intellect is freed. "The world's law was no law for her mind. . . . She assumed a freedom of speculation. . . . In her lonesome cottage, by the sea-shore, thoughts visited her, such as dared to enter no other dwelling in New England." Chillingworth, a learned physician, ruins himself by his remorseless researches in the mind of the unhappy Dimmesdale. With Dimmesdale's escape and death he falls into annihilation. "All his strength and energy—all his vital and intellectual force—seemed at once to desert him; insomuch that he positively withered up, shrivelled away, and almost vanished from mortal sight, like an uprooted weed that lies wilting in the sun."

These parallels between Byron and Hawthorne have been presented as interesting relationships, mutually fertilizing; not as proofs of literal and particular influence. It has been shown that Hawthorne was well acquainted with Byron's life and with his poetry, and that he alluded directly to Byron at intervals for a considerable period of time. Consequently, the influence is probable enough, though not to be attributed flatly to any precise passage in either writer; in any event, the idea of literal transmission (or transcription) would be denigrating to Hawthorne and perhaps, by association, to Byron. As was earlier remarked, Hawthorne's literary interests were widely and rather evenly distributed, and his fiction is less allusive than that of most well-read authors. Whatever his sources, he transformed and re-created them thoroughly. For him, as for other sensitive readers, Byron would have been simply an unquestioned part of his cultural heritage, a large and nearby monument which he could not have failed to see. In sum, it seems to me that the relationship was considerable and is stimulating.

NOTES

1. See "Books Read by Nathaniel Hawthorne, 1828–1850," *Essex Institute Historical Collection*, LXVIII (1932), 65–87; and Marion L. Kesselring, "Hawthorne's Reading, 1828–1850," *BNYPL*, LIII (1949).

2. Hubert H. Hoeltje, *Inward Sky: The Mind and Heart of Nathaniel Hawthorne* (Durham, North Carolina, 1962), p. 28.

3. See *The American Notebooks by Nathaniel Hawthorne*, ed. Randall Stewart, (New Haven, 1932); *The English Notebooks by Nathaniel Hawthorne,* ed. Randall Stewart (New York, 1941); and *Passages from the French and Italian Note-Books* (Boston and New York, 1887). In the last-named work references to Byron continue as late as 1859, when Hawthorne and his family visited the Castle of Chillon, staying at the Hotel Byron.

4. Hawthorne's treatment of children is predominantly Wordsworthian, although he is capable of portraying them as fiends, as in his long short-story "The Gentle Boy."

5. See for instance Doris Langley Moore, *The Late Lord Byron* (London, 1961); and Malcolm Elwin, *Lord Byron's Wife* (London, 1962).

6. *English Notebooks*, p. 382.

7. *Ibid.*, p. 564. In 1857 Hawthorne visited Newstead Abbey and recorded his impressions at some length (pp. 487–491). His landlady filled him up with gossip about the "taint in the Byron blood, which makes those who inherit it wicked, mad, and miserable." He speculates on "the evil fate which is supposed to attend confiscated church-property," but concludes that "Nevertheless, I would accept the estate, were it offered me" (p. 491).

8. Randall Stewart's "Character Types . . ." and his "Recurrent Themes in Hawthorne's Fiction" (*American Notebooks*) do the groundwork for all subsequent discussions of isolation and isolated characters in Hawthorne.

9. ". . . his pleasant path-way among realities seems to proceed out of the

Dreamland of his youth, and to be bordered with just enough of its shadowy foliage to shelter him from the heat of the day" (1851 Preface to *Twice-Told Tales*).

10. See Randall Stewart, *Nathaniel Hawthorne: A Biography* (New Haven, 1948).

11. For image patterns in *Manfred* see W. Paul Elledge, *Byron and the Dynamics of Metaphor* (Nashville, Tennessee, 1968), pp. 82 ff.

SHELLEY'S VEILS: A THOUSAND
IMAGES OF LOVELINESS

Jerome J. McGann

Because Neville Rogers rightly saw that the veil was "one of the most subtle and complex of all Shelley's poetical concepts," he discussed the nature of this symbol at some length. "It is," he goes on to say, "a vital clue, symbolically, to his whole attitude towards Life and Death." Quite properly approaching his subject from the vantage of its Platonic context and implications, he concludes that "What the veil comes to signify . . . throughout Shelley's mature work is the illusory world of impermanence that hides or half hides the ideal world of reality." In themselves Shelleyan veils are indeed images of impermanence, figured curtains which stand between the One that remains and the Many that change and pass. But Rogers insists that Shelley's veils embody only things which are "imaginary, not really existent."[1] For him, the veil is always equivalent with "evil and error," or all those sublunary phenomena which it is the business of the imagination to strip away in order to reveal the One which stands unchangeably behind them.

This understanding of Shelley's veils seems to me too reductive. Rogers himself suggests a further possible significance for Shelley's veils when, after quoting *Prometheus Unbound* III. iii. 113-123, he observes:

> There are times when Shelley's doctrine of Mutability comes close to the New Birth idea: in this passage, for instance, there is an implication of a natural process of regeneration, something productive of new bloom, beauty and vigour, which will begin when the Veil is lifted. But Mutability does not in itself imply this: it is used rather to indicate Shelley's consciousness of a Heracleitean flux in earthly and human experience in contrast to the permanence of the ideal, divine realm beyond the Veil —it is this *impermanence* that the word implies, without necessarily implying more.[2]

198

But in the passage which he quotes, as we shall see more fully in a moment, the veil does in fact imply more than a negative idea of impermanence, nor is it the only passage where a further range of significance is suggested. These additional implications of the veil image are important because they point to some peculiar modifications which Shelley introduced into the Platonic scheme lying behind his poetry, modifications which do suggest a New Birth idea through regenerative process. And within that process veils, both in nature and in art, assume significant positive functions.

In the *Defence of Poetry* Shelley says that "Poetry . . . may be defined to be 'the expression of imagination,'"[3] and after some Coleridgean observations on the nature of metaphorical language as well as a lengthy excursus on the "critical history of poetry," he comes back to his proper theme. The poetic imagination, he says, "strips the veil of familiarity from the world, and lays bare the naked and sleeping beauty, which is the spirit of its forms" (p. 137). Imagination creates the world in the image of the poet's most sublime conceptions: "It compels us to feel that which we perceive, and to imagine that which we know" (p. 137). Shelley reiterates this idea often in his essay, and frequently the image of removing a veil or a covering of some sort is expressed or implied. Thus: "Poetry is a sword of lightning, ever unsheathed, which consumes the scabbard that would contain it" (p. 122). Greek tragedy, he says, strips away "all but that ideal perfection and energy which everyone feels to be the internal type of all that he loves, admires, and would become" (p. 121). The frequency with which Shelley comes back to this idea of imaginative unveiling, in his poetry and prose alike, suggests the deep anti-natural strain in his convictions.

At the same time—and it is this aspect of Shelley's attitude toward veiling which Mr. Rogers has neglected—imagination "spreads its own figured curtain."

> Poetry . . . makes immortal all that is best and most beautiful in the world; it arrests the vanishing apparitions which haunt the interlunations of life, and veiling them, or in language or in form, sends them forth among mankind, bearing sweet news of kindred joy to those with whom their sisters abide—abide, because there is no portal of expression from the caverns of the spirit which they inhabit into the universe of things (p. 137).

Earlier, speaking of the qualities of the "highest class" of poetry, Shelley says that "it is doubtful whether the alloy of costume, habit, &c., be not necessary to temper this planetary music for mortal ears" (p. 117). The reason is to be found in the nature of language itself. Shelley insists that we must be careful to "distinguish words from thoughts" (p. 127). They are not equivalents, and hence "when composition begins, inspiration is already on the decline, and the most glorious poetry . . . is probably a feeble shadow of the original conception of the Poet" (p. 135). The very metaphorical character of poetry, which he had been at pains to emphasize near the beginning of his essay, throws a shadow across the soul's highest intuitions. "How vain it is to think that words can penetrate the mystery of our being," Shelley says in the short essay "On Life"; and in still another context he exclaims that "words are ineffectual and metaphorical. Most words are so—No help!" ("On Love").

This paradoxical attitude toward veil images and the act of veiling persists in Shelley's poetry and is of crucial importance for understanding the nature of his art. We can distinguish three kinds of Shelleyan veils, all of which are variants upon the single idea developed by Rogers that for Shelley "Veil" is the equivalent of "Mutability." But if Shelley's veils always represent appearances, he attaches very different values to the different types. First is the veil of old and worn out ideas which cover the true beauty of life. Shelley calls them the "recurrence of impressions blunted by reiteration." Poetry tears away this veil and thereby frees men from a bondage to someone else's law. The most famous illustration of this veil—which Shelley always regards as evil—is at the end of the third act of *Prometheus Unbound.*

> The painted veil, by those who were, called life,
> Which mimicked, as with colours idly spread,
> All men believed or hoped, is torn aside;
> The loathsome mask has fallen, the man remains
> Sceptreless, free, uncircumscribed, but man
> Equal, unclassed, tribeless, and nationless,
> Exempt from awe, worship, degree, the king
> Over himself . . . .
>   (*P.U.*III.iv.190–197)

The second kind of veil is that which Nature lays over the world as a garment of beautiful appearances. Again *Prometheus Unbound* provides a good example. Shelley begins with a reference to the first kind of veil, the veil of familiarity or common perception which is really death.

> Death is the veil which those who live call life:
> They sleep, and it is lifted . . . .
> (*P.U.*III.iii.113–114)

Before the veil is raised for the last time, however, man must suffer a world still covered by a veil:

>   and meanwhile
> In mild variety the seasons mild
> With rainbow-skirted showers, and odorous winds,
> And long blue meteors cleansing the dull night,
> And the life-kindling shafts of the keen sun's
> All-piercing bow, and the dew-mingled rain
> Of the calm moonbeams, a soft influence mild,
> Shall clothe the forests and the fields, ay, even
> The crag-built deserts of the barren deep,
> With ever-living leaves, and fruits, and flowers.
> (*P.U.*III.iii.114–123)

This—the veil of natural appearance—is obviously beneficent in the context. But it need not be. To the poet-youth of *Alastor*, for example, the earth veiled in natural beauty seems "garish" and "vacant" (192 ff.). He ignores this beauty because he is obsessed with his visionary longing. Though Shelley is deeply sympathetic to the poet-youth, he regards his aspirations as a mistaken form of apocalypticism ("He overleaps the bounds. Alas! Alas!" [p. 207]).

The third kind of veil is that which poetry itself lays upon the visionary intuitions of the poet. In the Prologue to *The Witch of Atlas* Shelley says that "the vest of flowing metre" with which he covers his witch is "Light" and delicately woven. Emilia Viviani, who symbolizes that which inspires all poetry as well as that which all poetry aspires to become, is beautifully veiled.

> Seraph of Heaven! too gentle to be human,
> Veiling beneath that radiant form of Woman
> All that is insupportable in thee
> Of light, and love, and immortality!
> Sweet Benediction in the eternal Curse!
> Veiled Glory of this lampless Universe!

Thou Moon beyond the clouds! Thou living Form
Among the Dead! Thou Star above the Storm!
(*Epipsychidion*, ll. 21–28)

This veiled ideal in Shelley's poetry takes on many forms: she is also Asia, the veiled vision in *Alastor,* and the witch of Atlas.

Because Shelley's apocalyptic impulsions are so strong, however, we often turn up poems and fragments which evidence his dissatisfaction with veils of any sort. This famous stanza from *Adonais* is a prominent example:

The One remains, the many change and pass;
Heaven's light forever shines, Earth's shadows fly;
Life, like a dome of many-coloured glass,
Stains the white radiance of Eternity,
Until Death tramples it to fragments.—Die,
If thou wouldst be with that which thou dost seek!
Follow where all is fled!—Rome's azure sky,
Flowers, ruins, statues, music, words, are weak
The glory they transfuse with fitting truth to speak.
(LII)

Nature, Art, Poetry itself are inadequate to the full revelation of "the glory they transfuse." When composition begins, vision is already in flight from us. Shelley's consciousness of this is the basis of his sympathy with the poet-youth of *Alastor,* as the self-referential lines which introduce that poem clearly indicate. *Alastor* is not only a poem of brutally honest self-criticism, but Shelley's first significant attempt to find an answer to the problem of outer versus inner, expression versus vision. But *Alastor* does not solve the problem. In 1818 Shelley again writes a poem about a sensitive youth doomed by his own highest aspirations.

Lift not the painted veil which those who live
Call Life: though unreal shapes be pictured there,
And it but mimic all we would believe
With colours idly spread,—behind, lurk Fear
And Hope, twin Destinies; who ever weave
Their shadows, o'er the chasm, sightless and drear.
I knew one who had lifted it—he sought,
For his lost heart was tender, things to love,
But found them not, alas! nor was there aught
The world contains, the which he could approve.
Through the unheeding many he did move,
A splendour among shadows, a bright blot
Upon this gloomy scene, a Spirit that strove
For truth, and like the Preacher found it not.

The sonnet is a bitter statement upon a no-exit theme, for the "tender" heart of the "one who had lifted" the veil can be satisfied neither with the "unreal shapes" on the veil nor with the "sightless and drear" shadows of Hope and Fear which lurk behind it. The sonnet, like stanza LII of *Adonais,* is a general comment upon veils of any kind. It is also related to *Alastor.* The poet-youth forswears everything except identity with his own highest intuitions and desires, but he finds that his "insatiate hope" is forever coordinated with "despair." Wordsworth calls this typical Romantic experience the "anxiety of hope." The "pardlike spirit" of *Adonais,* who is Shelley at the poem's allegorical level, is presented exactly like the youth in *Alastor* and the one who had lifted the veil in the sonnet.

> Midst others of less note, came one frail Form,
> A phantom among men; companionless
> As the last cloud of an expiring storm
> Whose thunder is its knell; he, as I guess,
> Had gazed on Nature's naked loveliness,
> Actaeon-like, and now he fled astray
> With feeble steps o'er the world's wilderness,
> And his own thoughts, along that rugged way,
> Pursued, like raging hounds, their father and their prey.
> (XXXI)

The connections seem to proceed indefinitely, for this "phantom among men" looks very like the Rousseau of *The Triumph of Life.* Further, the image of Actaeon, who "gazed on Nature's naked loveliness," ought to recall Shelley's general definition of the poet, who "lays bare the naked and sleeping beauty" of Life. In the last two instances, equivalent images assume different meanings in each context. This difference seems a significant indication of Shelley's own ambivalent attitudes. Nature, Art, and poetic expression all possess positive and negative values depending upon one's point of view. But now we see that the poet's visionary capability ("his own thoughts") is itself positively and negatively charged at various junctures.

We shall look in vain to find these apparent contradictions resolved definitely in Shelley's philosophic or critical writings. On the other hand, his poetry does not seem to suffer from the presence of such ambivalences. In fact, the poetry frequently provides the resolutions that Shelley was unwilling or unable to formulate conclusively in sober prose. Shelley suggests two functions for the imagination in his *Defence,* both of which are the means to a higher end: "And whether it spreads its own figured curtain, or withdraws life's dark veil from before the scene of things, it equally creates for us a being within our being" (p. 137). The latter part of the statement is thoroughly consonant with the most Idealistic strains of philosophic thought. Shelley defines poetry as a search for identity, the ego's quest for the ego-ideal, the attempt to penetrate to the epipsyche and become one with it. That he often showed a skepticism not only about the practicality of an apocalypse of this sort, but also about the creative possibilities which it could afford, seems quite clear. I will return to this point in a moment. Shelley's statement also says that imagination has a double office: taking old veils away and putting new veils on. Once again we are back at the root doubleness of his thought, for he does not distinguish at this point between the kind of veil that poetry weaves and the kind that it takes away. The following piece of lyric from *Prometheus Unbound,* along with numerous other similar passages in the poetry, suggests that the veil of poetry somehow conceals and reveals at the same time.

> Child of Light! thy limbs are burning
>   Through the vest which seems to hide them;
> As the radiant lines of morning
>   Through the clouds ere they divide them;
> And this atmosphere divinest
> Shrouds thee wheresoe'er thou shinest.
>   (II.v.54–59)

Contrariwise, veils of old, dead perceptions only obscure one's vision, hence poetry must replace them with its own. But Shelley's mind has yet another level of awareness—that basic dissatisfaction with language itself. Poetry, he says, can never truly recapitulate vision so that the quest for the epipsyche apparently must remain fruitless.

One of Shelley's most important, and neglected, poetic techniques can help solve this riddle born of his intense self-consciousness. Let us examine the following two passages, one taken from the *Defence* and the other from *To a Skylark:*

Poets are the hierophants of an unapprehended inspiration; the mirrors of the gigantic shadows which futurity casts upon the present; the words which express what they understand not; the trumpets which sing to battle, and feel not what they inspire; the influence which is moved not, but moves. Poets are the unacknowledged legislators of the world.
                                                                 (p. 140)

What thou art we know not;
    What is most like thee?
From rainbow clouds there flow not
    Drops so bright to see
As from thy presence showers a rain of melody.

Like a poet hidden
    In the light of thought,
Singing hymns unbidden,
    Till the world is wrought
To sympathy with hopes and fears it heeded not:

Like a high-born maiden
    In a palace-tower,
Soothing her love-laden
    Soul in secret hour
With music sweet as love, which overflows her bower:

Like a glow-worm golden
    In a dell of dew,
Scattering unbeholden
    Its aëreal hue
Among the flowers and grass, which screen it from the view!

Like a rose enbowered
    In its own green leaves,
By warm winds deflowered,
    Till the scent it gives
Makes faint with too much sweet those heavy-wingèd thieves:

Sound of vernal showers
    On the twinkling grass,
Rain-awakened flowers,
    All that ever was
Joyous, and clear, and fresh, thy music doth surpass:

Teach us, Sprite or Bird,
    What sweet thoughts are thine:
I have never heard
    Praise of love or wine
That panted forth a flood of rapture so divine.

Chorus Hymeneal,
    Or triumphal chant,
Matched with thine would be all
    But an empty vaunt,
A thing wherein we feel there is some hidden want.

What objects are the fountains
    Of thy happy strain?
What fields, or waves, or mountains?
    What shapes of sky or plain?
What love of thine own kind? what ignorance of pain?
                            (ll.31–75)

Both passages are attempts at definition: what is a poet, what is the skylark? Further, the method of definition is the same in each instance. "What is most like thee," he asks and produces a sort of image anthology that attempts to capture the epipsyche of bird and poet. All the images strike somewhere just off the mark, however, so Shelley continues to pour them out even though he senses that "there is some hidden want" in them. "What objects are the fountains / Of thy happy strain?" he asks of his bird, but no answer can be found to this question either. The deepest truth is imageless. Neither passage can be called a failure at statement, however, for if we cannot define the object of the bird's song of love neither can we define the object of the poet's. The bird is "unseen," only heard (hence the bird's symbolic identification with the poet himself and with the act of imagination in general). Both bird and poet sing about "unapprehended" things, though their songs are themselves quite palpable. Thus Shelley gains an identification with the bird who is his epipsyche by reproducing a song like to its song. Just as he cannot see the sources of the bird's inspiration, so we cannot see the source of the poet's.

The song of the poet is a veil of imagery. In this case there is no stripping away of obscuring veils but only a successive process of re-veiling. The process is itself the crucial thing, for if words are helplessly ineffectual and metaphorical, the activity of continuous and related image-making reveals the self-creative powers of the mind (making the outer inner and the inner outer). The epipsyche is not revealed, but the activity of this ego-ideal is. Such an activity is not an apocalyptic rending of the "inmost veil of Heaven," but an imaginative resort to successively different figurations drawn from the world of perception. Certain images in Shelley's repertoire may be regarded as better than others for defining the activity of the epipsyche, like the beautifully symbolic veil image (drawn from a purely natural source) which is the basis of the "Child of Light" passage. But in every case language cannot offer an equivalent of the epipsyche itself, only of its powers. Nor should we expect any more; the epipsyche is a spirit, whatever the sense we give to that idea. Shelley hints at this function of poetry rather frequently in his prose. Perhaps the most suggestive passage is this from the *Defence*: "the impersonations [of poetry] . . . stand . . . as memorials of that gentle and exalted content which extends itself over all thoughts and actions with which it coexists" (117-118).

The "gentle and exalted content" is the ego-ideal which is the
source of all life, and poetry is the act of impersonating that
power and memorializing its truth. The thing itself remains
"unapprehended," for "words . . . express what they understand not."

In *Epipsychidion* Shelley lays to rest the problem posed in
Alastor, for the later poem is the story of Shelley's successful
recovery in the world of men of the veiled vision of his youth,
just as *Alastor* records the poet-youth's failure at such a recovery. "I never thought before my death to see / Youth's vision
thus made perfect," Shelley says near the beginning of *Epipsychidion* (ll. 41-42), but Emily is that vision in human form.

> I knew it was the Vision veiled from me
> So many years—that it was Emily.
> (ll.343–344)

Like the veiled maid in *Alastor*, Emily is herself a veiled spirit
whose epipsyche only "darkens through" (l. 38) even that
brightest portion of her materiality, her eyes. This being the
case, Shelley again resorts to his image anthology technique
whenever he attempts to define the deepest reality of his inspira-
tional source:

> Art thou not void of guile,
> A lovely soul formed to be blessed and bless?
> A well of sealed and secret happiness,
> Whose waters like blithe light and music are,
> Vanquishing dissonance and gloom? A Star
> Which moves not in the moving heavens, alone?
> A Smile amid dark frowns? a gentle tone
> Amid rude voices? a beloved light?
> A Solitude, a Refuge, a Delight?
> A Lute . . .
>
> . . . a buried treasure?
> A cradle of young thoughts of wingless pleasure?
> A violet-shrouded grave of Woe?
> (ll.56–69)

"I measure / The world of fancies, seeking one like thee," Shelley says (ll. 69-70), but the "dim words" (l. 33), however
"lightning-like" (l. 34), always strike obliquely to the deep
truth. In the end he finds only his imaginative "infirmity." But
the apocalyptic failure of metaphoric language is nothing against

the theme of an epipsychidion, for Emily herself is an "image" (l. 115) and a "Metaphor" (l. 120). Just as she impersonates the outer and the inner worlds (both "Eternity," [l. 115], and "Spring and Youth and Morning," [l. 120]), so Shelley's poetry recapitulates her status and functioning power. *Epipsychidion* is his veiled vision.

This fundamental meaning in the poem helps to explain its conclusion, when Shelley attempts to define his "far Eden of the purple East" (l. 417) where he and Emily are to be imparadised. The image anthology technique is used throughout the description of the visionary "isle and house" (l. 513), as we would expect. In an effort to consummate a definition, Shelley drives his poetry to a peak of intensity:

> One hope within two wills, one will beneath
> Two overshadowing minds, one life, one death,
> One Heaven, one Hell, one immortality,
> And one annihilation.
> (ll.584–587)

At this point the artistic flight seems to falter seriously, and Shelley appears to sustain a fall from vision:

> Woe is me!
> The wingèd words on which my soul would pierce
> Into the height of Love's rare Universe,
> Are chains of lead around its flight of fire—
> I pant, I sink, I tremble, I expire!
> (ll.587–591)

Is this really a fall from visionary surmise? In one sense, yes, for even "winged words" are "chains of lead" around the imaginative impulse. "Weak Verses," Shelley calls his poetry (l. 592). But nothing in the concluding twelve lines of *Epipsychidion* suggests that Shelley's mood has darkened because of his apparent failure of expression. He says his language is his master, it is true, but he also commands his language like a Prospero, telling it what to do and where to go. Moreover, at the conclusion he sends his poem to league with the company of all the great poems of the past. Their chorus will chant an invitation to all men to join Shelley at the banquet of Love where he is *even now*:

> Then haste
> Over the hearts of men, until ye meet
> Marina, Vanna, Primus, and the rest,
> And bid them love each other and be blessed:
> And leave the troop which errs and which reproves,
> And come and be my guest,—for I am Love's.
>
> (ll.599–604)

Again we are faced with a paradox, this time with the apparent failure of Shelley's poetic language and the manifest success of his poetic attitude. The poem does not conclude in an emotional disequilibrium. The explanation of this curious event seems to depend to some extent upon the often-ridiculed "I pant, I sink, I tremble, I expire!" I think we wrongly interpret the line if we read it as in any way suggesting the swan-song of a beautiful but ineffectual angel. The line is not self-pitying, but the climax of the symbolic death-motif which runs throughout the poem.

Carlos Baker has cogently argued the close relationship between the patterns of meaning in *Epipsychidion* and *Adonais*.[4] Perhaps the most important of these is the significance of Death as Shelley conceives it, and the relation which this idea has to the poetic faculty. At the end of *Adonais* Shelley asserts the necessity of dying into full life:

> Life, like a dome of many-coloured glass,
> Stains the white radiance of Eternity,
> Until Death tramples it to fragments.—Die,
> If thou wouldst be with that which thou dost seek!
>
> (LII)

Some readers seem not to have recognized that this focal idea in *Adonais* is also a key to the meaning of *Epipsychidion*. In fact, this famous passage from *Adonais* received its initial formulation when Shelley was working on the first draft of *Epipsychidion*.

> Free love has this, different from gold and clay,
> That to divide is not to take away,
> Like ocean, which the general north wind breaks
> Into ten thousand waves, and each one makes
> A mirror of the moon—like some great glass,
> Which did distort whatever form might pass,
> Dashed into fragments by a playful child,

Which then reflects its eyes and forehead mild;
Giving for one, which it could ne'er express,
A thousand images of loveliness.[5]

The significance of these lines can be judged by the measure of
their resemblance to two of the most important passages in
Epipsychidion. Both are attempts at a definition of Love, the
central motif in the poem.

True Love in this differs from gold and clay,
That to divide is not to take away.
Love is like understanding, that grows bright,
Gazing on many truths; 'tis like thy light,
Imagination! which from earth and sky,
And from the depths of human fantasy,
As from a thousand prisms and mirrors, fills
The Universe with glorious beams, and kills
Error, the worm, with many a sun-like arrow
Of its reverberated lightning. Narrow
The heart that loves, the brain that contemplates,
The life that wears, the spirit that creates
One object, and one form, and builds thereby
A sepulchre for its eternity.
(ll.160–173)

In this passage the closest analogue to Love is Imagination, the
power of the mind which can create a universe of its own as
diverse and populated as that of Nature's. Imagination is an
image-making faculty, and its vitality is to be measured in terms
of the diversity of its realizations. In this connection we can
hardly fail to recall Shelley's image anthology technique.

The MS lines also relate to the following passage in *Epipsychidion*:

The day is come, and thou wilt fly with me.
To whatsoe'er of dull mortality
Is mine, remain a vestal sister still;
To the intense, the deep, the imperishable,
Not mine but me, henceforth be thou united
Even as a bride, delighting and delighted.
The hour is come:—the destined Star has risen
Which shall descend upon a vacant prison.
The walls are high, the gates are strong, thick set
The sentinels—but true Love never yet
Was thus constrained . . .
. . . like Heaven's free breath,

Which he who grasps can hold not; liker Death,
Who rides upon a thought, and makes his way
Through temple, tower, and palace, and the array
Of arms: more strength has Love than he or they;
For it can burst his charnel, and make free
The limbs in chains, the heart in agony . . . .
(ll.388–406)

The connections here are a bit more complicated and must be pieced together by comparing these lines with the two other passages from *Epipsychidion* just cited, as well as with the conclusion of *Adonais*. "True Love" is the equivalent of "Free love," a power "unconstrained" as regards its objects. Whereas this love-ideal is said to be most like Imagination in the other passage, here it is most like Death "Who rides upon a thought" and overpowers all mortal things. Love and Imagination at their highest powers move out toward an indefinite range of connections and creations. Death, imaged in *Adonais* as one who shatters the "narrow" and "constrained" world of life into a multiplicity of new (and vital) mirrors of the One, is not only a likely image of Love, but also of Imagination. Shelley's is a "moth-like Muse" (l. 53) in *Epipsychidion* and seeks "A radiant death, a fiery sepulchre" (l. 223). This death toward which he yearns possesses attributes similar to Love's and Imagination's: it radiates ("as from a thousand prisms and mirrors"); further, it can burst the "charnel" which is unimaginative life (or death-in-life) since Shelley's death-ideal is a symbol of resurrection, a "fiery sepulchre" comparable to the symbolic pyramid outside the Protestant cemetery in Rome, which Shelley in *Adonais* describes as "flame transformed to marble" (L). The Love-Death-Imagination fire is the herald of a new day. It consumes "the last clouds of cold mortality" in *Adonais* just as it overcomes the poet's "dull mortality" in *Epipsychidion*.

Shelley admits that he never really expected to see the perfected vision of Love "before my death." His vision of Love "lured me toward sweet Death" (l. 73), he says, but the significance of the "story" in *Epipsychidion* is that the poet discovers a means for dying into an immediate life with Love through Imagination. "Sweet Death" is reached before the term of Shelley's human existence has run out. This death experience amounts to the attainment of an untrammeled Imagination and an infinite love-capability. It is a point which marks the transition from an incapacity to a capacity. It signals the death of

something established and inadequate, and the birth of a re-
newed and vital life.

Since *Adonais* deals most explicitly with the meaning of this
recreative death-encounter, we should look briefly at that poem
before returning to *Epipsychidion*. "What Adonais is, why fear
we to become?" Shelley asks. The question triggers the final
movement of the poem, in which Shelley determines not to
linger or shrink back any longer from "what Adonais is." In
one sense, of course, Adonais has been transported wholly beyond the realms of time, nature, and humanity. He lives in "the
abode where the Eternal are," beyond the last, the "inmost
veil of Heaven." John Keats is dead. But in his eternal form
as Adonais "he is not dead": "He lives, he wakes—'tis Death
is dead, not he." The truly dead are the dead in life ("The
herded wolves . . . The obscene ravens . . . The vultures
. . ." [XXVIII]), and those who mourn over the death of
Adonais thereby consign themselves to an existence among the
deadly company of this spectrous humanity:

> 'Tis we, who lost in stormy visions, keep
> With phantoms an unprofitable strife,
> And in mad trance, strike with our spirit's knife
> Invulnerable nothings.—*We* decay
> Like corpses in a charnel; fear and grief
> Convulse us and consume us day by day,
> And cold hopes swarm like worms within our living clay.
>
> (XXXIX)

Urania, Nature, and the brother poets of Adonais all grieve
over his passing, but their very grief is the sign that they have
submitted to the dominion of the dead in life. Like Prometheus,
they are enslaved by their own minds, and this slavery brings
death into the world. "He will awake no more" (VIII), the
poet says at the beginning of the elegy, and his remark summarizes the feelings of all who now grieve. Urania is the
heavenly Muse and the spirit of the creative Imagination. As
such she ought not to mourn for Adonais, for her office is the
understanding of the deathless nature of Imagination. The fact
that she too comes to weep at the grave seems the symbolic
representation of Shelley's attitude toward the poets and poetry
of his time: they have forgotten the prerogatives of poetry and
are sunk into an unenlightened self-despair:

Who mourns for Adonais? Oh, come forth,
Fond wretch! and know thyself and him aright.
(XLVII)

The poem's denouement involves the recognition that Adonais
is not dead, that the powers of death-in-life are mere spectres
who cannot harm the essential spirit of man, and that a fully
realized life is possible even for those "chained to Time." Like
Socrates, "Adonais has drunk poison" (XXXVI) and in so
doing has achieved his eternal form. The Socrates allusion hints
a purposiveness in Adonais's fate, as if he went gladly to the
realms of death. "When lofty thought / Lifts a young heart
above its mortal lair . . . the dead live there," Shelley finally
sees (XLIV). Adonais's "lofty thought" is a rebuke to all the
mourners, and in the end it is the spur to the poet's own pur-
posive advance upon the shores of darkness.

Adonais is now altogether beyond Time and Mutability, but
his mythologized history (told by Shelley in the poem) stands
as a symbol of what imaginative men can achieve in time. After
Shelley recognizes the deathless Adonais, he urges Nature back
to life: "cease to moan! / Cease, ye faint flowers and fountains,
and thou Air" (XLI). Adonais is "made one with Nature"
(XLII) and she participates in his principle of deathless life
even now:

> The splendours of the firmament of time
> May be eclipsed, but are extinguished not;
> Like stars to their appointed height they climb,
> And death is a low mist which cannot blot
> The brightness it may veil.
> (XLIV)

The rediscovery of this permanent vitality in Nature leads to a
similar rediscovery in man:

> Who mourns for Adonais? Oh, come forth,
> Fond wretch! and know thyself and him aright.
> Clasp with thy panting soul the pendulous Earth;
> As from a centre, dart thy spirit's light
> Beyond all worlds, until its spacious might
> Satiate the void circumference: then shrink
> Even to a point within our day and night;
> And keep thy heart light lest it make thee sink
> When hope has kindled hope, and lured thee to the brink.
> (XLVII)

The passage describes the vivifying function of Imagination, which can "satiate the void circumference" and create out of its own powers a universe of beauty. The heart must be kept "light" with imaginative hope and capability, not weighted down with a burden of self-constraining griefs. Thus, when Shelley determines at the end to sail forth upon a voyage toward the Kingdom of Death, he is driven not by a Freudian death-wish but by a desire to live a life of untrammeled imagination and creativity. Ordinary death has no real significance in this conclusion. Shelley strikes out for a Life in Death, which is a Life lived *in* time but *after* Imagination. It participates in Eternity in the immediate (though to do so it must constantly voyage toward the apocalyptic end). What he flees from is Death in Life, which is a death lived *in* time but *after* self-restriction. Death into Imagination shatters the "void circumference" of a constrained world ("a dome of many-coloured glass"), and the trampled fragments henceforth exist as an infinity of mirrors which reflect the infinity of true life, as well as the powers of the loving Imagination.

The Love-Death-Imagination motif traced earlier in *Epipsychidion* operates within a thought structure similar to the one I have just marked out in *Adonais*. Consequently, that problematical line near the conclusion ("I pant, I sink, I tremble, I expire!") ought to be read within Shelley's specialized poetic categories. In fact, only thus can we make sense of the last twelve lines of the poem. The notorious line in question records, successively, the final yearning, lingering, and shrinking back before the death which signals another movement forward. This expiration is not an end but the beginning of a new life, a new life of veiled beauties and veiled visions which themselves succeed to further deaths and lives. No one image of Life or a condition of Life—no one group of images—can be allowed a definitiveness. The Epipsyche, and the One, require a universe of imaginative fragments in an eternity of time to exhibit their full loveliness. The attitude is best expressed in terms of poetry (an *Epipsychidion*, like so many Romantic poems, is a poem about poetry). Language is a veiled vision, and the poet's veil of imagery must be destroyed if the power of vision is to be sustained, if fresh creations are to be brought forth and new figured curtains to be woven. "One object, and one form" for the poet's love are wholly inadequate. Thus, Shelley's last attempt at an image anthology in *Epipsychidion* rises to a crescendo of oxymorons and concludes with an image of "annihilation," which consummates and cancels the preceding series and introduces Shelley's last short descant on the self-destructiveness of poetry.

But this death of poetry signals the rebirth of imaginative power. As Shelley puts it in one of the *Fragments Connected with Epipsychidion:*

> There is a mood which language faints beneath;
> You feel it striding, as Almighty Death
> His bloodless steed . . . .
> (ll.139–141)

This "mood" which calls forth "Almighty Death" is associated with the most sublime reaches of human creativity. It is

> a Power, a Love, a Joy, a God
> Which makes in mortal hearts its brief abode,
> A Pythian exhalation, which inspires
> Love, only love.
> (ll.134–137)

Just before Shelley enters upon such a death in his act of composing *Epipsychidion* he tells us what life will be like in his island paradise:

> And we will talk, until thought's melody
> Become too sweet for utterance, and it die
> In words, to live again in looks, which dart
> With thrilling tone into the voiceless heart . . . .
> (ll.560–563)

Love dalliance here is a succession of talk and silence, with a "death" the point of mediation. What the lovers do here is what the "voluptuous nightingales" do in *Prometheus Unbound:*

> There the voluptuous nightingales,
>   Are awake through all the broad noonday.
> When one with bliss or sadness fails,
>   And through the windless ivy-boughs,
> Sick with sweet love, droops dying away
> On its mate's music-panting bosom;
> Another from the swinging blossom,
>   Watching to catch the languid close
> Of the last strain, then lifts on high
> The wings of the weak melody,
> 'Till some new strain of feeling bear

The song, and all the woods are mute;
When there is heard through the dim air
The rush of wings, and rising there
Like many a lake-surrounded flute,
Sounds overflow the listener's brain
So sweet, that joy is almost pain.
(*P.U.*II.ii.24—40)

This mutual interchange is what throws Shelley's idea of imagination beyond solipsism. The interchange is love, or the imaginative sympathy between gifted souls which results in a process of mutual invigoration. Lovers bring new life to each other just as, in history, time weaves a cyclic poem in which the great poets of past ages create a music which dies into the life of the future. In itself expression is neither self-consummating nor self-perpetuating, but must achieve itself in and through that silence which is an immediate experience of love—an experience directed out from the ego toward "the beautiful which exists in thought, action, or person, not our own" (p. 118).[6] Imagination cannot be sustained without this love-encounter with otherness:

> For if the inequalities, produced by what has been termed the operations of the external universe were levelled by the perception of our being, uniting, and filling up their interstices, motion and mensuration, and time, and space; the elements of the human mind being thus abstracted, sensation and imagination cease. Mind cannot be considered pure.[7]

This is why Shelley says that "this cold common hell" of contingency is "a doom / As glorious as a fiery martyrdom" (214-215), and that the "strife" of Life "Tills for the promise of a later birth / The wilderness of this Elysian earth" (188-189). Everything in the Shelleyan universe sympathizes—echoes, or reflects ("as from a thousand prisms and mirrors"). In so doing that universe images the power of imagination not to echo or reflect the hidden One in a single item or instance: that spirit which "creates / One object and one form" of its love builds only "A sepulchre for its eternity." Rather, because the deep truth is imageless, the imagination rises to upbuild itself into ever new forms, and only by describing this endlessly generative process itself does it approximate the ideal source of all generation and life. Thus, the imagination is both a veiling and an unveiling power.

The frequency with which Shelley images such a process of death and rebirth cannot be ignored, nor can it be explained by

Rogers's rigorous Platonic schema. *The Cloud* also describes this process of death and rebirth, of course, and so does the analogous passage in *Prometheus Unbound* (II.ii.41-82). "Free love," operating through imagination, deals out "A thousand images of loveliness" by undergoing this cycle of death and rebirth, of rending the veil and weaving again new veils of beautiful apparitions. So the cloud is an image of this regenerative activity: "I change, but I cannot die." We are like clouds, he says again in one of the *Epipsychidion Fragments,*

> Which rain into the bosom of the earth,
> And rise again, and in our death and birth,
> And through our restless life, take as from heaven
> Hues which are not our own, but which are given,
> And then withdrawn, and with inconstant glance
> Flash from the spirit to the countenance.
> (ll.128–133)

Shelley's life/death sequences are at the basis of art and life alike. Poetic expression "faints" and "dies" under the pressure of the imaginative "mood" of love, which yearns for otherness in order to preserve its vitality; and new materials of poetic expression are born from those experiences with the non-ego seen with an imaginative eye. Poetic expression (image-making) is itself crucially important, for only thus can the activity of imagination and the experience of love be memorialized and impersonated.

NOTES

1. Neville Rogers, *Shelley at Work*, 2nd ed. (Oxford, 1967), pp. 120, 123, 124.

2. *Ibid.*, pp. 124–125. Richard Harter Fogle's discussion of Shelley's veils (*The Imagery of Keats and Shelley* [Chapel Hill, N. C., 1949], pp. 230–239) suggests a wider range of meanings in Shelley's veils. His analysis seems closer to mine than to Mr. Rogers's.

3. In *The Complete Works of Percy Bysshe Shelley*, ed. Roger Ingpen and Walter E. Peck (London, 1930), VII, 109. All further references to the *Defence* are made to this edition and are noted in the text. All poetry quotations are taken from *The Complete Poetical Works of Shelley*, ed. Thomas Hutchinson (Oxford, 1956).

4. *Shelley's Major Poetry* (Princeton, 1948), pp. 215–224.

5. Neville Rogers (p. 121) has noted "A slight anticipation" of the phrase "many-coloured" in *The Voyage* (1812).

6. See also, *e.g.*, *The Question*. The poem enacts an imaginative flight which concludes in the poet's (apparently unsuccessful) attempt to establish a connection between vision and reality. He seeks a sympathy in the world, but does not find it. For my purposes, the poem is interesting because it suggests Shelley's desire to establish such a connection.

7. "Speculations on Metaphysics," *Complete Works*, VII, 61.

LEIGH HUNT IN PHILADELPHIA[1]

Lewis Leary

In 1775 Isaac Hunt was carried through the streets of Philadelphia in a wooden cart to the accompaniment of beating drums and the jeers of spectators, protected from "gross insults from the populace" and a "good American coat of tar and feathers laid on with decency" only by a company of Associators who accompanied him and by his own forthright, and humble, acknowledgment of Loyalists sins. His crime against his colonial countrymen was not only that he had dared defend a peddler accused of selling British goods,[2] but also that he had been the author of a temporizing pamphlet entitled *The Political Family*, in which he had pled for "uninterrupted union between Great Britain and her American colonies."[3] Not long afterwards he escaped to England by way of the West Indies, perhaps in one of the vessels with which his father-in-law, Stephen Shewell, carried on an active and profitable trade during the Revolution. There, putting behind him the profession of law in which he had been making progress in America, he took Holy Orders and became a popular preacher at Paddington.[4]

Theatrical, fond of good society, strong tobacco, and rich port, Isaac Hunt was perhaps too pleasant a companion to rise among his more steady Anglican brethren, even if he had not been a colonial, born in Barbados and educated at Provost William Smith's promising but provincial small college in Pennsylvania. Ready to make the best of what he had, he prepared a fifteen-page defense of *The Case of Isaac Hunt, Esq; of Philadelphia*,[5] which helped bring him the small loyalist pension he was to mortgage before it ever came to his hands. It is sometimes suggested that he sought an easy road to preferment when in 1784, while tutor in the household of the Duke of Chandos, he named the youngest of his sons James Henry Leigh in honor of his high-born pupil. But that seemed finally to bring him little

219

advantage. Isaac Hunt died in 1809, impoverished but never embittered, and with little, in addition to the titles mentioned above, to show for his life-long itch for writing except a handful of satirical tracts (with which as "Isaac Bickerstaff" he had scandalized Philadelphia when he was a young man just out of college),[6] two "discourses" published in London,[7] and a pamphlet on *Rights of Englishmen,* which in 1791 was smothered among dozens of better replies to what Leigh Hunt called the "whimsical attacks" of Thomas Paine—only these, plus a handful of titles of books he might someday write, a list longer, said his son with some sympathy, than that of Rabelais.[8]

James Henry Leigh Hunt never forgave his American grandfather Shewell or his grandfather's country for the manner in which his father had been treated, but especially for the strain and suffering his mother had been allowed to undergo as she watched her husband's ignoble passage through Philadelphia streets, as she worried through his escape from that turbulent city, and as two years later she bundled up her three young children for the perilous, storm-tossed voyage which would allow them to join him in London: "My father's danger, and the war-whoops of Indians which she heard in Philadelphia, had shaken her soul as well as frame." She always seemed old to Leigh Hunt, and with cause. Among other things, the countenance of Tom Paine, who had visited at her father's Philadelphia home, had "inspired her with terror." The skirmishing she had seen in America during the early days of the Revolution so affected her that, years later, "the sight of two men fighting in the streets would drive her in tears down another road." Walking with her small son through a London park, "she would take me a long circuit out of the way rather than hazard the spectacle of the soldiers" who drilled there. To her last days, however, she was American, retaining occasional colonial eccentricities of speech: *haive* for have, *shaul* for shall. She was darker than most Englishwomen, as if "Anglo-Americans already began to exhibit the influence of their climate in their appearance." Always a little homesick, timid and with "no accomplishments but the two best of all, a love of nature and a love of books," his mother was permanently marked by her experiences in America and by the hardships which her wealthy colonial father allowed her to suffer in exile from it. "Never shall I forget her face," her son vowed, "with that weary hang of the head on one side, and that melancholy smile!"[9]

Mary Shewell Hunt was proud of this youngest son who became a good companion to her. "My Boy Leigh," she wrote to her father in Philadelphia, "is a steady sensible boy and I copy some of his exercises for your perusal. They are serious and uncommon for his years. He is not yet fifteen."[10] Her pride must have increased when two years later young Leigh became the talk of literary London, as his verses began to appear regularly in such periodicals as the *Morning Chronicle* and the *Monthly Mirror*, and were represented—nine of them—in the impressive *Poetical Register, and Repository of Fugitive Verse, for 1801,* which spoke of him as a young man "of taste and genius," many of whose "pieces would not disgrace authors of more advanced age."[11] His collected *Juvenilia,* "dedicated by permission to the Hon. J. H. Leigh," contained "proofs of genius, and literary ability . . . taste and ingenuity" seldom found in one so young.[12] More than eight hundred people had subscribed for this volume of poems, announced as having been "written between the ages of twelve and sixteen." Important among the subscribers were Americans, some of them resident in England: the Ambassador of the United States, Rufus King; John Trumbull, the painter from New England, who, arrested in London years before in retribution for the death of Major André, considered his deliverance in large measure due to the friendly intervention of Isaac Hunt;[13] the young author's great-uncle, Benjamin West, whom some Americans thought a renegade, but of whose position as President of the Royal Academy most of them were proud; and William Corbett, known to every Pennsylvanian as "Peter Porcupine," whose satirical quills had and would prick them sorely. There were others, from Philadelphia: Joseph Gilpin, Samuel Sitgreaves, D. Murgatroyd, and the poet's oldest brother, Isaac.[14] Then, as the young man's reputation grew through publication in England of a second and a third edition of his astounding first volume, Philadelphia claimed him as her own:

A youth, of American origin, whose native powers, fostered by the discernment of friends . . . have produced . . . a variety of original poems, which, in fertility of invention, brightness of imagination, and vivacity of expression, may be compared with many of the tardier productions of veteran wit.[15]

Samuel Shewell, grown old and increasingly wealthy in Philadelphia, seems also to have been proud, but worried also, about this grandson he had never seen. "My grandfather," Leigh Hunt reported blandly, "sensible of the new fame of his family, but probably alarmed at the fruitless consequences to which it might lead, sent me word, that if I would come to Philadelphia, 'he would make a man of me.' " Still resentful of what he considered Shewell's "niggardly conduct to my mother," the young poet declined the invitation, apparently with some heat: "men grew," he replied, "in England as well as America." Better perhaps! Leigh Hunt never visited the country which he later characterized as a nation of linendrapers, standing behind a gigantic counter which stretched along their coast from Massachusetts to Mexico: "Americans are Englishmen with the poetry and romance left out of them."[16] But America, especially Philadelphia, did not easily forget Leigh Hunt, or that, except for the accident of birth in England, he might have been one of theirs.

The boy poet, or perhaps his relatives in Philadelphia, did, however, go to some pains to nourish the interest that America showed in him. When the third edition of the *Juvenilia* appeared in London in 1803, not only was there an increase in number of American subscribers, but many of them were identified—introduced, as it were, to English readers—with words of high praise. David Rittenhouse was "one of the greatest philosophers of the present age," as John Ewing was "one of the first mathematicians and philosophers of the United States." Benjamin Rush was identified as the physician "whose tender care of the lives of his fellow citizens, at the risque of his own, when the yellow fever raged, endears his name to every philanthropist in the old, as well as the New World." John Dickenson was "the celebrated author of the Farmer's Letters—member of the American Congress—good, as well as great." Nicholas Waln was explained as "in his youth an eminent barrister at Philadelphia, and for some years as eminent a preacher in the Society of Friends—a people simple, yet for the most part subtle." More equivocally, William Franklin was "son of the late ingenious Benjamin Franklin, *prima conductor* of the American revolution, and *principal founder* of the United States of America—without his *type* in our days."[17] We suspect the hand of the grandfather in these fine descriptive words, for he stands out, naked in comparison among them, simply listed as "S. Shewell, esq."[18]

Philadelphia responded by printing, on 2 April 1803, the young man's *Ode to Contemplation* in *The Port Folio*, with a headnote explaining that

A rare instance of that early maturity of genius in some, Quos aequus Jupiter amavit, is exemplified in the history of a living poet in England. A Mr. Hunt, a youth of seventeen, has, from a still tenderer age, been in the habit of composing in a style of correct elegance, poems, which display not merely fertility of invention, but a wonderful accuracy and delicacy of taste. We shall, occasionally, copy the productions of this juvenile bard, and rejoice that Genius can overleap the vulgar bounds of time.

(III,112).

On 14 May twenty-six untitled lines appeared, identified as by Mr. I. H. L. Hunt (*The Port Folio,* III, 157), and on 4 June appeared, reprinted without title from *The Poetical Register* (pp. 175-176), Hunt's *Translation of Horace's Ode 'Descende Coelo, &c.'—A Fragment,* done "in a style of energy and animation not unworthy of the original *(The Port Folio,* III, 184).

Philadelphia responded even more cordially with a long essay by "Samuel Saunter" which recommended young Hunt as a deserving object of American patronage. "Such juvenile merit naturally challenges the curiosity of mankind, and such splendour nothing can long conceal." It listed with commendation the dukes, lords, and bishops among Leigh Hunt's English patrons —"two thousand names," including the "most eminent characters in England." It spoke with modest approval of the "distinguished Americans, whom our author, with patriotic partiality," had listed with "affection and respect." It made the most of the boy's kinship with Sir Benjamin West—*The Port Folio,* as edited by Joseph Dennie, was never loath to mention a title— and suggested with some pardonable local pride that as "Sir Benjamin has transplanted himself from the genial soil of a republic to the cold and comfortless region of a Monarchy, he may be curious to discover whether another Scion, from America, may not shoot luxuriantly, under all the disadvantages of a foreign clime" ("From the Shop of Messrs. Colon and Spondee," *The Port Folio,* III [11 June 1803], 186). Yes, Leigh Hunt, Philadelphians thought, belonged to Philadelphia. He was her gift to the English world of letters. Samuel Saunter reproduced in his essay the apostrophe *To Genius* entire, as "one of the earliest odes of our juvenile bard"; lines from Hunt's *Ode on Painting* were reprinted, with some variations in phrasing and punctuation—American improvements perhaps —as a "charming" adaptation of the manner of Collins; his

The Palace of Pleasure was quoted with high approval: the critic wondered whether in *The Faerie Queene,* in Shenstone's *Schoolmistress,* or in Thomson's *Castle of Indolence* "more vivid personification . . . can be found" (III, 167).

Then, in the final two paragraphs, comes the practical point of Samuel Saunter's essay: "A proposal has been issued, in this city," he reported, "for the republication of these poems, for the *benefit of the author.*" A nation of linendrapers, indeed! Such a young man, with American antecedents, deserved American patronage. "We are not to calculate, with a pedlar's slate and pencil . . . a Poet's receipt and expenditure." Philadelphia's would be "but a tribute which Opulence owes to Genius," which *"when paid, honours* the *giver* and the *receiver.*" On this note, he ends his essay:

> I have now imperfectly fulfilled a voluntary and pleasing task. I recommend a boy of genius, blest by the Author of Intelligence with a mind of premature strength, fertile to the tiller's care, and copious of the fairest flowers. I give him, it is but a little, my solitary subscription and suffrage. I hope others may give much more to one, who, glowing with the flame of Fancy, has always repressed its unhallowed fire, and who is not less the friend of Virtue, than the darling of the Muses.[19]

Joseph Dennie, editor of *The Port Folio,* may have been author of "The American Lounger," though the style of that essay is florid even beyond his more exalted moments.[20] But the editor, intent now as always on correcting vulgar errors and improving the literary taste of his American countrymen, did present two weeks later, under his long-familiar heading, "From the Shop of Messrs. Colon and Spondee," his own effusion on young Leigh Hunt, as "one of those etherial spirits, who glitter in the van of life, and are so copiously endowed with mental stores, that, like the exquisite pulp of certain generous fruits, they burst forth before the tardy period of ordinary maturity." Dennie's critical boiling point was not ordinarily so easily reached; yet it is perhaps unfair to note that the proposed Philadelphia edition of the *Juvenilia* was at that time planned to be printed "for the *benefit of the author,*" to be sure, but by Hugh Maxwell, from whose shop at 25 North Second Street in Philadelphia *The Port Folio* was also issued. Dennie offered his name as a subscriber to the proposed volume: "Although Fortune does not permit me to be a Maecenas, yet I shall cheerfully cast in my mite of subscription for the American edition of the poems of this boy bard." Dennie reminded American readers that "this early blooming genius is a blossom from *our own* garden, that his mother is a *native* of *Philadelphia*," and that Philadelphia should claim her own.

"Studious to advance the reputation, promote the interest of Mr. Hunt," Dennie continued, "I have endeavoured to obtain some of his latest products." He had extracted them, he said, "from a volume so recent, and scarce in this country, that, to a great majority of his readers, they must be entirely novel." Then from the *Poetical Register* he presented the *Sonnet, Written at the Close of Eve* (p. 300), the *Ode to Thomas Campbell* (pp. 224-225), the *Song in Imitation of Sir John Suckling* (pp. 129-130), which Dennie thought "superior to the original" (and reprinted Suckling's verses beginning "Why so pale and wan, fond lover," to prove it), and the *Anacreontic* (pp. 110-111) as a "festive song, which has not been often surpassed by the bacchanalian lays of much older, and more experienced votaries of the jolly god."[21]

The Port Folio of 11 June had also announced a rare treat for American readers: "An original manuscript from Mr. Hunt, the juvenile poet of so much renown, shall be inserted with alacrity" (III, 191). Dennie was without doubt sincere in believing that he would publish an entirely new poem from the young author whom he considered such "an honour to that country from which he is descended." Leigh Hunt's cousins and aunts in Philadelphia undoubtedly passed around among their friends examples of such of their young relative's "exercises" as we have seen his mother proudly forwarded to America. The mistaken notion that Dennie printed an original poem[22] seems therefore a natural one to have been made.

The poem in question was undoubtedly the one submitted to *The Port Folio* by a person who signed himself "J.E.H.," and who was probably John Elihu Hall, then a young man reading law, an occasional contributor to the magazine, and a Philadelphian whose interest in poetry would soon bring him kindly attention from Thomas Moore. Hall, only one year older than Leigh Hunt, was enough his admirer to be listed among subscribers to the Philadelphia edition of the *Juvenilia*. His friendship with the Shewell family through his grandfather Samuel Ewing would have placed him in a position to have access to an original manuscript, if such had existed. He did undoubtedly believe that what he submitted was an original manuscript. It

might even have been a copy, in Leigh Hunt's hand, that someone among the family in England had sent to his American
relatives. In truth, Hall did not quite claim the poem to be
original: "I send you," he wrote Dennie, "a short piece on
Melancholy, from the pen of that youthful bard." It may well
be that neither he nor Dennie knew that the poem had appeared
eighteen months before in the *European Magazine and London
Review*.[23]

None of Leigh Hunt's poems in *The Port Folio* was a first
printing. They continued occasionally to appear during the next
several months. *The Shade of Collins, an Ode* was reprinted on
18 June from the *Poetical Register* (pp. 46-50) as another example of the poet's "maturer muse." On 10 September appeared
twenty-six lines of a "spirited apostrophe, and affecting description" excerpted from *Retirement, or the Golden Mean*, just as
they had appeared in *Juvenilia* (3rd ed., pp. 33-34). A week
later appeared, without title, Hunt's "sweetly" rendered *Translation of Horace's Ode . . . to Septimus* and, also without title,
his *Paraphrase of Horace's Ode 'Inter Vitae'* (*Juvenilia*, pp.
41-42, 45-46), so sophisticated in response to the attractions of
Horace's mistress that it "causes us to forget that the translator
was a schoolboy." Dennie wondered whether the "epigram of
Erasmus on Prince Arthur" was not applicable to the genius
of Mr. Hunt—

> Praecoqua nec tardam expectat sapientia pubem,
> Praeverit annos indoles ardens suos.

The *Parody on Dr. Johnson's 'Hermit Hoar'* and *Anacreon.
Ode 19* (*Juvenilia*, pp. 7, 34) were printed on 15 October as
"lively specimens of Mr. Hunt's poetry, when inspired by the
gayer muses." On 29 October, *Wandles Wave* (*Juvenilia*, pp.
130-131) was exhibited, untitled, as proof that Hunt could also
write in the "style and cadence of . . . popular songs" (*The
Port Folio*, III, 352).

Philadelphia was not to be allowed to forget her poet. Note
was made of his present occupation in composing a tragedy,
called *The Earl of Surrey*.[24] A complimentary English review
was reprinted from the *Poetical Register* (pp. 430-431).[25]
Nonetheless, subscriptions for the proposed Philadelphia edition
seem to have come in slowly. It was now announced that it would
be printed "elegantly, in a portable volume," by James Hum-

phreys, "one of the most assiduous of our booksellers," as soon
as "justified by an adequate suscription."[26] But it was not until
a year after the project had first been broached that Dennie
was able to inform his readers that "after a lingering delay, the
natural effect of the base, ignominious, and *republican* mode of
printing books by *subscription,* the ingenious Poems of Mr. Hunt
have made their appearance." He again quoted stanzas from
The Palace of Pleasure, a poem which, he thought, "nearly
rivals Thomson's 'Castle of Indolence,' in the happiest imitation
of Spenser, in directness and boldness of poetic painting, and in
the rainbow brightness of the tints of fancy."[27]

The American edition made a handsome volume of just over
two hundred pages. Three hundred and fifty-two subscribers
had signed in advance for three hundred and seventy-two copies,
and with Joseph Dennie at the head of the list. John Blair Linn
was represented, and Samuel Ewing and John Elihu Hall, but
the roll of Hunt's Philadelphia patrons is unimpressive and
must have been disappointing. Clearly the book did not do well,
for printer or author. Nor did everyone share Dennie's enthusiasm for the young poet. Charles Brockden Brown's *Literary
Magazine, and American Register* was candidly severe: "Men
do not go forward in poetry as they are accustomed to in other
intellectual paths. . . . Age may be expected in some degree to
refine the taste, and enlarge the stores of imagery, but the ultimate exaltation is not proportioned to the height of the point
from which we set out. . . . We may venture to predict that
Hunt will not reach a higher station than Campbell, Moore, or
Bloomfield."[28]

Leigh Hunt had other American admirers, then and later.
Washington Irving is said to have thought him a finer poet than
Wordsworth, though with an occasional "dash of flippancy"
marring his writing.[29] Lowell praised him; Bayard Taylor enjoyed visiting him; Emerson in 1848 found him "very agreeable";[30] and Hawthorne, meeting him a few years later, thought
him "thoroughly American, and of the best type"—the American of the future.[31] And Hunt reciprocated in kind: he admired
Bryant and Emerson and Lowell. But not Americans in general,
not the linendrapers. After *The Story of Rimini* appeared in
1816, the poet reports that one day in London he was surprised
to receive a strange, new edition. It was "like witchcraft," he
said: "the identical poem, in type and appearance, bound in calf
and sent to me without any explanation." He turned it over in his

hands a dozen times, "wondering what it could be, and how it could have originated." Then he turned to the title page, to discover that it had been printed, and without authorization, by Mathew Carey of Philadelphia. Hunt consoled himself by thinking "how the sight would have pleased my father and mother." Some years later, he received a copy of another American edition, with which was enclosed an impertinent letter—or so he thought it—wherein the publisher, having heard of still another work soon to appear, suggested that he would be happy to reprint it also, if the author would send him a copy. "Not a syllable did he add about the happiness of disbursing a doit for the permission." How many of his works were thus pirated in America, and with no recompense to him, Hunt did not know, but he believed that he had been paid the "shabby compliment" of having all of them reissued there. "Being a cousin-germane of the Americans I am very popular in their country," he explained, "and receive from them every compliment imaginable, except a farthing's payment."[32]

"How came my mother to have been born in such a country?" he asked. Leigh Hunt returned little of the admiration that Philadelphia offered, but was never quite able, to shower on him. "Why do they not get a royal court of two among them," he jibed, "and then learn that there is something else in the world besides huffing and money-getting?" He did respect those few Americans who differed from the bookmongers, those "parasites who do us so much honor in taking our books, and giving us nothing in return." Lastly, and chivalrously, for his mother's sake, he admired all American women, "and all Philadelphia women in particular." That was all. He made it sufficiently plain that, for himself, he would have no part of the "arrogant" and "slave-holding" and "payment shirking"[33] America in which, but for its ill-use of his parents, he might have been born.

NOTES

1. A somewhat briefer version of this essay, subtitled "An American Literary Incident of 1803," appeared in *The Pennsylvania Magazine of History and Biography*, LXX (July 1946), 270–280.

2. See William Duane, Jr., ed., *Passages from the Remembrancer of Christopher Marshall* (Philadelphia, 1839), pp. 43–45; Alexander Graydon, *Memoirs of a Life*

Chiefly Passed in Pennsylvania within the Last Sixty Years (Harrisburg, 1811), p. 112; and *The Autobiography of Leigh Hunt, with Reminiscences of Friends and Contemporaries* (New York, 1850), I, 17–18.

3. *The Political Family: or a Discourse Pointing Out the Reciprocal Advantages Which Flow from an Uninterrupted Union between Great-Britain and Her American Colonies* (Philadelphia, 1775).

4. See Louis Landré, *Leigh Hunt (1784–1859): Contribution à l'histoire du Romantisme anglais* (Paris, 1936), I, 16–18.

5. (London, 1776).

6. Carl and Jessica Bridenbaugh, *Rebels and Gentlemen: Philadelphia in the Age of Franklin* (New York, 1942), pp. 123–131, present a delightful exposition of the background of Hunt's pamphleteering. There is some doubt that the thirteen pamphlets and broadsides attributed to Isaac Hunt between 1764 and 1765 in Charles Evans, *American Bibliography*, are all his; see C. R. Hildeburn, "Authorship of a Pennsylvania Pamphlet of 1764," *The Pennsylvania Magazine of History and Biography*, VI (1882), 251.

7. *Discourse Delivered at St. Paul's Church, Shadwell, for the Benefit of the West Indian Sufferers of the Islands of Jamaica and Barbadoes* (London, 1782) and *A Discourse . . . with . . . Remarks on the Present Miserable Situation of the (Once Happy) United States of America* (London, 1786).

8. *Autobiography*, I, 23.

9. *Autobiography*, I, 29–32, 101.

10. Landré, *Leigh Hunt*, I, 30.

11. (London, 1802), p. 430.

12. *Monthly Mirror*, XI (April 1801), 254.

13. *Autobiography, Reminiscences and Letters of John Trumbull, from 1756 to 1841* (New York, 1941), pp. 319–320.

14. Little is known of Isaac Hunt, Jr. He had left England to seek his fortune in the new world, probably by 1791, when a letter from young Leigh to his aunt, Lydia Shewell of New York, records the seven-year-old's precocious observation concerning his brother that "a roaming stone gathers no moss." Mrs. Hunt worried about Isaac in a letter to her father in 1799, and in 1804 spoke of him to her sister, Mrs. Frances Smith of Philadelphia, as her "long lost Isaac." See Landré, *Leigh Hunt*, I, 21. To the best of my knowledge, this recording of "Hunt, I. Mr. Philadelph." among the subscribers to the *Juvenilia* (p. xix) is the only evidence of his residence in that city. Leigh Hunt, *Autobiography*, I, 141, mentions his oldest brother, "who had been 'wild,' " who nearly fifty years before had been in America, and who "has never been heard of since."

15. *The Port Folio*, III (28 May 1803), 169.

16. *Autobiography*, I, 129–130; II, 18–19.

17. This last description, if Hunt's, is at best ironic, at worst sycophantic, for he later tells us (*Autobiography*, I, 130) that at this time "I acquired a dislike for my grandfather's friend Dr. Franklin, author of *Poor Richard's Almanack*; a heap, as it appeared to me, of 'Scoundrel maxims.' "

18. On the other hand, they may have represented belated apologies from the Rev. Isaac Hunt, who in pamphlets of 1764 and 1765 had attacked most of these gentlemen.

19. "The American Lounger," *The Port Folio*, III (28 May 1803), 169–170.

20. Authorship of this number of "The American Lounger" is not identified in

Randolph C. Randall, "Authors of the *Port Folio* revealed by the Hall Files," *American Literature*, XI (January 1940), 379–416.

21. *The Port Folio*, III (11 June 1803), 186–187.

22. See, for example, Harold Milton Ellis, *Joseph Dennie and His Circle* (Austin, 1918), p. 169, and Frank Luther Mott, *A History of Early American Magazines, 1741–1850* (New York, 1930), p. 231, both of whom state that Dennie printed an "original" poem of Hunt's.

23. XL (December 1801), 448. *Melancholy* was printed in *The Port Folio*, III (18 June 1803), 200.

24. *The Port Folio*, III (23 June 1803), 207; the statement is reprinted, with slight chauvinistically identifying expansion, from a note which had appeared in the London *Monthly Magazine*, XII (June 1802), 553.

25. *The Port Folio*, III (18 June 1803), 197.

26. *The Port Folio*, III (9 July 1803), 222.

27. *The Port Folio*, IV (19 May 1804), 158.

28. II (October 1804), 532.

29. Stanley T. Williams, *The Life of Washington Irving* (New York, 1935), I, 178, 434.

30. Ralph L. Rusk, ed., *The Letters of Ralph Waldo Emerson* (New York, 1939), IV, 86.

31. *English Note-Books* (Boston, 1863), I, 323.

32. Leigh Hunt is not quite accurate. *The Story of Rimini* was published by Wells and Lilly of Boston and by Mathew Carey of Philadelphia in 1816. *The Feast of the Poets* had been pirated in New York two years before; *Foilage, or Poems Original and Translated* appeared in Philadelphia in 1819, and *Byron, and Some of His Contemporaries* in 1828; during the 1840s several of his volumes were printed in Boston and New York. The extent of the piracy does not, however, seem to have been as great in his case as he would make it seem; it is certainly minor beside the number of unauthorized editions of Longfellow and other American authors which appeared during these years in London, as shown in Clarence Gohdes, *American Literature in Nineteenth-Century England* (New York, 1943).

33. *Autobiography*, I, 129–130; II, 18–19.

ARCHIBALD ALISON AND THE
SUBLIME PLEASURES OF TRAGEDY

W. P. Albrecht

Critics and writers on aesthetics have frequently taken pains to
analyze the pleasures of tragedy, for a play, poem, or novel that
deals with evil and terror is not patently delightful. One explanation current in seventeenth- and eighteenth-century Britain
was that the dramatist's artistry, rather than anything distinctively tragic, is responsible for tragic pleasure. Another explanation, and probably the most widely accepted one until the
latter half of the eighteenth century, was that a tragedy both
pleases and instructs by distributing rewards and punishments
after the manner of Divine Providence. According to a third
explanation, the emotions excited by tragedy are the enjoyable
agents of morality. Pity, it was supposed, makes the audience
compassionate, whereas fear combats pride. In addition, the
strong excitement of fear or terror became increasingly valued
as pleasing in itself when the audience could take comfort in its
own safety from threatening dangers.[1] Edmund Burke's *A Philosophical Enquiry into the Origin of Our Ideas of the Sublime
and Beautiful* (1757) identified the tragic as sublime and, more
than any other work, established emotion as the principal source
of tragic pleasure. Among Burke and his followers evil in tragedy became a cause both of delightful terror and of pleasantly
moral sympathy. Gone, or at least greatly diminished as part
of the tragic experience, was any reasoned definition of evil
such as could be drawn from a moral fable.

However, during the course of the eighteenth century and
the beginning of the nineteenth, the imagination acquired new
powers, and consequently the pleasures of tragedy came to include an immediate knowledge of evil communicated not by a
moral fable but through the imaginative molding of sensory
materials by thought and feeling. Intense emotion, on the part

231

of both poet and audience, was still important, not merely for
its own sake, however, but for its power both to promote and
to control the imagination's fusion of images, thoughts, and
feelings. The important kind of unity in a tragedy became the
imaginative unity of thought and feeling rather than any of the
traditional three. As the most intensely emotional kind of poetry,
tragedy seemed to some critics to provide the greatest opportunity for the imagination to unify a wide range of images and
ideas and thus to harmonize both the poet's and his audience's
faculties in a creative act which embodies "truth" and morality.
Through this sort of imaginative complex, evil could be both
known and enjoyed. As Hazlitt pointed out, in a great tragedy
intense emotion has fused the images of pain and suffering with
other images, thoughts, and feelings to create a symbol providing the keenest insight into human life, the securest of values,
and the resulting impetus to moral action. In *King Lear,* said
Keats, the "disagreeables evaporate" when they are fused with
the knowledge and evaluation that a great poet can bring to the
creative act, the whole complex being given immediate force
by vivid and striking imagery. Like Burke, Hazlitt and Keats
merge the tragic and the sublime, and, also like Burke, they use
the word *sublime* in a precise sense and not, as it was sometimes
used, merely to designate intense or exciting emotions. But
whereas Burke traces sublime emotions principally to a physiological response to certain objects, a response which excludes
cognition, Keats and especially Hazlitt are concerned with the
psychological process, which includes cognition and to which
they have transferred the element of size traditionally linked
with sublimity.[2]

When it comes to the pleasures of tragedy, Archibald Alison
does not go so far as Hazlitt and Keats in explaining that tragedy both defines evil and renders it pleasant as part of the whole
imaginative complex. Alison only approaches this explanation,
but finally justifies evil passions in tragedy as emphasizing, by
contrast, the amiable ones. Nevertheless, he establishes a number of assumptions which underlie Hazlitt's and Keats's conclusions. Beauty and sublimity, according to Alison, are not
qualities of matter but depend on association. Aesthetic experience comprises trains of associated ideas and the emotions
excited by these ideas. These trains suggest generalizations
about human life and carry the moral impact derived from
feelings associated with natural objects and with human beings.

Aesthetic pleasure increases with additional trains, which, in turn, require the emotional unity called "simplicity," "purity," or "harmony." This is true of pleasure derived from either beauty or sublimity, but sublime pleasure—which is the more intense—evidently has the greater call for additional trains. Thus Alison makes the connection between simplicity and the expansion of the mind that is found among earlier writers on the sublime. An important difference from these earlier writers, and a similarity to Hazlitt and Keats, is that the expansion of the mind, for Alison, comprises a psychological process of aggregating images and ideas, and is not dependent on the size of external objects but on the intensity and unity of emotion. Consequently, Alison finds sublimity in dramatic as well as descriptive poetry, and makes unity of emotion—or simplicity—a prime requisite for each kind and therefore necessary to the pleasures of tragedy.

i

Alison published his *Essays on the Nature of Taste* in Edinburgh in 1790. Although favorably reviewed, the book did not require a second edition until 1811. Four more Edinburgh editions appeared by 1825. These *Essays*—which are perhaps best known through Jeffrey's 1811 review and for their influence on Wordsworth—had considerable effect on contemporary thought.[3] Alison is probably the most consistent of eighteenth-century writers on the sublime in translating the sublime, and the beautiful as well, into psychological terms—that is, in seeing all aesthetic experience as comprising trains of associated ideas and the accompanying emotions. For Alison, sublimity and beauty do not inhere in any external object but depend entirely on association. ". . . The qualities of matter are in themselves incapable of producing emotion . . . yet . . . from their association with other qualities" they become "signs or expressions" of emotion-exciting qualities (pp. 106-107; II, i).[4] The term *association*, as Alison uses it, seems to include all the relationships of resemblance, contiguity, and cause and effect stated by Hume;[5] but "the principal relationship" in these aesthetic trains is "resemblance; the relation . . . the most loose and general, and which affords the greatest range of thought for our imagination to pursue" (p. 23; I, i, 2 [3]). The "emotion of taste"

—which is Alison's term for aesthetic experience—goes beyond "the simple perception of the object" to embrace a whole complex of associated images, thoughts, and emotions assembled by the imagination.

> Thus, when we feel either the beauty or sublimity of natural scenery—the gay lustre of a morning in spring, or the mild radiance of a summer evening, the savage majesty of a wintry storm, or the wild magnificence of a tempestuous ocean—we are conscious of a variety of images in our minds, very different from those which the objectcs themselves can present to the eye. Trains of pleasing or of solemn thought arise spontaneously within our minds; our hearts swell with emotions, of which the objects before us seem to afford no adequate cause . . . .
> (p. 18; I, i, 1)

These trains may probe deeply into the mind's intellectual and moral resources. In a passage recalling Hobbes's distinction between "unguided" and "regulated" trains of thought and Lord Kames's "reverie,"[6] and anticipating Hazlitt's "disinterestedness" and Keats's "negative capability," Alison writes: "That state of mind . . . is most favourable to the emotions of taste, in which the imagination is free and unembarrassed" by any practical or rational purpose (pp. 20-21; I, i, 2 [1]). However, it would be inaccurate to conclude that "Alison makes taste entirely dependent on the imagination, to the exclusion of judgment and reason."[7] For Alison, as for such others before him as Sir Joshua Reynolds and Abraham Tucker, the imagination, without any effort of the will, draws on accumulated experience for comparisons and generalizations, to become thereby an act of immediate cognition as well as pleasure.[8] Alison's trains include "pleasing or solemn thoughts" and "analogies with the life of man." Autumn scenes, for instance, inspire "that current of thought, which, from such appearances of decay, so naturally leads him to the solemn imagination of that inevitable fate, which is to bring on alike the decay of life, of empire, and of nature itself" (p. 24; I, i, 2 [3]). Rendered intuitive by experience, these comparisons and generalizations come "immediately." The same kinds of trains characterize our enjoyment of painting, music, or poetry (p. 18; I, i). Alison, like Johnson, recognizes that at its best metaphor not only pleases but also instructs—and pleases, at least partly, *because* it instructs.[9] Alison's insistence on the subjectivity of beauty and sublimity casts some doubt on the objective truth of these comparisons and generalizations, but nevertheless Alison assumes, as a stable base for the highest aesthetic pleasure, a network of associations that is widely shared, at least among the educated and leisured classes (pp. 60-61; I, ii, 2 [1]; pp. 303-304; II, iv, 3).

Alison also finds a strong moral and religious component in the "emotion of taste." That beauty and sublimity depend on an "expression of the mind" rather than any quality inhering in an object is, in fact, evidence of God's beneficence as the final cause of aesthetic pleasure. Even "the rocks and the deserts" nurturing a savage will have pleasing associations for him; and the marks of age or disease, rather than disfiguring a loved one, will become signs of the lasting affection that cements pleasure with the principles of duty (pp. 423-424; II, vi, 6). The "Divine artist" has endowed us with susceptibility to moral feelings which association then comes to bind with certain objects, animate or inanimate. "While the objects of the material world are made to attract our infant eyes, there are latent ties by which they reach our hearts; and wherever they afford us delight, they are always the signs or expressions of higher qualities, by which our moral sensibilities are called forth" (p. 428; VI, vi, 6). The "latent ties" imply, it would seem, not some power inherent in the object—which Alison always denies —but a disposition in the child, antedating any association, to respond to certain objects with a kind of pleasure which purifies the mind of evil. Once the object and the moral pleasure have been associated, this and similar objects continue to provide moral strength. Like the "high objects" mentioned in *The Prelude* as "purifying . . . / The elements of feeling and of thought," they may be recalled in "maturer seasons" (I. 409-410, 595) to reinforce "those sentiments and principles" which bring happiness to others and honor to ourselves (p. 430). This "great purpose of nature" is "yet more evident" in the sublimity and beauty of works of art and most evident in the sympathetic virtues expressed by *"the human countenance and form"* (p. 429). Ultimately, as signs of God's power, wisdom, and goodness, beauty and sublimity lead us "directly to RELIGIOUS sentiment" (p. 430).

ii

Aesthetic pleasure is increased by "additional trains of imagery" (pp. 37, 48; I, i, 3 [2-3]), which in turn depend upon "the degree in which . . . uniformity of character prevails" (p. 24; I, i, 2 [3]). Or, to use a term which Alison shares with earlier writers on the sublime, this expansion of the mind depends on *simplicity.* In itself, Alison's distinction between the effects of beauty and of sublimity is commonplace enough. Like others, Alison confines aesthetic experience to sounds and, more especially, to "objects of sight." "Fine and winding lines" are most beautiful since they are associated with delicacy and ease, while "strong and angular lines" are least beautiful, since they express "harshness, roughness, etc." (pp. 186-187, 206; II, iv, 1 [2, 3]). Beautiful sounds, too, are rather gentle, familiar, and undisturbing: "the sound of a waterfall, the murmuring of a rivulet, the whispering of the wind, the sheepfold bell, the sound of the curfew, &c." (p. 124; II, ii. 1 [2]). On the other hand, as one might expect, sublime sounds are associated with "ideas of danger, or power, or majesty, &c." Thunder, for its expression of awe and terror, is the most sublime of the sounds in nature (pp. 114-115; II, ii, 1 [1]). Sublime forms, which also express "qualities capable of exciting very strong emotions," include bodies having "magnitude" of height, depth, breadth, or length, or "bodies connected . . . with ideas of Danger or Power" (military weapons), with "great duration" (Gothic castles), with "splendour or magnificence" (thrones, triumphal arches), and with "awe or solemnity" (temples, religious services, Jupiter's thunderbolts, the Heavens) (pp. 178-182; II, iv, 1 [1-2]). In its references to size and power, especially with religious significance, Alison's list of sublime objects and qualities is hardly unique. What is more interesting and less commonplace is Alison's explanation of the mind-stretching that is stimulated by both sublimity and beauty, the relation of simplicity to this mind-stretching, and the similarity of dramatic and descriptive poetry in these respects. Because of its frequent application to large objects and to the elevated, even religious emotions they inspire, the word *sublime* had seemed more appropriate to descriptive poetry or to the epic, especially *Paradise Lost,* than to the dramatic. Alison's thoroughgoing attribution of both beauty and sublimity to trains of associated ideas makes the sublime less dependent on descriptions of natural objects.

The word *sublime,* as used in the eighteenth century, often describes vast, sometimes irregular objects and the emotions—such as awe, reverence, and terror—that these objects inspire. Beautiful objects, as distinguished from sublime ones, are smaller, more delicate, and more regular; they arouse less intense, less violent, and less mind-filling emotions. The word *sublime* is also applied, as Longinus used it in *On the Sublime,* to style that elevates the soul; and of course it was Longinus's term that came to describe elevated emotions and great thoughts and the objects that were supposed to produce them. The concept of the "natural sublime," as distinguished from the Longinian or rhetorical sublime, emerged in seventeenth-century England before Longinus had been well known there.[10] With the discovery of a universe no longer limited in time and space, emotions once reserved for the Deity were transferred first to interstellar space and then to large terrestrial objects, especially mountains. It was the natural sublime, rather than the Longinian, that was mainly responsible for the importance of religion and visible size in the concept of the sublime.[11]

In its literary use during the eighteenth century, the word *sublime* achieved a range of meaning including almost any sort of intense emotion and the causes thereof. However, in more precise senses principally derived from the natural sublime, the word was more often applied to descriptive or epic rather than dramatic poetry, for the natural sublime originally implied visible magnitude with a close relationship to the religious or the supernatural. Dennis finds the religious insights of "Enthusiastick Passion"—his term for sublime emotion—in "those parts of Epick Poetry, where the Poet speaks for himself, or the eldest of the Muses for him," and excludes them from "those parts of an Epick and Dramatick Poem, where the Poet introduces Persons holding Conversation together."[12] Addison does not exclude sublimity, in the Longinian sense, from tragedy; but for the natural sublime, or "greatness," he turns to "reading the *Iliad,* [which] is like travelling through a Country uninhabited, where the Fancy is entertained with a thousand Savage Prospects of vast Desarts, wide uncultivated Marshes, huge Forests, mishapen Rocks and Precipices" (*Spectator* 39, 417). The distinction between the tragic and the sublime was probably also enforced by the tendency to separate sublime rapture from the distracting "agitation" of the "pathetic," a distinction permitted by Longinus, acknowledged by Addison, insisted on by Baillie, and only partly repudiated by Gerard.[13] Gerard, who like Burke values the agitation of terror for increasing the scope of mental activity, comes close to identifying the sublime and the tragic; but his literary illustrations of sublimity emphasize the images of physical size, especially in the epic (pp. 23-27; I, ii). For Johnson, the sublime is agitating, but it is still a quality of external nature rather than human life; like others, Johnson turns to the epic, especially *Paradise Lost,* for sublimity, and to descriptive rather than dramatic poetry—which he calls "pathetick."[14] Kames regards the sublime as "applicable to every sort of literary performance intended for amusement" (I, 238; iv); but his illustrations, although frequently drawn from Shakespeare's tragedies, principally describe large or elevated objects (I, 217-221; iv). Like Gerard, he readily admits figurative or moral elevation to the sublime, but this is found more in the epic than in tragedy. Kames shows the important place "the social affections" had taken in tragedy when he writes "that tender passions are more peculiarly the province of tragedy, grand and heroic actions of epic poetry" (II, 375; xxii). The exclusion of tragedy from at least the highest flights of sublimity persisted into the next century. Coleridge finds sublimity mainly in the Scriptures and in Milton. Wordsworth would add Spenser. According to De Quincey, "in Milton only, first to last, is the power of the sublime revealed."[15] Even Hazlitt, for whom Shakespeare's tragedies represent the highest reach of sublimity, on at least one occasion likens the sublime effect of Egyptian pyramids and Gothic ruins to the "admiration and delight" excited by epic poetry, whereas dramatic poetry "affects us by sympathy."[16]

Alison removes these distinctions between the sublime and the tragic. We have already noticed that he admits the agitation of terror to sublime emotions and that he regards *all* aesthetic experience, sublime or beautiful, as ultimately religious. Alison makes a more interesting contribution toward identifying the tragic and the sublime, however, by substituting psychological size for physical size in his concept of sublimity. The mental activity aroused by the sublime had, of course, already been subject to a good deal of analysis. In addition to exciting high and religious feelings, the sublime was thought of as giving the mind some pleasant exercise and relieving that disagreeable vacuity which the eighteenth century so consistently deplored.[17] The natural sublime was supposed to offer the special pleasures of encompassing great size. Addison, Baillie, Gerard, and Kames suggest the analogy—made most explicit by Hume—between physical and mental activity: it is as if the mind, while "imagining itself present in every part of the scene," actually expanded and as if the difficulties involved were measured by the physical strains of traversing, bodily, a large object or extended space.[18]

The mind's expansion was also viewed more literally in terms of its own rather than the body's powers, that is, as a process combining images and other ideas and harmonizing the various faculties to provide pleasure and, in varying degrees, cognition and moral direction as well. Dennis's "Enthusiastick Passion" is moved by "Ideas in Contemplation," into which the idea of an object has been expanded by "Thought" or "Meditation." This expansion, although it would seem to involve association, cannot be explained entirely in empirical terms; for the faculty that organizes the mind in a moment of moral knowing is reason, and reason, for Dennis, includes supersensory insight.[19] Addison regards the mind's activity during aesthetic experience —whether incited by sublimity or beauty—not only as a sort of physical extension but also as a process combining simple ideas into a complex one; and, as evident in Addison's analysis of the secondary pleasures of the imagination, these pleasures increase as the trains of associated ideas are multiplied (*Spectator* 412, 413, 416, 417). Gerard takes the compounding process farther than Addison does, beyond a collection of visual images: the "one grand sensation" necessary to sublime emotion includes related ideas supplied by the moral sense and by the judgment (pp. 137-138, 266; II, vii, IV, v).

To promote sublime mind-stretching—or, to use Gerard's term, to "spread" the mind "to the dimensions of its object"— the sublime object was required to have "simplicity," which meant the absence of distracting detail. Addison cites the "poor and weak Effects" of the excessive detail in a "*Gothick* Cathedral" compared with the "Greatness of Manner" which distinguishes the "*Pantheon* at *Rome*" (*Spectator* 415). For Gerard "objects are sublime, which possess *quantity,* or amplitude, and *simplicity,* in conjunction" (p. 11; I, ii). Gerard was drawing on John Baillie, according to whom the intrusion of small or dissimilar parts breaks the magnitude of a scene and "destroys the creative Power of the Imagination" to extend the soul (pp. 9-10). Samuel Johnson's well-known comment on "the grandeur of generality" in the *Life of Cowley* expresses the usual concern for that "comprehension and expanse of thought which at once fills the whole mind" and for sublime "aggregation" unbroken by "minuteness." Johnson seems to refer both to visual extension ("the prospects of nature" and "the wide effulgence of a summer noon") and to widely general thoughts ("not limited by exceptions"). The integrity of the former must not be broken by distracting detail, and its inclusiveness must not be limited by nonrepresentative particulars.[20]

Alison, too, makes simplicity necessary to the kind of mind-stretching he requires of both sublimity and beauty, that is, to an extended concatenation of associated images. For Alison simplicity is unity of emotion or unity of "character." It is one of the two qualities that distinguish aesthetic trains from "ordinary" ones, the other quality being the "simple emotion" excited by each idea within the train (pp. 51-55; I, ii, 1).

> In those trains . . . suggested by objects of sublimity or beauty . . . there is always some general principle of connexion which pervades the whole, and gives them some certain and definite character. They are either gay, or pathetic, or melancholy, or solemn, or awful, or elevating, &c. according to the nature of the emotion which is first excited. Thus the prospect of a serene evening in summer, produces first an emotion of peacefulness and tranquility, and then suggests a variety of images corresponding to this primary impression.
>
> (p. 55; I, ii, 1 [2])

The delight attending "every operation of taste" is not merely the sum of the simple emotions produced by each image or idea but includes "a higher and more pleasing kind" attributable to the exercise of the imagination as it produces a unified train (pp. 98-99; I, Conclusion). This kind of pleasure increases as the imagination extends itself to supply "additional trains of imagery" (p. 48; I, i, 3 [3]), but this extension is impossible if there are details which suggest incongruent emotions. "When our hearts are affected, we seek only for objects congenial to our emotion: and the simplicity [of a landscape or painting] permits us to indulge, without interruption, those interesting trains of thought which the character of the scene is fitted to inspire" (p. 82; I, ii, 3 [2]). This simplicity, with the additional trains it permits, is required of both beauty and sublimity; but since sublime emotions are more intense than those excited by beauty and since aesthetic emotions are proportioned to "uniformity of character" and to the "range of thought" it encourages (p. 23; I, i, 2 [3]), one might infer that sublimity calls on the imagination to produce the more abundant trains.

Alison distinguishes "simplicity" from "uniformity or regularity," such as that of primitive art. He prefers the greater detail, variety, and realism of modern art, as long as the details are selected in "accord with the general expression of the scene" (pp. 78, 258-260; I, ii, 3 [1], II, iv, 2 [1]). This same sort of simplicity is as necessary in poetry as in painting. In fact, it is more important to the poet, who must blend together qualities perceived not only by sight but by other senses and, in addition, "the sublimity and beauty of the moral and intellectual world" (p. 83; I, ii, 3 [3]). Alison applies this requirement not only to descriptive poetry but "to every other branch of poetical imitation, to the description of characters, the sentiments, and the passions of men" (pp. 91-92; I, ii, 3 [3]). "The same unity of emotion is demanded in dramatic poetry, at least in the highest and noblest species of it, tragedy" (p. 94; I, ii, 3 [4]). Of course, Kames and other associationist critics had suggested kinds of unity based on relations other than the more formal ones of time, place, and action; and Kames had also found "simplicity . . . a chief property" of tragedy if its subject is to occupy "our whole attention." But in this context "simplicity" apparently depends on unity of action, which for Kames, as for Johnson, remains the most important kind in tragedy.[21] However, for Alison "unity of character," along with the emotional abundance it promotes, is "fully as essential as any of those three unities, of which every book of criticism is so full" (p. 94; I, ii, 3 [4]). Indeed, Alison's emphasis usually makes it seem a good deal more essential.

Alison, therefore, has no difficulty ascribing sublimity to tragic drama. For one thing, as we have noted, he admits the agitation of terror to sublime emotions. For another, he considers all aesthetic experience—sublime or beautiful, descriptive or dramatic—as ultimately religious. However, more interesting in view of Hazlitt's and Keats's analyses of tragedy, is Alison's explanation of psychological size and emotional simplicity as needed for the highest reaches of beauty and sublimity, and his identification, on this basis, of the sublime and the dramatic. It may be inferred that the sublime emotions, because they are more intense, require more abundant trains than the emotions of beauty; but this inference, although helpful, is clearly not necessary to the classification of tragedy as sublime. What is more important is that Alison has removed visual extension as a requirement of sublimity. Alison's list of sublime objects, it is true, still reflects the influence of physical size, and his emphasis is still on the visual sign, large or otherwise, of beauty or sublimity. On the stage it is the "attitudes or gestures" which he finds "expressive . . . of amiable or unamiable dispositions" (pp. 388-389; II, vi, 4 [1]). But these signs need not be in external—rather than human—nature to produce the highest aesthetic feelings and therefore religious sentiment. Nor is it necessary to have the signs linked by *visual* simplicity. Thus Alison removes certain distinctions which had tended to keep the tragic and the sublime apart.

iii

Alison's sublime pleasures of tragedy, like Burke's, are mainly, if not entirely, emotional, with little insight into the nature of evil. The sublime, of course, had not always implied sheer emotionalism. Dennis's "enthusiasm" harmonizes sensation, emotion, and reason in a moment of insight. Addision accompanies the pleasure of the imagination with at least rudimentary operations of the other faculties, although these are not comparable with the "more serious Employments" of reason and judgment (*Spectator* 411, 412). Gerard echoes Addison in considering the pleasures of taste "less improving than such as are intellectual" (p. 182; III, v), but he nevertheless goes farther than Addison in joining reason and judgment to the imagination. However, having identified the sublime and the tragic, Burke leaves a knowledge of evil out of his description of tragic pleasure. The source of the sublime is "whatever is fitted . . . to excite the ideas of pain, and danger"; and when we are not actually imperiled, the "terrible" produces "delight," which along with the pleasures of sympathy accounts for the enjoyment of tragedy.[22] Burke explains that one may rationally infer something of the role of evil in human life from a study of the passions, which will suggest that the Creator wisely made evil a force for good; but this is not the effect of tragedy itself, the pleasures of which are compounded of sensation and emotion.[23] The imagination does not involve the reason; since it merely reproduces or combines sensory impressions, it is only memory's substitute for sensation.[24] Alison, on the other hand, defines the imagination as offering, in the immediate impact of a work of art, knowledge derived through comparison and generalization; but he does not make use of this cognitive power in defining the pleasures of tragedy. The moral force of tragedy is derived, not from a definition of evil, but—as in Burke—from the kind of emotions tragedy evokes. Tragedy, at its best, awakens "only the greatest and noblest passions of the human soul," thus rendering the theater "a school of sublime instruction" (p. 95; I, ii, 3 [4]).

Hence the need for unity of emotion or character. Alison's elevation of this kind of unity does not, however, lead him to make very liberal judgments. He finds tragi-comedy, for want of unified character, "utterly indefensible" and, therefore, Shakespeare's taste inferior to his genius. For "an uniform character of dignity," Alison therefore turns to a writer with somewhat more classical tastes: Corneille, who disregarded "whatever of common, of trivial, or even of pathetic in the originals from which he copied" that might distract us from the "greatest and noblest passions." Without citing any of Corneille's works, Alison admits his "extravagance and bombast" but would make "some allowance . . . for a poet, who first shewed to his country the example of regular tragedy" (pp. 95-96; I, ii, 3 [4]). Alison, perhaps, is less confident of the power of imaginative trains to unify diverse materials than he sometimes might seem; whereas, writing thirty years later, Hazlitt has fully attained this confidence: Greek tragedy, which closely imitates "the external object," requires the unities of time, place, and action "to give [it] coherence and consistency"; while English tragedy attains unity, and thereby a less rigid and higher kind of beauty, by seeking "to identify the original impression with whatever else, within the range of thought or feeling, can strengthen, relieve, adorn, or elevate it."[25]

Alison's lack of confidence in the fusing power of the imagination, despite his able argument for this power, appears again when he explains how the evil characters in tragedy contribute to tragic pleasure. In his "Introduction" Alison proposes to examine "the qualities of sublimity and beauty . . . in objects that are in themselves productive of PAIN" (p. viii). As it turns out, he never does this in any systematic way, but he provides some scattered comments which help in guessing how he would have analyzed this kind of enjoyment. The usual delight in perceiving an accurate imitation—which Alison dismisses as a "cold pleasure" (p. 82; I, ii, 3 [2])—would have played but a small part. Instead, the emotional contribution to expressing "one pure and unmingled character" (p. 82) would have been the important thing. To be pleasing in a work of art, an object, viewed in the context of that work, only has to have associations which contribute to the delightful emotion characterizing the whole scene, picture, or person. As one learns to appreciate art for "character" rather than for mere imitation, he comes to enjoy even "the representation of desert or of desolate prospects" for its characterizing feeling of solitude, desolation, or wildness (pp. 81-82). Similarly, the withered signs of age or the honorable scars of combat may characterize the portrait of a beloved friend or a national hero (pp. 372, 388-390, 395; II, vi, 2-3). This contribution of unpleasant materials to an overall effect of pleasure is not quite the same as the "conversion" of feeling described by Hume and Gerard, according to whom painful feelings in tragedy are pleasantly resolved by the "prevailing" emotions of imitation, energy of expression, power of numbers, etc. Thus, the emotions of terror and moral disapproval are changed qualitatively and add their component, quantitatively, to the general pleasure.[26] Alison, on the other hand, does not see any qualitative change in somber emotions but only a direct contribution, or a contribution by contrast, to the prevailing effect.

When it comes to immoral human beings rather than harsh scenery or mere physical decay, Alison uses the principle of contrast to justify the expression of "dark, or malignant, or selfish affections" (p. 389; II, vi, 4 [1]). The beauty of the "representation of *Richard* or *Iago*" lies in the contrast that "gives effect to the character and the expression of virtue." That is, the representation of such characters has only the "artificial" beauty appropriate to the purpose of the composition. Attitudes and gestures which are "beautiful *in themselves*" are those that express "amiable dispositions," *i.e.*, those of "gaiety, gentleness, pity, humility, &c.," and not those expressing "fear, rage, envy, pride, cruelty, &c." (pp. 389-390). Richard III and Iago are, of course, about as villainous as tragic characters are likely to become. Alison does not discuss the kind of character whose attitudes and gestures express both good and bad qualities. In such a character, perhaps, he would see the evil as making the good stand out more clearly.

As this shift in standards of beauty from harsh objects in external nature to harsh passions in human nature suggests, the unifying emotion does not have quite the same components in dramatic as in descriptive poetry. As we have seen, God—by providing "latent ties" between "our hearts" and the "objects of the material world" and, in addition, the capacity to store up associations—has made these material objects a continual source of moral delight and religious sentiment. Even the harsher natural objects have their place in supplying aesthetic pleasure for the local inhabitants and for the more sophisticated tastes that have learned to enjoy unified scenes of desolation, danger, and wildness. God has also accommodated our aesthetic emotions to the physical signs of disease or age; but, unlike "the rocks and deserts" and "the collapsed cheek," the "attitudes and gestures" expressing fear, rage, cruelty, etc. are not susceptible to pleasant associations. According to Alison's aesthetic, a play comprising only evil characters doing evil acts could not be enjoyable, for, despite the unified expression of character, the "simple ideas" comprised by the trains would be unpleasant. Such unpleasant ideas, therefore, find a place in tragedy only because, by contrast, they intensify the pleasure derived from the amiable ideas and the trains comprising them. Alison takes no notice of the possibility that the unpleasant ideas, in the context of imaginative trains, might become enjoyable through a recognition of their truth and an awareness of the poet's evaluation of evil. Of course, the audience might infer that evil exists to make good seem more attractive; but even so, as Burke suggests, this would be an inference from a study of the passions rather than an immediate effect of tragedy. But perhaps Alison would have dealt more satisfactorily with the problem of evil if he had completed that part of the *Essays* which was to deal with those "noblest productions of the fine arts . . . founded upon subjects of TERROR and DISTRESS" (p. viii; Introduction).

iv

In Alison we find another step—beyond Burke and Gerard— in identifying the sublime and the tragic. Alison is not unusual, of course, in finding sublimity an intense sort of aesthetic experience, tragedy an intense sort of poetry, and therefore a close relationship between the sublime and the tragic. He is more unusual for his translation of sublime size with physical integrity into psychological size with emotional integrity and for his identification, on this basis, of the sublime and the dramatic. By Alison's time the transfer of sublime size to moral qualities

—magnanimity, virtue, fortitude, etc.—was nothing new, and as early as Dennis and Addison the enjoyment of the sublime had been traced to a sizable mental operation explained in psychological terms. But the sublime importance of external nature and its religious implications persisted, as is shown by the continued linking of sublimity with descriptive and religious poetry rather than dramatic. Alison's thoroughness in ascribing beauty and sublimity to association rather than any quality in external objects removes the reason for such a distinction. On the basis of the emotional integrity necessary to abundant trains, and therefore the greatest aesthetic pleasure, Alison sees no difference between descriptive poetry and dramatic poetry. Tragedy, especially, requires this sort of integrity, since its "greatest and noblest passions" must not be contaminated. This sort of integrity is, of course, required of both beauty and sublimity; but its correlation with the most intense and most elevated feelings makes it a further link between the sublime and the tragic.

Although he analyzes sublimity as an extended fusion of images, thoughts, and feelings, Alison is a little disappointing when he specifies the sublime pleasures of tragedy. He has no difficulty explaining the pleasure derived from the harsher aspects of material objects: all of these may be beautiful or—more likely—sublime in their contribution to the moral pleasure of an emotionally integrated scene, painting, or description. Alison has satisfactorily integrated such aspects with his own conception of God's benevolent design; for, he points out, divine benevolence has made all kinds of material objects susceptible to pleasing associations. But this cannot be true of evil actions. Therefore, the evil characters in tragedy have only an "artificial" kind of beauty derived from their power to increase, by contrast, the amiable pleasures of viewing the good characters. In his analysis of the pleasures of tragedy, Alison does not come to grips with the problem of evil in human life—or with the function of tragedy in defining the role of evil—but then he does not pretend to have made a systematic or searching approach to this problem.

Nevertheless, Alison helps lay the psychological basis for a much more profound treatment of evil in Hazlitt and Keats. Aesthetic pleasure, he says, increases as the imagination's trains —speeding along the same emotional track—range most widely, and bring into the complex of ideas more and more of our accumulated experience and the resulting thoughts and feelings, finding more analogies between visual images and "the life of man," exercising "our moral sensibility," and "leading us directly to RELIGIOUS sentiments." Although the hampering restraints of reason and judgment are lifted during the reverie necessary to extended trains, previous conclusions of reason and judgment are nevertheless available for fusion within the imaginative complex. It might be concluded, therefore, that even the grimmest aspects of human as well as material nature—seen, known, and evaluated in and through this complex—could become pleasing. But, ignoring the cognitive power he has found in the imaginative process and perhaps content with amiable religious sentiment strengthened by contrast with evil, Alison does not reach this conclusion, which was nevertheless drawn, from a similar identification of the tragic and the sublime, by Hazlitt and Keats.

NOTES

1. See Samuel H. Monk, *The Sublime: A Study of Critical Theories in XVIII-Century England* (Ann Arbor, Mich., 1960), pp. 61–62, 67–68; Earl R. Wasserman, "The Pleasures of Tragedy," *ELH*, XIV (1947), 283–307; Baxter Hathaway, "The Lucretian 'Return upon Ourselves' in Eighteenth-Century Theories of Tragedy," *PMLA*, LXII (1947), 672–689; Eric Rothstein, "English Tragic Theory in the Late Seventeenth Century," *ELH*, XXIX (1962), 306–323.

2. See my article "Hazlitt, Keats, and the Sublime Pleasures of Tragedy," in *The Nineteenth-Century Writer and his Audience*, ed. H. Orel and G. J. Worth, University of Kansas Humanistic Studies No. 40 (Lawrence, Kansas, 1969), pp. 1–30.

3. See Martin Kallich, "The Meaning of Archibald Alison's *Essays on Taste*," *Philological Quarterly*, XXVII (1948), 314–324; Francis Jeffrey, "Alison on Taste," *Contributions to the Edinburgh Review* (New York, 1869), pp. 13–39; Arthur Beatty, *William Wordsworth, his Doctrine and Art in Their Historical Relations*, 3rd ed. (Madison, Wis., 1960), pp. 38, 45–51, 159; Walter J. Hipple, Jr., *The Beautiful, the Sublime, and the Picturesque in Eighteenth-Century British Aesthetic Theory* (Carbondale, Ill., 1957), pp. 158–181; Monk, pp. 148–153.

4. All references will be to the edition of the *Essays* published in Boston in 1812, which is based on the Edinburgh edition of 1811.

5. *An Enquiry Concerning Human Understanding*, Section III. See Hipple, pp. 168–169.

6. Thomas Hobbes, *Leviathan*, ed. M. Oakeshott (Oxford, 1957), pp. 14–15 (I, iii); Henry Home, Lord Kames, *Elements of Criticism*, 6th ed. (Edinburgh, 1785), I, 93 (ii, 1), 173 (ii, 5), 315 (ix).

7. Kallich, p. 315.

8. Sir Joshua Reynolds, *Discourses on Art*, ed. R. R. Wark (San Marino, Cal., 1959), pp. 230–234 (Discourse XIII); Abraham Tucker, *The Light of Nature Pursued*, 2nd ed. (London, 1805), II, 1–6.

9. *The Works of Samuel Johnson* (Oxford, 1825), VI, 42; VIII, 329–330.

10. Marjorie Nicolson, *Mountain Gloom and Mountain Glory* (Ithaca, N. Y., 1959), pp. 185–270; Ernest Tuveson, "Space, Deity, and the 'Natural Sublime,' " *Modern Language Quarterly,* XII (1951), 20–38; and *Imagination as a Means of Grace* (Berkeley and Los Angeles, 1960), pp. 56–71; Monk, p. 21.

11. Longinus had designated large bodies of water, the stars and the planets, and erupting volcanoes as "great" and "more divine" than lesser phenomena, but he does not call these large objects "sublime." The enjoyment of this greatness, rather, is evidence of man's capacity for elevated thoughts ([Cassius] Longinus, *On the Sublime,* trans. B. Einarson and Sir Joshua Reynolds, *Discourses on Art,* with intro. by Elder Olson [Chicago, 1945], pp. 4–5, 13, 62–63 [i, vii, xxxv–xxxvi]). The Longinian and the "natural" concepts of sublimity, of course, reinforced each other in various ways, but the idea of size is central to the latter and only incidental to the former.

12. John Dennis, *Critical Works,* ed. Edward N. Hooker (Baltimore, 1939–1943), I, 338–339.

13. *On the Sublime,* pp. 14–15 (viii); *Spectator* 339; John Baillie, *An Essay on the Sublime* (1747), Augustan Reprint Society (Los Angeles, 1953), pp. 10–11, 23–24, 33; Alexander Gerard, *An Essay on Taste,* 3rd ed. (Edinburgh, 1780), p. 13 (I, ii), pp. 51–52 (I, iv), p. 160 (III, i).

14. *Works,* I, 221–222; VI, 145, 339–340; *Johnson on Shakespeare,* ed. Walter Raleigh (London, 1908), pp. 150–152; J. H. Hagstrum, "Johnson's Conception of the Beautiful, the Pathetic, and the Sublime," *PMLA,* LXIV (1949), 134–157.

15. *Coleridge's Miscellaneous Criticism,* ed. T. M. Raysor (Cambridge, Mass., 1930), p. 164; *Poetical Works of William Wordsworth,* ed. E. de Selincourt and H. Darbishire, 2nd ed. (Oxford, 1952), II, 439; "On Milton," in the *Collected Writings of Thomas De Quincey,* ed. D. Masson (Edinburgh, 1889–1890), X, 400–402; Clarence De Witt Thorpe, "Coleridge on the Sublime," in *Wordsworth and Coleridge: Studies in Honor of George McLean Harper,* ed. E. L. Griggs (Princeton, 1939), pp. 207–218; Sigmund K. Proctor, *Thomas De Quincey's Theory of Literature* (Ann Arbor, Mich., 1943), pp. 78–92; John E. Jordan, *Thomas De Quincey, Literary Critic* (Berkeley, Cal., 1952), pp. 55–68; and "Hazlitt, Keats, and the Sublime Pleasures of Tragedy," pp. 17–20.

16. *The Complete Works of William Hazlitt,* ed. P. P. Howe (London, 1930–1934), V, 52.

17. See [Jean-Baptiste] Du Bos, *Réflexions critiques sur la poésie et sur la peinture,* 5th ed. (Paris, 1746), I, 5–11 (I, i); [Bernard le Bovier de] Fontenelle, "Réflexions sur la poétique," in *Œuvres* (Paris, 1758), III, 162–163 (xxxv–xxxvi); Wasserman, pp. 289–290.

18. *Spectator* 412; Baillie, pp. 4–7; Gerard, p. 12 (I, ii); Kames, I, 210–211, 225 (iv); David Hume, *A Treatise of Human Nature,* ed. L. A. Selby-Bigge (London, 1896), pp. 435–436 (II, iii, 8).

19. *Critical Works,* I, 188, 202, 263–264, 338–340, 345, 348, 350. See Monk, p. 49, and Nicolson, pp. 281–282, n.

20. *Works,* II, 16–17. See also *Rambler* 36, *Works,* II, 178; and Scott Elledge, "The Background and Development in English Criticism of the Theories of Generality and Particularity," *PMLA,* LXII (1947), 147–182, esp. 160–168.

21. Kames, II, 397–398 (xxii), 407–409 (xxiii); see also I, 200–201 (iii); Johnson, *Works,* III, 242; *Johnson on Shakespeare,* pp. 14–17, 24–25; Ralph Cohen, "Association of Ideas and Poetic Unity," *Philological Quarterly,* XXXVI (1957),

465–474. Kames would also have the unities of time and place observed within each act (II, 427–428; xxiii).

22. Edmund Burke, *A Philosophical Enquiry into the Origin of our Ideas of the Sublime and Beautiful*, ed. J. T. Boulton (London, 1958), pp. 35–40, 44–48, 51 (I, iv–vii, xiii–xv, xviii).

23. *Ibid.*, pp. 49–54, 57, 61, 131, 138 (I, xvi, xvii, xix; II, ii, iv; IV, iii–ix).

24. *Ibid.*, pp. 16–17 ("Introduction on Taste").

25. *Complete Works*, VI, 350. Cf. A. W. Schlegel, *A Course of Lectures on Dramatic Art and Dramatic Literature*, trans. J. W. Black (London, 1846), pp. 24–27 (Lecture I), and Hazlitt's review of the 1815 edition, *Complete Works*, XVI, 60–62.

26. David Hume, "Of Tragedy," *Essays, Moral, Political, and Literary*, ed. T. H. Green and T. H. Gosse (London, 1889), I, 261, 263–264; Gerard, pp. 51–52 (I, iv).

ON THE INTERPRETATION OF *ENDYMION:*
THE COMEDIAN AS THE LETTER E

Jack Stillinger

In 1940, well before the Wallace Stevens critical industry got under way, Hi Simons began an essay on *The Comedian as the Letter C* with the observation, "Since it was brought out in *Harmonium,* in 1923, eight theories for its interpretation have been proposed. But these hypotheses are mutually contradictory. . . . So their net effect is to cancel each other out."[1] This is not quite the situation with criticism of Keats's *Endymion,* but there have been many interpretations—well over a hundred since F. M. Owen's *John Keats: A Study* appeared in 1880, and some thirty of them of major proportions. While it can hardly be said that they are all "mutually contradictory" or that they cancel one another out, they do in many ways conflict, and none has been found (except perhaps by its author) wholly satisfactory as a comprehensive explanation of Keats's intentions in the poem.[2] My purpose here is not to arbitrate among the principal interpretations, nor even to offer one of my own, but rather—much less ambitiously—to attempt to explain why there have been so many.

i

My main point, if I may set it down at the beginning rather than at the end, is that there are a number of central themes running through Keats's poem. Interpretations have dealt with one or more of these, sometimes with several, but not, at once, with all of them. I shall single out five for brief discussion, giving partial documentation of the relevant passages in quasi-tabular form.

250

(1) *"Fellowship with essence"*—*a kind of imaginative join-ing or identification with things and persons outside oneself that leads, at its highest reach, to union with some ideal.* Many critics before, and all critics after, Newell F. Ford[3] have been aware of this theme, which not only is the subject of an impressive speech by Endymion (I.777 ff.)[4] and is easily seen as one description of Endymion's quest throughout the poem, but also is a concept imbedded in much of the incidental language—in the verbs "bind," "commune," "melt into," "blend," "mingle," "interknit," "combine," "commingle," for example. It is obviously related to Keats's notion of Negative Capability, though the letters most frequently cited for that idea (27[?] December 1817 and 27 October 1818, *Letters,* I, 193-194, 386-387) were written after the first draft of the poem was completed, and the earlier of them seems to speak of it as a recent discovery ("several things dovetailed in my mind, & at once it struck me"). Among passages relevant to this theme are the following:

I.30–31, 36–37 (two brief instances of identification with "essence") ; 98–100 ("melt out . . . essence . . . Into the winds") ; 540–678 (Endym-ion's dream-union with Cynthia—see especially ll. 594–595, 600) ; 777–849 (the full-scale explanation—note the language of ll. 784–785, 796, 798–799, 810–813, 833) ; 902 ("Bathing my spirit"). II.12 ("in our very souls, we feel") ; 274–284 (self and solitude, the opposites of "fellowship") ; 707–827 (another dream-union with the goddess—note ll. 739–740, 752, 815–817) ; 835–839 (poet's immersion in a "sleeping lake"). III.55 ("thine airy fellowship") ; 162–173 (the moon's blending with Endymion's "ardours") ; 380–391 (Glaucus's self-destroying entangle-ment with the ocean) ; 766 ff. (the "mighty consummation" of Glaucus and Scylla and the other lovers) ; 963 ("blend and interknit"). IV.92 ff. (Endymion's love for the Indian maiden) ; 477 ("no self-passion or identity") ; 512–551 (the Cave of Quietude) ; 977–1002 (the final union with Cynthia).

(2) *"Gradations of Happiness"*[5]—*the idea of a valuation scale of "essences."* This, again based on Endymion's speech in I.777ff., is clearly subordinate to, or a part of, the preceding motif. But it has been treated separately in so many critical dis-cussions that it has acquired independent status as a theme of the poem. The principal passages are the following:

I.540 ff. (Endymion's dream experiences begin with nature and the moon, and end with the goddess) ; 777 ff. (progression from rose leaf and music to friendship, mortal love, and immortal love).

In Book II there is a progression of sorts from solitude to concern for nature (from which Endymion is separated) and then love (the Venus and Adonis episode and the second dream-union with Cynthia). III.23–40 (describing a "ladder" to heavenly "regalities") ;[6] 142–179 (Endymion's retrospective account of his relationship with the moon —again a progression beginning with nature and going on to higher fellowship). IV.851–854 (distinction between "pleasures real" and "higher ones"). At the end of Book IV Endymion achieves the highest fellowship on the scale.

(3) *The conflict of self and solitude with love and humanitarian activities.* This would be at least partly subsumable under (1), the theme of "fellowship," were it not that at certain points in the poem human and divine relationships are directly opposed to one another. In any case, because of the peculiar connection between Keats's poem and Shelley's *Alastor* (see section II, below), which prominently treats solitude and self-love, the theme must be listed separately. In his quest for union with Cynthia, Endymion renounces the world and worldly activities; in much of the poem he is a "solitary." A sizable group of critics,[7] pointing to Endymion's actions in sympathizing with Alpheus and Arethusa in Book II, freeing the drowned lovers in Book III, and pitying and falling in love with the (seemingly) mortal Indian maiden in Book IV, take it as Keats's main point that Endymion must be schooled in the ways of *human* existence before he can gain immortality. The following may be cited:

I.721 ff. (the whole exchange between Peona and Endymion, especially the conflict of earthly fame and "high and noble life"—ostensibly the performance of humanitarian deeds—with love, as in ll. 757–760 and 816–842).

II.77–78 (Endymion in "a solitary glen, / Where there was never sound of mortal men": he is separated from the human world for all of Books II and III and much of Book IV) ; 274–293 ("habitual self," the "deadly feel of solitude") ; 586–587, 590, 633, 681–682, 706, 857–860 (six references to solitude and loneliness) ; 1012–1017 (Endymion's sympathy for Alpheus and Arethusa, and prayer to Cynthia to aid them).[8]

III.282–290 (Endymion's heart "warm[s] / With pity") ; 386 (Glaucus's "Forgetful utterly of self-intent" again relates anti-self to "fellowship," the idea of "self-destroying" enthralments in I.798–799) ; 714 ff. (Endymion's "achievement high" in freeing the lovers, for which he is apparently rewarded—see ll. 1023–1024).

IV.475–477 ("no self-passion or identity"). Book IV is largely concerned with love, and especially with Endymion's human feelings (pity, love, perplexity) in relation to the Indian maiden.

(4) *The opposing claims of human and immortal realms of existence.* This is partly related to the preceding concern, and involves some of the same passages cited for it, but is primarily a metaphysical or "ontological"[9] rather than a social or moral theme. Endymion's rhetorical question of I.777 asks, among other things, whether happiness lies in the actual world or in some ideal realm,[10] and through much of his quest he is intent on freeing himself from the one in order to gain entrance to the other. This motif especially shows up in incidental details of the poem, as in the first three instances below:

I.7 ("bind us to the earth"); 68–72 (the lamb straying out of the actual world); 176–177 ("like one who dream'd / Of . . . groves Elysian"); 360–393 (the old shepherds' ideas of heaven—note the tone of "wander'd," "vieing to rehearse," "fond imaginations" in ll. 371, 372, 393); 404 ("Like one who on the earth had never stept"); 473–474 ("Can I want . . . aught nearer heaven"); 505–507 (Endymion knows of "things . . . Immortal, starry"); 621–622 and 681–705 (immortal dream vs. reality); 721 ff. (again, Peona's speech on the claims of this world, and Endymion's reply justifying his longing for the higher realm); 972–977 (Endymion's temporary resolution "to fashion / My pilgrimage for the world's dusky brink"—and not beyond).
II.123–125 (the idea of wandering "far . . . past the scanty bar / To mortal steps"); 142–162 (Endymion's analogy for human life, which he rejects); 185–187 (more bursting of mortal bars); 302–332 (Endymion's plea, as "exil'd mortal," for deliverance "from this rapacious deep"); 463–464 (Adonis failed to seize "heaven"); 904–909 ("earthly root . . . bloom of heaven").
III.374–378 (Glaucus's "distemper'd longings" for another world); 906–907 (the idea of escape "from dull mortality's harsh net"); 1007 ("far strayed from mortality"); 1024–1027 ("Immortal bliss . . . endless heaven").
IV.36–37 (the Indian maiden's plea for "one short hour / Of native air"); 298–320, 614–723, 851–854 (Endymion's internal conflict in these passages and throughout much of Book IV over the choice between the Indian maiden and his goddess). At the end of Book IV, when the Indian maiden reveals herself as Cynthia, Endymion in a sense wins both worlds.

(5) *The authenticity of dreams, which here (as in a number of Keats's later poems) are meant to symbolize the visionary imagination.* The invitation to make much of this theme and a guarantee of the symbolism of dreaming in the poem are offered by Keats himself in the letter to Benjamin Bailey of 22 November 1817 in which he affirms his certainty in "the authenticity of the Imagination": "you may know my favorite Speculation by

my first Book" (of *Endymion,* presumably referring especially
to Peona's questioning of dreams—"how light / Must dreams
themselves be . . . Why pierce high-fronted honour to the quick
/ For nothing but a dream?"—and Endymion's reply urging
the reality of the dream he is pursuing). "What the imagination
seizes as Beauty must be truth," Keats says, and he goes on to
compare imagination to Adam's dream in Book VIII of *Paradise Lost:* "he awoke and found it truth" *(Letters,* I, 184-185).
Critics[11] have seen Endymion's quest as a testing of the authenticity of dreams, and there is, most prominently in Books I and
IV, a good deal of evidence to support the idea:

I.22–24 (tales as "immortal drink" from "heaven's brink"); 176–177
(Endymion's seeming to dream of Elysium is an early clue); 288–289
and 293–302 (Pan as a symbol of imagination, giving "clodded earth
. . . a touch ethereal"); 324–325 (history sending "A young mind from
its bodily tenement"); 360–393 (again, the old shepherds' "fond imaginations," which, while not dreams, are nevertheless types of visionary
experience); 455–463 (sleep, dreams, visionary "enchantment"); 540–
678 (Endymion's dream experiences—note ll. 573–578, 581–586);
717–722 and 747–760 (Peona's remarks on Endymion's "weakness"
and the lightness of dreams—"whims," "mere nothing"); 769 ff.
(Endymion's reply—see especially ll. 770–771 and 850–861).
II.43 (Endymion is said to be "Brain-sick"—cf. I.758); 437–439 (the
presentation of "immortal bowers to mortal sense"); 703–708 (dreaming as an escape from solitude).
III.440–443, 460, 476 (Glaucus's "love dream" is a "specious heaven").
IV.407–436 (Endymion dreams of heaven and his goddess, and then
"Beheld awake his very dream"); 636–659, 669 (Endymion's renunciation of dreams[12]—in a passage, however, described as "fancies vain and
crude," 722, the product of his desperation and frustration). At the end
of the poem Endymion's dream turns out—as since Book II we knew
it would—to be a "truth."

There are other preoccupations in the poem—one might include (6) "the playing of different Natures with Joy and Sorrow" *(Letters,* I, 219—for the *Endymion* references see "joy,"
"grief," "sorrow" in the Keats concordance); (7) Keats's
curious emphasis here and there on *midway-ness* (see "bourne,"
"brink," "half," "middle," "midway" in the concordance); and
(8) the extent to which Endymion is, as Keats wrote in two
letters of 23 January 1818, "led on . . . by circumstance" and
"overshadowed by a Supernatural Power" *(Letters,* I, 207, 213

—in the poem see II.123-128, 293, 574-575, III.297-299, 708, 759, 1023, IV.976, 990). Still other topics could be added to the list. But the first five items I have set out briefly above are, I think, the main themes of the poem.

Now comes the knotty problem of relationships among them. All five of the themes appear in the dialogue between Peona and Endymion in the last half of Book I, and there are obvious connections made (or to be made) among them: the idea of gradations (2) is embodied in the exposition of "fellowship with essence" (1); self and solitude (3) are opposed to "fellowship" (1), while love and humanity (3) are high on the scale; both the human and the divine realms (4) are areas in which love and, in a sense, humanity (3) are possible; dreams (5) are posited as a means to highest fellowship (1), which is a type of immortal existence (4); and so on. On the other hand, certain oppositions may be observed: dreaming (5) is antithetical to human love and humanitarian deeds (3), and these—and the whole human realm (4)—are renounced for higher fellowship (1); dreaming (5) also may ultimately be opposed to highest fellowship (1)—in the commonest critical reading of the poem it is necessary for Endymion to repudiate his ideal in order to win it. All five themes have to be considered in any comprehensive interpretation of the poem, and, as I suggested at the outset, the critics, while dealing with one or more of them, or even with partial elements of all of them, have not managed to reconcile them in a single, unified explanation of the poem. There is good reason for this.

All five of the themes are, loosely speaking, "philosophical," but they do not all belong to the same branch of philosophy. In varying degrees they have implications that are social (1-4), moral (1, 3, 4), metaphysical (1, 2, 4, 5), psychological (1, 3, 5), and aesthetic (1, 2, 5), but there is no one category in which all five can be related into a consistency. In particular, owing to Keats's peculiar emphases in the poem, there is a point at which the social-moral concerns on the one hand (very roughly, 1-4) and the psychological-aesthetic concerns on the other (taking for the moment 5 by itself)[13] do not seem to impinge on one another. It is not so much that they conflict as that they simply have nothing to do with one another. The difficulty may, of course, be merely our own (or my own) critical shortsightedness, but I prefer to offer another explanation.

ii

I think a clarification, though not a resolution, of the problem can be found in Shelley's *Alastor* (published in March 1816, thirteen months before Keats began his poem), which has long been recognized as a precipitating element in *Endymion*.[14] It is, of course, possible to read *Alastor* in a number of different ways. Two of these are more relevant than the others to the question at hand, and I shall outline them briefly.[15] (1) *Alastor* is, among other things, an allegorical representation of an unfortunate state of mind and the effects that follow from it. The state of mind is self-love; the effects are loss of sympathy or response in nature, physical wasting away, and ultimately death. Shelley's Poet goes happily about seeking and gathering knowledge until the need for love suddenly and necessarily awakens in him, and he has a vision. This vision, combining the attraction of a be-loved woman with certain attributes of nature, is the creation of the Poet's imagination, and it comes near being an idealization of the Poet's self, his own soul, stripped of all imperfections (Shelley's fragmentary essay "On Love" is frequently cited in connection with this aspect of the vision; see also the first para-graph of Shelley's Preface to *Alastor* and ll. 153-161 of the poem). In the course of his long search, for a human embodi-ment of this vision or reunion with the prototype, the Poet's quest gradually turns into one of yearning after self (and hence the Poet's rejection of humanity and his increasing involvement in solitude, the "self-centred seclusion" of Shelley's Preface). If there is an *alastor* in the poem, it is the Poet's self-love. He wastes away and dies at the end principally because he has, in seeking after his love-vision, become enamored of himself (the narcissuses in ll. 406-408 are one of several clues), and because he has excluded "sweet human love" (see especially ll. 60-63, 129-139, 203-205, 266-271).

(2) *Alastor* may also be read as an exposition of an epistemo-logical dilemma involving imagination, creativity, and association psychology. Here the question would be how, if (in the theories of Locke and Hartley) dreams and visions are no more than simple and complex recollections of sense experience, can any new truths outside the material world be apprehended?—or, to put it in Keats's terms, how can the imagination be "au-thentic"? *Alastor* has clearly an associationist bias—note "sinks . . . into the frame of his conceptions," "modifications," "intel-

lectual faculties, the imagination, the functions of sense," "attaching . . . to a single image" in the first paragraph of the Preface, and "vacant mind" in line 126. Shelley's Poet takes in impressions until his mind is saturated, and he has exhausted the natural world. He then, in quest of novelty, creates a love-vision which, because it is actually based on his own past sensations, is too much like his knowledge of himself. He seeks in vain for a prototype that in reality has no existence outside himself, and then dies, "Blasted by his disappointment." In this reading,[16] *Alastor* is a denial of the imagination's ability to provide authentic transcendental truths—"What the imagination seizes as Beauty" proves to be a false lure—and the poem is a calmly despairing lament over the situation.

We have here, then, two thematic preoccupations in Shelley's poem that, while they are not incompatible, are not really relatable any more than the social-moral and psychological-aesthetic themes of *Endymion*. It is primarily these two concerns that I think Keats responded to in his own poem. To the one he provided a positive answer. Where the Poet in *Alastor* had renounced the world, spurned human love, pursued a vision of idealized self, failed in his quest, and died, Endymion, beginning on the same course, learns sympathy, performs humanitarian deeds, experiences human love, and finally succeeds, being rewarded with "Immortal bliss." In the other matter Keats is less conclusive. Although Endymion's love-dream does turn out to be a truth, as the *Alastor*-Poet's did not, Endymion seemingly has serious doubts toward the end of the poem—

> I have clung
> To nothing, lov'd a nothing, nothing seen
> Or felt but a great dream! . . .
> . . . gone and past
> Are cloudy phantasms. Caverns lone, farewel!
> And air of visions, and the monstrous swell
> Of visionary seas! No, never more
> Shall airy voices cheat me . . .
> (IV.636–654)

—and there is good reason, especially in the light of his later poems, to think that Keats shared them, in spite of the happy ending he wrote into his poem. My point, however, is not once again to argue for Keats's skepticism concerning the visionary imagination, but rather to show how an unrelatedness of themes in *Endymion* is paralleled in a similar unrelatedness of themes in

Alastor, known to be one of the sources of Keats's poem. If we are assigning blame for faulty unity, then part of it must fall on Shelley.

iii

I do not, however, think blame is called for, and I would maintain that such thematic unrelatednesses are quite common in long poems. I began this essay, and chose my title, in anticipation of making a concluding point using parallels in a more modern allegory. Though Wallace Stevens read *Endymion* at least twice, in 1899 and 1909,[17] one would hardly call it an immediate stimulus to *The Comedian as the Letter C,* which was written in the early 1920s. Yet Stevens's poem does in some ways begin where *Endymion* leaves off, and it vaguely bears something of the same thematic relationship to Keats's poem as *Endymion* bears to *Alastor.*

In Part I, "The World without Imagination," Stevens's Crispin (who is both a poet in search of an aesthetic and a pilgrim-wanderer in search of an inhabitable world) is on the first leg of a voyage from "Bordeaux to Yucatan, Havana next, / And then to Carolina" (54-55). At sea, tempest-tossed and overwhelmed by the immensity of the ocean, he is reduced to "some starker, barer self / In a starker, barer world" (61-62): "The last distortion of romance / Forsook the insatiable egotist" (76-77). In Yucatan (Part II) Crispin, arriving "destitute" (96), engorges himself on "savage color" (103) and "Green barbarism" (125), finding "A new reality in parrot-squawks" (148). Part III plays off "moonlight" yearnings against "the essential prose" of realistic detail. Crispin's journey is "A fluctuating between sun and moon" (234), and as he approaches Carolina "The moonlight fiction disappeared" (257): "He gripped more closely the essential prose / As being, in a world so falsified, / The one integrity for him" (274-276). In Part IV Crispin projects a colony on the premises of the value of essential prose. Romance is banished ("Exit the mental moonlight" [284]), and fiction and dreams as well ("All dreams are vexing. Let them be expunged" [377]); the sole value is "veracious page on page, exact" (381). In Part V Crispin, further reducing his scope "To things within his actual eye" (394), builds a cabin, marries, and settles down to "what is" (438)—a "quotidian" that, if it saps philosophers (460), nevertheless consists of food, birds, flowers, and lovemaking. Part VI, which introduces his four daughters, shows the hero now leading the same kind of life he led in Bordeaux. The realization of the circularity of his pilgrimage engenders a fatalistic skepticism, which produces the "doctrine" of lines 540 ff.:

> Crispin concocted doctrine from the rout.
> The world, a turnip once so readily plucked,
> Sacked up and carried overseas, daubed out
> Of its ancient purple, pruned to the fertile main,
> And sown again by the stiffest realist,
> Came reproduced in purple, family font,
> The same insoluble lump.

The lines, which may be read as retracing the "action" of the poem, conclude with the idea that Crispin's new world is "the same insoluble lump" with which he began.

I suppose the general drift of the story is clear enough: Crispin the romantic settles down as Crispin the realist. But there are a number of things that stand in the way of more detailed interpretation. The progress from section to section is sometimes confusing—for example, the shifts from romanticism to bare realism to "exotic realism" and then back to bare realism in Parts I-III seem arbitrary rather than reasonably motivated. And one is left in doubt about the attitude of the poem toward Crispin's situation in the final section: is it supposed to be an arrival or a falling-off? A special difficulty, which may relate the poem more immediately to the present discussion of *Endymion* and *Alastor,* is the introduction of a social theme. "Mythology of self" and "insatiable egotist" at the outset (20, 77) have primarily an epistemological reference, and are related to an initial theory of imagination in lines 1-2 ("man is the intelligence of his soil, / The sovereign ghost") that is subsequently discarded for that at the opening of Part IV ("his soil is man's intelligence. / That's better. That's worth crossing seas to find" [280-281]). So too with "the relentless contact he desired" (215) and "The liaison, the blissful liaison, / Between himself and his environment" in Part III, even though this liaison is said to be "chief motive, first delight . . . *and not for him alone*" (221-224, italics mine). But at least beginning in Part V, if not earlier in the notion of colonizing, social considerations appear in the poem: Part V opens with "Crispin as hermit"

(382), and in the next 150 lines he enters into marriage and the rearing of a family. And though the marriage serves in part to build up the picture of the "quotidian," and the four daughters are almost certainly symbolic (they are "Four questioners and four sure answerers" [539], which may, however, strike some fathers as a believable description of real daughters), still they involve Crispin in social ties that he has earlier been conspicuously free from. Line 489, "The return to social nature," is an additional clue.[18] Other critics besides Hi Simons have discovered social preoccupations in the poem, and others besides him have foundered in interpreting Parts V and VI. Some of the difficulty may be the same that I have set forth to explain why critics have written incompletely about *Endymion*: the social-moral and psychological-aesthetic concerns do not always cohere.

Stevens declared in 1935, in connection with *The Comedian*, that he had "the greatest dislike for explanations. As soon as people are perfectly sure of a poem they are just as likely as not to have no further interest in it; it loses whatever potency it had."[19] I do not agree, but there is a risk, in the kind of monothematic explanation that Stevens probably had in mind, of oversimplifying and distorting the works we seek to clarify. For some reason not clear to me, in dealing with a "difficult" modern like Stevens the critics tend to accept what they cannot work into their systems, while in dealing with earlier poets like Keats and Shelley they more often take a condescending view, blaming the poets for the immaturity of their conceptions. It is more reasonable all around, it seems to me, to understand that long poems like *Endymion, Alastor,* and *The Comedian* can have unrelated themes, and that we do not, in *reading* them, really object to these unrelatednesses. All three poems were, for their authors, serious efforts, and we read and reread them with a comparable seriousness, responding to their various concerns as they are offered to us. It is only when we write our critical explanations, seeking some neat, unified schematization of the allegory, that such unrelatednesses become a problem. It may be, ultimately, that the reading of long poems and the writing of critical interpretations are totally different classes of activity. If the latter is to be more realistically aligned with the former, we shall have to relax a little in the matter of coherence. I would not go so far as to invoke Keats's description of the long poem (in this instance *Endymion,* when he had just begun writing it) as "a little Region [for readers] to wander in where they may pick and choose" *(Letters,* I, 170). But surely, as a critical value, "unity" is overrated these days.

NOTES

1. " 'The Comedian as the Letter C': Its Sense and Its Significance," *Southern Review,* V (1940), 453–468 (reprinted in *The Achievement of Wallace Stevens,* ed. Ashley Brown and Robert S. Haller [Philadelphia and New York, 1962], pp. 97–113).

2. Among criticism of the last two decades I would cite Jacob D. Wigod, "The Meaning of *Endymion,*" *PMLA,* LXVIII (1953), 779–790; Glen O. Allen, "The Fall of Endymion: A Study in Keats's Intellectual Growth," *K–SJ,* VI (1957), 37–57; Carroll Arnett, "Thematic Structure in Keats's *Endymion,*" *Texas Studies in English,* XXXVI (1957), 100–109; Clarisse Godfrey, *"Endymion,"* in *John Keats: A Reassessment,* ed. Kenneth Muir (Liverpool, 1958), pp. 20–38; Albert Gérard, "Keats and the Romantic *Sehnsucht,*" *UTQ,* XXVIII (1959), 160– 175 (reprinted in Gérard's *English Romantic Poetry* [Berkeley and Los Angeles, 1968], pp. 194–214); Stuart M. Sperry, Jr., "The Allegory of *Endymion,*" *SIR,* II (1962), 38–53; Walter H. Evert, *Aesthetic and Myth in the Poetry of Keats* (Princeton, 1965), pp. 88–176; Bruce E. Miller, "On the Meaning of Keats's *Endymion,*" *K–SJ,* XIV (1965), 33–54; Mario L. D'Avanzo, "Keats's and Vergil's Underworlds: Source and Meaning in Book II of *Endymion,*" *K–SJ,* XVI (1967), 61–72; Helen E. Haworth, "The Redemption of Cynthia," *Humanities Association Bulletin,* XVIII (1967), 80–91; Northrop Frye, *"Endymion:* The Romantic Epiphanic," *A Study of English Romanticism* (New York, 1968), pp. 125–165. For surveys of the views of important earlier critics—among them Robert Bridges, Ernest de Selincourt, Sidney Colvin, Amy Lowell, Clarence D. Thorpe, J. M. Murry, Leonard Brown, Douglas Bush, C. L. Finney, and Newell F. Ford —see in particular the articles by Wigod, Sperry, and Miller. Evert, pp. 115– 118, has a fine note illustrating some of the "inconsistencies and contradictions with which the interpreter of the poem must contend." I have assumed from the outset that the question of whether or not the poem is allegorical is no longer an issue, and that the main problem is (once again) the interpretation of the allegory.

3. See especially his "The Meaning of 'Fellowship with Essence' in *Endymion,*" *PMLA,* LXII (1947), 1061–1076.

4. A speech perhaps made more impressive by Keats's assurance to his publisher John Taylor, 30 January 1818, "that when I wrote it, it was a regular stepping of the Imagination towards a Truth. My having written that Argument will perhaps be of the greatest Service to me of any thing I ever did" *(The Letters of John Keats,* ed. Hyder E. Rollins [Cambridge, Mass., 1958], I, 218).

5. In the same letter to Taylor (see note 4) Keats goes on to say that Endymion's speech in Book I "set before me at once the gradations of Happiness even like a kind of Pleasure Thermometer."

6. It should be noted, however, that these lines are philosophically quite unspecific. Though a ladder is mentioned in line 26, there is otherwise no suggestion of gradations or scales—simply the assertion that "A thousand Powers" exist,

largely unseen except as they are represented in clouds and other elements of the sky. The passage is an introduction to Keats's eulogy of the moon.

7. Douglas Bush's writings, from *Mythology and the Romantic Tradition in English Poetry* (Cambridge, Mass., 1937) through *John Keats: His Life and Writings* (New York, 1966), have been notably influential. The fullest explications in terms of "spiritualization-through-humanization" are those by Wigod and Evert. It is probably fair to say that, among more recent discussions, this is the majority view of the principal meaning of Keats's allegory.

8. The point of the Alpheus-Arethusa incident may indeed be Endymion's awakening humanitarianism. But much more is made of the fact that it is Cynthia and Arethusa's vow of chastity to her that cause the trouble between the lovers, just at a time when Cynthia herself secretly burns for Endymion, with whom (in a dream) she has just made love. The irony is emphasized in Endymion's addressing his prayer to the unknown "Goddess of my pilgrimage," who is, of course, Cynthia.

9. See Miller's essay, cited in note 2.

10. In my introduction to *Twentieth Century Interpretations of Keats's Odes* (Englewood Cliffs, N. J., 1968), pp. 2–3, I provide a simple diagram of the two realms and a collection of terms commonly applied to them. This "ontological" theme, like that concerning the authenticity of dreams (see the next paragraph), is of course particularly relevant to Keats's later poems.

11. Most notably Allen and Sperry, in the articles cited in note 2, and Earl R. Wasserman, *The Finer Tone: Keats' Major Poems* (Baltimore, 1953), especially the chapter on *The Eve of St. Agnes*.

12. It is worth noting that Keats wrote these lines only a few days after his 22 November 1817 letter to Bailey.

13. If the question of authenticity of dreams (5) is thus isolatable from the others, it might be thought the easiest solution to the problem simply to drop the theme from the list. But its importance to Keats in several hundred lines of Books I and IV, especially in view of the fervor with which Endymion defends the idea at the beginning of his wanderings and attempts to renounce it near the end, cannot be denied.

14. See Leonard Brown, "The Genesis, Growth, and Meaning of *Endymion*," *SP*, XXX (1933), 618–653. There are enough similarities and echoes of narrative and descriptive detail in *Endymion* as to leave no doubt that Keats had *Alastor* in mind while writing his poem.

15. I am aware that in dealing with *Alastor* I have at hand another of those Romantic poems (there is a distinguished group of them that includes *Tintern Abbey*, the *Intimations* ode, *The Rime of the Ancient Mariner*, *Kubla Khan*, and several of Keats's odes) that have not been definitively interpreted and on which there is an immense body of critical literature. Here, however, I am not so much concerned with what Shelley may have intended in the poem (in any event, the Preface and the poem do not cohere, and the second paragraph of the Preface has seemingly unresolvable internal inconsistencies) as with two meanings that I think, on the evidence of *Endymion*, Keats himself was most concious of. If the interpretations depend more than they should on Shelley's Preface, it ought to be remembered that Keats read that Preface, and without benefit of the critical explications of the last four decades.

16. Among critical studies of the poem, the interpretation closest to the one offered in this paragraph is that by Albert Gérard, *"Alastor,* or the Spirit of

Solipsism," *PQ*, XXXIII (1954), 164–177 (reprinted in revised form in Gérard's *English Romantic Poetry*, pp. 136–162).

17. *Letters of Wallace Stevens*, ed. Holly Stevens (New York, 1966), pp. 28–29, 147–148. He also saw Keats's fair copy of the poem, now in the Pierpont Morgan Library, in 1908 (p. 110).

18. Outside the poem, Stevens's letter to Hi Simons of 12 January 1940 may also be relevant to the mixing of aesthetic and social themes. Approving Simons's interpretation of *The Comedian* (see note 1, above) as "correct, not only in the main but in particular, and not only correct but keen," Stevens comments, "I suppose that the way of all mind is from romanticism to realism, to fatalism and then to indifferentism, unless the cycle re-commences and the thing goes from indifferentism back to romanticism all over again." He then goes on, in the next paragraph, to speculate on "a new romanticism"—not the "imaginative realism" that we have come to see as a main theme in Stevens's work generally, but Communism! (*Letters of Wallace Stevens*, pp. 350–351).

19. *Letters of Wallace Stevens*, p. 294.

JOHN CARLYLE IN GERMANY AND THE
GENESIS OF *SARTOR RESARTUS*

John Clubbe

Dr. John A. Carlyle, younger brother of Thomas, spent about
sixteen months, from November 1827 through February 1829,
in Germany and Austria, during which time he attended the Universities of Munich and Vienna, heard celebrated professors
lecture and was introduced to some of them, and underwent a
variety of adventures. These experiences he described in many
long letters to his brothers Thomas and Alexander and to his
mother Margaret. G. B. Tennyson, in the only book-length study
of Carlyle's *Sartor Resartus*, has claimed that "there are
too many echoes in *Sartor* of Carlyle's extensive reading and
writing on German subjects to credit John's adventures with
more than a small share in forming Carlyle's picture of
Germany."[1] My examination of this correspondence has led me
to draw a somewhat different conclusion: though no one will want
to deem John's letters a major influence on *Sartor*, they affected
its "picture of Germany" more than scholars have hitherto admitted. In a general way, John's descriptions of German life
helped shape the German setting of *Sartor*. His account of the
new University of Munich acquainted Carlyle with the German
university scene and supplied him with many details for the
"New University" of Weissnichtwo. More particularly, John's
character sketches of Lorenz Oken, Professor of Physiology at
Munich, played a significant role in Carlyle's conception of
Diogenes Teufelsdröckh. Furthermore, John's letters contain
detailed pen portraits of the literary critic August Wilhelm
Schlegel and the philosopher Friedrich Schelling as well as noteworthy (and unpublished) records of their literary opinions.
Not only did John's lively descriptions of the German scene
serve to sharpen Carlyle's image of Germany and to influence the

development of *Sartor,* but they have also intrinsic importance in themselves. At a time when both Britain and the conglomerate of states that constituted "Germany" had gropingly begun to recognize common strands in their national cultures, the correspondence offers important glimpses into English (more accurately, Scottish) attitudes toward Germany. Two major cruces of argument will thus develop: one analyzing John's travels and their effect upon him, and one their effect on Carlyle's vision of Germany and on his writing of *Sartor.*

By the late 1820s the idea of visiting Germany once again aroused interest among Englishmen; for many, the extended trip up the Rhine replaced in the years around 1830 the Italian journey, the fashion in travel during the decade following Waterloo. John Carlyle, a recent graduate in medicine of the University of Edinburgh, had accepted the position in Munich of private physician and companion to Baron David von Eichthal (1776-1851)—uncle of the Saint-Simonian Gustave d'Eichthal whom Thomas Carlyle was to meet and befriend in London early in 1832—with the understanding that his duties would leave him ample time to pursue a course of study at the University. John went to Germany to obtain a fuller knowledge of the land whose literature his brother had already begun to promote in Britain, to widen also his experience of life, but chiefly—his "principal errand,"[2] as he called it—to learn the latest techniques of German medicine. No one carried higher hopes that he would attain his goals in regard both to personal self-improvement and to professional education than did Carlyle. He followed him about in his imagination, and through his brother's letters he came to live vicariously in the land he greatly desired to see and to which he had long felt strong spiritual attachment. From his concern that John profit to the utmost from this unique opportunity, we sense Carlyle's own frustrated wish to visit Germany and call upon the man whom he admired above all others—Goethe.

Born in 1801 and now twenty-six, John was six years younger than his brother Thomas and still a somewhat unsettled young man. Literary ambition in part, and financial need even more, had led him to translate Bernardin de Saint-Pierre's *Paul et Virginie* and a novel, *Elisabeth, ou les exilés de Sibérie,* by Sophie Cottin, a now-forgotten French authoress.[3] The Edinburgh firm, Oliver & Boyd, published both together in 1824. In a life that lasted until 1879, John never did quite abandon the notion that through literature he might one day gain recognition. He heard Coleridge talk in London, and intelligence lies behind his finely perceptive observation of him in 1830: "I believe there is no man in the island 'puts more thought through himself.'"⁴ In 1849 he published "a literal prose translation" of Dante's *Inferno* which contemporaries praised and which ran through many editions. It is still in print. John never brought to completion, however, his projected translations of the *Purgatorio* and the *Paradiso*.

For a while in the early 1820s literature competed with medicine for his none-too-abundant energies. He inclined first toward a literary life. But with Thomas's stern admonitions about the insecurity and hardship that such a life entailed echoing in his ears, he turned toward medicine and in 1826 took his degree at Edinburgh, then the leading center of medical study in Britain, with a dissertation on mental illness, *De Mentis Alienatione*. In 1827 his medical interests demanded first attention, and in these interests no one more willingly gave him moral support and financial backing than did Carlyle. "The real explanation of John Carlyle's opportunity" to study medicine, observes Mabel Davidson, author of the only article I have found on the elusive brother, "is to be found first, in his brother Thomas's preference for and generosity to him, and second, in his own natural acquiescence in any plan looking toward ease and requiring not too great exertion and initiative on his part."⁵ Thomas had largely financed John's medical studies in Edinburgh, and even after his marriage to Jane Welsh in October 1826 he continued to aid his brother. In 1827, when his financial resources were meager and his literary prospects uncertain, he readily agreed to help support John for further study in Germany. Toward this favorite brother, Thomas always showed uncommon understanding and tenderness, pardoning faults in him that, if present in another, would have called forth his thunder.

During the year and a half John remained abroad he wrote letters home that, if not equal to his brother's in brilliance and metaphorical splendor, nonetheless abound in keen observations and in fine psychological insights, notably in the pen portraits of Schlegel, Schelling, and Oken. In addition, they range informatively over a wide field of subjects. Several are of importance in Carlyle's biography—for instance, Goethe's opinion of Carlyle's life of Schiller. Even if we see Germany and the Germans refracted through the eyes of a conservative Scot, the image, though distorted, is extremely sharp. Once we recognize the biases of John's Scottish make-up when they intrude we may discount them: the clarity of his sight remains unaffected. But much of the interest of these letters from Germany lies precisely in the prejudice his Scottish viewpoint reveals. While blind to much in the Catholic culture of southern Germany and Austria, John at least does not veer toward the more lamentable position of identifying himself totally with his hosts' point of view. Throughout, he maintains a firm sense of his own identity. And for all his prejudice and narrow experience, John does attempt to be fair. When "in a strange country," he affirmed after nine months abroad, "one must see all that one can in honesty";[6] it stands to his credit that, in his way, he always strove for this objectivity. Though in earlier letters he admits to *"bewilderment* & giddiness . . . in this strange land where the language is but imperfectly understood by me, and where each object is new and unprecedented,"[7] a natural sentiment for a young man making his first extended trip to a foreign land, the later letters, though less enthusiastic, show no slackening of interest in the life flowing around him.

On 6 October John Carlyle left England for an indefinite stay in Munich. After taking the packet from London to Rotterdam, where he stayed several days, John walked to The Hague; to his brother he quoted Lady Mary Wortley Montagu's description of the Dutch capital as the "finest village in the world." The people left him singularly unimpressed, however: "The three or four days I staid in Holland had made me weary of Dutch uniformity. . . ." While he "admired the neatness and cleanliness of the houses," he "disliked the avaricious and phlegmatic character of the inhabitants."[8] From The Hague he took the diligence and journeyed, via Utrecht, Nimwegen, and Krefeld, to Cologne, where he stayed one night, time enough to admire the unfinished cathedral. Thence to Bonn, where he remained two days and delivered letters of introduction.

On one of his evenings in Bonn, John "was with [A. W.] Schlegel for about an hour and was received by him very kindly and politely." The account he sent to Carlyle of his interview with Schlegel, then sixty and since 1818 *Professor der Literatur und Kunstgeschichte* at Bonn, opens with a physical sketch:

Schlegel lives in an elegant house furnished in some measure after the English mode. He is a littlish man though not very slender squints somewhat with his dark grey eyes, and when he is speaking to you throws his head a little backwards so that he is in some measure looking along his face and pointing his chin to the person hearing him. He wears a wig of brownish hair. He had no neckloth [sic], wore a black coat silk vest and grey trowsers. From his round and broad snuff-box he is continually taking snuff on the tip of his fore-finger but he did not make much use of the large mirror on its lid. He speaks English almost quite perfecctly, and in a mild and cultivated tone of voice.[9]

John's precise description of *Herr Professor* Schlegel cannot rival in brilliance Heine's bravura portrait of *"Herrn Dichter"* Schlegel in *Die Romantische Schule* (1836). There, a rollicking though obviously negative account of Schlegel's qualities as poet, critic, and translator serves as prelude to Heine's personal reminiscences of the dandyish professor whose lectures in Bonn he had attended in 1819 as a brash young student—a portrait which has gained notoriety as a classic of satire. Heine observes Schlegel lecturing with "kid gloves" and "attired in quite the latest Parisian style; he was still perfectly scented with high society and *eau de mille fleurs;* he was daintiness and elegance incarnate. . . ." And further: "On his delicate little head still shone a few silver hairs, and his form was so slender, so emaciated and transparent that he seemed to be all spirit, almost a symbol of spiritualism."[10] John's portrait of eight years later, not etched in acid, is fairer to Schlegel than Heine's caricature. Under John's steady gaze he emerges less a dandy, more a believable human being.

During the interview John brought the conversation around to literary topics, among them his brother's translation, published in 1824, of Goethe's *Wilhelm Meisters Lehrjahre.* Schlegel "enquired how it had succeeded in England and asked if its morality had not offended English taste, praised the 'exquisite beauty' of the style & composition as a piece of Art, said it had little in it to excite violent emotion. . . ."[11] The German critic "thought his brother's [Friedrich Schlegel's] 'Characteristics['] of Meister good, and on my suggesting the propriety of prefixing it to an English translation he seemed to think it might be well to do so, for he would have no manufacturing of such works to the public taste." Rather, he would "have them presented in their original and complete form and received and studied as foreign works and thus [?] it might be [good?—letter torn] to have some knowledge of the sentiments of the nation from which they might be brought."[12] Goethe's tale "The New Melusina" he judged "perhaps the finest tale that had ever been published." John also recorded that Schlegel considered the *"Fantasiestücke"* of "my friend Louis Tieck" "youthful attempts"; he "supposed his work on the Dramatic authors before [Shake]speare is not known in England. It is perhaps the best thing he ever wrote." At the time of John's visit only the first volume of Tieck's *Shakspeare's Vorschule* (1823; 1829) had appeared; his *Phantasien über die Kunst, für Freunde der Kunst,* in which he collaborated with Wackenroder, first came out in 1799.

Jean Paul Richter, Carlyle considered "by a good many degrees the strangest and most gifted novellist, or indeed writer of his country, except Goethe, and quite unknown here."[13] In reference to Richter's *Des Feldpredigers Schmelzle Reise nach Flätz* (which Carlyle translated as *Army-Chaplain Schmelzle's Journey to Flaetz* for his *German Romance*), Schlegel commented that "there would be [much?—word effaced by seal] to offend the English taste in Richter's Works." Obviously unfriendly, he added:

> Richter has more capacity than Sterne but less dexterity. Richter was not a man of the world and delighted to dwell amid the scenes with which his early life had been familiar. He could never tell a story, and his transitions had always something clumsy about them. He had not succeeded so well in any of his works as Sterne in his Tristram Shandy—Uncle Toby—Corporal Trim &c.

Schlegel also spoke of Coleridge's translations of Schiller. In 1800 Coleridge had translated *Die Piccolomini (The Piccolomini)* and *Wallensteins Tod (The Death of Wallenstein),* parts II and III of Schiller's tragedy *Wallenstein*. The prelude or first part, *Wallensteins Lager (Wallenstein's Camp),* he did not translate. Schlegel "thought the *Lager* in Wallenstein should by no means have been left out and that it was not more difficult to translate than many passages of Shakespeare which have been very well rendered." We can only surmise why Coleridge neither translated *Wallensteins Lager* nor wrote his projected essay on the genius of Schiller.[14] Perhaps he found, as Schlegel implies, the dialogue too difficult to render—dialogue "cast into a rude Hudibrastic metre," as Carlyle was later to describe it, "full of forced rhymes, and strange double-endings, with a rhythm ever changing, ever rough and lively. . . ."[15] In any event, though in after years he looked back on it with pleasure, Coleridge regarded the translation during the time he toiled on it as "my irksome & soul-wearying Labor."[16] Schlegel went on to say that "it is a general opinion (which you [Carlyle] already know) that Goethe had some share in writing the *Lager*."[17] When John mentioned to his host that he purposed going to Munich for study, Schlegel "spoke somewhat slightingly of the University"; "München [was] not a very good place," he thought, for there "the better classes speak French but strange and the lower are totally unintelligible."

John's detailed account prompted Thomas to reply before the month was out: "We were *greatly* entertained with your graphic sketch of Shlegel [*sic*]."[18] And well might Carlyle be pleased: having acknowledged German writers, and especially Goethe, as determining influences upon his development, Schlegel's opinions held for him the greatest interest.

John reached Munich on 1 November. Upon leaving Bonn, he had journeyed to Frankfurt, then to Würzburg, before taking the diligence to the Bavarian capital, then as now a European cultural center. There Baron von Eichthal and his family welcomed him with much kindness.

Within less than a month John had become "tolerably expert at speaking German and at least understand all that is said to me in that tongue."[19] But already by year's end the first exhilaration of living in a foreign land had begun to wane. The " 'fairy land' of Germany had been disenchanted," John announced to Thomas on 29 December, and he "found it to be in reality a country of this earth as well as my own which I had so abruptly left." Now that he had "got footing" on *"Terra firma,"* he continued to think he had "done well taking all in all" in coming to Germany, but there were "perhaps two or three hours a week when the evil genius comes over me"; at those times "I think differently. . . ." Yet a positive note concludes his train of reflection: "I feel more & more convinced that this stay in Germany will be of lasting importance to me in many respects."[20] He knew that his *Lehrjahre* abroad would be his last chance for self-improvement before he returned to take up the "earnest duties" of medical practice at home. Furthermore, he had ample opportunity to meet people in Munich from whose acquaintance he came to profit greatly. And if we judge a man's education by what he learned from others, John fared well.

"I had almost forgot to tell you that I met with a Gentleman here who is acquainted with Goethe whom he had see[n] shortly before," wrote John to his mother on 30 November. He continued: "Goethe had since written to him and mention[ed] the translation and biogr[ap]hical criticism in the German Romance of which he spoke with much applause. I am to see the letter from Goethe and then I will tell you about the whole matter." It was at the mansion of Baron von Eichthal that John had met the "Gentleman . . . acquainted with Goethe"—Sulpiz Boisserée, archaeologist and art collector of renown. To him Goethe had written, mentioning Carlyle's translations "as one of the *Merkwürdigkeiten* [remarkable things] that had occurred at Weimar."[21]

Earlier in the year Carlyle had sent Goethe, along with his letter of 15 April, copies of his *Life of Schiller* (1825) and the four volumes of *German Romance* (1827). The first three volumes contained translations of tales by contemporary German writers (Musäus, Fouqué, Tieck, Hoffmann, and Richter), the fourth his translation of Goethe's *Wilhelm Meisters Wanderjahre*. Goethe, writing to Boisserée, praised both the Schiller biography and *German Romance*. He commended Carlyle for his knowledge of German literature and for the respect mixed with critical acumen he showed toward Schiller; the biographical notices prefacing each translation he admired for their ability to recapture a living image of the man. Though written, as Goethe remarks, with partiality, as was the life of Schiller, Carlyle's portraits yet emerge clearly. From Goethe's letter to Boisserée, John copied out for his brother these extracts:

Indessen war mir aus Edinburgh eine Sendung zugekommen, mit einem Schreiben von einem Manne, der im mittlern Alter seyn mag und sich mit der deutschen Literatur [auf eine wundersam-innige Weise] bekannt gemacht hat. Eine Biographie Schillers zeugt von der reinsten Antheil, von einer warmen und zugleich einsichtigen Verehrung dieses ausserordentlichen Mannes.

Ein Werk in vier Bänden eben dieses Herrn Thomas Carlyle, *German Romance*, liefert Übersetzungen aus den Werken unseren deutschen Erzähler: Musäus, Tieck, La Motte Fouqué, Hoffmann, mit kurzen Lebensnotizen von diesen sämmtlichen; der vierte Band enthält meine Wanderjahre und von meinem Leben eine freundliche Darstellung.

Uberhaupt ist hier zu bemerken, was schon früher von der Schillerischen
Biographie dieses Verfassers gesagt worden; alle diese kurzen Biographien
sind mit Neigung, aber mit Klarheit geschrieben; was er als Mängel
seiner Autoren tadeln konnte, das behandelt er als Eigenschaften und
Eigenheiten, und so entsteht doch zuletzt das Bild eines lebendigen, wenn
auch nicht durchaus lobenswürdigen Menschen.

[Meanwhile I have received a parcel from Edinburgh with a letter
from a man who seems to be in middle age and who has made himself
familiar with German literature (in a wonderfully intimate way). A
biography of Schiller creates the most unalloyed interest through a warm
and at the same time judicious admiration of this extraordinary man.

A work in four volumes, *German Romance*, also from this Mr. Thomas
Carlyle, provides translations from the works of our German story-
tellers: Musäus, Tieck, La Motte Fouqué, Hoffmann, with short biographies of all of them; the fourth volume contains my *Wanderjahre*
and a sympathetic portrayal of my life.

On the whole, one should note what was already said earlier about this
author's biography of Schiller; all these short biographies are written
with affection yet with clarity; what he could censure as shortcomings
in his authors, he treats rather as distinctive qualities and idiosyncrasies,
and thus the portrait of a living if not altogether praiseworthy human
being emerges at last.][22]

In addition, Goethe proposed in a later letter to Boisserée
(a passage also extracted by John) the circumstances he deemed
necessary for "world literature" to emerge: "Hierbei lässt sich
ferner die Bemerkung machen, dass dasjenige was ich Welt-
literatur nenne dadurch vorzüglich entstehen wird, wenn die
Differenzen, die innerhalb der einen Nation obwalten, durch
Ansicht und Urtheil der übrigen ausgeglichen werden." ["In
this connection, one can make the observation moreover that
what I would call world literature will thus arise above all when
the distinctions which prevail within one nation will be compen-
sated for by the conviction and judgment of other nations."][23]
Influenced by the German poet, Carlyle was to become the first
British critic to advocate a world literature: in several early
essays on German writers but most fervently in the conclusion
to his "Historic Survey of German Poetry" (1831), he asked
if "a new era in the spiritual intercourse of Europe is approaching; that instead of isolated, mutually repulsive National Litera-
tures, a World Literature may one day be looked for?"[24] A
passage in which Goethe speaks of his progress on the second
part of *Faust* ends the remarks which John had thought of "spe-

:ial interest" for his brother; Goethe's commendation to Boisserée of Carlyle's work carried particular weight, John claimed,
because it derived from "an unbiassed unflattering opinion."[25]

Undoubtedly amused by Goethe's placing him "in mittlern
Alter" yet clearly pleased by his mentor's praise, Carlyle in his
reply of 1 February 1828 launched with enthusiasm into John's
opportunities: "Would I had Dr Boisserée for my Cice-
rone. . . !" And on 16 April he asked John for news of the
man whom he most revered: "Is he greater than man; or in
his old days growing less than many men? The former to me is
unexampled, the latter incredible. Go see and tell us truly."[26]

At the University of Munich, John attended courses of lectures, among them "the Anatomical Lectures of [Ignaz] Döllin-
ger," lectures he first found "excellent" but later concluded were
"no better than at Edinburgh perhaps not so good," for "the
state of pathological Anatomy here is not as advanced as in
Edinburgh."[27] A deeper impression was left by the philosopher
Schelling, who in 1827 had accepted a professorship at Munich.
In the opportunity to hear Schelling's well-attended lectures, to
which not only students but also colleagues and professional
men came, lay a chief reason behind John's decision to accept
the position in Munich. The detailed and lively characterizations
of Schelling that he sent home constitute a major interest of the
letters. John attended his course of lectures on the "Allgemeine
Methodologie des Academischen Studiums zugleich als Einleit-
ung in das [sic] Studium der Philosophie" ["General Meth-
odology of Academical Study as well as Introduction to the
Study of Philosophy"];[28] of a second course of lectures, the
"System der Weltalter (in Verbindung mit einem philosophis-
chen Disputatorium u. Conversatorium[)]" ["System of Historical Periods (in conjunction with a Philosophical Disputation
and Discourse)"] John only mentioned that, though announced,
it had not yet begun. To Thomas he sent a graphic pen portrait
of Schelling as lecturer:

Schelling is a littlish man about the size of [name illegible—Mancrief?]
the Advocate and not unlike him in make and appearance, only the
features magnified, larger eyes, larger mouth and larger curved
nose, and gray hair, and a stronger voice though also somewhat
shrill and asthmatic. He reads slowly and with remarkable distinctness

and precision, pausing now & then to get breath and to take snuff—
which last by the by is almost universal here among the professors. His
style is an iron style with no superfluous ornament. He has many similes
it is true, but there [sic] are told in the firmest language, and no word
or idea comes forward that has not its meaning. What he says sometimes
excites violent laughter, but he himself never does more than smiles. He
has a very large number of hearers, many of them old people. He reads
for the first time in Munich, and as he says himself gives the first
complete account of his *Philosophie*. Hitherto he has been employed in
giving a review of the systems of Spinoza, Leibnitz, Kant, Fichte, and
has said almost nothing about his own as yet.

John quoted to Carlyle Schelling's striking metaphor on Fichte's
system: "The philosophy of Fichte was like lightning, it showed
itself only for an instant, but it kindled a fire which will burn
forever."[29]

Thomas delighted in John's account: "Your description of
Schelling interested us much; and warmly do I commend your
purpose of studying Philosophy under such a man." He continued with strong words of admonition: "For Heaven's sake
get some *real* Knowledge of this high matter: be not disheart-
ened with difficulties, for all things are possible to all men.
. . ."[30] Schelling's lectures, attended thrice weekly, were often
mysteries to him, John admitted to his brother, but he hoped,
nonetheless, to "derive great benefit from them. The spirit,
geniality, clearness and firm precision with which he states his
principles," he explained,

are not lost for me, and will banish that portion of selfsufficient scepticism, which one imbibed from the conclusions of Scotch philosophy—
about the vanity and uselessness of all speculations of the kind. I wish
you could see the toleration and compassionate gentleness with which
Schelling speaks of the Utilitarians in Philosophy, and the composure
with which he at length dismisses them from the scene of action. Hitherto
he has been giving an introduction, and has just commenced with his
own System, and the first peculiarity of it he is now engaged in showing,
by many illustrations and arguments which I yet comprehend almost
nothing of. External nature he says (if I have understood him) is something *"an und vor sich"* ["in and unto itself"]—it is not barely the
objective produced by the *Subjective* I. But I tread on hollow ground
and must not attempt to say more of these matters. . . .[31]

Boisserée introduced John to the philosopher. "We spoke of
Coleridge," John records, "whose translations of Wallenstein
and *'Biographia Litteraria'* he had seen." Schelling "thought
Coleridge understood the German Philosophy but did not speak

clearly of it"—a tantalizingly ambiguous remark in view of
René Wellek's convincing claims for Coleridge's heavy intellectual dependence in the *Biographia* and elsewhere on Kant, the
Schlegels, and especially Schelling himself.[32] Speaking "always
of Goethe with boundless praise in his lectures and in private,"
Schelling considered the recent article in the *Edinburgh Review*
"very *böse* [ill-spirited] and shallow."[33] Even his command of
the social graces impressed John favorably: "Schelling is lively
in society without frivolity, takes his share of the conversation
that is going without speaking in a dictatorial tone to anyone;
and his clear blue eyes seem to indicate that he is at peace with
himself."

In the *Edinburgh Review* for October 1827, Carlyle had published an article entitled "State of German Literature." "Two
or three nights ago I saw Schelling," John reported to him on
1 March,

> and he told me he had read it, and was much satisfied with the '*Edelmuth
> und hohen Geist*' ["generosity and noble-mindedness"] in which it is
> written, and with the justice of your remarks on the German philosophy;
> but that some of the opinions which you had expressed regarding German
> Literature might perhaps be disputed, *die man vielleicht bestreiten könnte*
> [which one might perhaps challenge].[34]

Though what these "opinions" were John had not opportunity
to discover, he was puzzled that it was with his brother's remarks on literature, rather than on philosophy, that Schelling
had expressed dissatisfaction. Diligent in his attendance of
Schelling's lectures, he rationalized his lack of headway in understanding the system thus: "the whole is so firmly connected together, and proceeds in such strict order that the result is not to
be known or represented till one can look back and consider all
the successive steps by which one has reached the summit." The
magnetism of Schelling's personality continued to elicit eloquent
tribute from John; the philosopher's elevation of thought was
set off effectively by his impressive podium manner:

> If I did understand no word of his philosophy, it would still be worth-
> while to hear his lectures for the episodes he makes. At the end of last
> lecture when he spoke of the limitation and uncertainty of human Knowl-
> edge and enquiry in this dim world, and of that better country where
> God had chosen more clearly to reveal himself to his creatures, his deep,
> earnest, stoical emotion worked on the spirit like tones from that very
> country of which he was speaking. Schelling only *seems* dry and cold;

when he speaks of things that move him, his eyes glisten and become larger[,] his features have a sort of convulsive aspect, he raises his head quicker from what he is reading, his words come closer upon each other but not louder, and are accompanied with no voluntary gesture. His eloquence speaks more emphatically to me than any that I have heard before.[35]

Thomas's letter of 7 March crossed his brother's of 1 March. "Above all," he stated in it,

I am glad to find both that you admire Schelling and know that you do not understand him. That is right my dear Greatheart: look into the deeply significant regions of Transcendental Philosophy (as all PHILOSOPHY *must* be), and feel that there are wonders and mighty truths hidden in them; but look with your clear grey Scottish eyes and shrewd solid Scottish understanding, and refuse to be *mystified* even by your admiration.[36]

Three of his brother's letters before him, John at last made his avowal of failure:

As to German philosophy it is still in a great measure quite unknown to me. After all my prattling about Schelling and his lectures, I must confess, at the conclusion I found that I had not understood him, and that setting aside the wholesome and spirit-stirring exercise which I often found in following him, his philosophy was a lost philosophy for me.[37]

Thus, in the end John's efforts to grasp the complexities of Schelling's thought seem to have come to little. "In Schelling," writes Harald Höffding, "we find the true Romantic impulse to revel in a content which is attained by intuition and symbolism, rather than as the result of critical thought. So he runs riot first in nature and art, afterwards in religion."[38] John responded sympathetically to Schelling's perceptions but understood few of them. In many ways Schelling is the typical philosopher of romanticism, but John understood philosophy to be "logic-chopping" and was of a most unromantic nature; thus by training and by disposition he was ill-equipped to fathom Schelling's transcendentalism. His lack of success notwithstanding, he determined to brave "the summer lectures of Schelling on the philosophy of mythology. . . ."[39] These lectures, together with those on the Philosophy of Revelation (*Philosophie der Offenbarung*), constituted the chief part of Schelling's own system and bodied forth his new philosophy of religion. They were given, however, at an hour which conflicted with John's "clinical course," and he stopped attending without regret after a few lectures.

Despite his lack of apparent success, John submitted to Schelling's influence more than he realized. He now saw the importance of going beyond the narrow rationalism of his native tradition. For Scotland he wanted a new synthesis, one which drew upon the best in Scottish rationalism and German idealism.

> I trust we shall live to see a better spirit in our own country also, in spite of the utilitarian, commercial, shallow philosophy which has the upperhand in these times, and I am vain enough to believe that my brother will contribute much to bring about that happy change. It seems to me as if this could be done only by one who has been trained up in Scotland, and who has studied its philosophy with fearless inquiry, and thoroughly understood, before he has begun to contemn it; who can think and write with Scottish clearness and German depth; for as shallow precision bears rule in our own country, so in Germany with all its pre-eminence there will be found a certain tendency to mystical speculation and extravagance among the multitude of its authors to which a Scotch education is the best and surest antidote.[40]

If any single man could effect this synthesis of Scottish and German, that man, John knew, was his brother. John himself never achieved this "better spirit," the "happy change" in inherited patterns of thought that he wished Thomas to help bring about. His Scottish rigidity, strict religious training, and uncompromising moral code were too deeply ingrained in his character for him ever to get outside himself and truly to understand a foreign philosophy—or culture. Despite his long stay in Germany and his willingness to acknowledge other than Scottish virtues, he never managed to transcend his inheritance.

In several letters to John, Carlyle had expressed interest in the German educational system and its possible use as model for Britain. John set down for him his firsthand impressions of professors and courses at the University, which had moved from Landshut to Munich only in 1826. Individual professors he portrays vividly. The contrasts of intellectual approaches and lecture styles left him agape with wonder:

> The university is indeed a strange 'mixture of good and evil.' Here you have the most perfect mysticism held forth with bare-faced confidence in spite of all reason, there, the deepest inquiries of a S[c]helling & a Thiersch conducted with a logical strictness and precision and an extent

of knowledge which perhaps are not surpassed in Europe. On the one hand reign the principles of Blair & the French school, on the other German *Aesthetik* in full purity. In natural history you may be entertained with fantastical earnest and sometimes eloquent strivings of Oken, the diseased but gentle, modest, poetical *'Ahndungen'* [*sic*; John means "*Ahnungen*," "presentiments"] of Schubert (with whom one could almost love to mysticise when he speaks of that better Age 'in which man stood in more strict combination with Nature and was taught by her to know higher things than he is at present capable of now that he is no longer in Harmony with her') ; & with the cold-blooded commonplace droning of Fuchs who safely keeps the old beaten tract reading like our own Jameson but with less costly apparatus and perhaps a little more dullness. In General History you can admire the classic purity & clearness of Ast or detest the headlong determined *Schwärmer-*[*r*]*egen* [literally "rain of gush"] of Görres, who was formerly a revolutionary, and is now converted to the *belief* of the R. Catholic Religion which he defends through thick and thin![41]

John's letters—and no doubt his subsequent conversations with Thomas about Germany upon his return to Scotland—had considerable influence upon *Sartor Resartus*. Moncure D. Conway, in his early biography of Carlyle, records John's reminiscing to him that the "quaint framework" of *Sartor* "was suggested by the accounts he . . . used to give of his experiences in Germany."[42] This has generally been interpreted, by G. B. Tennyson among others, to mean intellectual and philosophical "framework," but in that sense John's observation is surely misleading. Of "framework," in the sense of intellectual "structure," very little of the kind of material John gave his brother found its way into *Sartor*. But of "framework," in the sense of physical "milieu," then I would argue that much of what John wrote and said is probably reflected in *Sartor*. The German setting, the university scene, the eccentric professors, local customs and habitats—all these John observed closely. He sent back to Carlyle many detailed descriptions that later influenced what one might designate the physical "framework" of *Sartor*. (In this essay I have quoted from the letters only a few of the more important passages, chiefly on academic subjects.) Carlyle's own letters to John, in addition, teem with specific queries, to which John usually sent back lengthy replies.

That his brother keep a regular journal became an obsession with Carlyle. "Gather stores of Knowledge which may avail us both," he urged him. Exhortations that he make the entries full and detailed descended upon John with almost every letter: "Preserve your Journal! Preserve it, preserve it however stupid; so it be only *full* enough. *Write down* whatever strikes you and as it strikes you."[43] Presumably John did, and presumably Carlyle read his journal. Carlyle, when he wrote *Sartor,* had never set foot on German soil: John's memories would have been the likeliest source against which to test the authenticity of the impression of the German milieu which he had gained through reading. *Sartor,* of course, rose up out of Carlyle's creative imagination—what he once described to Goethe as "the wonderful Chaos within me"[44]—but no exaggeration lies behind my argument that John's letters from Germany and subsequent conversations at Craigenputtoch helped lay a firm substratum of fact. And upon fact—always for Carlyle the grand desideratum —the matrix of his imagination would work to form the symbolic universe of *Sartor.*

One of John's experiences that can with certainty be identified in *Sartor,* though much transmuted, is significant and probably representative of others. In Munich there existed a "Schelling Club," Conway writes,

which Schelling himself used to visit now and then, devoted to beer, smoke, and philosophy. The free, and often wild, speculative talks of these cloud-veiled (with tobacco-smoke) intelligences of the transcendental Olympus amused his brother Thomas much in the description and rehearsal, and the doctor said he recalled many of the comments and much of the laughter in "Sartor Resartus."[45]

In the scenes in *Sartor* that take place in the *Grüne Gans,*[46] "beer, smoke, and philosophy" mix in a manner that recalls the Schelling Club. Every evening Diogenes Teufelsdröckh came to the *Grüne Gans,* there to brood or to hold forth one of his "memorable utterances."

Mentioned in the first scene of *Sartor* is "Herr Oken of Jena" —who is none other than the Lorenz Oken whose "fantastical earnest and sometimes eloquent strivings" had "entertained" John as he listened to his lectures on "Natural History" at the University. Indeed, Oken had always been known for his "extraordinary lecturing ability."[47] That Oken left a deep impression upon him John reveals by presenting Thomas with a detailed pen portrait. Because I consider the character of Teufelsdröckh drawn, chiefly in its external lines, upon that of Oken (with a strong admixture of Schelling and other German professors as well), the passage deserves quotation in its entirety:

I have met with Professor Oken several times. Perhaps you have heard of him as the Editor of the "Isis," which he has published for some time— I believe seven or eight years in Jena where he was formerly professor.

He lectures here on what is called *"Naturgeschichte"* [Natural History] (a general idea of Botany, Mineralogy, Zoology) and on the *"Entwickelungs-Geschichte der Natur"* [History of the Development of Nature] a sort of air-philosophy, an intellectual *'fantasying'* [*Phantasieing, i.e.,* fantasia] with the philosophy of Nature, which is here listened to with avidity. He reads in the same room as Schelling, and just before him. I sometimes go to hear him, and really he is very amusing, I mean his conclusions. He ended his last lecture I heard with *"Ernstlich und wahrhaftig meine Zuhörer ist Venus aus dem Meeres Schaum entstanden"* ["Seriously and truly, ladies and gentlemen, did Venus emerge from the foam of the sea"]. I have not met with any thing resembling these combinations of Ideas without principles. . . . Oken is an extremely little, care-worn, man. He squints perceptibly with his large black eyes, and there is a sort of convulsive simper or grin which gives a painful expression to his whole countenance. He speaks in a solemn tone of voice, and that even in society. You would laugh if I could send you one of his *aabers* [*aber*: but] which present themselves so oft in his lectures and discourse. But enough of him. He is a sort of phenomenon here and his lectures have certainly something *original* in them, if they have nothing else worthy of recommendation.[48]

"We are greatly pleased with your sketches of 'German character,'" replied Thomas; "your Oken . . . your Schelli[n]g &c must surely be pictures from the Life."[49] Oken, a lifelong "phenomenon," had had a checkered, stormy career before he came to Munich in 1827. The following characteristic description of Teufelsdröckh in *Sartor* could apply, with equal aptitude, to him: "the man Teufelsdröckh passed and repassed, in his little circle, as one of those originals and nondescripts, more frequent in German Universities than elsewhere."[50] Oken's independent, at times high-handed, character had left him many enemies, few friends. Though he gave lectures at the University of Munich, he was at first without an official academic position; but already by the year's end he was named to a professorship. Teufelsdröckh's university career at Weissnichtwo and Oken's at Munich show intriguing parallels. "Considerable also was the wonder at the new Professor," writes Carlyle in *Sartor,* "dropt opportunely enough into the nascent University; so able to lecture, should occasion call; so ready to hold his peace for indefinite periods, should an enlightened Government consider that occasion did not call."[51] Of Oken's later career, it suffices to say that he soon found the "enlightened Government" of the Bavarian régime deciding "that occasion did not call" and indeed forcing him to resign his professorship in 1832.

In *Sartor,* Carlyle explicitly related Teufelsdröckh's one "practical tendency" to Oken and his journal *Isis*:

If through the high, silent, meditative Transcendentalism of our Friend [Teufelsdröckh] we detected any practical tendency whatever, it was at most Political, and towards a certain prospective, and for the present quite speculative, Radicalism; as indeed some correspondence, on his part, with Herr Oken of Jena was now and then suspected; though his special contributions to the *Isis* could never be more than surmised at.[52]

Oken, like Teufelsdröckh, had hardly any "practical tendency whatever"; he was driven from Munich, as he had been from Jena, for his "Radicalism" and for his disputes with the régime. Teufelsdröckh resembles Oken in other ways: in physical appearance and in career, in personality and in style of lecturing, and in ideas. Physically, Teufelsdröckh has a "little figure . . . in loose ill-brushed threadbare habilments" and "eyes . . . deep under their shaggy brows"; Oken is "an extremely little, careworn, man . . . with large black eyes."[53] Teufelsdröckh is a "stranger" in Weissnichtwo (Know-not-where), "wafted thither by what is called the course of circumstances";[54] so too is Oken, newly arrived from Munich after years of living in Jena, "a sort of phenomenon here." Surely Carlyle's decision to place Teufelsdröckh in a milieu John knew intimately cannot be accidental. Teufelsdröckh does not give formal lectures at the University, but his nightly discourses at the *Grüne Gans*—both it and the *Wahngasse* where he lived actually existed in Munich and were visited by John—resemble Oken's "intellectual '*fantasying*' with the philosophy of Nature."

Teufelsdröckh's lecture style seems compounded of that of Schelling and Oken: he "speaks-out with a strange plainness,"[55] says Carlyle. Schelling, it may be remembered, "conducted [his lectures] with a logical strictness and precision."[56] Carlyle speaks also of "the force of that rapt earnestness" of his professor's Work on Clothes, of its "untutored energy. . . . Many a deep glance, and often with unspeakable precision, has he cast into mysterious Nature, and the still more mysterious Life of Man."[57] Such insight into Nature and the "mysterious Life of Man" thus seems to combine Oken's "fantastical earnest and sometimes eloquent strivings" on Natural History with Schelling's "logical . . . precision" of speech. Oken's lecture subjects moreover—"*Naturgeschichte*" and the "*Entwickelungs-Geschichte der Natur*" a sort of air-philosophy"—become favorite Teufelsdröckhian topics of discourse, while his substanceless "air-philosophy" may foreshadow the substantive "clothes philosophy" of Carlyle's hero. C. F. Harrold points out that the "symbolical, *hieroglyphical* character of nature" found in *Sartor* reveals indebtedness, among other sources, to the philosophy of Schelling,[58] but Oken's lectures, from John's account, also touch upon this idea.[59]

Although Teufelsdröckh and Oken parallel each other's careers at other points, I have limited myself here to their life circumstances, physical characteristics, and personal eccentricities. Parallels between their views of Nature exist, but in a general way only: Carlyle, as Harrold has shown, drew upon a bevy of writers and philosophers, English as well as German, for his philosophical concepts. But he drew strongly upon his brother John's character sketches of the Munich professors, including Schelling but especially Oken, for the genesis of his finest creation: Diogenes Teufelsdröckh enthroned in his chair of "Professor of Things in General."

John Carlyle's attendance at the lectures of Schelling and Oken marked the high point of his German experience: frustration and anticlimax characterize the remainder of his stay abroad. Much of his time during the spring and summer of 1828 he spent "pent up amid books, in my studies always attempting much and always accomplishing very little. . . ."[60] Increasingly, he found himself responding adversely to the German society he encountered at Baron von Eichthal's home. Though he assured Alexander Carlyle that he was "too old to be corrupted by the irreligion or hypocrisy of those around me," we see, as his stay in the Bavarian capital wore on, John reaffirming the homely virtues of his Scottish and Protestant upbringing. Nothwithstanding the pleas he received from Thomas and the family to return to native soil, he decided to go instead, in September 1828, to Vienna. "What you specially want," Thomas wondered, "or how you hope to *better* your fortune, in that stupid Sybarite Metropolis is not clear to any of us." But despite grave reservations he continued to show generosity of heart and purse to John, urging him to travel "till that maggot is *fully* cleared out of your head."[61]

In the "stupid Sybarite Metropolis" John pursued his medical studies. "The school of medicine here is infinitely superior to any thing of the Kind which I have seen," he wrote his mother, "and it will be my own fault if I do not learn much."[62] The Viennese he judged "on the whole . . . the stupidest common people I have seen in my life." Nor did their Catholicism escape his censure: "they are extremely prejudiced and even supersti[ti]ous in what regards religion."[63] By mid-winter he could stand no more of Vienna. Hard indeed was his final judgment on his hosts: "a rude, gluttonous, ignorant, enslaved immoral nation."[64] And on Friedrich Schlegel, whom his brother had urged him "by *all* means, go and see . . . and tell us what manner of man he is,"[65] his judgment showed only slight gain in charity. The conversion of the Schlegels, husband and wife, to Roman Catholicism in 1803 passed John's understanding:

> I could not alas, pay a visit to F. Schlegel. He spent the whole winter in Dresden and as you have by this time heard died there after a few hours illness just when on the eve of his departure for Vienna—Poor Schlegel! endowed with the finest gifts he had sold himself to the Austrian government and turned the advocate of superstition.

"The people of Vienna," he concluded, "seemed to have entirely lost sight of him, and his death cited almost no sensation."[66] Carlyle, more understanding of the man and his achievement, recorded the event sorrowfully in his journal: "Friedrich Schlegel dead at Dresden on the *9th* of January!—Poor Schlegel what toilsome *seeking* was thine: thou knowest now whether thou hadst *found*—or thou carest not for knowing!"[67]

Carlyle's letter of 5 March to his brother in Paris marks the end of their correspondence during John's sojourn abroad. John returned to Scotland early in April. Without immediate prospects of earning his living, he gladly accepted Thomas's hospitality at Craigenputtoch, where he and Jane had resided since Whitsuntide 1828. "His presence was very welcome," remarks Mabel Davidson, "and did much to lessen the gloom and loneliness of Jane Carlyle's life there."[68] His German adventure, which began in hope but ended in disillusionment, closed an epoch in his life. Though often painful, his *Wanderjahre* had yet been years of seeking after knowledge unobtainable at home, of seeing new lands and different ways of life, of conversing with men in other tongues than his own. He did not deny that he had learned much. But John remained in essence a person who, as he gradually had come to realize himself, drew his firmest support from his own native tradition. Scotland had marked his innermost being. If his sixteen months abroad did leave an imprint upon his character, it cannot be said that it was either deep or lasting. The trip's chief value lay in supplementing Thomas Carlyle's extensive reading in German subjects with vivid firsthand impressions. Through having a brother whom he greatly loved and trusted in Germany and through the wealth of information about the complex German scene recorded in John's letters, Carlyle's knowledge of German life, especially German academic life, became considerably enlarged. No doubt it was further augmented during the conversations the two brothers, both great talkers, had on German subjects during the months to come at Craigenputtoch.

In the autumn of 1829 John Carlyle left for London, slowly to wend his way in the great world for which he had made such extensive preparation.[69] A year later, Thomas Carlyle began to write "Thoughts on Clothes," the first draft of what later became *Sartor Resartus*.[70] His image of Germany sharpened by John's letters and conversation, he was now well able to present a compelling picture of German life.

NOTES

1. *SARTOR Called RESARTUS* (Princeton, 1965), p. 129. It seems unlikely that Tennyson examined John's letters.

2. National Library of Scotland (hereafter NLS), Edinburgh, 1775A–99. Letter to Thomas Carlyle, 5 May 1828. Almost all of John's letters remain unpublished. The passages quoted from them in this study, as well as those from Carlyle's letters already published or published in part, I have transcribed whenever possible directly from xeroxes of the originals, most of which are in the NLS. They are cited with the kind permission of the Trustees of the NLS and of Professor Charles Richard Sanders of Duke University, general editor of the forthcoming Duke–Edinburgh edition of the collected letters of Thomas and Jane Welsh Carlyle. To Professor Sanders, in addition, I am indebted for first pointing out to me the importance of John's German stay for *Sartor Resartus*. As far as I could determine, the correspondence between Thomas and John Carlyle for the duration of John's trip is—one or two letters excepted—complete. Within quotations from the letters I have used brackets to indicate both conjectures of missing words or parts of words and editorial insertions.

3. See Edwin W. Marrs, Jr., "Carlyle, Bernardin de Saint-Pierre, and Madame Cottin," *Victorian Newsletter,* 33 (Spring 1968), 43–45.

4. NLS, 1775A–118. Letter to Thomas Carlyle, 17 May 1830.

5. "The Record of a Broken Friendship," *South Atlantic Quarterly,* XXIV (July 1925), 278. The friendship was with Jane Welsh Carlyle. John got on her nerves increasingly in later years. Information about John can of course be found in most books on the Carlyles. Carlyle's correspondence with him is more extensive than with any other person.

6. NLS, 1775A–101. Letter to Alexander Carlyle, 13 June 1828.

7. NLS, 1775A–87. Letter to Thomas Carlyle, 3 November 1827.

8. *Ibid.*

9. *Ibid.*

10. *Sämtliche Werke,* ed. Hans Kaufmann (München, 1964), IX, 69–70. All English translations in this essay are my own.

11. John records Schlegel's literary opinions in his letter to Carlyle of 3 November 1827.

12. Carlyle had slightly abridged, for fear of offending British taste, his translation of the *Lehrjahre.* "In many points, both literary and moral," he wrote in the Preface to the edition of 1824, "I could have wished devoutly he had not written as he has done. . . . Except a few phrases and sentences, not in all amounting to a page, which I have dropped as evidently unfit for the English taste, I have studied to present the work exactly as it stands in German" *(Works,* XXIII, 10). Friedrich Schlegel's essay *Über Goethes Meister* appeared in 1798.

13. NLS, 3823.2. Letter to William Tait, 3 November 1825. Carlyle had published in the *Edinburgh Review* for June 1827 the first of his several articles on Richter.

14. E. K. Chambers, *Samuel Taylor Coleridge* (Oxford, 1938), p. 125; Lawrence Hanson, *The Life of S. T. Coleridge* (London, 1938), pp. 410–411.

15. In the *Life of Schiller* (1825): *The Works of Thomas Carlyle* (hereafter *Works*), ed. H. D. Traill (London, 1896–1899), XXV, 129–130.

16. *Collected Letters of Samuel Taylor Coleridge,* ed. Earl Leslie Griggs (Oxford, 1956), I, 332. Letter to Josiah Wedgwood, 21 April 1800.

17. Cf. Carlyle's *Works,* XXV, 131, where Carlyle in a note to the 1845 edition of his biography of Schiller comments that the Capuchin's sermon is "said to be by Goethe." Carlyle, when he wrote his biography in 1823–1824, could not obtain a copy of Coleridge's translation. From the "many large specimens" which he had seen, however, he rated it, "excepting Sotheby's *Oberon,* to be the best, indeed the only sufferable, translation from the German with which our literature has yet been enriched" *(ibid.,* p. 151). Modern scholarship judges that Schiller, though he constantly discussed the cycle of plays with Goethe, wrote *Wallensteins Lager* unaided.

18. NLS, 522.64–1958. Letter of 29 November 1827.

19. NLS, 1775A–89. Letter to Margaret A. Carlyle, 30 November 1827.

20. NLS, 1775A–93. Letter of 29 December 1827.

21. Quoted by John in *ibid.*

22. I cite the text of Goethe's letter to Boisserée of 25 September 1827 from *Goethes Werke* (Weimar, 1908), XLIII, 79–80, rather than from John's transcription in his letter to Carlyle of 29 December 1827. John omitted in his transcription the phrase in brackets. Goethe had written to Carlyle on 20 July 1827, praising the biography of Schiller and singling out for particular commendation the biographical notices of Musäus, Hoffmann, and Richter *(Correspondence between Goethe and Carlyle,* ed. Charles Eliot Norton [London and New York, 1887], pp. 14–15, 22–23).

23. *Goethes Werke,* XLIII, 106. Letter of 12 October 1827. Several paragraphs in Goethe's letter to Carlyle of 20 July affirmed his belief in cultural internationalism and in the importance of translators in promoting cultural exchange.

24. *Works,* XXVII, 369. See G. B. Tennyson, pp. 96–97, and René Wellek, *A History of Modern Criticism, 1750–1950* (New Haven, 1965), III, 98 ff.

25. Letter of 29 December 1827.

26. NLS, 522.65–1959 and 522.68–1962. Carlyle's admiration for the German poet, which began in 1820 with his reading *Faust,* cannot be exaggerated. To Goethe he wrote on 20 August 1827: "As it is, your Works have been a mirror to me; unasked and unhoped-for, your wisdom has counselled me; and so peace and health of Soul have visited me from afar" *(Correspondence between Goethe and Carlyle,* p. 34).

27. NLS, 1775A–93 and 95. Letters to Thomas Carlyle, 29 December 1827 and 6–7 February 1828.

28. Schelling's popular handbook, *Vorlesungen über die Methode des akademischen Studiums,* first published in 1803, reached a third edition by 1830. It is a large-scale presentation of Schelling's philosophy as he conceived it toward the end of his first period. John mentions reading the *Methode* in his letter to Thomas of 6–7 February 1828 and Carlyle probably first read it the summer before—indeed it is the one work by Schelling he is known to have read (see Charles Frederick Harrold, *Carlyle and German Thought: 1819–1834* [New Haven, 1934], pp. 10, 15). From the course title which he gives, John must have attended lectures based on a much-revised version of the *Methode.* According to the article on Schelling by Friedrich Jodl in the *Allgemeine Deutsche Biographie* (hereafter *ADB),* the philosopher now gave in Munich in the form of lectures the long-awaited "results of the last fifteen or eighteen years of tranquil reflection: that which [he] . . . now understood to be philosophy and designated his system." The winter semester of 1827–1828 he offered (I cite Jodl again) "an Introduction 'to the Nature of Philosophy as Knowledge,' which he had already given at Erlangen . . . and a 'History of Modern Philosophy since Descartes.' " John seems to have attended both courses of lectures.

29. Letter of 29 December 1827.

30. NLS, 522.65–1959. Letter of 1 February 1828.

31. Letter of 6–7 February 1828.

32. *Ibid.* Wellek restates in the Coleridge chapter of his *History of Modern Criticism,* vol. II, the argument he first developed in *Kant in England* (Princeton, 1931).

33. Schelling referred to Francis Jeffrey's notice of Carlyle's translation of *Wilhelm Meisters Lehrjahre* in the *Edinburgh Review,* XLII, no. 84 (August 1825). Jeffrey summed up ambiguously: "While we hold out the work therefore as a curious and striking instance of that diversity of national tastes, which makes a writer idolized in one place who could not be tolerated in another, we would be understood as holding it [the *Lehrjahre*] out as an object rather of wonder than of contempt; and though the greater part certainly could not be endured, and indeed could not have been written in England, there are many passages of which any country might reasonably be proud, and which demonstrate, that if Taste be local and variable, Genius is permanent and universal" (p. 449). Carlyle, in essence, concurred with Schelling in his opinion of Jeffrey's article: "I think the critic very honest," he wrote to James Johnston on 26 October 1825, "and very seldom unjust in his feeling of individual passages; but for the general whole, which constitutes the essence of a work like this, he seems to have no manner of idea of it, except as a heap of beautiful and ugly fragments" *(Early Letters of Thomas Carlyle,* ed. C. E. Norton [London and New York, 1886], II, 330–331). Though they later became good friends, Jeffrey at the time he wrote the review did not know Carlyle. Not until the late 1830s did Goethe's works,

in large part because of Carlyle's efforts, lose their stigma of immorality and gain popularity in England.

33. Letter of 6–7 February 1828.

34. NLS, 1775A–97. John had reported in his letter of 6–7 February that Schelling (told by Baron von Eichthal of Carlyle's article) had said he was "very anxious of knowing what can appear in the Ed*r* Review in favour of German Literature."

35. Letter of 1 March 1828.

36. NLS, 522.66–1960.

37. NLS, 1775A–99. Letter of 5 May 1828.

38. *A History of Modern Philosophy* (New York, 1955), II, 162.

39. Letter of 5 May 1828.

40. Letter to Thomas Carlyle, 1 March 1828.

41. Letter of 5 May 1828. John's expression—"mixture of good and evil"—in the first sentence of the passage quoted is coterie speech (see *The Love Letters of Thomas Carlyle and Jane Welsh,* ed. A. Carlyle [London and New York, 1908], II, 174). Friedrich Thiersch (1784–1860), German philologist. Hugh Blair (1718–1800), Scottish Presbyterian clergyman and Professor of Rhetoric at Edinburgh. Lorenz Oken [Okenfuss] (1779–1851), naturalist and philosopher who sought to unify the natural sciences. Gotthilf Heinrich von Schubert (1780–1860), philosopher influenced by Schelling who later turned to mysticism; his *Die Geschichte der Seele* appeared in 1830. Johann Nepomuk von Fuchs (1774–1856), mineralogist and chemist who discovered water glass in 1823. Robert Jameson (1774–1854), Scottish mineralogist. Georg Anton Friedrich Ast (1778–1841), philologist and writer on philosophy. Joseph von Görres (1776–1848), after opposing Napoleon fought against Prussian reactionary measures by founding *Der Rheinische Merkur,* suppressed in 1816; in his despair at the triumph of reaction in Germany he became an ardent Ultramontane. He was Professor of History at Munich during 1827–1828.

42. *Thomas Carlyle* (New York, 1881), p. 71.

43. Letter of 7 March 1828. The whereabouts of John's journal today, if it has survived, is unknown.

44. *Correspondence between Goethe and Carlyle,* p. 210. Significantly, Carlyle makes no reference to German academic life in his two previous attempts at fictional narrative: *Wotton Reinfred,* begun in January 1827 and put aside incomplete in June of the same year (thus anterior to John's German sojourn), and an even earlier work, the recently discovered fragmentary novel "Illudo Chartis" (probably written during 1825–1826). No character in *Wotton Reinfred,* not even the "old Doctor," bears resemblance to a German professor. Later, Carlyle would transfer passages, almost word for word, from *Wotton Reinfred* into *Sartor.* "Illudo Chartis" also makes no use of the German scene, though it reflects, as does *Wotton Reinfred,* Carlyle's German reading. See Marjorie P. King, "'Illudo Chartis': An Initial Study in Carlyle's Mode of Composition," *MLR,* XLIX, no. 2 (April 1954), 164–175.

45. Conway, *Thomas Carlyle,* p. 71. In his *Autobiography* Conway quotes a passage from his diary of 5 April 1866 recording a conversation with John: in Munich, John told him, "he went a great deal to see Schelling. He belonged to a choice club of German beer-drinkers, who drank, smoked, and gave one another their views on the universe; and it was from his accounts and stories of these

men told to Thomas that the idea of Teufelsdröck came into his head" ([Boston and New York, 1904], II, 103). Conway presumably accepted at face value John's recollections in old age. He told C. E. Norton similar stories (see *Letters of Thomas Carlyle 1826–1836,* ed. C. E. Norton [London, 1889], pp. 554–555, and David Alec Wilson, *Carlyle to "The French Revolution"* [London, 1924], p. 184).

46. *Sartor Resartus,* ed. Charles Frederick Harrold (New York, 1937), pp. 15–16, 19–20, 296.

47. [Lang, Arnold] *ADB,* XXIV, 217. My analysis of Oken's career paraphrases or closely follows Lang's account in the *ADB* (pp. 216–226). The quotations from Alexander Ecker's biography are also taken from this source.

48. Letter of 6–7 February 1828. No account I have seen of the genesis and development of *Sartor* examines Oken's serving as a model for Teufelsdröckh. That the character of Teufelsdröckh is partly Carlyle's disguised autobiography substantiates rather than invalidates my argument: it is chiefly in ways that Teufelsdröckh is not like Carlyle that he bears greatest resemblance to Oken. As Harrold observes: "while much of the external character of Teufelsdröckh had little in common with himself, the whole story of the inner struggle and victory was essentially his own" *(Sartor,* p. xxxii). John's account of Oken and other German professors provided Carlyle with a ready-made "external character" with which he could clothe his spiritual development.

49. Letter of 7 March 1828.

50. *Sartor,* p. 18.

51. *Ibid.,* p. 19.

52. *Ibid.,* p. 15. The *Isis,* like Diogenes Teufelsdröckh, maintained an interest in "Things in General" ["*Allerley-Wissenschaft*"]. It published articles in all fields of knowledge except Law and Theology. Lang writes: "Indeed the *Isis* was for years a central organ for many branches of the natural sciences as no journal has been since" (p. 217).

53. *Sartor,* p. 16. John's description of Oken's physical appearance tallies with that of Alexander Ecker, his first biographer and a man who knew him personally. Ecker noted "the tiny, haggard form; the striking, dark, southern complexion; the glossy curly black hair; the large brown flashing eyes" *(Lorenz Oken. Eine biographische Skizze* [Stuttgart, 1880]. All quotations translated from the *ADB* article).

54. *Sartor,* p. 17.

55. *Ibid.,* p. 29.

56. John's letter to Carlyle, 5 May 1828.

57. *Sartor,* p. 30.

58. *Ibid.,* pp. xxxix–xl.

59. I have found no evidence that Carlyle ever read any of Oken's works, several of which had been published by the time John heard him lecture in Munich. Oken's greatest achievement was his lifelong attempt to prove the unity of nature (for a concise summary and critique of his theories, see Lang's *ADB* article, especially p. 220). His *magnum opus,* bringing together all his thought, was the *Allgemeine Naturgeschichte für alle Stände,* 7 vols. (Stuttgart, 1833–41). The first volume examined minerals, the second and third the vegetable kingdom, the last four the animal kingdom. Alfred Tulk translated parts of it as *Elements of Physiophilosophy* (London, 1847). Preposterous as Oken's theories may seem now, they had wide circulation in his day and influenced many contemporaries. A precursor to Darwin, he foreshadowed theories of the cellular structure of

organisms and of the protoplasmic basis of life. Emerson, whose intellectual debt to Carlyle is well known, took up Oken's theory of the evolutionary development of different kinds of life in his essay "Fate" *(Works,* ed. E. W. Emerson [Boston and New York, 1904], VI, 14, 341 n).

60. Letter to Alexander Carlyle, 13 June 1828.

61. NLS, 522.71–1965. Letter dated 10 October 1828 (probably written several days later).

62. NLS, 1775A–107. Letter of 19–28 October 1828.

63. *Ibid.*

64. NLS, 1775A–111. Letter from Munich to Thomas Carlyle, 9–10 February 1829.

65. NLS, 522.72–1966. Letter of 26 November 1828.

66. Letter of 9–10 February 1829.

67. *Two Note Books of Thomas Carlyle,* ed. C. E. Norton (New York, 1898), p. 135.

68. Davidson, p. 281.

69. Several years later he was still without regular employment and still supported by his long-patient brother. (The facetious may wish to claim that John's greatest contribution to *Sartor* was the gospel of work, which Thomas felt it necessary to stress as a spur for him.)

70. G. B. Tennyson (pp. 337–338) dates the writing of this first draft to September-November 1830, the completed and expanded book to March-August 1831.

TENNYSON READS *MAUD**
Gordon N. Ray

i

The book which I am going to describe in this essay came to me in the course of building a library of Victorian first and other early editions, and I propose to treat it as an example of the way in which rare books, examined in the context provided by a research library, can enrich literary study.

The Victorian age is not so far in the past that those of my generation have lost all sense of personal contact with it. Among my English friends of earlier years was W. T. D. Ritchie, Thackeray's grandson. As a boy he had often been taken by Lady Ritchie to visit Tennyson at Farringford, and his impressions of the poet remained vivid. He liked to tell an anecdote whose resonances Tennyson particularly relished. It concerned a parrot of local celebrity which called from its perch on a tree to a passing yokel, "Good evening." Whereupon the startled man replied, touching his forelock: "Beg pardon, sir, I thought you was a bird." Mr. Ritchie had another story, this time about rather than from Tennyson. The Laureate, walking with a young lady at a garden party, was disturbed by a series of rumblings. He left her abruptly, with a disapproving glare, but returned a few moments later to remark apologetically: "It was the mowing machine."

With this background Tennyson inevitably came to be present in my mind as a person as well as a poet. He was a swarthy, "mole-blind,"[1] large, gaunt, shaggy-headed man. (Indeed, he once said that he relied on "chance burnings" from unregarded candles to keep his hair trimmed.[2]) He dressed with a careless outlandishness, he smoked constantly, and he was not always scrupulously clean. His favorite photograph among the several

that Julia Margaret Cameron took of him was one that he himself entitled "The Dirty Monk."[3] It is not surprising that Henry
James, disappointed at finding in the man no trace of the elegance, urbanity, and careful finish of his poetry, should have remarked that "Tennyson is not personally Tennysonian."[4]
Though a consciousness of his extraordinary appearance helped
to make him taciturn and ill at ease in unfamiliar company, he
did not allow himself to become unduly oppressed by this
awareness. Sir Charles Tennyson tells a pleasant story of his long
walks through the London streets, dressed in "his great Spanish
cloak and sombrero," and accompanied by the small daughter of
friends. When their passage attracted attention, he gravely
admonished her: "Child, your mother should dress you less conspicuously, people are staring at us."[5]

Had I been concerned with Tennyson's work alone, I should
have been content in my collecting to assemble his first editions,
editions in which he made textual revisions, and editions with
contemporary illustrations. But being equally interested in the
man, I have sought as well his autograph letters, the fragments
of his manuscripts which occasionally turn up, and inscribed
copies of his books. In June of 1968 I was fortunate enough to
visit the firm of Walter T. Spencer at a time when the gaps on
the shelves of the rare book room on the top floor of their
house on Upper Berkeley Street had just been replenished
from their reserve. I found there nine volumes of Tennyson's
poems presented by him to his friends, volumes for the most part
acquired by old Mr. Spencer at Sotheby's before the first World
War, when family collections containing such material came on
the market with some frequency. The recipients included Mrs.
Cameron, among the closest of his Isle of Wight friends, and her
son Hardinge Hay Cameron; Blanche Guest, who with her
father Sir Ivor Guest printed small private editions of several of
Tennyson's poems at their Canford Manor press; John Leigh-
ton, the illustrator and binding designer; Franklin Lushington,
Tennyson's friend since Cambridge days, and Vernon Lushington; and the Rev. Drummond Rawnsley, who officiated at the
Tennyson marriage in 1850. All were welcome trophies, the
more desirable to a collector because Tennyson was relatively
chary of presentation inscriptions.

The final book, however, was something more than an ex-
hibition piece. This was volume four, containing *In Memoriam*
and *Maud,* of the six-volume *édition de luxe* of Tennyson's

THE WORKS OF

ALFRED TENNYSON

POET LAUREATE

VOL. IV.   IN MEMORIAM AND MAUD

Anchora Spei

STRAHAN & CO., PUBLISHERS

56, LUDGATE HILL, LONDON

1872

Works published by Strahan and Company in 1872. Opposite section one of *In Memoriam* in this book appear the
words: "The following notes were made by me from Tennyson's
dictation as he read the poem to me in August 1870—& March
1871. James Knowles. (The original notes were made by me in
pencil in an American copy of his poems published by Harper
Brothers, of New York, in 1870. JTK.)" At the beginning of
Maud there is a similar attestation, though this time the date of
Tennyson's reading is not given. After Knowles had transcribed
his notes, he brought the 1872 volume back for validation to
the poet, who wrote on the title page: "J. T. Knowles from
A. Tennyson." Tennyson's comments on *In Memoriam* run to
about 1,180 words, those on *Maud* to about 540 words.

Sir James Thomas Knowles was born in 1831.[6] The son of
a well-known architect, he was trained to the same profession in
his father's office, and he practiced it successfully for several
decades. His great avocation, however, was literature, and
Tennyson was his favorite author. The reading of *In Memoriam* in 1850 "made an epoch in his life," and he soon knew
Tennyson's poetry "almost by heart." When he quarried a little
book about King Arthur and his knights out of Malory, he
asked and received Tennyson's permission to dedicate it to him.
Vacationing on the Isle of Wight in the autumn of 1866,[7] he
found the courage to present himself at Farringford. He was
cordially received there, and after some conversation Tennyson
read "Boädicea" and other poems to him.

Their friendship was confirmed through a chance encounter
the following year on the platform of the Haslemere railway
station. Tennyson had come up from Farringford to look at a
small plot of land two miles outside of Haslemere, where he
hoped to build a house that would serve as a refuge from the
tourists who pestered him on the Isle of Wight. The location
high on Green Hill, overlooking "the whole of woody Sussex
to the South Downs and the sea," could not have been improved, particularly since its seclusion was complete. After telling
Knowles of his intentions, Tennyson inquired: "You are an
architect, why should you not make a plan of it for me?"
Knowles agreed on the understanding that he would accept no
fee.[8]

Tennyson had in mind a four-room cottage, but after Knowles
had enlarged on the possibilities of the site, he was authorized

to proceed with what he called "a less unimportant dwelling."
The most strenuous debate took place over an "arcaded porch"
which Knowles proposed "to complete the design." Tennyson

> put his foot down and said he would have nothing to do with it—that
> he would have no more additions—that it would ruin him and could not
> be entertained for a moment. He walked to and fro, coming back from
> time to time to the table where the drawing lay and looking at it. He
> admitted that he liked it more and more the more he looked at it, but
> presently cried out with simulated fury, 'Get thee behind me, Satan,'
> and ran out of the room. Then I knew that the porch was won.[9]

Tennyson laid the foundation-stone of Aldworth, as the new
house was called, on Shakespeare's birthday in 1868 and followed its construction with keen interest. Nor was his satisfaction at all diminished after he took possession. "It was delightful to see his enjoyment of everything in the new house, from
the hot-water bathroom downwards," Knowles recalled, "for
at first the hot-water bath seemed to attract him out of measure.
He would take it four or five times a day, and told me he thought
it the height of luxury 'to sit in a hot bath and read about little
birds.' "[10]
Knowles's admiration for Tennyson, both as a poet and as a
seer, was complete. Laid in the 1872 volume already described
are four pages of pencil notes on *In Memoriam,* his homework
(so to speak) for the poetical initiation he was to receive as
Tennyson read the poem to him, which make it clear that he
regarded the doctrine of this work with all the reverence which
students of an earlier age had reserved for holy writ. His whole
attitude toward the poet, indeed, was a perpetual compliment.
Nor was he deficient in verbal praise when the occasion arose.
Contemplating Aldworth just after its completion, Tennyson
said to its architect: "You will live longer than I shall. That
house will last five hundred years." Knowles's reply was: "I
think the English language will last longer."[11]
Yet there was nothing obsequious in Knowles's attitude; he
was merely displaying suitable deference toward a great man
twenty years his senior. Moreover, he was quite alive, though
in the friendliest possible way, to Tennyson's oddities and
foibles. If Tennyson indeed came in later years to be "sunk in
coterie worship, and (I tremble to say it) in the sympathy of his
most lady-like, gentle wife," as Edward FitzGerald maintained

to Lord Houghton in 1872,[12] Knowles brought a current of fresh air into this incense-laden atmosphere. Deeply involved in the practical world himself, he did his best to make Tennyson less of a recluse, persuading him to visit London and even to take part in the meetings of the Metaphysical Society. The brooding poet was duly grateful to his cheerful, energetic, and sensible friend. "You certainly are a jolly good fellow," Tennyson told him. "You do encourage me so much." And on another occasion he added: "I'm very glad to have known you. It has been a sort of lift in my life."[13]

Knowles became a frequent visitor to Aldworth, where his status as one of Tennyson's intimates was soon confirmed. There the Laureate's evening routine was unvarying. After an early dinner, during which he took a leading part in the conversation, he would drink his pint of port and retire to his study for a solitary pipe. On his return to the drawing room, he could often be persuaded to read his poems, though Knowles recalls that "it was not reading as generally understood, but intoning on a note, almost chanting." Then, after the ladies had retired, the evening would conclude with "confidential discussions and soliloquies" in his study with a favored friend or two.[14]

This was the setting, then, for the readings of *In Memoriam* and *Maud* during 1870 and 1871 recorded by Knowles. They presumably took place late in the evening in Tennyson's study, since Knowles specifies that "he read the poem *to me*." At any rate, the poet's commentary on these occasions was of a different character from that which Hallam Tennyson quotes in his *Memoir* of his father[15] or includes in the notes to the Eversley Edition of Tennyson's *Works*.[16] There one finds a careful selection, formal, discreet, and sometimes portentous, from Tennyson's remarks about his poems over half a lifetime. They give us a Tennyson washed, combed, and put into clean linen. Knowles, on the other hand, shows us the poet talking freely at a specific point in time and without thought of effect.[17] "He is captivating with his frankness, confidingness and unexampled naïveté," Mrs. Browning wrote after a similar experience of Tennyson's reading. "Think of his stopping in 'Maud' every now and then 'There's a wonderful touch! That's very tender! How beautiful that is!'"[18] In Knowles's jottings we come close to Tennyson the natural man, to the Tennyson "who was not Tennysonian."

ii

A good many of Tennyson's observations as he read *In Memoriam*, including most of those of greatest interest, were printed in the memorial article which Knowles wrote about his friend in his own magazine, *The Nineteenth Century*,[19] and are consequently familiar to students. They appear in their entirety in Appendix I below. Tennyson's remarks while reading *Maud*, on the other hand, deserve detailed examination. Except for a few sentences quoted by Knowles in his memorial article, they have been unknown to students of the poem. Moreover, of all Tennyson's works, *Maud* is perhaps the one concerning which his candid and unrehearsed commentary is most to be desired.

Since the publication of Sir Charles Tennyson's biography of his grandfather in 1949, the profoundly autobiographical nature of *Maud* has been sufficiently clear. Tennyson's able but erratic father, though the oldest son of the wealthy George Tennyson, had been disinherited in favor of a younger son. While he, his wife, and his eleven children led an obscure and difficult existence at Somersby Rectory, his younger brother, who had changed his name to Tennyson d'Eyncourt, became a leader of county society, serving as a member of parliament and spending vast sums in rebuilding Bayons Manor, the family seat. Thus, Tennyson grew up under an oppressive sense of the unfairness with which he and his family had been treated, a feeling exacerbated by the protracted spectacle of his father's drinking himself to death. When it was revealed after his grandfather's death in 1835 that little had been done to rectify the injustice visited on the Somersby family in the distribution of his property, Tennyson's bitterness was intensified. As Professor Ralph Rader has recently shown, what slight chance he had of marrying Rosa Baring, a young lady belonging to the branch of the great banking clan that resided at Harrington Hall, two miles from Somersby Rectory, were altogether destroyed by this development. Though he fell in love with Emily Sellwood the following year, Tennyson still found it difficult to accept with equanimity Rosa's *mariage de convenance* in 1838 with Robert Duncombe Shafto, whom she had accepted because he was the son of an old and wealthy Durham family.[20]

Into the unnamed protagonist of *Maud*, far more than into the speaker in *Locksley Hall* some years earlier, Tennyson put himself as he was as a young man. Almost twenty years of intermittent melancholia and hypochondria, passed in morbid brooding over the maltreatment of his father, the threat of insanity that haunted his entire family, the failure of his poetry to attain recognition, his impecuniousness, his consequent inability to marry, and the suspicion with which he was regarded by respectable acquaintances as a person of irregular habits and doubtful piety had made him painfully at home with the state of mind of his hero at the opening of his poem. In some moods he too was given to "railing against the whole system of society,"[21] though in others he could see how unprofitable was such an intellectual stance. Indeed, it must have been a profound relief for so reserved and taciturn a man to speak out freely and forcibly through his creation. No doubt the phases of his hero's growing love for Maud also had their parallels in Tennyson's experience. And if the remaining events of the poem—the duel in which he kills Maud's brother, his flight to Brittany, his temporary insanity, and his redemption through remembered love and pugnacious patriotism—were imagined by Tennyson, they were imagined as happening to someone very like himself. Thus, *Maud* was for Tennyson, as Mr. Rader has pointed out, "a very special kind of document with deep roots in his emotional being."[22]

When *Maud* appeared in 1855, it baffled and irritated the public, which found its subject matter disagreeable and its tone unhealthy. A reviewer observed that one of the two vowels in the title should have been omitted, and it didn't matter which. Among the anonymous letters which Tennyson received was one which ran:

Sir, I used to worship you, but now I hate you. I loathe and detest you. You beast! So you've taken to imitating Longfellow.
Yours in aversion * * *[23]

The protagonist was particularly abused as extravagant, incoherent, and bloodthirsty. Nor did Tennyson himself, as the creator of such a figure, escape criticism. "If an author pipe of adultery, fornication, murder and suicide," wrote one reviewer, "set him down as the practitioner of these crimes." Tennyson was at least able to deny suicide.[24] *Maud* came to be better understood with the passing years, but the aura of suspicion created by its initial reception was never entirely dissipated. When Gladstone, who had noticed the poem unfavorably in the *Quarterly*

Review in 1855, in part withdrew his strictures after hearing
Tennyson read it in 1878, he still ventured to doubt in his stately
way whether *Maud* had "the full moral equilibrium which is so
marked a characteristic of the sister-works."[25]

Tennyson was greatly disturbed by *Maud*'s seeming failure.
He did not lose faith in his poem, but he did seize every opportunity to explain and justify it. In particular he sought to read
it to those whose judgment he especially respected. Among such
auditors were the Brownings, Dante Gabriel and William Michael Rossetti, and the Carlyles, all of whom noted how he lost
himself in his reading. The skeptical Mrs. Carlyle, to whom
Tennyson eagerly read his poem four times within a few weeks,
remarked concerning the final occasion at "a large party" assembled at Lord and Lady Ashburton's country house that Tennyson "seemed strangely excited about *Maud*—as sensitive to
criticisms as if they were imputations on his honor."[26] Nor did
this sensitivity and proselytizing zeal greatly diminish as the
years passed.

Before he began to read *Maud* to Knowles, Tennyson observed: *"No other poem (a monotone with plenty of change and
no weariness) has been made into a drama where successive
phases of passion in one person take the place of successive persons. It is slightly akin to Hamlet."* And he called his poem not
simply *Maud,* but *Maud "(or the Madness),"* thus restoring the
title he had first given it.[27] Knowles records no remarks of Tennyson about the first ten sections of Part One, perhaps because
he knew that the explanation with which Tennyson "generally
prefaced his reading" was available in Dr. R. J. Mann's *Maud
Vindicated,* published in 1856.[28] During the remainder of Part
One, however, Tennyson's commentary was abundant, and it
took the form chiefly of an effort to exculpate his protagonist,
or at least to palliate his offences. These are the pages of the
poem, of course, where such an enterprise has the best chance
of success, since it is here that he appears in the most amiable
light.

Until Maud first shows him favor, Tennyson's hero has been
wholehearted in his denunciation of life. But by section XI of
Part One her attentions have pierced his armor:

> O let the solid ground
>   Not fail beneath my feet
> Before my life has found
>   What some have found so sweet.

"The poor madman," was Tennyson's comment. *"He begins to soften."* He continues:

> Then let come what may,
> What matter if I go mad,
> I shall have had my day.

Concerning these lines Tennyson inquired anxiously: *"It's terrible, isn't it?"* After his rebuff by Maud's brother, the protagonist falls into what Tennyson described to Knowles as *"a counter passion—passionate & furious."* Yet at the end of this tirade he is capable of saying to himself:

> Peace angry spirit, and let him be!
> Has not his sister smiled on me?

"He makes allowances for the man," Tennyson pointed out, adding indignantly: *"Yet he is called a mere brute!"*

Section XV is a further exploration of the protagonist's state of mind. Tennyson's summary for Knowles was: *"He begins with universal hatred of all things & gets more human by the influence of Maud."* In the following section he has a new problem to ponder. Can it be that Maud is promised in marriage to the vacuous son of a recently ennobled coal magnate?

> Should I love her so well if she
> Had given her love to a thing so low?
> Shall I love her as well if she
> Can break her word even for me?

"You see he is the most conscientious fellow," Tennyson pleaded, *"a perfect gentleman tho' semi-insane! he would not have been so, had he met with happiness."* By section XVIII the protagonist is able to tell himself: "It seems that I am happy," which led Tennyson to the fond if mocking observation: *"Isn't that a change for the man?"* And when he expressed a wish not to "die, but live a life of truest breath," Tennyson exclaimed, by this time virtually at one with his creation: *"I won't die!"* In section XXII, as the protagonist sits in the garden while Maud dances at the Hall, he asks himself:

> O young lord-lover, what sighs are those
> For one that will never be thine?

And Tennyson thereupon scores another point for him by remarking: *"No reproach for the young lover—now that he feels successful."*

This concluded Tennyson's defence of his maligned hero except in one respect. Hostile critics of *Maud* had taken particular exception to the protagonist's exaltation of the Crimean War as the salvation both of his country and of himself. On this issue Tennyson was prepared neither to defend his hero, nor to disavow him. Confined to a madhouse in section V of Part Two, he contrasts the carnage of war with his killing of Maud's brother:

> Friend, to be struck by the public foe,
> Then to strike and lay him low,
> That were a public merit, far,
> Whatever the Quaker holds, from sin;
> But the red life spilt for a private blow—
> I swear to you, lawful and lawless war
> Are scarcely even akin.

Of this sudden swerve in his hero's line of thought, Tennyson observed sardonically: *"He feels that he is getting a little too sensible in this remark."* And concerning the poem's much-debated final lines—

> It is better to fight for the good than
>   to rail at the ill;
> I have felt with my native land, I am
>   one with my kind,
> I embrace the purpose of God, and
>   the doom assign'd—,

Tennyson offered a cool comparison rather than a firm endorsement: *"Take this with the first where he railed at everything. He is not quite sane—a little shattered."*

Tennyson's commentary on section V of Part Two, which shows his hero *"mad in Bedlam,"* is also particularly interesting. The whole section extending to 104 lines *"was written in 20 minutes,"*[29] Tennyson told Knowles, an astounding feat but physically just possible, since many of the lines are short. In the third division one of the hero's fellow-Bedlamites is described as "a lord of all things, praying / To his own great self, as I guess." Tennyson informed Knowles that, for "a lord of all things," *"I put 'a God Almighty' first, which is a usual form of madness."* No doubt this telling phrase was replaced lest pious readers should find it blasphemous. The "vile physician, blabbing / The case of his patient" Tennyson identified as *"the doctor of the madhouse,"* not another inmate. The elliptical "Tell him now" which begins the seventh division Tennyson expanded to tell *"the old father . . . how we met in the garden,"* that is, taunt Maud's father with the fact that she and the hero had once had their hour together. After further clarifying identifications in division nine, came the ironical comment on lawful and lawless murder already mentioned. Tennyson's concluding remark on section V was: *"Some mad-doctor wrote to me—'Nothing since Shakespeare has been so good for madness as this.'"*[30]

Among Tennyson's other comments were directions for reading certain sections of the poem. The words already noted concerning section XIII of Part One, *"passionate & furious,"* fall into this category. His remark about the first three subsections of section XVIII, *"These might not be divided,"*[31] implies that there should be no pause in reading them. At the end of section XX he noted: *"The verse should be read here as if it were prose. Nobody can read it naturally enough,"* an admonition to which he returned at the end of section I of Part Two: *"It all has to be read like passionate prose."* Then, since *Maud* by Victorian standards was highly elliptical and allusive, Tennyson provided a number of narrative clues and identifying asides. These need not delay us, however, since the points thus illuminated hardly give pause to modern readers, accustomed as they have become to this kind of poetry.[32]

The rest of Tennyson's comments were of a more miscellaneous nature, but in several cases none the less interesting for that. In explanation of the lines in section XII of Part One—

> For her feet have touched the meadows
> And left the daisies rosy—

he remarked: *"If you tread on daisies—they turn up underfoot & get rosy."*[33] And when he came to his description of the gate of Maud's garden in the following section—

> A lion ramps at the top,
> He is claspt by a passion-flower—,

he offered a comment with profound implications for the interpretation of his poetry generally: *"a token—I hardly write anything without some meaning of that kind."* In section XVIII Tennyson's protagonist, ecstatic with delight over Maud's love for him, apostrophizes the "happy stars":

> Has our whole earth gone nearer to the glow
> Of your soft splendours that you look so bright?
> *I* have climbed nearer out of lonely Hell.

Concerning the last line, Tennyson exclaimed: *"a wonderful line, surely!"* He ended his reading by remarking: *"I've always said that Maud and Guinevere were the finest things I've written,"*[34] thus reaffirming his faith in his beloved though much abused poem.

iii

Several of Tennyson's already cited observations on *Maud* invite extended interpretation, but I here propose to explore only the implications of his comments on sections III and IV of Part Two, about which I have as yet said nothing. In section III Tennyson's protagonist *"comes back to England and London"* from Brittany, and there *"he learns of her* [Maud's] *death."* In section IV he dreams that he is led through the London streets at evening by the phantom of Maud. After a variety of other visions,

> there rings on a sudden a passionate cry,
> There is someone dying or dead,
> And a sullen thunder is roll'd;
> For a tumult shakes the city,
> And I wake.

"Perhaps the sound of a cab in the street suggests this cry of recollection," was Tennyson's gloss. His protagonist then revisits in person the scenes about which he had been dreaming.

> And I loathe the squares and streets,
> And the faces that one meets,
> Hearts with no love for me:
> Always I long to creep
> Into some still cavern deep,
> There to weep, and weep, and weep
> My soul out to thee.

MAUD.   **293**

III.

Here he comes back to England and London.

OURAGE, poor heart of stone!
   I will not ask thee why·
   Thou canst not understand

re leaves

That thou art left for·ever alone:

i death -

Courage, poor stupid heart of stone.— "
Or if I ask thee why,
Care not thou to reply: "
She is but dead, and the time is at hand
When thou shalt more than die.

There was another poem in [about] London & the streets at night — where all the scum of night & hell boils, [leave the] cellar & the sewer" was part of it—

Tennyson remarked about these last lines: *"I've often felt this in London."*

Section IV is a substantially revised version of "Oh, that 'twere possible," the poem in *The Tribute* of 1837 which *"was the nucleus of all the rest of Maud,"* so Tennyson told Knowles, *"woven round it at the request of Sir John Simeon."* It fits exactly the state of mind of the shattered protagonist, by now "a wasted frame" incapable any longer of active response. Yet it is fascinating to learn from Tennyson's commentary at this point that *"There was once another poem about London & the streets at night—'When all the scum of night & hell boils from the cellar & the sewer' was part of it."* These lines resemble in tone the tirades at the beginning of *Maud,* in which Tennyson's hero vents his rage against life, and they would clearly be out of place at this juncture, even if his wanderings about London had not been already described in the lines which were *Maud's* starting point. Yet one greatly regrets the loss of the poem of which they were a part, for it evidently offered a nightmare vision of the streets of London after dark such as one finds nowhere else in Tennyson's work.

At any rate, the discovery that such a poem once existed suggests certain reflections on the response of the great Victorian writers to the spectacle of the streets of London at night, the most obvious reminder to prosperous and respectable Englishmen of the seamy side of that nineteenth-century urban civilization of which they were so proud. The subject began to impose itself inescapably upon them in 1850 when the abortive first instalments of what was to become Henry Mayhew's *London Labour and the London Poor* appeared. Thackeray wrote in *Punch*:

> A clever and earnest-minded writer gets a commission from the *Morning Chronicle* newspaper, and reports upon the state of our poor in London; he goes amongst labouring people and poor of all kinds—and brings back what? A picture of human life so wonderful, so awful, so piteous and pathetic, so exciting and terrible, that readers of romances own they never read anything like to it; and that the griefs, struggles, strange adventures here depicted exceed anything that any of us could imagine.[35]

Mayhew resumed his revelations in weekly pamphlets published by himself in 1851. Beginning with number 37 in this series he alternated pamphlets on "Those Who Will Not Work," that is to say vagrants, beggars, cheats, thieves, prostitutes, and their dependents, with his initial series on "Those Who Will Work." In the following year this venture too came to an abrupt end, the series on "Those Who Will Work" breaking off in the middle of a word with number 63 of 21 February, and that on "Those Who Will Not Work" ending in the middle of a sentence with number 61 of 7 February.[36] It was not until 1862 that the publication, thus so recalcitrantly received by the public, was at last brought to a conclusion.

In the third number of the series on "Those Who Will Not

Work" Mayhew, who was nothing if not systematic, added to his outline-analysis of the total English population a final category of "Those Who Need Not Work." No doubt there was a hint of irony in his mention of this group, which was of course no part of his concern in *London Labour and the London Poor*.[37] At any rate, it was from just these "landlords, fund holders, shareholders, annuitants, pensioners, sinecurists, sleeping partners, royalty men, protégés, dependents, wives and children" that the respectable Victorian reading public was largely drawn, and the last topic about which they wanted to be informed was poverty, misery, and vice in London. "The times are such," Thackeray had written in *Vanity Fair* (chapter 49), "that one scarcely dares allude to that kind of company which thousands of our young men in Vanity Fair are frequenting every day, which nightly fills casinos and dancing-rooms, which is known to exist as well as the Ring in Hyde Park or the Congregation in St. James's—but which the most squeamish if not the most moral of societies is determined to ignore." Hence London poverty and still more London vice were for the most part avoided by the great authors of the time, and even Dickens's vast prestige was threatened when he dwelt too pointedly upon the darker aspects of the metropolis in his later novels.

Yet out of sight was not necessarily out of mind. Consider, for example, the way in which Anthony Trollope, to the Victorians perhaps the closest counterpart in fiction to Tennyson in poetry, allowed himself to touch upon this subject. Again and again when a character is at the end of his tether in one of Trollope's novels, he is sent wandering through the London streets at night. So it is with Burgo Fitzgerald, the handsome, feckless dandy of *Can You Forgive Her?*, whose only remaining hope in life lies in persuading Lady Glencora Palliser to elope with him, after he realizes that she is going to remain true to her husband.[38] So it is with Ferdinand Lopez in *The Prime Minister*, after he has been exposed as a complete blackguard and "it was all blank and black with him."[39] So it is with young Tom Tringle in *Ayala's Angel* after he has been brought finally to realize that his beloved Ayala is not for him but for his hated rival Colonel Stubbs.[40]

In each case Trollope provides a detailed itinerary of his character's wanderings. Here is what we are told of Lopez the night before he throws himself under a train at the Tenway Junction station of the underground railway.

At about twelve o'clock he left the club and took his way homewards. But he did not go straight home. It was a nasty cold March night, with a catching wind, and occasional short showers of something between snow and rain,—as disagreeable a night for a gentleman to walk in as one could well conceive. But he went round by Trafalgar Square, and along the Strand, and up some dirty streets by the small theatres, and so on to Holborn and by Bloomsbury Square up to Tottenham Court Road, and back to Manchester Square by Baker Street. He had more than doubled the distance,—apparently without any object. He had been spoken to frequently by unfortunates of both sexes, but had answered a word to no one. He had trudged on and on with his umbrella over his head, but almost unconscious of the cold and wet. And yet he was a man sedulously attentive to his own personal comfort and health, who had at any rate shown this virtue in his mode of living, that he had never subjected himself to danger by imprudence. But now the working of his mind kept him warm, and, if not dry, at least indifferent to the damp.

Similarly, we follow Burgo Fitzgerald from Grosvenor Square to Park Lane, Oxford Street, Bond Street, and back to Grosvenor Square, and Tom Tringle ("wet through, muddy, still tipsy, a sight miserable to behold"), from Lancaster Gate to Queen's Gate, Leicester Square, and the Haymarket, before he is taken to the Vine Street police station.

It will be noted that Lopez was "spoken to frequently by unfortunates of both sexes, but he answered a word to no one." Of Tom Tringle in Leicester Square we learn that "he did not make his way round the square without being addressed, but he simply shook off from him those who spoke to him." Burgo Fitzgerald is less fastidious:

At the corner of Bond Street, a girl took hold of him and looked up into his face.[41] "Ah!" she said, "I saw you once before." "Then you saw the most miserable devil alive," said Burgo. "You can't be miserable," said the girl. "What makes you miserable? You've plenty of money."—"I wish I had," said Burgo. "And plenty to eat and drink," exclaimed the girl; "and you are so handsome! I remember you. You gave me supper one night when I was starving. I ain't hungry now. Will you give me a kiss?"—"I'll give you a shilling, and that's better," said Burgo. "But give me a kiss too," said the girl. He gave her first the kiss, and then the shilling, and after that he left her and passed on. "I'm d———d if I wouldn't change with her!" he said to himself.

In these passages Trollope shows himself to be as expert in dealing with failure and defeat as with success and triumph. Having stripped each of these lost or doomed men of the defences of privilege and self-esteem that normally protect him, he sends him wandering into "regions of the town with which he had no business, and which he never frequented," hardly knowing where he goes or wherefore.[42] The hopeless blankness of his mind is driven home by Trollope's flat recital of his movements as if apart from the weather there was nothing else to report. Yet all the while we are not allowed to forget, through his brushes with the city's "unfortunates," the abyss that gapes for him beyond the limits of respectable society. The result is a powerfully dramatic confrontation, crystallizing the human significance of his situation, which stands out sharply from the placid flow of Trollope's customary narrative.

Returning finally to *Maud*, I remind you of Tennyson's remark that he hardly wrote anything without some meaning of a symbolic kind. It was natural enough that he too should have thought of sending his protagonist in *Maud* through the streets of the metropolis,

> When all the scum of night & hell
> Boils from the cellar & the sewer,

thus paralleling the anarchy and despair in his mind with the anarchy and despair of London's midnight Saturnalia. Unfortunately, it was also natural enough that, having written such a poem, Tennyson should have discarded it. Even in the early eighteen-fifties he had no desire to be found "wallowing" in what he was later to call "the troughs of Zolaism."[43]

By discussing Tennyson's comments to Knowles about *Maud* in a broad context, I have tried to illustrate the usefulness of the pattern of collecting which is followed in research libraries. The Victorian age, it should be emphasized, particularly lends itself to such a program. This is the earliest period for which printed and manuscript material of real importance may still be acquired in some abundance. Think of the excitement that would be generated by the discovery of a series of observations on his poems by Spenser, or Dryden, or Pope, or even Keats, not because these poets are greater than Tennyson, but because the little authoritative personal commentary that we have about their work has long since been thoroughly assimilated. Our knowledge of Victorian authors, in fact, is of a different order of magnitude from our knowledge of earlier authors. Before the second World War this fact tended to operate as a deterrent to students eager to make a definitive contribution to scholarship. During the last two decades, as the academic world has grown greatly in size, this abundance of data has served on the contrary as a powerful incentive to an ever-growing band of Victorian scholars, whose interests in these days of interdisciplinary study range far beyond the biographical and the editorial. A great deal has already been done, but enough remains to engage the attention of students for generations to come. No well-stocked Victorian research collection is likely to remain unused.

NOTES

*This is a shortened version of the Sedgwick Memorial Lecture for 1968. I am grateful to the authorities of the University of British Columbia for allowing me to republish it.

1. So Tennyson describes himself in a manuscript letter in my possession.

2. Sir Charles Tennyson, *Alfred Tennyson* (London, 1949), p. 357.

3. Helmut Gernsheim, *Julia Margaret Cameron* (London, 1948), p. 83.

4. Quoted by Leon Edel, *Henry James: The Conquest of London* (Philadelphia and New York, 1962), p. 374.

5. *Alfred Tennyson*, p. 425.

6. Knowles's reminiscences of Tennyson are set down in "Aspects of Tennyson II (a Personal Reminiscence)," *Nineteenth Century*, XXXIII (January 1893), 164–188; and "Tennyson and Aldworth," *Tennyson and his Friends*, ed. Hallam, Lord Tennyson (London, 1911), pp. 245–252. He also contributed a memorial poem, *Apotheosis: Westminster, October 1892*, to *Nineteenth Century*, XXXII (November 1892), 843–844.

7. So Knowles writes (*Tennyson and his Friends*, p. 246), but I have a letter from Tennyson to him of 31 January 1866, which suggests that the meeting took place before that date.

8. *Tennyson and his Friends*, pp. 247–248.

9. *Ibid.*, pp. 248–249.

10. *Ibid.*, pp. 249–251.

11. *Nineteenth Century*, XXXIII, 173.

12. Quoted by Harold Nicolson, *Tennyson* (London, 1949), p. 200.

13. *Nineteenth Century*, XXXIII, 174.

14. *Tennyson and his Friends*, pp. 251–252.

15. Hallam Tennyson, *Alfred Lord Tennyson: A Memoir by His Son* (London and New York, 1897), chapters 14 and 19.

16. Volumes III and IV (1908).

17. It should be noted that Tennyson in no sense regarded Knowles as his

Boswell. "Only upon the few occasions which are here recorded," Knowles wrote in his memorial article, "did I make any note in writing of all Tennyson's talk." (*Nineteenth Century*, XXXIII, 164)

18. Quoted by Sir Charles Tennyson, *Alfred Tennyson*, p. 290.

19. XXXIII, 182–187. Knowles's few quotations from Tennyson's comments on *Maud* appear on pp. 166 and 187. They are identified in the notes that follow.

20. See Ralph Wilson Rader, *Tennyson's "Maud": the Biographical Genesis* (Berkeley and Los Angeles, 1963), chapter two *passim* and pp. 92–93. Mr. Rader suggests a number of other biographical parallels not mentioned in the brief summary above.

21. See Rader, *Tennyson's "Maud,"* p. 77.

22. *Ibid.*, pp. 10–11.

23. *Memoir*, I, 400.

24. *Alfred Tennyson*, p. 286.

25. *Memoir*, I, 399.

26. See Charles Richard Sanders, "Carlyle and Tennyson," *PMLA*, LXXVI (March 1961), 91–92.

27. *Memoir*, I, 402. These preliminary comments were quoted by Knowles, *Nineteenth Century*, XXXIII, 187. Here and afterwards Tennyson's comments will be italicized.

28. See *Memoir*, I, 394–395.

29. Quoted by Knowles, *Nineteenth Century*, XXXIII, 187.

30. *Ibid.*

31. They have remained divided in all editions of the poem.

32. Many of these, in any event, are recorded in Hallam Tennyson's notes to volume IV of the Eversley Edition of his father's *Works*, or in *Memoir*, I, 402–405.

33. Quoted by Knowles, *Nineteenth Century*, XXXIII, 166.

34. *Ibid.*, 187.

35. "Waiting at the Station," *Punch*, 9 March 1850; *Works*, (London, 1908), VIII, 256.

36. These details are drawn from a set of the 1851–1852 part issues, bound with the covers and "Answers to Correspondents," in my possession.

37. Number 41, 20 September 1851, p. 27.

38. Chapter 66.

39. Chapter 60.

40. Chapter 44.

41. Burgo Fitzgerald's earlier encounter with this girl is described in chapter 29.

42. These words come from Trollope's account of Adolphus Crosbie's similar meanderings "through the gloom of a November evening" in London as he tries to make up his mind to jilt Lily Dale for Lady Alexandrina de Courcey in chapter 28 of *The Small House at Allington*.

43. *Locksley Hall Sixty Years After*.

APPENDIX I

In Memoriam

The following notes were made by me from Tennyson's dictation as he read the poem to me in August 1870—& March 1871.

James Knowles

(The original notes were made by me in pencil in an American copy of his poems—published by Harper brothers of New York, in 1870   JTK.)

* * * *

[IN MEMORIAM. A.H.H. OBIIT MDCCCXXXIII:]

Born in Bedford Place Feby 1st 1811—Eton Octr/22   Went to Cambridge October 1828   died 15th September 1833   buried on 3d of January 1834 in the Chancel of Clevedon Church in Somersetshire, the property of his grandfather Sir Abraham Elton In the summer of /27 went to Italy with his parents—In autumn of /30 & Spring of /31 wrote the poem of the two Sisters 'Mary & Emily'

* * * *

Divisions of the Poem[1]
```
  1 to 8—
  9 to 20 all connected—about the Ship
 21 to 27
 28 to 49
 50 to 58
 59 to 71
 72 to 98
 99 to 103
104 to 131
```

* * * *

In the Poem altogether private grief swells out into thought of & hope for the whole world. It begins with a funeral & ends with a marriage—begins with death & ends in promise of a new life—a sort of divine comedy—cheerful at the close. It's a very impersonal poem as well as personal. There's more about myself in Ulysses which was written under the sense of loss and that all had gone by, but that still life must be fought out to the end. It was more written with the feeling of his loss upon me than many poems in 'In Memoriam.' It is rather the cry of the whole human race than mine

* * * *

[I. 1:]   perhaps Goethe?
[VII:]   This & 119 are pendant poems.
[VII. 1-2:]   67 Wimpole St.

[VII. 10:] say in Oxford St.

[VII. 12:] see the altered view of the same street in 119—

[IX:] This was the first written

[IX. 1–4:] IX to XX are all connected—about the Ship

[XVII:] The bringing home

[XVIII:] The burial

[XIX:] After the burial these thoughts come

[XIX. 3–8:] The Grave

[XIX. 9–12:] Written at Tintern (supposed to be)

[XXIV. 4:] Spots on the Sun

[XXVIII. 1–4:] Christmas & the thoughts of it

[XXXV. 8–12:] The vastness of the future—the enormity of the ages
to come after your little life would act against that love—

[XXXVIII:] The Spring now comes

[XL:] See Poem 97 where the writer is compared to the female—*here*
the spirit becomes the female in the parable—

[XI. 19. concerning "offices as suit":] I hate that. I should not write
so *now*. I'd almost rather sacrifice a meaning than let two S'S come
together.

[XLI. 4–8:] Love fears to be lost in the advance of the dead beyond
the Survivor.

[XLII. 4–8:] Sympathy of the teacher & taught

[XLIII. 4–8:] Sympathy of equal learning in the new life

[XLIII. 11:] painted with the past life—

[XLIV. 6. concerning "the hoarding sense":] the memory—

[XLIV. 10:] in the same way as the infancy is forgot—

[XLIV. 13–16:] if you *have* forgot all earthly things—yet as a man has
faint memories, even so in the new life a sort of vague memory of the
past would come. This is fortified by considering that the use of flesh
& blood were lost if they do not establish an identity.

[XLVI. 4:] If there were a perfect memory of all sorrows & sins we
should not be able to bear it

[XLVI. 12. after "five years":] of our acquaintanceship (only 5 years!)

[XLVI. 13: after "were":] then

[XLVI. 15–16:] —as if Lord of the whole life—

[XLVII. 1–4:] Love protests against the loss of identity in the theory
of absorption—

[XLVII. 11. concerning "vaster":] less defined

[XLVII. 14:] into the universal spirit—

[XLVII. 15:] —but at least one last parting! & always would want it
again—of course—

[XLIX. 4–8:] referring to the previous stanzas

[XLIX. 9. concerning "look thy look":] the reader

[LI. 1–4:] But aren't you ashamed for the dead to see you?

[LII. 3:] There is so much evil in me that I don't really reflect you &
all my talk is only words

[LII. 5-6:] Then the Spirit of true love replies—all life fails in some measure.

[LIII. 4-8:] There is a passionate heat of nature in a rake sometimes— The nature that yields emotionally may come straighter than a prig's

[LIII. 9-12:] Yet don't you be making excuses for this kind of thing— it's unsafe. You must set a rule before youth

[LIII. 13-16:] There's need of rule to men also—tho' no particular one that I know of—it may be arbitrary—

[LVI:] There's a deeper tone about these than the last lot (of speculative stanzas)—

[LVII. 5. concerning "your cheeks":] the auditor's

[LVII. 7. concerning "richly shrined":] in half a life!

[LVII. 13-16:] I thought this was too sad for an ending—

[LIX:] Added afterwards but one of the old poems nevertheless

[LIX. 7:] A time has now elapsed & he treats sorrow in a more familiar & less dreading way—

[LXI. 15-16:] —perhaps he might, if he were a greater soul—

[LXIII. 1-4:] Man can love below as well as above himself; So surely it cannot be a weight on the Spirit to remember the writer—

[LXV:] Another higher thought now comes—a great lift-up—part of mine will live in thee.

[LXVI. 1. concerning "You":] the auditor

[LXVI. 3-4:] my old blind grandmother

[LXVI. 5-8:] The very sense of loss makes me social—

[LXVI. 15:] The remembrance of the day—

[LXVII:] One I like very much. The visions of the night

[LXVII. 3:] The Bristol channel

[LXVII. 7:] 'Arthur Hallam'—buried at Clevedon

[LXVIII:] The visions of the night—

[LXVIII. 15. concerning "trouble of my youth":] Your own death.

[LXIX. 5-12:] I tried to make my grief into a crown of these poems— but it is not to be taken too closely— To write verses about sorrow grief & death is to wear a crown of thorns which ought to be put by—as people say—

[LXIX. 14-15:] The divine thing in the gloom.

[LXXI. 7. concerning "blindfold sense of wrong":] The 'trouble in thine eye'—(stanza LXVIII)

[LXXII:] Another death day Sept 15th (see stanza 99)

[LXXXIV:] I like that one—

[LXXXVI:] This is one I like too— The West wind—written at Bournemouth—

[LXXXVI. 12:] Imagination—The Fancy—no particular fancy—

[LXXXVI. 13-16:] The west wind rolling to the Eastern Seas till it meets the evening Star—

[LXXXVII. 21-24:] The 'water club' because there was no wine— They used to make speeches— I never did—

[XCIV. 9–12:] I figure myself in this rather—
[XCV:] This happened in my native place—
[XCV. 10: concerning "filmy shapes":] moths
[XCV. 28. concerning "his":] its
[XCV. 36:] *The* living Soul, perchance of the Deity— The first read-
ing was His living Soul was flash'd on mine—but my conscience was
troubled by 'his'. I've often had a strange feeling of being wound &
wrapped in the Great Soul—
[XCVII:] A running comment on life. The Soul left behind is only
acquainted with the narrow circle of the old house—thus resembling
a wife married to a mighty man of Science.
[XCVII. 18. concerning "He loves her":] *She* says—
[XCVII. 21:] metaphysician
[XCVII. 22:] astronomer—
[XCVII. 29–32:] Just as this poor gift of Poesy is exercised because
he loved it—
[XCVII. 31:] of earth
[XCVII. 32:] of Heaven
[XCVIII. 7. concerning "wisp that gleams":] the ghosts
[XCIX:] The *death* day September
[CI. 1–4:] Sir John Simeon's last quotation on leaving England—
[CIII. 3:] the dead man
[CIII. 6. concerning "maidens within me":] all the human powers &
talents that do not pass with life but go along with it
[CIII. 7. concerning "hidden summits":] The high—the divine—the
origin of life
[CIII. 8. concerning "river":] life—
[CIII. 16. concerning "the sea":] eternity
[CIII. 25–28:] The great progress of the age as well as the opening
of another world—
[CIII. 33–36:] All the great hopes of Science and men.
[CIII. 45–48:] He was wrong to drop his earthly hopes & powers—
they will be still of use to him.
[CVII. 5–6:] February
[CXIX:] See poem 7 (pendant poems)
[CXIX. 7:] 4 o'clock on a Summer morning
[CXX. 8:] to one who would not stay
[CXXI. 1–4:] The grief over the end of things—
[CXXI. 8:] sleep, image of death
[CXXI. 9–12:] The progress of mankind is the undermeaning which
he has before referred to, alluding—all the previous poem—to the
greater thing which is to come
[CXXII. 1:] If any body thinks I ever called him "dearest" in his
life they are much mistaken, for I never even called him '*dear*'
[CXXII. 2:] of grief

[CXXII. 9. concerning "If thou were with me":]   at all helping me—
then
[CXXVII. 15:]   The back stroke of lightning—The people rise
[Epilogue:]   This was written on the marriage of another sister—not
the one engaged to A.H.—but Mrs. Lushington

* * * *

It's too hopeful, this Poem (In Memoriam)—more than I am myself—

* * * *

The general way of its being written was so queer that if there were a
blank space, I would put in a poem.

* * * *

I think of adding another poem—a speculative one bringing out the
thoughts of the higher Pantheism and showing that all the arguments are
about as good on one side as the other—& thus throw man back more
& more on the primitive impulses & feelings—

---

1 Knowles's recapitulation (in pencil) of Tennyson's divisions as marked in the
text.

APPENDIX II

Maud

The following notes were made by me from Tennyson's dictation as he read the poem to me.—JTK.

* * * *

No other poem (a monotone with plenty of change and no weariness) has been made into a drama where successive phases of passion in one person take the place of successive persons. It is slightly akin to Hamlet.

* * * *

[MAUD:]   (or the Madness)

[PART ONE]

[XI:]   The poor madman— He begins to soften
[XI. i. 5-7:]   It's terrible—isn't it?
[XII. i. 3:]   rooks
[XII. iii. 3:]   the little birds
[XII. vi. 3-4:]   If you tread on daisies—they turn up underfoot & get rosy—
[XIII:]   a counter passion—passionate & furious
[XIII. iv:]   He makes allowances for the man— Yet he is called a mere brute!
[XIV. i. 7-8:]   A token— I hardly write anything without some meaning of that kind.
[XIV. ii. 11-12:]   alludes to the time when she did come out
[XV. 4. concerning "some one else":]   Maud
[XV. 7-10:]   He begins with universal hatred of all things & gets more human by the influence of Maud.
[XVI. i. 1. concerning "lump of earth":]   the brother
[XVI. i. 8. concerning "My Oread":]   She lives on the hill near him.
[XVI. iii:]   You see he is the most conscientious fellow—a perfect gentleman tho' semi-insane! he would not have been so, had he met with happiness—
[XVIII. i, ii, and iii:]   These might not be divided
[XVIII. iii. 14-16:]   Snow in contrast with the dark black cedars
[XVIII. iv. 8. concerning "sad astrology":]   modern astronomy
[XVIII. vi. 5:]   Isn't that a change for the man?
[XVIII. vii. 1:]   I won't die!
[XVIII. viii. 19:]   a wonderful line, surely!
[XX. i. 4. concerning "The Sultan":]   the brother

[XX. ii. 2. concerning "ponderous squire":]   the brother

[XX. iv. 9–13:]   The verse should be read here as if it were prose—Nobody can read it naturally enough!

[XXII. v. 3–4:]   No reproach for the young lover—now that he feels successful.

[PART TWO]

[I. i:]   He has fled to the top of the next hill after the duel.

[I. ii:]   It all has to be read like passionate prose.

[II. i:]   He has fled—he has gone to Brittany

[II. viii. 3:]   I remember that *shell* did rhyme to *well*—but I forget how it dropped out of the rhyme.

[III:]   Here he comes back to England and London. There was another poem about London & the streets at night—"When all the scum of night & hell boils from the cellar & the sewer" was part of it—

[III. 4:]   Here he learns her death.

[IV:]   This poem in "The Tribute" was the nucleus of all the rest of Maud—woven round it at the request of Sir John Simeon.

[IV. iv.:]   In London

[IV. vi:]   his dream still

[IV. vi. 4:]   of the old hall

[IV. vii. 4–6:]   Perhaps the sound of a cab in the street suggests this cry of recollection—

[IV. xiii. 7–10:]   I've often felt this in London.

[V:]   This was written in 20 minutes—

[V. i:]   Here he is mad in Bedlam

[V. iii. 3. concerning "a lord of all things":]   I put "a God Almighty" first, which is a usual form of madness.

[V. iii. 7. concerning "a vile physician":]   the doctor of the madhouse

[V. iii. 10–11:]   A glance at the whole world

[V. vii. 1. concerning "him":]   her old Father

[V. vii. 1. after "now":]   how we met in the garden—

[V. ix. 3. concerning "a friend of mine":]   his own father

[V. ix. 6. concerning "second corpse":]   of his own son

[V. x. 6–7:]   He feels that he is getting a little too sensible in this remark

[At the end of Section V:]   Some mad-doctor wrote to me—"Nothing since Shakespeare has been so good for madness as this"—

[PART THREE]

[VI. i:]   Now he is out of the Asylum—but shattered

[VI. iii. 8. concerning "dreary phantom":]   of Maud

[VI. iv. 8:]   The Czar—

[VI. v. 4:]   Take this with the first where he railed at everything—He is not quite sane—a little shattered—

* * * *

I've always said that Maud and Guinevere were the finest things I've written—

DEATH AND BROWNING'S DYING BISHOP
G. *Malcolm Laws, Jr.*

Browning's *The Bishop Orders His Tomb at Saint Praxed's Church* has been universally admired since its publication in 1845 as one of the poet's supreme achievements in the dramatic monologue. Most commentators have seen it both as a superb character study and as a brilliant depiction of the Italian Renaissance spirit. It is not the purpose of this paper to elaborate on those aspects of the poem praised by John Ruskin in the frequently reprinted passage from *Modern Painters*.[1] Nor do I intend to dwell upon the various poetic and dramatic techniques and psychological implications discussed by Roma King, Park Honan, and others.[2] I do not even propose to offer any new or startling interpretations of individual passages, most of which have been satisfactorily explicated. Rather it is my intention to reanalyze the Bishop's statements about death and to show that his views are presented in a precise and meaningful sequence which must be closely followed if the monologue is to be fully understood.

This paper is designed in part to answer the following related questions: 1) What are the Bishop's concepts of death and of his future state? 2) How closely are these concepts related to the tomb which he desires? 3) How are these concepts related to Gandolf and his tomb? 4) What kind of tomb is the Bishop likely to get? and 5) What is his state of mind at the end of the poem? While most of the answers to these questions are imbedded in the scholarship, they are frequently combined with statements which seem to me misleading or erroneous.[3] Thus my method is eclectic and I find myself in partial agreement with almost all who have written on the subject. But the following view of the full sequence of the Bishop's thoughts on death, particularly as they relate to his present and future states, has not, I believe, been set forth previously.

318

The Bishop speaks in several voices during the course of his monologue. The first is his public voice, the voice of a preacher. This is formal, sententious, orthodox, the voice of an actor experienced enough to ad lib his lines and always ready with a store of appropriate quotations. As the poem begins, the Bishop is using this voice: "Vanity, saith the Preacher, vanity!"[4] But immediately his tone changes as he assumes the direct, conversational tones of the sophisticated father to his illegitimate sons: "Draw round my bed: is Anselm keeping back?" The third voice is the confidential one in which he admits that he has stolen the lapis lazuli from the ruins of his former church. And the last is the voice of his delirium, which comes over him most strongly toward the end of the poem. In this final voice he is usually musing half incoherently. Typically, Browning gives the reader little or no warning of these shifts of voice, and in a number of places his presentation is ambiguous; that is, it is not clear whether a particular statement expresses inner conviction or simply verbalizes familiar formulas.

The Bishop's first mention of death occurs in lines 6-13, in which he has a good deal to say on the subject. He has been referring to Gandolf's envy of his mistress, the mother of his sons:

> What's done is done, and she is dead beside,
> Dead long ago, and I am Bishop since. . . .
>
> (ll. 6-7)

This passage is revealing because it indicates the enormous gulf in the Bishop's mind between physical presence and absence, being and nonbeing. His mistress, being dead, has ceased to exist for him. She has no continuing reality except, occasionally, in his memory. "And I am Bishop since" is but one of numerous indications of his total self-centeredness. His own achievement is truly meaningful and important to him. Yet he goes from this to the observation that "as she died so must we die ourselves," and to the conclusion, "thence ye may perceive the world's a dream." Now this might be regarded as a philosophical observation, except that it is inconsistent with almost everything else he says and thinks, and more important because he does not develop the thought in any Christian or even pagan context. If matter is only a temporary manifestation, if life is a momentary state within eternity, as the Christian religion may be said to imply, then truly the world may be called a dream.

But the Bishop is no transcendentalist, Christian or otherwise, and it becomes increasingly clear as he continues to speak that the remark is simply another of his preacher's saws, that it comes from his public position rather than from his convictions. The remainder of the monologue shows that the world is everything to the Bishop and that all else is less than a dream.

The Bishop then poses two questions:

> Life, how and what is it? As here I lie
> In this state-chamber, dying by degrees,
> Hours and long hours in the dead night, I ask
> "Do I live, am I dead?"
>
> (ll. 10-13)

Here we have the first inkling of a concept of death more fully developed later. "What is life?" asks the Bishop, or how is the life of deathly stillness in the long, lonely night different from death itself? Thus the question, "Do I live, am I dead?" But he knows at the moment of speaking that he is still alive, and he begins to talk about his tomb. There is evidence later in the poem that he has broached the subject before (lines 56-57: "The bas-relief in bronze ye promised me, / Those Pans and Nymphs ye wot of. . ."), but he must have given only the sketchiest of suggestions, for his main requests have not been uttered and even these are subject to revision. Such a rich and powerful prelate could surely have ordered his tomb in advance from the craftsmen or could at least have made certain that his wishes were committed to writing and were legally binding on his heirs. His failure to give such instructions until he is sure he is dying suggests a reluctance to think about death. This unchristian fear of facing the reality of death is borne out both by his reactions toward dissolution and by his unique conception of his own afterlife. Since he has kept the subject from his mind, he is free to improvise thoughts about death as they occur to him.

First, the Bishop has a serious complaint against a former colleague:

> . . . I fought
> With tooth and nail to save my niche, ye know:
> —Old Gandolf cozened me, despite my care;
> Shrewd was that snatch from out the corner south
> He graced his carrion with, God curse the same!
>
> (ll. 15-19)

His first reference to a dead body, in its use of the term "carrion," suggests not only utter contempt for the corpse but an image of it in a state of decomposition. This seems an unusual reaction for an official of a church which honored its dead with elaborate monuments and which venerated the relics of its saints. But as will emerge, the Bishop's highly personal reactions have little to do with tradition or orthodoxy. He now shifts his thinking to the niche his tomb will occupy and tries to rationalize its location as superior in some ways to Gandolf's. Next, he speaks specifically of the materials of his tomb:

> And I shall fill my slab of basalt there,
> And 'neath my tabernacle take my rest,
> With those nine columns round me, two and two,
> The odd one at my feet where Anselm stands:
> Peach-blossom marble all, the rare, the ripe. . . .
> (ll. 25-29)

The significance of this phrasing should not be overlooked. "I" now means, though he has not said so, a recumbent statue of the Bishop, which will rest on a slab beneath a tabernacle supported by marble columns. Having just mentioned Gandolf's dead body, he says nothing of his own, which will be contained, as Gandolf's is, beneath the slab and within the tomb. Obviously, he is suppressing thoughts of his own dissolution and taking refuge in the idea of continued existence in a sculptured likeness. But whence arises the strange idea of the transmigration of his being into a statue on a tomb-top? Browning provides the clue in the lines which follow:

> —Old Gandolf with his paltry onion-stone,
> Put me where I may look at him!
> (ll. 31-32)

Recalling the statue of Gandolf on the top of his tomb, the Bishop asks to be placed where he can see him. While the word "him" is not an absolute indication that the Bishop now regards Gandolf's statue as a living being, this passage is followed by three others which cannot logically be interpreted in any other way. The reader should not forget that the Bishop is old and ill, that he has been long confined to his bed, and that he has received varying impressions of his surroundings. The statue is an exact likeness of Gandolf lying at full length and partially covered by marble drapery. The Bishop now sees the statue as one old man might see another in a nearby hospital room or across a ward. In the flickering candle light the white marble face could easily resemble a pale living one and might even seem to change expression. Gandolf seems alive to him now and in so seeming gives the Bishop his own key to a future life. He, too, will continue to live, reclining on a tomb-top in his church.

Now he indicates what the alternative would be:

> My sons, ye would not be my death? . . .
> (l. 36)

and proceeds to give instructions for finding the stolen and buried piece of lapis lazuli. He reminds them that he is leaving them his villas and all the rest of his estate, and continues:

> So, let the blue lump poise between my knees,
> Like God the Father's globe on both his hands
> Ye worship in the Jesu Church so gay,
> For Gandolf shall not choose but see and burst!
> (ll. 47-50)

Here it is plain that "my knees" means the knees of the statue and that Gandolf, the statue, is to burst with envy when he sees the Bishop's jewel. In other words, carrying out the Bishop's instructions regarding tomb, statue, and jewel will assure him of a future life, while failure to do so will bring his life to an end. Again the Bishop's thoughts return to death, and in one of those ambiguous passages he paraphrases Job:

> Swift as a weaver's shuttle fleet our years:
> Man goeth to the grave, and where is he?
> (ll. 51-52)

Perhaps the Bishop has had another vision of the contents of his tomb. At any rate the passage suggests despair rather than any Christian hope for eternal life. Here and throughout the poem the interior of the tomb is equated with annihilation; only the exterior of the tomb, and specifically the effigy on top of it, offer a continuation of existence.

The Bishop then proceeds to order for the frieze of his tomb the Christian and pagan symbols which produce so ironic and humorous an effect:

> The Saviour at his sermon on the mount,
> Saint Praxed in a glory, and one Pan
> Ready to twitch the Nymph's last garment off,
> And Moses with the tables. . . .
>
> (ll. 59-62)

But he sees his sons whispering and begins to suspect that they will give him no fine tomb and statue. He speaks accusingly:

> Ah, ye hope
> To revel down my villas while I gasp
> Bricked o'er with beggar's mouldy travertine
> Which Gandolf from his tomb-top chuckles at!
>
> (ll. 64-67)

The word "gasp" suggests that he fears that he would quickly breathe his last inside a cheap, statueless tomb, while Gandolf remained alive on top of his. But this grim thought passes and hope returns as he tries to bribe his sons with promises of prayers to St. Praxed.

In his imagination he is once more safe on his tomb-top, and he muses:

> And then how I shall lie through centuries,
> And hear the blessed mutter of the mass,
> And see God made and eaten all day long,
> And feel the steady candle-flame, and taste
> Good strong thick stupefying incense-smoke!
>
> (ll. 80-84)

Here it is obvious that the Bishop sees no essential difference between his present state and the death which he anticipates. His senses will still be dominant as they respond to physical stimuli. But how can he visualize himself as a marble statue? Browning cleverly shows how easily a confused, ill person might make the mental transition from bed to tomb-top:

> For as I lie here, hours of the dead night,
> Dying in state and by such slow degrees,
> I fold my arms as if they clasped a crook,
> And stretch my feet forth straight as stone can point,
> And let the bedclothes, for a mortcloth, drop
> Into great laps and folds of sculptor's-work. . . .
>
> (ll. 85-90)

Here the Bishop acts out his dream of the tomb and the effigy. The proposed statue would be as exact as possible (though, no doubt, somewhat idealized) a likeness of the Bishop. It would be his size and shape, would have his features, and would display the signs and symbols of his office. It would probably represent the Bishop lying in such calm repose that an observer might ask whether the sculptor intended to represent death or peaceful sleep. It would be as if the Bishop's weak fleshly body had been magically transformed without decay into a permanent and beautiful body possessing the all-important ability to enjoy sense experiences. Such a process would have some striking similarities to the Christian doctrine of the resurrection of the body—and some equally striking differences. It could represent the Bishop's distortion of those teachings in terms of his own nature and his own desires. Looking in both directions from the foregoing passage, we can see that the Bishop's reveries about his future state are entirely limited to the concept of the sentient statue.

As the poem progresses the Bishop's mental state deteriorates further, and he begins to speak deliriously, confusing the Savior with St. Praxed and thinking once more of his mistress, his life both before and after entering the Church, and the pure Latin he wants inscribed on his tomb. In a last desperate threat, he says:

> All *lapis,* all, sons! Else I give the Pope
> My villas!
>
> (ll. 102-103)

He tells them that he has really asked for very little, and he lists a number of additional pagan symbols which could be added to his "impoverished frieze" to "piece out its starved design," and, as he says in his confusion:

> To comfort me on my entablature
> Whereon I am to lie till I must ask
> "Do I live, am I dead?"
>
> (ll. 111-113)

While this rephrasing of what he had said earlier is probably a mental slip, like "all *lapis*" for the "all of jasper" of line 68, it is psychologically interesting in suggesting that the transition

from one state to the other will be imperceptible to the Bishop.
His recent uncertainty about being alive will simply be replaced
by a like uncertainty about being dead. The afterlife which he
envisions is, as Perrine observes, passive, but it is also largely
limited to sense impressions connected with religious observances
and experiences, activities which are hardly among the Bishop's
chief interests. Thus, if his present state as he lies dying is
indistinguishable from the future state he envisions, it follows
that his future state would leave a good deal to be desired, and
the question "Do I live, am I dead?" to be asked on his slab
suggests some dissatisfaction with the product of his own fancy.

The Bishop now becomes convinced that his sons are too
selfish to carry out his wishes and that he will have neither fine
tomb nor recumbent statue holding its beautiful jewel for all to
see. Without them his life must end. Thus, the image he uses is
one of murder:

> There, leave me, there!
> For ye have stabbed me with ingratitude
> To death—ye wish it—God, ye wish it!
> (ll. 113-115)

Now he clearly visualizes his own decaying corpse, and one is
reminded of his earlier reference to Gandolf's:

> Stone—
> Gritstone, a-crumble! Clammy squares which sweat
> As if the corpse they keep were oozing through—
> And no more *lapis* to delight the world!
> (ll. 115–118)

Death and physical corruption alone await him, rather than
centuries of pleasant sensations.

But this mood of horror again changes to one of calm resig-
nation as he dismisses his sons:

> Well go! I bless ye. Fewer tapers there,
> But in a row: and, going, turn your backs
> —Ay, like departing altar-ministrants,
> And leave me in my church, the church for peace,
> That I may watch at leisure if he leers—
> Old Gandolf, at me, from his onion-stone,
> As still he envied me, so fair she was!
> (ll. 119-125)

The poem has come full circle. The Bishop is exactly where he was when he began to speak, without any prospect of a tomb (except for a cheap container for his body), despite his earnest pleas. And Gandolf, who will continue to live on his tomb-top, will leer and chuckle in triumph over the Bishop's defeat and death. How, then, can he accept so calmly the knowledge of his coming annihilation and the denial of his passionate wishes for an elaborate monument? The answer seems to be that once more the present and the future are merging in his thoughts. The row of tapers is replacing the row of wished-for columns, the bed is replacing the tomb, and he himself is becoming the substitute for the statue he had earlier pretended to be. Thus, he gains peace by creating for himself in the seemingly endless present the state which he knows his sons would deny him in the future. He can still take pleasure in his surroundings, in the memory of his love affair, and in his earlier victory over Gandolf.

In creating the concept of the sentient statues, Browning supplies a key to the Bishop's nature. He is a man totally involved with the physical and material and hence totally unable to comprehend the spiritual. He lives entirely in the world of sense experience and can imagine nothing beyond it. (The angels that he mentions early in the poem presumably decorate the inner dome of St. Praxed's.[5] God the Father is a statue in the Jesu Church.) No bodiless ghost or immortal soul in this world or the next seems comprehensible to the Bishop. He is a Christian prelate by historical accident, but he would not have made a good pagan either, if that term implies some belief in the gods of antiquity. The Bishop's paganism, like his Christianity, is limited to the physical symbol or object of art. There is no ethical principle or dogma which he accepts, no example which he follows. The Savior and Moses are appropriate symbols for a bishop's tomb, as is St. Praxed, after whom the Bishop's church is named. But the Sermon on the Mount, the Ten Commandments, and the charity of the Roman virgin are expressions of ethical principles beyond the comprehension of the Bishop of St. Praxed's.

Concepts of an after-life different from his life on earth are equally beyond the Bishop's ken. One might suppose that a Christian bishop after a sinful life would realize the peril to his immortal soul, would summon his confessor, and would hope for the absolution necessary to avoid eternal damnation. But merely to state such a hypothetical situation is to show how inappropriate it is in the Bishop's case. In only one passage of the entire monologue does he show a glimmer of moral sense. In the long speech uttered during his delirium he says:

> Evil and brief has been my pilgrimage
> (l. 101)

and a couple of lines later he says to his sons:

> Ever your eyes were as a lizard's quick,
> They glitter like your mother's for my soul.
> (ll. 104-105)

The first line seems specific enough and might be regarded as indicating a sense of sin welling up from the Bishop's subconscious. The second passage is more ambiguous. It could refer either to the danger to his soul represented by the fatal attraction to the mother of his sons, or, in this context, merely to their apparent desire for his demise. Since the moral conflicts hinted at here are not developed, these ideas may be regarded as the vague wanderings of a disoriented mind. Thus the irony is intensified for the reader, who may expect the Bishop to become aware at last of his sinfulness, only to have him revert within a line or two to the pagan decorations of his tomb.

Heaven and hell and their pagan counterparts are all equally meaningless to the Bishop. Lacking in imagination, he is unable to project himself into a totally different environment where all values have changed and where soul rather than body is the living unit. He does not worry about his soul because he is not aware of having one. Yet he does not want to die. The statuary likeness on a handsome tomb offers him the only kind of immortality he can understand, that of the physical object. He has no concept of eternity, but centuries are meaningful to him, for the solid objects in which he puts his faith are of finite endurance. In contrast to the corruption of the body, the statue is relatively incorruptible. But it is a far cry from the incorruptible heavenly body of orthodox belief. Without the tomb and statue there is only the dark but painless finality of the grave.

NOTES

1. Ruskin said, in part: "I know no other piece of modern English, prose or poetry, in which there is so much told, as in these lines, of the Renaissance spirit,

—its worldliness, inconsistency, pride, hypocrisy, ignorance of itself, love of art, of luxury, and of good Latin" (*Modern Painters*, IV [London, 1856], 479).

2. An excellent detailed analysis of the entire poem is that of Roma A. King, Jr., who devotes a chapter to its intricacies in *The Bow and the Lyre: the Art of Robert Browning* (Ann Arbor, 1957), pp. 52–75. Park Honan explores many of its verbal devices and implications in *Browning's Characters: a Study in Poetic Technique* (New Haven, 1961), pp. 140–141, 149–150, *et passim*. In a reply to Francis W. Bonner's note in *Explicator*, XXII (1964), item 57, Laurence Perrine gives an admirably succinct and perceptive interpretation of the Bishop's character and situation in *Explicator*, XXIV (1965), item 12. Barbara Melchiori concentrates on the pagan symbols of the poem in "Where the Bishop Ordered His Tomb," *Review of English Literature*, V, iii (1964), 7–26. Robert Langbaum in *The Poetry of Experience: the Dramatic Monologue in Modern Literary Tradition* (New York, 1957), p. 183 *et passim*, offers several keen observations. Particularly helpful notes to the poem are supplied by Edward Berdoe, *The Browning Cyclopedia*, 2nd ed. (London, 1897), pp. 80–82; by William J. Rolfe and Heloise E. Hersey, *Select Poems of Robert Browning* (New York, 1886), pp. 165–167; and by Walter E. Houghton and G. Robert Stange, *Victorian Poetry and Poetics*, 2nd ed. (Boston, 1968), pp. 204–206. I acknowledge a debt to all who have written about this poem as well as to my students of Victorian poetry.

3. For example, I do not accept Professor Honan's idea that the Bishop regards Gandolf as "living a ghostly existence confined to his sepulcher" or as moving up to his tomb-top (p. 150). And to look for a tomb like the Bishop's in the Roman Church of Santa Prassede, as Barbara Melchiori and others have done, is to ignore the evidence that the order for a tomb was to go unfilled. It seems to me that both Professor King and Professor Perrine fail to make clear the connection between the Bishop's cheap tomb and his extinction. I hope to elucidate these and other matters during the course of this essay.

4. The text I am using is *The Works of Robert Browning*, Centenary Edition, ed. F. G. Kenyon (London, 1912; reprinted, New York, 1966), IV, 125–128.

5. Barbara Melchiori writes: "Santa Prassede is one of the few Roman churches without a sunny or even a sunless dome" (p. 7). Did Browning forget this fact, or did he simply need a dome and create one for the poem?

BROWNING'S *RED COTTON*
NIGHT-CAP COUNTRY
Clyde de L. Ryals

Like most of Browning's later poems, *Red Cotton Night-Cap Country* (1873) remains unappreciated. Indeed, it has been almost universally deplored. It has, however, been deplored briefly, with a phrase or with an adjective like "sordid" or "grotesque." Even the most sympathetic of Browning's critics have apparently been at a loss to know what to make of it: Mrs. Sutherland Orr was content to dismiss it as a "manifestation of an ungenial mood of Mr. Browning's mind," and G. K. Chesterton agreed that it reflects "one of the bitter moods of Browning."[1] To my mind such criticism evidences a complete misunderstanding of the poem, and I should like here to suggest that, far from being "grotesque" or "bitter," *Red Cotton Night-Cap Country* is both a carefully planned poem and an affirmation of the poet's most highly prized beliefs.

In mode *Red Cotton Night-Cap Country* is a conversation poem. Structurally it is divided into four parts plus coda. It is perhaps helpful to think of it as modeled on the sonata form.[2] Beginning with a slow introduction, the first movement, with its interplay between "white" and "red" leading to the story, is allegro, rapidly and intricately setting forth the major themes. The second movement, telling the love story, is andante, lyrical and melodic. The third, developing the conflict between "turf" and "tower," is scherzo vivace in character, speedily and relentlessly leading to the tragedy. The fourth movement, which reviews, elaborates, and comments upon the story previously told, is a triumphal climax resolving the aspiration and struggle of the earlier parts, "white" at last proved "red." Last, the coda, alluding to the initial point of departure in the speaker's conversation, reaffirms the tonic.

Thematically the poem has four major motifs: (1) the illu-

329

sory nature of the phenomenal world, (2) the necessity of change in men's formulations of truth, (3) the concentration of one's energies on a desired goal and the deleterious effects of compromise, and (4) the power of the creative imagination to reduce multiplicity to unity.

Like the conversation poems of Coleridge, *Red Cotton Night-Cap Country* begins in an unassuming and deceptive fashion: so casual is the manner of exposition that one initially believes that he is reading a loosely constructed descriptive idyll. The first thousand lines or so seem, like the strollers themselves, to ramble on about the Norman countryside. In fact, the speaker is busily and ingeniously setting up the themes which will inform his narrative.

Things are not necessarily what they look to be, he says. The creative "soul" can, however, pierce through the false shows of the phenomenal world and arrive at the truth which lies hidden behind appearances; at least the soul can gain "intimations" of the truth. This idea is first implied in the speaker's description of walking through a field of wild-mustard flower on his way to the sea:

> Of that, my naked sole makes lawful prize,
> Bruising the acrid aromatics out,
> Till, what they preface, good salt savors sting. . . .[3]
>
> (737a)

And then the idea is expounded in more forthright terms: the countryside which the strolling pair now view is totally unexceptional, yet the speaker likes it

> just because
> Nothing is prominently likable
> To vulgar eye without a soul behind,
> Which, breaking surface, brings before the ball
> Of sight, a beauty buried everywhere.
> If we have souls, know how to see and use,
> One place performs, like any other place,
> The proper service every place on earth
> Was framed to furnish man with: serves alike
> To give him note that, through the place he sees,
> A place is signified he never saw,
> But, if he lack not soul, may learn to know.
>
> (737b)

This is, of course, one of Browning's most passionately held beliefs: the soul, appropriately oriented and employed, can penetrate the falseness and see the truth of things.

In developing this idea the speaker touches on the theme of anachronism—that is, the Carlylean philosophy of worn-out clothes, which, as we shall presently see, is subsumed under the theme of permanency and change. He alludes to a notice on a barn which "repeats / For truth what two years' passage made a lie" and to signs proclaiming the Emperor's confidence in a war which has already been lost. What is needed is removal of these vestiges from the past: "rain and wind must rub the rags away" (738a). Quite beguilingly then does the poet establish three of the primary motifs of his poem, the theme of compromise remaining unannounced until, at the end of Part I, the story proper is introduced.

In a manner reminiscent of the beginning of *The Ring and the Book*, in which the speaker tosses the Old Yellow Book in the air and thinks on the meaning locked in this account of some ancient trials, the narrator considers in Part I the appellation "white Cotton Night-cap Country" applied by his friend to the section of France which the two are now visiting for the summer.[4] In this "lazy land untroubled" (738a) the nightcap is a fitting head covering, symbolizing not only the idleness of the inhabitants but also their insulation from the busy world. Suspicious of the light, the people cover their heads and, "with advancing years, night's solace soon / Intrudes upon the daybreak dubious life / Persuades it to appear the thing it is [,] / Half-sleep." So though "Their usage may be growing obsolete, / Still, in the main, the institution stays" (738d).

Yet, as the narrator ponders further the use and meaning of nightcaps, he asks: is this land properly *White* Cotton Night-cap Country? Behind the seemingly innocent drowsiness of the inhabitants might there not lie some evil or some horror? Might not the land also be called Red Cotton Night-cap Country? Aroused by his own suggestion, he seeks with fervor to prove that the color red is the more appropriate epithet. "You put me on my mettle," he says to his companion, who reasonably accuses him of argumentativeness; "suppose we have it out / Here in the fields, decide the question so" (740a). And without awaiting her reply, he urges, "Quick to the quest, then—forward, the firm foot" (740b).

The walk, here as in *Fifine at the Fair*,[5] thus becomes a quest, an exploration into history, human psychology, and phenomenal existence. Though the speaker puts words into the mouth of his companion, in essence his is a dialogue with himself, an accompanied sonata (to use an analogy previously referred to) designed primarily for one instrument: it is a disquisition undertaken not only out of a perverse wish to argue but also out of a desire to penetrate appearances and explain why things appear as they do.

As they begin their stroll the two rise to an elevated place and survey the whole countryside with its many churches and spires. His eye lights on the spire of the famous shrine La Ravissante: "There now is something like a Night-cap spire" (740c). Only recently the church had received as a gift gold crowns for its Virgin and Child, the Virgin's topped with an extremely precious stone. A week ago there had been a festive celebration of the event, for which people came from miles around. The narrator had, however, "stuck to my devotions at high-tide" and "never had a mind / To trudge the little league and join the crowd" (741b). Yet why should he be contemptuous of the multitude's belief in miracles? For, though "sceptical in every inch of me," suddenly "Even for me is miracle vouchsafed." In thinking of the shrine and the name of the donor of the Virgin's jeweled crown, there comes an illumination, a possible answer as to why this should be *Red* Cotton Night-cap Country. "Did I deserve that, from the liquid name / 'Miranda' . . . a shaft should shine, / Bear me along . . . till, lo, the Red is reached, / And yonder lies in luminosity!" (741c).

Through a series of associations the narrator had got to the French Revolution, a hangman, a red cotton nightcap. Now he further associates the jeweler Miranda with the story recounted by Carlyle of a scandal concerning a diamond necklace. Miranda's was "no unsuggestive craft" (741d). And at this moment the pair of strollers see in the distance the edifice, Clairvaux, which had been the residence and architectural plaything of the jeweler Miranda who died two years previously.

Originally the building had been a priory, but since "nothing lasts below" (742a), it had been taken over by the state at the time of the Revolution and later sold to private owners. By Miranda it had been utterly transformed, and to the narrator it is upon closer inspection entirely different from what it seemed to be from a distance:

> Those lucarnes which I called conventual, late,
> Those are the outlets in the mansard-roof . . .
> And now the tower a-top, I took for clock's
> Or bell's abode, turns out a quaint device,
> Pillared and temple-treated Belvedere—
> Pavilion safe within its railed-about
> Sublimity of area. . . .
>
> (742c)

The point is that Clairvaux, once a religious edifice but now secularized, is decorated to *appear* what it originally was. And in yet another way Clairvaux is also deceptive: with its *Parc Anglais* it represents an attempt on the owner's part to carry Paris, the city from which he escaped, to the country, so that "Clairvaux thus renovated, regalized / Paris expanded thus to Normandy" (743a). Regarding this establishment the narrator says: "a sense that something is amiss, / Something is out of sorts in the display, / Affects us, past denial, everywhere" (742d). What is right for Paris is perhaps wrong for Normandy.

The owners of the place were a "happy husband and as happy wife." The man was both generous and devout, and the wife was likewise. Where then lies the "red"? Going on to describe the wife, whom he has seen the day before, the speaker tantalizingly enumerates only "white" facts about the pair who lived at Clairvaux. Finally, at the end of Part I, he reveals the "red" in his story: Miranda met a tragic death two years ago, "and not one grace / Outspread before you but is registered / In that sinistrous coil these last two years / Were occupied in winding smooth again" (745c). At last the narrator is ready to prove by example that things are not what they seem.

The story of Léonce Miranda recounted in the second movement is a tale of a divided life. From his father he inherited "the Castilian passionate blind blood" and from his mother a "spirit, French, critical and cold" (746c). It was an unfortunate mixture, making "a battle in the brain, / Ending as faith or doubt gets uppermost" (746c). Trained in strict religious principles, he gave full assent to Christianity as embodied in the Roman Catholic Church: he believed in miracles and an earthly life of pietistical purity. This is the side of his nature symbolized in the poem by "towers." Yet this part was not long to predominate, for at the age of twenty-two the young man, stimulated by his French blood, found that "there spread a standing-space / Flowery and comfortable, nowise rock / Nor pebble-pavement" (747b); in short, he discovered the "turf" alluded to in the subtitle to the poem. What then should he do: forsake the towers for the turf? Believing that his life should properly be lived among the towers, he nevertheless is unwilling to forgo the all too earthy turf. So at this point Miranda is seduced by the spirit of Molière's pusillanimous Sganarelle to accept a compromise. He decides to remain on the turf but to "keep in sight / The battlement, one bold leap lands you by" (747c). The voice of Sganarelle urges:

> Resolve not desperately 'Wall or turf,
> Choose this, choose that, but no alternative!'
> No! Earth left once were left for good and all:
> 'With Heaven you may accommodate yourself.'
> (747d)

Heeding this advice Miranda joins the "Ravissantish" with the "Spirit of the Boulevard" (747d), thereby planting the seed of his downfall. He gave blind assent to the tower, never stopping to inquire whether the tower be partially damaged or whether, in fact, it be merely a ruin still standing as a monument from some former age. He made no effort to determine how much of the tower was sound, how many "obstructions choke what still remains intact." Moreover, he did not listen to the "voice / Not to be disregarded," which said: "Man worked here / Once on a time; here needs again to work; / Ruins obstruct, which man must remedy" (745d). Instead he simply accepted the tower for what it seemed to be or for what it might once have been:

> because the world lay strewn
> With ravage of opinions in his path,
> And neither he, nor any friendly wit,
> Knew and could teach him which was firm, which frail,
> In his adventure to walk straight through life
> The partial-ruin,—in such enterprise,
> He straggled into rubbish, struggled on,
> And stumbled out again observably.
> (746b)

Settled on compromise, he works hard in his jewelry business and is a model of what pious bourgeois parents wish their child to be, but on holidays he seeks occasional pleasure with women:

nothing serious, nothing indiscreet, only "sport: / Sport transitive—such earth's amusements are" (748d). So thus "realistic" and "against illusion armed" (749a) he goes one night to a playhouse aptly named "The Varieties," and sees a woman who captivates him and makes him "For life, for death, for heaven, for hell, her own" (749b). Ceasing to be "realistic," he gives up his "sport" and devotes his energy to gaining her love. For, says the narrator, " 'tis the nature of the soul / To seek a show of durability, / Nor, changing, plainly be the slave of change" (748c).

More than once the speaker guarantees that "this love was true" (749c), on the lady's part as well as her lover's. Clara is a beautiful flower grown in inferior soil: "Social manure has raised a rarity" (749d). Reared in poverty, exposed to sordidness and humiliation, married to an unsuccessful tailor, she nevertheless remains "a flower of flowers" (749d), her youthful "artless innocence" uncorrupted (750b). And though, because of her divorce, she can never wed Miranda, she is to him "very like a wife / Or something better" (762a).

Superficially regarded, Miranda's alliance with Clara is unlikely. A son of the Church, he chooses to live with her in defiance of the Church's teaching. A dutiful child, he elects a way of life which his pious parents cannot approve. A believer in the transiency of all things terrestrial, he opts for an earthly love which he fears is opposed to his love of God. In brief, he seems in every case to choose the turf in preference to the tower. Yet in actuality he refuses to make any choice at all: he will both have his cake and eat it. Moreover, both Church and parent join with his own "Saint Sganarelle" to countenance, somewhat grudgingly and half-heartedly to be sure, his relationship with Clara.

Avoiding the social ostracism of Paris, the couple retire to Normandy and make of their home, Clairvaux, a pale imitation of life in the French capital. Miranda knew, deep within himself, that his every act was "provisory" (753d), but he tried to blot out from his conscious mind just how temporary is all of man's earthly existence. The world had offered its advice:

> Intrench yourself,
> Monsieur Léonce Miranda, on this turf,
> About this flower, so firmly that, as tent
> Rises on every side around you both,
> The question shall become,—Which arrogates

Stability, this tent or those far towers?
May not the temporary structure suit
The stable circuit, co-exist in peace?—
Always until the proper time, no fear!
'Lay flat your tent!' is easier said than done.
                                                    (753c)

This counsel he receives favorably, and so repairs to Normandy to make of Clairvaux his pavilion on the turf. Clairvaux became the Earthly Paradise, its owners crying out: "Permanency,—life and death / Here, here, not elsewhere, change is all we dread!" (754a). But Miranda and his lady did not accept the necessarily provisional nature of their Eden, deluding themselves that they were "Proprietors, not tenants for a term" (754a).

Unlike the truly perceptive ("folk of individuality"), the pair did not want to understand that all material building "only harbors man / The vital and progressive" who was indeed meant to build, but to build "with quite a difference, / Some time, in that far land we dream about, / Where every man is his own architect" (754a). The building which Léonce and Clara undertake is mere mimetic reconstruction, their impulse being "to live, / In Norman solitude, the Paris life" (754b).

The imitative nature of their building is exemplified in Léonce's taste in art. Sufficiently perceptive to recognize that genuine artistic endeavor requires enormous expenditure of physical and spiritual energy in the artist's fight with outmoded forms, Miranda "nowise cared to be / Creative" (754b-c). In dilletantish fashion he played at art and life, blotting out of his mind the fact that "Soon or late will drop / Pavilion" (754d): "Wrong to the towers, which pillowed on the turf, / He thus shut eyes to" (755a).

For five years Léonce and Clara lived the "Paradisiac dream" (755b) recounted in Part II, and "self-entrenched, / They kept the world off from their barricade" (768b). Yet, in Part III, the world intrudes and the sleepers wake when Léonce's mother summons him to Paris and berates him for his extravagant and sinful life. The return is disorienting. When he is confronted with "Madame-mother" and "Monsieur Curé This and Sister That" (756a)—all in short that represents the towers—he is forced to acknowledge that his life with Clara at Clairvaux had been in clear violation of what he was reared to accept as good and true. " 'Clairvaux Restored:' what means this Belvedere?"

he mother asks. "This Tower, stuck like a fool's-cap on the
roof—/ Do you intend to soar to heaven from thence? /
Tower, truly! Better had you planted turf" (755d).

The anxiety occasioned by his return to Paris resulted not so
much from a conviction of sinfulness as from an unwillingness
to choose either the tower or the turf. If, says the narrator, he
had been forced to make a choice, then he might have done so
and lived happily. But he was told, "Keep both halves, yet do
no detriment / To either! Prize each opposite in turn!" (756a).
Believing that he has wronged both halves, Léonce plunges into
the Seine, seeking thereby to avoid making a decision in favor
of either one. He is rescued, however, and goes back to Clairvaux.

No sooner is he recovered than he is recalled to Paris to find
his mother dead. Made to feel responsible for her death, he
decides to give up Clara and make his cousins his heirs. And
so, in an instant, the pavilion built for permanency collapses:

> down fell at once
> The tawdry tent, pictorial, musical,
> Poetical, besprent with hearts and darts;
> Its cobweb-work, betinselled stitchery,
> Lay dust about our sleeper on the turf,
> And showed the outer towers distinct and dread.
>   (757d)

Yet before the final arrangements are completed, he reads over
Clara's love letters, and in a paroxysm of guilt he burns both
the letters and his hands so that he might be purified. But the
result is once again the same: in time he returns to Clara and
Clairvaux.

Having vacillated between tower and turf, Miranda now
admits the validity of each: "Don't tell me that my earthly love
is sham, / My heavenly fear a clever counterfeit! / Each may
oppose each, yet be true alike!" (761b). He realizes that it had
been a mistake to attempt to build, independent of the towers,
a durable pavilion on the turf. He now must harmonize the
two, "Unite the opposites . . . / And never try complete aban-
donment / Of one or other" (761b). As to how this is to be
done he seeks, in this "native land of miracle," "guidance of
The Ravissante" (762a).

The narrator does not hesitate to point out Miranda's false
move in looking to the reputedly miraculous for aid. From all

recorded time, he claims, no miracle was ever wrought to help
whoever wanted help (761c). To resort to the miraculous for
direction is, in effect, to ask that truth stand fully revealed. In
the phenomenal world, however, the truth can never be completely disengaged from the false (762b). To be sure, certain
aspects of truth may be grasped, but the achievement result.
from occasional penetrations of truth's false covering. One must
therefore, deal with phenomena which lie at hand: "When
water's in the cup, and not the cloud, / Then is the proper time
for chemic test" (762d). The world is a vale of soul-making
and one becomes a living soul, sharing some aspects of truth
with the Divine, only through experience with the phenomenal

To the narrator "our vaporous Ravissante" is water in the
cloud. He refuses to speculate upon how "fable first precipi-
tated faith," but he does say that such faith as the shrine represents belongs to the past. The monk, the nun, the parish priest—
all, in fact, who go to La Ravissante "for the cure of soul-
disease"—do but "practise in the second state of things," bringing "no fresh distillery of faith" but only "dogma in the bottle
bright and old" (762d). For Browning, theirs is an outmoded
faith, one inherited rather than proved on the pulses and therefore hardly worthy of the name. However, Miranda "trust
them, and they surely trust themselves. / I ask no better"—
which is to say, if accepted, faith must be embraced whole-
heartedly: "Apply the drug with courage!" (763a).

For two years Miranda deluded himself that "by gifts / To
God and to God's poor, a man might stay / In sin and yet stave
off sin's punishment" (763d). At the end of such time Léonce
one spring day climbed to the top of the Belvedere and gazing
at La Ravissante began, in Part IV, the meditation which end.
with his death.

Stepping off the Belvedere he believed that he would be
miraculously transported to La Ravissante. Instead he landed on
the turf. The world adjudges Miranda insane for putting his
faith in the Virgin to the test. The narrator, however, consider.
him sane, because, given his premises, he at last acted on what
he believed:

> Hold a belief . . . ,
> Put faith to proof, be cured or killed at once! . . .
>   In my estimate,
> Better lie prostrate on his turf at peace,
> Than, wistful, eye, from out the tent, the tower.
>   (767d)

Or as Browning had said years earlier, in "The Statue and the Bust": "Do your best . . . / If you choose to play!" Finally Miranda settled his wavering between turf and towers.

In the opinion of the narrator, Léonce can be condemned only for having waited so long to choose. The wish to reach the tower was thoroughly vain, one worthy of the Middle Ages perhaps, but not of the nineteenth century:

> the sense of him should have sufficed
> For building up some better theory
> Of how God operates in heaven and earth,
> Than would establish Him participant
> In doings yonder at The Ravissante.
> The heart was wise according to its lights
> And limits; but the head refused more sun,
> And shrank into its mew, and craved less space.
>
> (771b)

Yet if this was his belief he did right to act on it.

A more enlightened man would have found love enough, which is the means by which God is "participant" in time. But Miranda never properly understood what it means to love: "The man's love for his wife exceeded bounds / Rather than failed the limit" (743c). In the beginning he came close to realizing the full power of love, for in his relationship with Clara he arrived at a profounder understanding of life than would have otherwise been possible: "Such potency in word and look has truth" (749c). And through his love he comes "to learn that there exists / A falsish false, for truth's inside the same, / And truth that's only half true, falsish truth" (749c). Yet ultimately his love was but an escape: "to live / Hers and hers only, to abolish earth / Outside" (743c). Only at the last, in his apostrophe to the Virgin, does he penetrate to the perception that his was a "mock love, / That gives while whispering 'Would I dared refuse!'" (766c).

Clara, on the other hand, is more worthy of praise: "She only has a claim to my respect" (771b). Throughout the poem she is represented as a white flower or "like some foreign cabinet, / Purchased indeed, but purifying quick / What space receives it from all traffic-taint" (744c). Her fault was that she regarded love as an end in itself, not as a means to truth. No doubt she loved Miranda, no doubt she was to be preferred to the statue of the Virgin at La Ravissante. She was both the nurturing mother and the doting wife: "All love could do, I did for him" (768b). Yet, says the narrator, "I do not praise her love" (772b): "One should not so merge soul in soul" (755b). For properly conceived, "Love bids touch truth, endure truth, and embrace / Truth, though, embracing truth, love crush itself" (772b). Like the grub which is to become a butterfly, Clara fed on her leaf, Miranda, and did not stop till she had "eaten her Miranda up" (773c). She did not urge, "Worship not me, but God," which is the expression of "love's grandeur" (772b). So, though Clara is "the happier specimen," she still must be judged morally a failure. For she simply accepted what was given. In no instance did she attempt to "Aspire, break bounds" (771b).

At the end of his story the narrator leaves his listener with no uncertainty as to the causes of the tragedy. First, the spirit of compromise—that is, an unwillingness to commit oneself fully—infected the personality and ended by poisoning all of Miranda's relationships. He was encouraged in his indecision by parents, mistress, and representatives of the Church, but he was no less wrong not to choose and thenceforth to act. Thus what the world sees as his madness was, correctly viewed, the moment of his triumph. Perhaps the choice was a poor one, but at any rate it was consonant with his belief. Second, Miranda did not use what intelligence had been granted him. He simply accepted an inherited faith, not only its doctrines and dogmas but its superstitions as well. If he had put his mind to work, then he would have seen that the religious faith which La Ravissante signifies belongs to history and should, with the past, remain buried. The attempt to "bring the early ages back again" (766b) was the vainest kind of activity. Third, neither Léonce nor Clara ever comprehended the meaning of love. For them, it was a means by which "self-entrenched / They kept the world off" (768b). Seeking for constancy amidst the flux of life, they built a pavilion on the turf which had the "show of durability" (748c) but which they mistook for permanency itself, forgetting that "Soon or late will drop / Pavilion, soon or late you needs must march" (754d). Love for them, in other words, was the end-in-itself instead of the means by which the soul conquers the false on its journey toward perfection. In the last analysis all the "white" facts of life proved the "red" of Miranda's undoing.

At the end of his quest, begun with the walk in the fields,

the speaker has attained his goal: he has shown that things are not always what they appear. He has proved that it is not enough to regard an object or an incident as "normal, typical, in cleric phrase / *Quod semel, semper, et ubique*" (739d). Everything has its own special truth. A nightcap is not just a nightcap any more than a fiddle is "just a fiddle" (739a). A man must "recognize / Distinctions" (739a), examine thoroughly the nightcap, and, if need be, "rub to threads what rag / Shall flutter snowily in sight" (740b).

This is, of course, the business of the creative imagination, especially as exercised in poetry. For the imagination deals with the multitudinousness of phenomena by piercing through the false covering of reality to see the thing-in-itself, reducing multiplicity to unity, and turning thought and action into language. In the coda the poet, identifying himself as narrator, reveals that such indeed has been the aim of his poem. Moreover, he suggests that *Red Cotton Night-Cap Country* is ultimately a poem about poetry and what it means to be a poet.

Speaking in his own voice, the poet tells that the endeavor of making the poem out of his few sordid facts has meant a step forward in self-articulation and, thus, a triumph of personality over seemingly meaningless data. The moment of insight which, he says in the postscript addressed to his walking companion, came "months ago and miles away"—"that moment's flashing" has been "amplified" and "Impalpability reduced to speech": "Such ought to be whatever dares precede, / Play ruddy herald-star to your white blaze / About to bring us day" (773c).

The overcoming of the false outer shows of things and the subsequent advance toward Ultimate Truth is the meaning of poetry. Just as, in the beginning, the narrator spoke of making "lawful prize" of the wild-mustard flower from which he had forced "the acrid aromatics out" (737a), so his extraction of meaning from the Miranda story is likewise a personal victory. Referring in Part I to Clara, the narrator asks:

> Yet is there not conceivably a face,
> A set of wax-like features, blank at first,
> Which, as you bendingly grow warm above,
> Begins to take impressment from your breath?
> Which, as your will itself were plastic here
> Nor needed exercise of handicraft,
> From formless moulds itself to correspond

> With all you think and feel and are—in fine
> Grows a new revelation of yourself,
> Who know now for the first time what you want?
> (744a)

Indeed, the poem itself becomes for its maker a new revelation of himself, for in penetrating to the truth of another's personality he adds a new dimension of truth to his own and thus gains an understanding of the self otherwise unrealized: "The revelation of the very truth / Proved the concluding necessary shake / Which bids the tardy mixture crystallize / Or else stay ever liquid" (752a).

Yet because the poet's apprehension of truth is always and necessarily in advance of any accepted formulation of it, he finds himself set apart from his fellows. The "life-exercise" of poetry means, then, that the poet assumes an almost intolerable burden:

> such exercise begins too soon,
> Concludes too late, demands life whole and sole,
> Artistry being battle with the age
> It lives in. . . .
> To be the very breath that moves the age
> Means not to have breath drive you bubble-like
> Before it—but yourself to blow: that's strain;
> Strain's worry through the lifetime, till there's peace;
> We know where peace expects the artist-soul.
> (754c)

It was precisely because he recognized the "strain" of art that Miranda did not wish to be a creative artist, choosing instead "the quiet life and easy death" of "Art's seigneur, not Art's serving-man" (754d).

The artist-soul, on the other hand, refuses to work with other men's formulae. In art as in religion nothing is so damning in Browning's eyes as acceptance of inherited beliefs and practices. To work in traditional modes is to submit to the world with all its falseness. Being an artist means breaking rules and bounds; being an artist means attempting the impossible. What matter whether the result is, in the world's opinion, a success? "Success is naught, endeavor's all" (771b). Art's value lies in its revelation of truth hitherto undisclosed. Whether the world judge it incomplete and unpolished, if it gain a grasp on the truth then "there the incomplete, / More than completion" (771c).

Undoubtedly Browning was speaking out of his own experience

when he referred to the burden of loneliness and misunderstanding to which the modern poet is subject.[6] Though in the 1870s he was widely admired, he could, in a work published two years later, *The Inn Album,* have one of the characters say of an unknown rhymer: "That bard's a Browning; he neglects the form." Mindful of the kind of criticism leveled against him, Browning nevertheless refused to heed the demands of his critics, who would prefer "work complete, inferiorly proposed, / To incompletion, though it aim aright" (771b). No, a poet is ever attempting a task impossible to finish: submitting life itself to the control of language:

> Along with every act—and speech is act—
> There go, a multitude impalpable
> To ordinary human faculty,
> The thoughts which give the act significance.
> Who is a poet needs must apprehend
> Alike both speech and thoughts which prompt to speak.
> Part these, and thought withdraws to poetry:
> Speech is reported in the newspaper.
>
> (765a)

The triumph of the artist lies in his endeavor to "break through Art and rise to poetry." If he succeeds, "Then, Michelagnolo against the world!" (771c).

To ascribe either ungeniality or bitterness to *Red Cotton Night-Cap Country* is to catch the wrong tone. There is no bitterness reflected in the observations on the loneliness of the artist. On the contrary, the narrator maintains that more than a compensatory joy is to be derived from the artistic exercise. Furthermore, there is nothing harsh about the narrator's reflections on religion as practiced by Miranda. Though written soon after the first Vatican Council and under the shadow of the ultramontanism of Pius IX, *Red Cotton Night-Cap Country* gives expression to Browning's belief that even the superstitious faith embraced by Léonce, benighted though it be, is preferable to doctrinaire materialism, which affirms the body while denying the soul. The only sardonic note in the whole poem is to be found in the narrator's description of the anticlerical doctor with his "new *Religio Medici*" which refuses to admit the existence of spirit (759d). Far from being acerb, then, *Red Cotton Night-Cap Country* is gay in tone. Friendly, playful, even self-mocking—"Ready to hear the rest? How good you are!"

(764d)—it disguises a profundity of ideas under a surface of conversational banter.

The manner in which the poem is related—the blending of casual humor and philosophical observation—is in itself suggestive of the ultimate "meaning" of this work of some four thousand lines. For Browning's great achievement in *Red Cotton Night-Cap Country* lies in the fusion of the universal and the particular. George Santayana, in describing the supposed "barbarism" of Browning's poetry, objected that the poet offered no ideal to his readers because he was entirely enmeshed in the particularity of the real.[7] Yet an examination of *Red Cotton Night-Cap Country* substantiates Arthur Symons's evaluation that "it is the special distinction of Mr. Browning that when he is most universal he is most individual."[8] Santayana was unable to discern this truth which is, I think, the essence of Browning's poetry. For the poet was able to discover not only the universal in the particular but also the divine in the real: "To reach the real truth behind a person, a flower, or an historical event is to reach not only the particular secret of a particular existence, but always and everywhere to encounter the divine truth itself."[9] Even in the distasteful and seemingly unpromising story of Léonce Miranda, Browning beheld the illuminating "flash" which enabled him to "imbibe / Some foretaste of effulgence" (773c).

NOTES

1. Mrs. Sutherland Orr, *Life and Letters of Robert Browning* (Boston and New York, 1892), II, 433; G. K. Chesterton, *Robert Browning* (New York, 1903), p. 124. Contemporary reviewers generally disliked the poem (See William Clyde DeVane, *A Browning Handbook* [New York, 1955], p. 374). Modern critical literature on it is slight. Books on Browning contain only the most cursory and derogatory treatment, Arthur Symons's *An Introduction to the Study of Browning* (London, 1890) being a notable exception in praising the poem (pp. 161–163). So far as I can find, there have been only three published essays concerned primarily with the work in the past fifty years. Lola L. Szladits, "Browning's French Night-Cap," *Bulletin of the New York Public Library*, LXI (1957), 458–467, studies Joseph Milsand's contributions to the poem; Charlotte C. Watkins, "Browning's 'Red Cotton Night-Cap Country' and Carlyle," *Victorian Studies*, VII (1964), 359–374, points out echoes of Carlyle; Barbara Melchiori, "Robert Browning's Courtship and the Mutilation of Monsieur Léonce Miranda," *Victorian Poetry*, V (1967), 303–304, suggests parallels between the story and the poet's

biography. Among essayists who have even mentioned the poem, John M. Hitner, in his "Browning's Grotesque Period," *Victorian Poetry*, IV (1966), 1–13, is typical. He calls it "another morbid newspaper story, dealing with mental disease and abnormal sex, culminating in suicide" (p. 5). Browning's whole point is that Miranda is sane, and of course there is no question of suicide, nor is there any suggestion of sexual abnormality between Miranda and his mistress.

2. J. Hillis Miller is the only critic I can discover who has even commented on the arrangement of the poem. Calling it "a huge, rough, awkward monstrosity, with its parts blown all out of size," he compares it with "the buildings of the Spanish architect Gaudí" (*The Disappearance of God* [New York, 1965], p. 132).

3. Citations of the poem are to the Cambridge Edition, *The Complete Poetical Works of Browning*, ed. Horace E. Scudder (Cambridge, Mass., 1895). Because the lines are not numbered in this dual-column edition I have added, for easier reference, the letters *a, b, c,* and *d* following the page numbers to indicate the quarter of the page on which a quotation may be found. Thus, "737a" means that the quoted material is located in the upper half of the first column. I have used this edition, rather than the Florentine or Centenary Editions, because to most readers it is more readily available.

4. Also like *The Ring and the Book, Red Cotton Night-Cap Country* is based upon a historical incident, the poet once again drawing upon legal documents for his facts. See the letter in which Browning explains how the subject came to him, quoted in DeVane's *Handbook*, p. 371.

5. See my essay, "Browning's Amphibian: Don Juan at Home," *Essays in Criticism*, XIX (1969), 210–217.

6. After the unfavorable reviews of *Red Cotton Night-Cap Country*, Browning wrote to Annie Thackeray, to whom the poem is dedicated: "Indeed the only sort of pain that any sort of criticism could give me would be by the reflection of any particle it managed to give *you*. I dare say that, by long use, I don't feel or attempt to feel criticisms of this kind, as most people might. Remember that everybody this thirty years has given me his kick and gone his way" (Annie Thackeray Ritchie, *Records of Tennyson, Ruskin, Browning* [New York, 1892], p. 181).

7. "The Poetry of Barbarism," in *Selected Critical Writings of George Santayana*, ed. Norman Henfrey (Cambridge, 1968), I, 84–116.

8. *An Introduction to the Study of Browning*, p. 4.

9. *The Disappearance of God*, p. 116.

THE NECESSARY SURMISE: THE SHAPING
SPIRIT OF ROBERT BROWNING'S POETRY

Roma A. King, Jr.

The shaping reality of Robert Browning's poetry includes a great deal more than his philosophical and theological thoughts. Browning, not himself a systematizer, left no formal statement of his beliefs. We might, of course, bring scattered statements together to form a coherent system that would with some accuracy represent his position. Such a system, however, would provide only limited insight into that basic sense of reality from which his poetry emerged. Intellectual systems, products of the conscious will, are always partial, and often misleading. To reach the ground in which Browning's poetry is rooted, we must look beyond formal statement and system. The obscure, elusive origins of his ultimate reality arise from within, from his unstructured, pre-rational disposition toward a way of feeling and acting. The whole of his poetry is an attempt to get those implied meanings and values concretely embodied in symbolic structure. We better appreciate what Browning considered ultimate by studying his poetry, and, simultaneously, we grasp more fully his artistic achievement by understanding those amorphous forces which shaped it.

An attempt to comprehend Browning's sense of the real on that level invites problems. It encourages us to think of him as a static entity, and to draw upon his works without reference to chronology or context. Much confusion has arisen from this error. Browning himself insisted that life was a process of growth and development, and that no one fragment or combination of fragments necessarily contained the whole. It is equally distorting, having accepted the concept of growth, to assume that it occurs logically, coherently, cumulatively. Browning's evolving values did not always follow a consistently predictable pattern. It is not certain that his last thoughts were his

346

best, nor that they came closer than earlier ones to representing the authentic Robert Browning. Indeed, in light of his poetry (and with support of modern psychology) we question whether or not there was one Robert Browning. His ability to write what Elizabeth Barrett called "R. B., a poem"; his disposition to approach his materials through *dramatis personae*, from first one and then another perspective; his capacity to entertain diverse, sometimes contradictory positions—all underscore the complex multiplicity of the man and make us hesitate to think of him as an entity, either static or dynamic.

Nevertheless, we do sense a certain stability beneath this discontinuous and sometimes contradictory surface, something that we may call the potential out of which the diverse Brownings emerged. Clearly, about something so amorphous one must speak cautiously and tentatively. The remarks which follow are meant to be suggestive rather than definitive. That elusive centrality of Browning's being, I suggest, is more apparent in the recurring needs which he experienced and expressed than in the specific solutions that he provided for them; more obvious in the recurring questions he asked than in the answers he supplied. There is in his thinking and writing a direction which, properly sensed, provides some insight into the reality which is the shaping spirit of his poetry.

It is necessary that we dissociate Browning at least temporarily from traditional external systems which might be assumed to impose *a priori* form upon his poetry. It is often stated that Browning's aesthetic and moral values derived from his belief in the Christian doctrine of Incarnation. Response to his poetry has been determined too frequently by the *a priori* structure thus imposed upon it, with, I believe, devastating results. It has led again and again to the assumption that having finally formed his notions of the Incarnation, Browning achieved with *The Ring and the Book* an intellectual and spiritual position that remained static through the rest of his life. This and its corollary—that his poetry after 1868 deteriorated steadily—I believe to be demonstrably false. My interest, however, is less in whether Browning believed in the Incarnation in some simple catechetical manner than in what he conceived the Incarnation to mean and the way in which he thought belief in it possible. Was the Incarnation significant ontologically—that is, as a source of meaning and values; or epistemologically, that is, as an instrumental construct which enabled him to achieve meaning and value not necessarily inherent in the structure itself? It is important that we ask this question both to clear away misunderstandings, and to grasp more firmly the real source of Browning's values.

Pauline, Sordello, and *Paracelsus* each tell the story of a young man's search for meaning and self-realization in a world where traditional religious and enlightenment solutions no longer seem applicable. Unable to derive from the natural order or to discover within traditional institutions any system of values grounded in a divine order, Browning's young men experience alienation, frustration, despair. Isolated from their past with its ineffectual institutions and traditions; finding in the present no external structures to give definition and purpose to their lives, they grope tentatively toward uncertain ends. Browning reflects in these poems that shift of sensibility, occurring at the end of the eighteenth and the beginning of the nineteenth century, which left those sensitive enough to comprehend it, particularly the artists, with a profound sense of disorientation. Morse Peckham has traced brilliantly the intellectual and cultural aspects of this revolution in his book *Beyond the Tragic Vision.*[1] M. H. Abrams speaks more explicitly of its aesthetic implications.[2] Classical art, he says, was regarded as a mirror which reflected an order of values inherent in the external world; modern art is a lamp, a subjective creative force, an emanation from within the artist himself which illumines and shapes the world about him. At least part of the task of the modern artist, as Browning was to discover, is to impose his own subjectively conceived, meaningfully shaped structure upon an amorphous world.

Pauline's poet, Paracelsus (in the original edition), and Sordello could find in no structure, objective or subjective, a source of values. The Incarnation apparently did not seem a viable option. Pauline's poet flounders in Romantic escapism; Paracelsus achieves a transcendental vision which contradicts his earlier affirmation that truth resides within; and Sordello is destroyed when he despairs of realizing his infinite vision through the finite means available to him. Although Browning concludes *Sordello* in a state of obvious frustration, he had made positive gains since *Pauline.* He would not turn again to Romantic idealism as a ground of values in the modern world. Where such ground was to be discovered, however, still eluded him as late as 1845 when he printed an unfinished version of *Saul* because he could imagine no satisfactory solution to the King's problem.

The sequel to this failure is too well known to dwell upon.

In 1845, Browning began a correspondence with Elizabeth Barrett which culminated in their marriage the following year; in 1849, he reissued *Paracelsus* significantly altered to include a passage offering the Christian Incarnation as the source of values which had hitherto escaped him;[3] in 1850, he published *Christmas Eve*, confirming the commitment which he had made a year earlier; in 1855 he completed *Saul*, permitting the King a saving vision of the Incarnate Christ as the embodiment of power and love; in 1861 Elizabeth died. During this period, 1845-1861, Browning seems to have held a fairly orthodox view of the Incarnation as historical fact.

In 1863, however, he removed from *Paracelsus* the lines referring to the Incarnation, whether because he had come to doubt the historicity of the event or because he found the concept inconsistent with the rest of the poem. In 1864, with the publication of *Dramatis Personae*, he returned to the subject once again, displaying considerable skepticism. He wished obviously to clarify his own views and to place the concept in relation to the rest of his thinking. In *A Death in the Desert*, a poem which records a significant alteration in his treatment of the subject, he dissociates the significance of the Incarnation from its possible historicity, ascribing to it epistemological rather than ontological values. It serves initially, he proposes, as a hypothesis, an imaginative projection, to which man commits himself. It becomes the motive and the tentative shaping pattern for self-creating action. The result of man's commitment, the experience which ensues, is its own meaning. Whether Browning at this time regarded the Incarnation as historical event is uncertain, but it is clear that in response to the higher criticism which attempted to discredit Christianity by disproving the historicity of the event, Browning discarded a fundamentalist view as requisite for Christian faith. His response to the higher critics was not to disprove their argument, but to demonstrate its irrelevancy to man's real concern: a discovery of meaning in the contemporary world.

In the *Epilogue* to *Dramatis Personae*, a speaker, a dramatic "I," perhaps Browning himself, engages in a dialogue with the Old Testament King David and the modern Biblical critic Ernest Renan, rejecting the transcendental affirmation of the one (in contrast to Browning's position in *Saul*) and the skeptical despair of the other, who laments the disappearance of the historical Christ from the modern world, and the sad state of man "lone and left / Silent through the centuries." The speaker proposes to retain the essence of the Christian faith without support of transcendental assurance or historical evidence. Christ the historical figure becomes the mythical embodiment of what man requires in order to develop soul, to achieve meaningful self-realization:

> That one Face, far from vanish, rather grows,
> Or decomposes but to recompose,
> Becomes my universe that feels and knows!
> (ll. 99-101)

The consistently decomposing-recomposing Face becomes the dynamic external expression, the concrete actualization, of a reality that arises from within man. No longer the source of values, external and fixed, the vision of Christ is at any one time and in any of its diverse manifestations the expression of a subjective vision, one fragment in the dynamic process by which man achieves meaning in an apparently meaningless world.

Browning's last significant treatment of the Incarnation comes in *The Ring and the Book*. The Pope accepts it not because it is indisputable history or infallible dogma, but because, having loved it in his heart, he acts upon it and proves its meaning. Indeed, having loved it, he tests it with his reason and finds it "sound." He arrives at a validation independent of external sources. The point is that love (commitment) precedes reason (abstraction).

This brief examination renders suspect the popular contention that Browning found in the Incarnation as historical event an external, *a priori* source for his aesthetic and moral values. It does more than that. It begins to suggest the sense of reality which is the shaping spirit of his poetry. Let us summarize some of its implications. Browning begins with the agonizing modern dilemma of man in search of soul in a world rendered apparently meaningless by the demise of traditional values and institutions. No longer certain of a fixed order of values in the external world or in his rational capacity to apprehend such order as might exist, man is forced in upon himself and required to create his own order. Even the fullness of his own being is apprehended experientially, not given; it must develop through a process of creative action. Hence the importance of action in all Browning's poetry. But how in the absence of incentive and pattern can man act? Fear of stasis and stagnation, of the unrealized self, of nonbeing, becomes the terror of all Browning's sensitive characters. This paradox, man's simultaneous need to act and his inability to do so, is an anxious concern in all Browning's poetry. Sordello expresses the dilemma precisely:

> The real way seemed made up of all the ways—
> Mood after mood of the one mind in him;
> Tokens of existence, bright or dim,
> Of a transcendent all-embracing sense
> Demanding only outward influence,
> A soul, in Palma's phrase, above his soul,
> Power to uplift his power,—such moon's control
> Over the sea-depths,—and their mass had swept
> Onward from the beginning and still kept
> Its course: but years and years the sky above
> Held none. . . .
>
> (VI. 36-46)

Browning's own sky seemed even more empty, his soul-angst more poignant, once his faith was shaken in the Incarnation as the objective embodiment of values imposed upon man from without.

The resulting crisis, personal and artistic, led him to postulate what in the language of the later poem La Saisiaz (1878) we may call the necessary "surmise," the hypothetical projection to which man commits himself, not because it is necessarily true objectively but because it enables him to act and to achieve a subjective being that becomes true.[4] Browning's awareness of man's situation, his alienation, his impotency, his unfulfilled and frustrated desires, and his transformation of external structures from sources of values into hypothetical constructs which enable man to create values provide the basic reality that underlies his creative efforts. What is implicit in the earlier poems becomes increasingly explicit in the latter ones.

The process by which this deepening realization achieves clarity and focus must be traced through those poems written after The Ring and the Book. It becomes especially clear in La Saisiaz which (along with Parleyings With Certain People of Importance in Their Day) occupies in Browning's later works much the position that Saul and Christmas Day hold in his earlier. All are concerned with the problem of meaning and values. La Saisiaz is an elegiac poem written upon the death of Browning's good friend Miss Anne Egerton Smith. Like many of his predecessors—Milton, Gray, and Shelley, for example—

Browning chose the elegy as the form most appropriate for expressing his ultimate grasp of life's meaning. Ostensibly, like the traditional elegy, the poem is concerned with the immortality of the soul.

Upon closer examination, however, it is clear that the significance of Browning's poem lies more in its differences from than in its likeness to the traditional elegy. In the first place, Browning himself is more immediately, more personally, involved with the subject. His relation with Miss Smith was much more intimate than was that of any of the earlier poets with his ostensible subject. This closeness between poet and subject in *La Saisiaz* emphasizes the personal over the general, the concrete over the abstract. Moreover, unlike Milton, Gray, and Shelley, Browning draws neither upon the nature myth (as in the classical tradition) nor upon the divine revelation of Christ (as in the strictly Christian tradition) for supporting argument. The poem is further outside the traditional genre in that it denigrates the capacity of the human mind to discover in the universe outside itself a rational order that illuminates and structures the chaos of its being. Browning's ultimate vision is not of a regenerated man living harmoniously in a divinely ordered universe. The poem begins and ends with Browning's commitment, skeptical and tentative, to two crucial assumptions which are neither derived from nor genuinely supported by the intervening dialogue between Fancy and Reason, in which he employs all human resources to give the immortality of the soul rational and empirical support.

Actually, as an argument the poem lacks unity and conviction. Indeed, the central section in which the case for immortality is argued leads to the subordination not the triumph of reason. It functions in the total poem not to underscore a metaphysical system but to depict dramatically the movement of Browning's inner being, emotional and rational, as it gropes for meaning in the aftermath of meaninglessness wrought by death. The poem is another of Browning's studies in which assumptions and arguments are integral parts of the larger subject, the development of the soul. The poem is held together by psychological and associational rather than by logical means.

Clearly, then, the subject is not primarily immortality in a dogmatic sense. The poem, focusing perhaps more on the present than on the hereafter, laments the apparent meaninglessness and futility of a life in which man's deepest needs are thwarted by evil and pain, on the one hand, and by death, on the other. To Browning, in a new and intimate way, Miss Smith's sudden and totally unexpected death presented a bleak prospect of life and of the mystery which surrounds it. The poem, arising from Browning's soul-angst rather than from intellectual curiosity, is a deeply personal and painful cry for meaning in life now. He is unwilling to regard this world, like Shelley, as a dome of many-colored glass which must be fragmented before man is permitted his goal, a vision of eternity's white radiance. He probes the problem of immortality not as an isolated good but as part of a larger whole, hoping to find in it an answering counterpart to man's mortality, something which, in the face of evil, pain, and death, can give substance and purpose to life on earth. He contemptuously dismisses his earlier discussions with Miss Smith upon the subject as abstract, hence irrelevant. The atmosphere of "fence-play" which characterized that exchange gives way to unrestrained urgency: "I will ask and have an answer" (l. 208). Rational affirmation has become less important than personal commitment: "How much, how little, do I inwardly believe / True that controverted doctrine?" (ll. 209-210). The stakes now are not a case won, but a being saved.

Browning examines the traditional arguments to distinguish between certain knowledge and "mere" surmise or fancy. He concludes that proofs for the existence of God and a meaningful creation derived from design and from contingency are inconsistent with life as he has experienced it. The poem begins with what appears at first as a Romantic paean to nature, but its mood quickly darkens. In lines 225-234, Browning dismisses the cyclical rebirth of nature as providing by analogy a proof of man's immortality. His ultimate judgment of the creation is expressed in the following lines:

I survey it and pronounce it work like other work: success
Here and there, the workman's glory,—here and there, his shame no less,
Failure as conspicuous.

(ll. 297-299)

Browning no more than Kierkegaard could find in life about him convincing evidence to support belief in a benevolent God.

He does not consider in *La Saisiaz* the possibility of divine revelation, perhaps because, as William Clyde DeVane proposes,[5] he conceived the poem as his contribution to the symposium then appearing in the magazine *Nineteenth Century* called "The Soul and the Future Life." If so, as DeVane argues, Browning understandably would have accepted the editors' strictures against recourse to divine revelation. But this explanation is only partly satisfying. Browning himself, significantly, makes no such allowances. Indeed, both the substance and the tone of the poem undercut such speculation. Browning's obvious sincerity and his sense of urgency, his emphatic rejection of "fence-play," suggest that he is using all the resources available to him. Unlike Bishop Blougram, he has held nothing to fall back upon if present ground gives way beneath him. Furthermore, in the later poem *Parleyings With Certain People of Importance in Their Day*, a deeply speculative work which Browning himself said "ought to be my best," he attempts once more to make a statement about ultimate meaning, and, again, without relying on divine revelation. Certainly in *Parleyings* he worked under no restrictions save those self-imposed. The suggestion is that even if Browning were aware of external strictures when he wrote *La Saisiaz*, he discovered it possible to work satisfactorily within them.

In short, Browning establishes in *La Saisiaz* a line of thought (already anticipated in *A Death in the Desert* and *The Ring and the Book*) that he was to pursue consistently thereafter. He writes:

> Truce to such old sad contention whence, according as we shape
> Most of hope or most of fear, we issue in a half-escape:
> "We believe" is sighed. I take the cup of comfort proffered thus,
> Taste and try each soft ingredient, sweet infusion, and discuss
> What their blending may accomplish for the cure of doubt, till—slow,
> Sorrowful, but how decided! needs must I o'erturn it—so!
>
> (ll. 249-254)

Thus reluctantly but decisively asserting his freedom from the past and professing to find in its affirmation no reliable guide for the present, he dismisses the whole of his cultural heritage. He becomes intensively subjective, fixing upon his consciousness as the only source of certain knowledge:

> Cause before, effect behind me—blanks! The midway point I am,
> Cause, itself—itself efficient: in that narrow space must cram
> All experience—out of which there crowds conjectures manifold,
> But, as knowledge, this comes only . . .
> . . . I am, and, since I am, can recognize
> What to me is pain and pleasure: this is sure, the rest—surmise.
>
> (ll. 255-258, 261-262)

This seems to me one of the most significant statements in Browning's poetry. Here he establishes the limits of man's capacity to know, which are restricted indeed:

> Question, answer presuppose
> Two points: that the thing itself which questions, answers,—*is,* it knows;
> As it also knows the thing perceived outside itself—a force
> Actual ere its own beginning, operative through its course,
> Unaffected by its end,—that this thing likewise needs must be;
> Call this—God, then, call that—soul, and both—the only facts for me.
>
> (ll. 217-222)

But Browning does more than establish limits. These statements are not a total rejection of reason, as has often been asserted. His argument has its constructive side also. The point is less that Browning rejects Reason and Fancy (imagination) than that he casts them in new, still significant, roles. No longer capable of revealing an absolute order which gives meaning to life, they become instead instruments, as I shall later demonstrate, through which man creates for himself a means out of his dilemma. To say that Browning surrenders reason, forgoes imagination, is totally to misunderstand *La Saisiaz.*

With the little that man can positively know, how can he achieve a fully developed soul? The "I" and the "Not-I" are not enough. The concept of "a force / Actual ere its own beginning, operative through its course,/ Unaffected by its end" acknowledges a creating and sustaining force, but it confuses more than clarifies the human issues. It was not the power but the love of God that disturbed Browning. What can one say in defence of a God who because he lacks either power or will permits evil, pain, and death? These are the inescapable conditions which make life seem unbearable. The problem itself is an old one (Browning acknowledges indebtedness to the Book of Job) but the passionate intensity with which he confronted it gave it fresh significance. Moreover, the intellectual and metaphysical perspective from which he was forced to write made his response modern. Continually in his work, particularly in that appearing after 1868, he grappled with those characteristic twentieth-century preoccupations: nihilism, rebellion, existentialism.

There are moments, like that revealed in the epilogue to *Ferishtah's Fancies,* which "Sudden turns the blood to ice" (l. 26) and almost persuade him of the ultimate emptiness and meaninglessness of life. At such times surely he seems tempted to embrace the nihilism into which his contemporary Friedrich Nietzsche felt himself reluctantly forced.[6] More frequent and more characteristic, however, are his moments of impulsive rebellion. In *La Saisiaz,* for example, he writes:

> By necessity ordained thus? I shall bear as best I can;
> By a cause all-good, all-wise, all potent? No, as I am man!
>
> (ll. 335-336)

Certainly Browning shared a great deal with Nietzsche, but he was never able to make more than momentarily that final renunciation. He is more closely related by thought and temperament to their successor Albert Camus, who also was concerned to discover meaning and value in life from which, on the evidence supplied by the presence of evil, pain, and death, God had been excluded. Like Camus, Browning recognized that through acts of rebellion man may achieve some self-awareness, some sense of the "I." Camus goes so far as to suggest that cumulative acts of rebellion suggest a universal human nature, which Browning would have called the common "soul." Camus writes: "Analysis of rebellion leads at least to the suspicion that, contrary to the postulates of contemporary thought, a human nature does exist, as the Greeks believed."[7] In *Fifine at the Fair,* Browning says:

> Alack, our life is lent,
> From first to last, the whole, for this experiment
> Of proving what I say—that we ourselves are true!
>
> (ll. 1396-1398)

True in the context of the poem means real, authentic.

Both Camus and Browning held that man's purpose was to live life intensely, fully. Either might have written that he was, as Camus put it, "motivated by the concept of a complete unity, against the suffering of life and death and a protest against the human condition both for its incompleteness, thanks to death, and its wastefulness, thanks to evil" (p. 24). For this very reason, however, Browning rejected rebellion as the final answer to the problem. Rebellion, he argued, awakened and set into motion less than the whole of man's potential being. At this point, then, Browning and Camus part company. For Camus, the metaphysical rebel is "not definitely atheistic" but he is "inevitably a blasphemer." Browning experienced the impulse toward blasphemy ("No, as I am man!"), but ultimately he rejected not only the role of atheist but also that of blasphemer, because such positions, he felt, were negative, repressive, and a barrier to that wholeness which his being demanded. He could not rest in that paradoxical position which holds that the death of hope and idealism enriches rather than impoverishes this present life. He was impelled to look beyond acts of negation and rebellion for more positive acts of affirmation.

Camus described man's dilemma as "the desperate encounter between human inquiry and the silence of the universe" (p. 6). Browning, less concerned to preserve the autonomy of the mind, thought rather, as in *Sordello,* of the encounter between man's instinctive need for God (an external source of meaning and value) and the emptiness of the universe. His was that "either/or" predicament which his contemporary Kierkegaard reduced to a choice between despair and the leap of faith, and which Camus describes as an alternative between suicide and rebellion. For Browning the options are equally limiting. His response is closer to that of Kierkegaard than to that of Camus. Having rejected rebellion, he, in spite of the apparent emptiness of the universe, makes, with the help of reason and imagination, a soul-saving affirmation by projecting upon life an order and meaning validated not by objective evidence but by that sense of wholeness which he experiences when he commits himself to it.

Going beyond the facts available, exceeding the bounds of mere reason, Browning, then, made what he called the necessary "surmise," the tentative assumption of an external order and meaning. He postulates a future state of the soul as one way of giving life meaning and allowing man to experience a sense of wholeness in face of his mortality. Such a surmise may seem at first to fall under the indictment which Camus pronounces upon all Christianity: "Historical Christianity postpones to the point beyond the span of history the cure of evil and murder, which are nevertheless experienced within the span of history" (p. 303). Two observations. First, Camus subjects Christianity to a rational test, declaring that he can never accept the faith so long as the claim for a benevolent God is contradicted by the presence in life of evil, pain, and death. Although Browning was equally aware of the paradox, he approached the problem quite differently. Again, he was concerned less about the demands of reason than about human need. He asks not if the hypothesis of immortality (and all that its acceptance implies) is totally rational, consistent with the empirical evidence (clearly it is not), but if it is effectual, if it provides a tentative construct which enables man to act and to achieve a sense of wholeness.

In the second place, Browning is not interested primarily in a future state, as Camus presumes all Christians to be. It was precisely because he was unwilling to "postpone to a point beyond history" that desired sense of wholeness that he felt impelled, even in the face of universal emptiness (for all that he could certainly *know*) and of reason, to make the necessary "surmise." His problem, too, was experienced within history and he was interested in immortality not only as an end but also as a means. In *La Saisiaz* his mood is somber. The poem is not, like the earlier *Saul,* an ecstatic celebration of "the wild joys of living." Tempered by time, rendered cautious by experience, Browning nevertheless persists still in his assertion that life now has significance.

Such a vision as Browning's is necessarily personal. He admits the extreme possibility that "To each mortal peradventure earth becomes a new machine." He disclaims, at any rate, the authority to speak for any other than himself. In an obvious repudiation of John Milton and the tradition which he represented, Browning writes:

> But, O world outspread beneath me! only for myself I speak,
> Nowise dare to play the spokesman for my brothers strong and weak,
> Full and empty, wise and foolish, good and bad, in every age,
> Every clime, I turn my eyes from, as in one or other stage
> Of a torture writhe they, Job-like couched on dung and crazed with blains
> —Wherefore? whereto? ask the whirlwind what the dread voice thence explains!
> I shall "vindicate no way of God's to man. . . ."
>
> (ll. 349-355)

Out of his felt need, based upon his intuitive sense of wholeness, and concerned to speak only for himself, Browning makes the necessary surmise.

To ask if his needs and intuitions were "real" makes no sense in light of his position. He experienced them; they were thus among the few "facts" that he could certainly know. Imagination conceiving, reason pronouncing plausible, the system which he constructed adds to the two knowable facts, Self and God, four others: earth, heaven, hell, judgment. This becomes his private eschatology, a present reality, not a distant abstraction, to which he commits himself in creative action. He carefully avoids attributing objective meaning to the system itself:

> Break through this last superstructure, all is empty air—no sward
> Firm like my first fact to stand on "God there is, and soul there is,"
> And soul's earthly life-allotment: wherein, by hypothesis,
> Soul is bound to pass probation, prove its powers, and exercise
> Sense and thought on fact, and then, from fact educing fit surmise,
> Ask itself, and of itself have solely answer, "Does the scope
> Earth affords of fact to judge by warrant future fear or hope?"
>
> (ll. 518-524)

Browning's answer is personal and tentative: "I hope—no more than hope, but hope—no less than hope" (1. 535).

His final assumptions, thus summarized, sound enough like the old idealism to be deceptive until we note that for him they are surmises, not absolutes; personal, not universal. The ephemerality of his structure, however, in no way renders it fraudulent or invalidates its serious usefulness. Nor does the tentativeness with which he projects it suggest necessarily that it has no corresponding absolute. The point is that Browning rejects the role of oracle, and refuses to pronounce upon absolutes, preferring rather to discover a means by which he can render his own life meaningful on its terms. In this sense, his necessary "surmise" is both valid and useful. Not deduced from nature, not supported by archetypal myth, not arrived at by rationalization, not divinely revealed, it is incapable of empirical proof. It is rather Browning's intelligent, imaginative response to his existential situation, in which his needs exceed natural, rational, and revelatory response. The construction itself partakes of that mutability characteristic of religious, social, and aesthetic structures generally. To ask if it is true in the ordinary sense misses the point. We ask rather if it provides the motive and means by which man may act out his being and achieve a sense of wholeness. Its validity rests upon the quality of life which it makes possible.

This conclusion has far-reaching implications. It enables us to see Browning's formal statements of belief as symbolic constructs shaped by a subjectively apprehended rather than an objectively given reality, establishing them in an epistemological rather than an ontological role. It also sharply focuses attention upon the centrality of creativity in Browning's scheme of values. Man's own soul—his fully realized self—is achieved by aid of hypothetical surmises which he projects as tentative answers to his subjectively apprehended needs. It emphasizes the necessary mutability, the capacity for fluidity and change, in all external structures if they are to continue as one of the antithetical poles that make possible the process by which man's inner being unfolds and develops. It establishes art as the realization in meaningful structure of a man's existential cry for wholeness, and as a persuasive incentive to beholders to pursue the path of self-exploration and development with the artist. It grounds all constructs, religious and artistic, in the subjective and proposes the quality of experience which they render possible as their validation. Thus viewed, the structures which Browning spent his life creating take on a transparency which reveals beneath their surface the dynamic, pre-rational vortex that constitutes the reality which becomes the shaping spirit of his poetry.

NOTES

1. Morse Peckham, *Beyond the Tragic Vision* (New York, 1962).
2. M. H. Abrams, *The Mirror and the Lamp* (New York, 1953).
3. In 1835, the lines read:

> Yes; I see now—God is the PERFECT POET,
> Who in his person acts his own creations.
> Had you but told me this at first! . . . Hush! hush!
>
> (ll. 648–650)

In 1849:

> Yes; I see now—God is the PERFECT POET,
> Who in creation acts his own conceptions.
> Shall man refuse to be aught less than God?
> Man's weakness is his glory—for the strength
> Which raises him to heaven and near God's self,
> Came spite of it: God's strength his glory is,
> For thence came with our weakness sympathy
> Which brought God down to earth, a man like us,
> Had you but told me this at first! . . . Hush! hush!
>
> (ll. 648–656)

In 1863:

> Yes; I see now. God is the PERFECT POET,
> Who in His person acts His own creations.
> Had you but told me this at first! Hush! hush!
>
> (ll. 648–650)

See *The Complete Works of Robert Browning,* eds. Roma A. King, Jr., Morse Peckham, Park Honan, and Gordon Pitts (Athens, Ohio, 1969), I, 138.

4. Browning uses the word *surmise* ten times (*surmised,* once) and although its meaning remains constant, Browning's attitude toward it changes. At first he speaks depreciatingly of it as "mere" surmise; later he recognizes it as a necessary part of man's search for meaning in the contemporary world.

5. William Clyde DeVane, *A Browning Handbook* (New York, 1955), p. 422.

6. In 1885, Nietzsche wrote: "My life is now comprised in the wish that the truth about all things be different from my way of seeing it: if only someone would convince me of the impossibilities of my truths!" Quoted by Erich Heller in *The Artist's Journey into the Interior* (New York, 1965), p. 196.

7. Albert Camus, *The Rebel,* trans. Anthony Bower (New York, 1956), p. 16. All other quotations from Camus are taken from this book and edition, and are identified in text by reference to page number.

NOTES ON CONTRIBUTORS

W. PAUL ELLEDGE, co-editor of this volume, is Associate Professor of English and Director of Undergraduate Studies in English at Vanderbilt University. He has authored one book, *Byron and the Dynamics of Metaphor,* and has published articles and reviews in a number of scholarly journals.

RICHARD L. HOFFMAN, co-editor of this volume, is Associate Professor of English at Queens College, City University of New York; he is a medievalist and, more specifically, a Chaucerian. He is the author of *Ovid and the Canterbury Tales* (1967), *History of the English Language: Selected Texts and Exercises* (1968), and two dozen notes and articles on Old and Middle English, appearing both in collections of essays and in a wide variety of scholarly journals. Currently he is preparing a new edition of *The Tale of Beryn* for the Early English Text Society and three anthologies of Middle English literature—lyric, romance, and drama.

MORSE PECKHAM has published various books on nineteenth-century culture, art, and pornography. He has also edited Darwin, Browning, and Swinburne. His numerous essays and papers are on such subjects as literary history, particularly Romanticism, art history, history of science, and literary and critical theory. He is Distinguished Professor of English and Comparative Literature at the University of South Carolina.

LIONEL STEVENSON, B.A. (British Columbia), M.A. (Toronto), Ph.D. (California), B. Litt. (Oxford), F.R.S.L., has been James B. Duke Professor of English at Duke University since 1955. He was chairman of the department from 1964 to 1967, and was Berg Visiting Professor at New York University from 1967 to 1968. He is the author of *Appraisals of Canadian Lit-*

erature; Darwin Among the Poets; The Wild Irish Girl; Doctor Quicksilver; The Showman of Vanity Fair; The Ordeal of George Meredith; The English Novel—A Panorama; The History of the English Novel, vol. xi (*Yesterday and After*); co-author of *English Literature of the Victorian Period;* and editor of *Victorian Fiction—a Guide to Research.*

PETER L. THORSLEV, JR., B.A. (Dana College), Ph.D. (University of Minnesota), is Associate Professor of English at the University of California, Los Angeles, where he has taught, with the exception of a year as a Guggenheim Fellow, since 1960. He is author of *The Byronic Hero* (1962) and a number of essays in such learned journals as *Comparative Literature* and *Studies in Romanticism.* Somewhat paradoxically, he combines an enthusiastic appreciation of Romantic literature with a deep respect for analytic reason.

ERNEST J. LOVELL, JR., is Professor of English at the University of Texas at Austin. He is Executive Editor of *Texas Studies in Literature and Language, a Journal of the Humanities* and is the author of *Byron: The Record of a Quest* (1949; 1966); *His Very Self and Voice: Collected Conversations of Lord Byron* (1954); *Captain Medwin, Friend of Byron and Shelley* (1962); *Medwin's "Conversations of Lord Byron"* (1966); *Lady Blessington's "Conversations of Lord Byron"* (1969); an anthology of modern drama; and numerous articles, notes, and reviews in scholarly journals.

MICHAEL G. COOKE is Professor of English at Boston University, and editor of *Studies in Romanticism.* Author of a number of articles on Romantic and modern subjects, he has also written *The Blind Man Traces the Circle: On the Patterns and Philosophy of Byron's Poetry.* He is currently at work on a study of the concept of will in English Romantic literature.

CHARLES RICHARD SANDERS, educated at Emory University (Phi Beta Kappa) and the University of Chicago, is Professor of English at Duke University. He is the author of *Coleridge and the Broad Church Movement* (1942); *The Strachey Family, 1588–1932: Their Writings and Literary Associations* (1953); *Lytton Strachey: His Mind and Art* (1957); *The Correspondence and Friendship of Thomas Carlyle and Leigh Hunt*

(1963); editor of an abridgement of Malory's *Morte d'Arthur* (1940); and general editor of *The Collected Letters of Thomas and Jane Welsh Carlyle* (about 35 volumes, the first four of which [1812-1828] will appear in 1970).

BRIAN WILKIE is Associate Professor of English at the University of Illinois. He is the author of *Romantic Poets and Epic Tradition* (1965).

CARL WOODRING is the author of *Politics in English Romantic Poetry; Wordsworth; Politics in the Poetry of Coleridge; Virginia Woolf; Victorian Samplers: William and Mary Howitt;* and other studies. He has taught at the University of Wisconsin and at Columbia University, where he is currently Professor of English. He holds the B.A. and M.A. from Rice University and the A.M. and Ph.D. from Harvard. He has enjoyed several national fellowships.

ROBERT D. HUME is Assistant Professor of English at Cornell University. He is the author of *Dryden's Criticism* (1970), and has published articles in *PMLA, The Review of English Studies, The British Journal of Aesthetics, The Journal of Aesthetics and Art Criticism, Eighteenth-Century Studies,* and other journals on subjects ranging from Shakespeare to Rossetti.

RICHARD HARTER FOGLE is University Distinguished Professor of English at the University of North Carolina. Interested in English and American Romanticism, he is preparing a book on Hawthorne and the chief English Romantic poets. Author of two books on Hawthorne, he has written on Melville, Coleridge, Keats, and Shelley.

JEROME J. MCGANN, Associate Professor of English and Humanities, University of Chicago, is the author of *Fiery Dust: Byron's Poetic Development,* as well as numerous articles on Romantic, Victorian, and modern poetry. He has held a Fulbright Fellowship (1965-1966) and is currently working as a Guggenheim Fellow (1970-1971) in England on a study of A. C. Swinburne.

LEWIS LEARY, B.S. (University of Vermont), Ph.D. (Columbia University), is William Rand Kenan Jr. Professor of English at the University of North Carolina. He is the author of *That Rascal Freneau: A Study in Literary Failure; John Greenleaf Whittier; Mark Twain; Norman Douglas;* and others.

W. P. ALBRECHT, B.S. (Carnegie Institute of Technology), M.A. (University of Pittsburgh), Ph.D. (University of Chicago), has taught at all three of these institutions, at the University of New Mexico, and at the University of Kansas, where he is Professor of English and Dean of the Graduate School. His publications include articles on medieval, nineteenth-century, and recent literature, and four books: *William Hazlitt and the Malthusian Controversy* (1950); *The Loathly Lady in "Thomas of Erceldoune"* (1954); *The American Technical Writer* (with C. V. Wicker) (1960); and *Hazlitt and the Creative Imagination* (1965).

JACK STILLINGER is Professor of English and Director of Graduate Studies at the University of Illinois. He has published articles on Keats, Sidney, and J. S. Mill, among others, and has edited Mill's *Autobiography* and other works (1961; 1969); Anthony Munday's *Zelauto* (1963); a selection of Wordsworth (1965); the letters of Charles Armitage Brown (1966); and a collection of essays on Keats's odes (1968). He is the principal editor of the *Journal of English and Germanic Philology*.

JOHN CLUBBE, B.A. (Columbia College), Ph.D. (Columbia University), has been Lecturer at Columbia University, City College of New York, and the University of Münster, and is now Assistant Professor of English at Duke University. He is the author of "Byron in Switzerland" (*TLS*, 1969) and *Victorian Forerunner: The Later Career of Thomas Hood* (1970), Assistant Editor of *The Collected Letters of Thomas and Jane Welsh Carlyle* (first four volumes, 1970), and is working on an article on Byron and Shakespeare and on two books, one of which is a full-length study of Byron's Swiss period with a critical examination of his poetry of this period, the other a one-volume abridgement of James Anthony Froude's four-volume biography of Carlyle.

GORDON N. RAY, B.A. (Phi Beta Kappa, Indiana University) Ph.D. (Harvard University), is President of the John Guggenheim Memorial Foundation in New York. He has taught English and American Literature at Harvard; the University of Illinois (Head of Department, Vice President, Provost); the University of Oregon; New York University; and the University of California at Berkeley. Holder of nine honorary degrees, he has been a Trustee of the Guggenheim Foundation since 1963, the Modern Language Association of America since 1966, and the Pierpont Morgan Library since 1970. He is the author of *The Buried Life* (1952); *Thackeray: The Uses of Adversity* (1955); *Thackeray: The Age of Wisdom* (1958); (with Leon Edel) *Henry James and H. G. Wells* (1958); and editor of the four-volume *The Letters and Private Papers of William Makepeace Thackeray* (1945-1946).

G. Malcolm Laws, Jr. received his Ph.D. at the University of Pennsylvania, where he is Professor of English, teaching nineteenth-century English poetry and fiction. His publications include *Native American Balladry* (revised edition, 1964) and *American Balladry from British Broadsides* (1964).

Clyde de L. Ryals, B.A. (Emory University), Ph.D. (University of Pennsylvania), is Professor of English at the University of Pennsylvania. He is the author of two books on Tennyson and of numerous articles on nineteenth-century subjects.

Roma A. King, Jr., B.A. (Baylor University), Ph.D. (University of Michigan), is Distinguished Professor of English at Ohio University, Athens. Discharged as Major with Army Commendation Ribbon from the Army Signal Corps in 1946, he has taught at Baylor University, University of Missouri at Kansas City, and Colorado University, as well as at Ohio. He is cofounder and associate editor of *Mundus Artium: A Journal of International Literature and the Arts* (1967–   ), and is the author of *Robert Browning's Finances* (1947); *The Bow and the Lyre: The Art of Robert Browning* (1957); *The Focusing Artifice: The Poetry of Robert Browning* (1968); general editor of the 13-volume *The Works of Robert Browning, With Variant Readings and Annotations*; and has written numerous articles on nineteenth- and twentieth-century literature.